ESSAYS IN CONVEYANCING AND PROPERTY LAW

Essays in Conveyancing and Property Law

in Honour of Professor Robert Rennie

Edited by

Frankie McCarthy
Senior Lecturer in Private Law at the University of Glasgow

James Chalmers
Regius Professor of Law at the University of Glasgow

Stephen Bogle
Lecturer in Private Law at the University of Glasgow

OpenBook
Publishers

http://www.openbookpublishers.com

Digital material and resources associated with this volume are available at http://www.openbookpublishers.com/9781783741472#resources

ISBN Paperback: 978-1-78374-147-2
ISBN Hardback: 978-1-78374-148-9
ISBN Digital (PDF): 978-1-78374-149-6
ISBN Digital ebook (epub): 978-1-78374-150-2
ISBN Digital ebook (mobi): 978-1-78374-151-9
DOI: 10.11647/OBP.0056

Cover image: Lali Masriera, Edinburgh chimneys (2010), CC BY.

All paper used by Open Book Publishers is SFI (Sustainable Forestry Initiative) and PEFC (Programme for the Endorsement of Forest Certification Schemes) Certified.

Printed in the United Kingdom and United States by Lightning Source
for Open Book Publishers

Contents

Contributors

Ross G Anderson is a member of the Faculty of Advocates and an Honorary Research Fellow at the University of Glasgow.

Lord Bonomy is a former Senator of the College of Justice.

Stewart Brymer is the founder of Brymer Legal and an Honorary Professor in Law at the University of Dundee.

David Carey Miller is Emeritus Professor of Property Law at the University of Aberdeen.

Douglas J Cusine is a former Sheriff of Grampian, Highland and Islands and before that Professor of Conveyancing and Professional Practice of Law at the University of Aberdeen.

Lord Gill is Lord President and Lord Justice General.

George Gretton is Lord President Reid Professor of Law at the University of Edinburgh.

Gerald F Hanretty QC is a member of the Faculty of Advocates.

Lord Hodge is a Justice of the Supreme Court of the United Kingdom.

Lord Hope of Craighead is a former Deputy President of the Supreme Court of the United Kingdom.

John King is Business Development Director at the Registers of Scotland.

Angus McAllister is Emeritus Professor of Law at the University of the West of Scotland.

John MacLeod is a Lecturer in Commercial Law at the University of Glasgow.

Hector L MacQueen is Professor of Private Law at the University of Edinburgh and a Scottish Law Commissioner.

Bernadette O'Neill is a doctoral researcher at the University of Glasgow.

Roderick R M Paisley is Professor of Scots Law at the University of Aberdeen.

Lady Paton is a Senator of the College of Justice.

Kenneth G C Reid is Professor of Scots Law at the University of Edinburgh.

Ann Stewart is Head of Knowledge Management at Shepherd and Wedderburn.

Kenneth Swinton is Division Leader (Law) at the University of Abertay.

Professor Robert Rennie

firm's business, to handle the rapidly increasing volume of conveyancing transactions. Robert answered my call, and joined the firm in April of that year, before being assumed as a partner the following year. I remain of the view that acquisition compares favourably with the acquisition of Kenny Dalglish by Liverpool from Celtic. Robert would be a mainstay, ultimately *the* mainstay, of the firm for almost thirty years.

Those were the heady days of scale fees and little competition. The five fee earners worked long and intense hours which brought generous rewards to all. Although the routine Wimpey or Barratt house purchase or sale may not have provided the conveyancing challenge Robert had experienced in Glasgow, the tenements of Bellshill and the occasional rash undertaking given by others in the firm meant that his workload was rich in complexities, and he was often called upon as trouble-shooter, not to say fire-fighter.

The wicked sense of humour was never far away, even during arduous periods, of which there were many. It was the nature of a business like Ballantyne & Copland that some clients, both the rich and those of modest means, required the services of more than one solicitor. So it was that Miss W, Robert's conveyancing client, brought her Alsatian to the office to demonstrate to me that it had been wrongly identified as the dog which had bitten a child in a play park. Robert and I occupied adjacent offices separated by a wooden partition, topped at a height of about twelve feet by glass. As the client persisted, in increasingly strident tones, with her contention that an Alsatian identification parade was the only fair way forward, Robert's face, framed by hands flapping like pointed ears and with tongue out and panting, appeared at the glass atop the partition. Completing that consultation required reserves of concentration and determination that I did not believe I could summon.

The firm continued to grow rapidly. Soon there were seven partners with the addition of Jock Brown, who completed his apprenticeship with the firm and went on to be assistant and partner while pursuing a parallel career as a football broadcaster, and Tony Ireland who arrived as an assistant and was later assumed. Those two are, like Robert, still in practice. In the early 1980's it was a formidable unit. At that time and in subsequent years there were other assistants, some of whom became partners. One assistant who went to the Bar is now a Senator of the College of Justice, Lady Stacey. Ballantyne & Copland was professional home to a number of talented and extremely hard-working individuals, all interesting characters with wide-ranging interests. By 1982 there were eight offices. From every single one there were regular calls for advice to Robert as the fount of knowledge of conveyancing, and increasingly of inventive, practical and effective solutions to the novel problems that the transactions and title deeds of West Central Scotland contrived to throw up.

Then from 1983 onwards a combination of factors including the abolition of scale fees, the encouragement of advertisement and open competition among solicitors, and personal career choices led to some personnel changes and a reduction in the number of offices, including the hiving-off of the firm's Hamilton office to two of the partners. Throughout these changes, and indeed throughout the remainder of his time at Ballantyne & Copland, Robert was the linchpin that secured the firm's stability. He did that in a number of ways, including his ready availability and willingness to patiently and calmly consider and advise on the problems others in the firm had encountered, and his management of the financial affairs and business of the firm. He took on responsibilities that others were seen to avoid, largely, it has to be said, because they knew that he would handle them better. A good example is the role of partner responsible for staffing matters, which should have been shared around, but which he held more often than not, because not only did the staff warm to his personality, but he is also a good listener who treated and treats all with equal respect.

One role which he, surprisingly, was slow to master was that of advocate, by which I mean in-court litigator. Any who have enjoyed the privilege of observing his performance at student seminars, or experienced his wicked mimicry of the pompous, can be forgiven for viewing him as a frustrated actor, usually a reliable pointer to a natural aptitude for court advocacy. It is probably to the great benefit of Scots Law that Robert chose a different course. Having said that, it is only right to acknowledge that, on those occasions when he was summoned to action in court he willingly did his bit and did enjoy some major triumphs. His first recorded successful reparation outcome was on behalf of a second-year apprentice colleague at Bishop, Milne, Boyd & Co., Hector Cameron, who sustained a laceration through contact with the sharp ornamental spike of a wall lantern jutting out over the stairway from the Alpha Restaurant where they had enjoyed a good lunch. Robert led the case against the Stakis Organisation, owners of the restaurant, netting his colleague £50, which was just under 10% of the then second-year apprentice salary. To the great credit of the pursuer, his largesse briefly knew no bounds, and the damages were rapidly returned whence they came, but exclusively at the bar, the following Friday with the assistance of apprentices and assistants from far and wide, who had somehow got wind of the windfall.

Robert occasionally appeared before licensing boards on behalf of a variety of clients, from the enterprising Asian off-sales proprietor (remember that it was in Motherwell that cut-price alcohol was first introduced to the public by AA Brothers) to the Coral Organisation, for whom Ballantyne & Copland acted, from the days when Joe Coral himself and his sons Bernard and Nicholas managed a tightly run betting shop business and personally attended all the hearings until they grew to be a multi-million pound gambling empire extending to hundreds of shops and a number of casinos. However, his principal involvement with those clients remained the associated property acquisitions. Commercial transactions brought a welcome change from the principal diet of domestic conveyancing, and also the occasional invitation to a corporate entertainment event. The Coral Organisation held membership of the St Andrews Sporting Club (the sport then and to this day being boxing). The late 1970s were a golden age for Scottish boxing. Robert had the good fortune to be Coral's guest on the night in January 1973 when Jim Watt met Ken Buchanan, two Scottish legends of the ring, to contest the British Lightweight Championship. The party had ring-side seats. As the boxers made their way into the ring, Robert remarked to Jim Clinton of Corals that Ken Buchanan did not look very tough to him, only to hear Clinton, who was by then fairly relaxed, call out to Ken Buchanan: "Hey, Ken. He (pointing to Robert) thinks you're no' very tough." The trait of speaking his mind frankly and saying what he thinks, which has led to praise in Robert's expert opinion practice, produced one of those anxious moments when time seemed to stand still. It was not clear whether Ken had heard anything over the general hubbub. As it was, Buchanan defeated Watt to take the title. As he left the ring, he smiled and waved a glove in the direction of the Coral party, bringing an end to a memorable, if latterly rather subdued, evening. Perhaps another close call.

Robert's major adversarial triumph undoubtedly came in the protracted and convoluted battle ("war" is probably the more appropriate expression) in 1977 to secure the election of Jack Gillespie to the board of Glasgow Rangers FC. Following the failure to secure a position on the Board by negotiation, on two separate occasions a major assault was mounted at the Club AGM to persuade the undecided few shareholders necessary to tip the balance in Gillespie's favour to vote for him. The second attempt was a pure forensic triumph. At a number of earlier stages it had appeared that the necessary majority had committed themselves to supporting Gillespie only for some of those commitments to later turn out to be hollow. You can talk all you like before the game (and almost everyone with an interest in the sport seems to do so) but all that really matters is how the team play on the day, and how the shareholders actually vote at the meeting. Realising that, Robert advised his client that he would have to win the fight on the field of play, persuade the waverers on the floor of the AGM. So it was that a token number of shares in Rangers were somehow acquired by Robert for himself and one of Scotland's premier senior counsel of the day, Philip Caplan QC. Both spoke at the meeting and both harnessed the inevitable emotional tension of the occasion. There was nevertheless something surreal about Philip Caplan's final oratorical flourish commending Jack Gillespie's election to provide a driving force to restore Rangers to "the place where they belong – among the elite of Europe." The victory was secured. It was a far cry from the occasion some years earlier when he had been called into action unexpectedly as a late substitute for one of the court assistants. He strove manfully to persuade Sheriff Dickson to a point of view that the Sheriff did not find attractive. As matters went from bad to worse to terminal decline, the assistant suddenly appeared through the court door to the obvious gratitude of Robert, and also of the Sheriff who, addressing the assistant with a sigh of relief, said: "Your procurator seems to be in some difficulty."

Over his years of teaching, no doubt with the benefit of having had his expert opinion challenged from time to time, he developed court-room skills to demonstrate to students in his professional negligence class the elements of negligence and the issues to be addressed by the professional witness. He became quite good and latterly seemed to take a particular pleasure in putting colleague expert witnesses like Donald Reid, who "guested" at his seminars, to the sword. Although it was no coincidence that the guest was occasionally one who had been of a different opinion in a recent case, the cross-examination was always conducted in the best possible taste.

Through the many changes of the 1980's and the 1990's when some partners and assistants moved on, assistants became partners, new blood was recruited and the senior partners retired, Robert remained steadfastly on the bridge – and in the engine-room – providing stability and maintaining

2011) with Alan K. Simpson a work that may turn out to be of increasing importance, *Minerals and the Law of Scotland*. A clear pointer to his versatility was his production with Professor Stewart Brymer in 2008 of *Conveyancing in the Electronic Age*. Those for which he must assume full responsibility are *Solicitors' Negligence* (1997), *Land Tenure Reform* (2003), *Land Tenure in Scotland* (2004), *Land Tenure and Tenements Legislation* (2005, 3rd edition 2009), a volume of *Opinions on Professional Negligence in Conveyancing* (2004) and a collection of essays entitled *The Promised Land* (2008). There are also countless articles on a wide variety of issues in the property and professional negligence fields. However, this is a list that I suspect is far from complete. A new work on *Leases* in collaboration with a number of colleagues has recently been published,[2] and in the absence of his academic commitment, which he will miss greatly, an outlet for the product of his fertile mind will have to be found. I am not alone in hoping that he will take on further academic writing.

Besides Robert's academic works, there is unlikely to be any downturn in demand for his "short stories" or opinions, or his willingness to produce them, at least as long as he remains in practice. Since his appointment to the Chair of Conveyancing he has written a staggering 4000 opinions. He has always regarded being actively in practice as an important feature of his opinion practice. The changes in conveyancing and property law since he qualified in 1969 are extraordinary. Registration of title alone would make today's practice unrecognisable to the 1969 practitioner. Add to that all the changes associated with the sweeping away of the feudal system as well as current developments, such as the move towards fully electronic processes for the transfer of land, and it can be seen why Robert's career has been described as spanning the gap between two different worlds of practice. As a result the expert who is not currently in practice is exposed to challenges to the relevance of his experience and even to his expertise which are at the very least a distraction and can undermine his opinion. It is a tribute to Robert's adaptability and resilience that he has not only taken it all in his stride but he also still retains his initial enthusiasm for his subject.

When I asked him to pick out a highlight of his career, it took little more than a moment or two of reflection to alight on *Sharp v Thomson* 1997 SC (HL) 66 in which his opinion that the delivery of a disposition of the flat effectively removed it from the "property and undertaking" subject to a

---

2   Robert Rennie, Stewart Brymer, Tom Mullen, Mike Blair, and Frankie McCarthy, *Leases SULI* (2015).

floating charge granted by the company selling the flat was vindicated in the House of Lords after having found no support in the Court of Session. That vindication gave him particular satisfaction because floating charges were after all something of a speciality for Robert, being the subject of his PhD thesis, and because his had been a solitary voice and his opinion had been the subject of some fairly fierce criticism by academic colleagues.

For a court faced with competing persuasive expert opinions a central issue may be the degree of confidence engendered by the respective witnesses. Robert is now a fairly familiar face in our courts, especially the Court of Session, where his opinions tend to be highly regarded. So much so that in the reclaiming motion in *Compugraphics International Limited v Nikolic* 2011 SLT 955, which did not involve any expert but raised the issue of servitudes of support and overhang working in tandem to secure to a factory owner rights over pipework extending from the ground within his title onto that of his neighbour, Lady Paton presiding asked counsel at the outset: "Is this not a case for Professor Rennie?" Senior counsel on both sides did not disagree, but felt it was too late to change course. I hope that Robert, and his professional colleagues with an interest in this field, are not unhappy with the result. It is an area of our law that continues to give rise to problems that the experts are called upon to solve – see the article in *The Journal of the Law Society of Scotland* of 2 May 2003 referred to earlier.[3] It seems that there will always be a demand for expert opinions on problems arising in connection with the transfer of title to heritable property and the conduct of transactions by solicitors.

Among the academic community in Glasgow and throughout the rest of Scotland Robert is held in high regard and indeed affection. That is shown by the award to him of the title "Emeritus Professor" which ensures that, in spite of retirement from his teaching responsibilities, he remains the only surviving Professor of Conveyancing in Scotland. He will be greatly missed by the University staff from whom I have received many tributes, and unwittingly by future students who will never know the Professor widely described by those he taught as "Legend." He can reflect with pride on the contribution he has made to the law of conveyancing, property and professional negligence. But he can also look forward to a continuing steady demand for those opinions full of learning, wisdom and practicality.

---

3   R Rennie, "A Matter of Opinion" (n 1).

2. "Tell Me Don't Show Me" and the Fall and Rise of the Conveyancer

Professor Kenneth G C Reid

A. Conveyancers: From Emasculation to Emancipation

Property law, observed Robert Rennie in 2010, has come to be marginalised by registration practice.[1] With the move from a system of registration of deeds to one of registration of title, the rights of parties were determined by what, on first registration, the Keeper was prepared to allow on to the Land Register. No doubt, in making such decisions the Keeper had regard to the law of property. But the Keeper's property law might not be the same as the property law of the applicant's solicitor – or indeed, that solicitor might contend, as the property law of Scotland.[2] No matter. What counted was not the law but the Keeper's views, and unless an applicant was willing to challenge those views in the courts – and few were – it was the Keeper's views that were determinative. As for conveyancers, their role was in danger of being reduced to that of a clerk, filling in forms, collecting documents, and awaiting with anxiety the verdict from Meadowbank House. In concluding his article, Robert drew on his own long professional experience to contrast

---

1   R Rennie, "Land Registration and the Decline of Property Law" (2010) 14 *EdinLR* 62.
2   Rennie (n 1) at 64: sometimes there is "a conflict between the policy adopted at the Land Register and the law of property itself."

    http://dx.doi.org/10.11647/OBP.0056.02

the position of Sasine conveyancing with conveyancing under the Land Register:[3]

> Those who practice conveyancing today take decisions based on what they think the Keeper will or will not do rather than having regard to the principles of property law. When, many years ago, I was an apprentice and then an assistant in the Glasgow firm of solicitors of which Professor Halliday was senior partner, all of the partners (not just Professor Halliday) were prepared to take a view on the sufficiency or marketability of a title based on their own knowledge of the principles of property law and the practice of conveyancing. How many solicitors today would risk taking a view on a servitude or be prepared to argue that the principles of law relating to the interpretation of a Sasine description supported a larger area than the Keeper was prepared to include in a title plan and so advise a client to accept the title? It does seem a pity that these skills have been lost and with it, I would suggest, some of our property law.[4]

If, for conveyancers, there was frustration in the position as depicted by Robert, there was also, one must admit, a degree of comfort, for in the perilous enterprise of conveying property they were no longer alone. On the contrary, almost everything that could be checked was checked by the Keeper's staff, and mistakes eliminated accordingly. And even if mistakes went undetected, as inevitably some must, the fact that the title was accepted by the Keeper made future challenge unlikely. The name of the game was to "get the title past the Keeper"; that done, there was little to worry about either for solicitors or for their clients.

It is true that the law was less accommodating than the view just outlined might suggest. Under the Land Registration (Scotland) Act 1979, a title made good by registration could still be removed from the Register if fundamentally bad;[5] and not even possession, a standard safeguard against rectification, could protect the registered proprietor where his

---

3   Rennie (n 1) at 78-79. In similar vein, see the interview with Robert Rennie ("A Tale of Two Systems") (2014) 59 *JLSS* Nov/13 at 14.

4   The extent to which conveyancers really were prepared to "take a view" without the comfort, which the 1979 Act introduced, of the Keeper's protection may be open to question. Certainly the Reid Committee thought that "in the present system of conveyancing there is an undue insistence on the rectification of minor technical defects and ... there is an understandable reluctance on the part of the solicitor acting for a purchaser to overlook the technical defects because, when the property comes to be sold, the solicitor acting for the next purchaser might insist on rectification." See *Registration of Title to Land in Scotland* (Cmnd 2032: 1963; hereinafter the "Reid Report") para 150.

5   Land Registration (Scotland) Act 1979 (hereinafter the "1979 Act") s 9(1).

or her solicitor had been "careless" in the conduct of the conveyancing.[6] Indeed, through such carelessness proprietors could both lose the property and also be disqualified from claiming indemnity from the Keeper, leaving only a claim in professional negligence against the offending solicitor.[7] Yet cases like this were hardly common enough for much sleep to be lost on their account. By and large, the Keeper's quality control ensured titles which were good or at any rate unchallenged in practice. If the price was a loss of autonomy, then that was a price which conveyancers were often willing to pay.

Back in 2010 Robert Rennie could hardly have imagined that, within a mere four years of writing, the emasculation of conveyancers of which he complained would have given way to a sudden and unexpected emancipation. With the coming into force of the Land Registration etc (Scotland) Act 2012, on 8 December 2014, the Keeper has abandoned many of her previous checks on applications for registration. True, the application form is scrutinised, as before, and the deed itself is checked for obvious error. On first registrations, the property boundaries continue to be plotted on what is now called the cadastral map. But for much of the rest the Keeper relies on the judgment of the applicant's solicitor. "Tell me don't show me" has become the new mantra at Meadowbank House.

In this chapter I consider this dramatic change of policy and the reasons for its introduction. I also explore some of the implications for conveyancers, for titles to land, and for the public at large.

B. "Tell Me Don't Show Me"

(1) Introduction

"Tell me don't show me" was not unknown before 2014. The mechanised nature of automated registration of title to land (ARTL) meant that transactions which proceeded under that system – not very many, as it happened – relied to a considerable extent on the word of the applicant's solicitor. In non-ARTL transactions too, a role for "tell me don't show me" had evolved. This can be seen from part B of the old (application) forms 1-3, where a number of the questions sought to elicit information without

---

6   1979 Act s 9(3)(a)(iii).
7   Ibid ss 12(3)(n) 13(4).

independent verification by the Keeper. That was true, for example, of the inquiry as to whether a third party was in adverse possession, or in respect of the detailed questions about the legal capacity of the parties, the possible appointment of liquidators and the like, and compliance with the statutory procedures where property was being sold by a heritable creditor. Nonetheless, for important matters the policy was still one of "tell me *and* show me": in the interests of maintaining an accurate Register, the staff at Registers of Scotland invested much time and effort in checking that all was in order. That policy has now changed. "Tell me don't show" has spread to many of the central areas of registration practice and to the most crucial registration event of all: the first registration of a Sasine title in the Land Register.

(2) Examination of title

That only valid deeds should be accepted for registration seems a proposition too obvious to require defending; and indeed the 2012 Act, unlike its predecessor, makes validity a formal requirement of registration.[8] Now, in order for a deed to be valid, two things must be true. First, the deed must be granted by someone with the title and capacity to do so – which in practice usually means by the person who is the owner of the land; and secondly, the deed itself must be valid in respect to both content and mode of execution. The last of these the Keeper's staff continue to check insofar as they are able to do so, i.e. by an inspection of the deed itself. The first, however, they have wholly abandoned. Even for first registrations, where the granter's title depends on what may be an intricate progress of Sasine writs, examination of title is no longer undertaken. Instead there is reliance on the word of the applicant, or in practice on that of the applicant's solicitor.

The full position emerges only from a close reading of two interlinking sections in the (new) application form for registration.[9] Under the innocuous heading of "certification in relation to links in title" there appears the statement that: "By signing this application form you[10] are certifying to the Keeper that appropriate links in title are in place and that the granter has

---

8   Land Registration etc (Scotland) Act 2012 (hereinafter the "2012 Act") ss 23(1)(b), 25(1)(a), 26(1)(a). A definition of "valid" is given in s 113(2). Exceptionally, however, the registration of *a non domino* dispositions is allowed: see 2012 Act ss 43-45.

9   Land Registration Rules etc (Scotland) Regulations 2014, SSI 2014/150, reg 7 Sch 1 part 4. The relevant sections are on p 5.

10 By which is presumably meant the applicant.

the legal right to grant the deed." The sting, of course, is in the tail: links in title are usually an irrelevance, and not all readers may bother to continue past the opening words to the apparently unconditional certification or warranty of title at the end. This certification is linked to the previous section of the form where the applicant is asked whether there has been "any limitation or restriction on the examination of title." But even if the answer to that question is "yes" – for example, because the transaction is an *inter vivos* donation or a transfer by an executor – there is no escaping the certification of title which follows. Indeed the certification could be avoided only by declining to sign the form at all, a move which would invalidate the whole application. It follows that, in applying for registration, the applicant is certifying the title of the granter to make the grant; the one cannot be done without the other. And as Registers of Scotland have explained, that certification will be relied on:[11]

> The Keeper will rely on this certification and will carry out no further investigation in this regard. This means the Keeper will not need sight of much of the supporting documentation that would previously have accompanied an application for registration. For example, rather than submitting links in title for examination, or producing the prescriptive progress of title, applicants will certify that valid links in title exist and that there has been an examination of title.

The certification is by the applicant, not by the applicant's solicitor;[12] but the judgment to be made here is that of the solicitor.

(3) Real burdens

A significant task on first registration is to populate the D section of the new title sheet with the real burdens affecting the property. The relevant writs can usually be identified easily enough, by consulting the lists of burdens in prior dispositions. Determining whether particular burdens are still enforceable in the light of the abolition of the feudal system and

---

11 Registers of Scotland, *General Guidance on the One-Shot Rule* (30 Oct 2014) 4. The passage continues, rather ominously: "This approach is underpinned by the duty of care and offence provisions under sections 111 and 112, respectively. In respect of applications for registration, both applicants and granters (and their solicitors) are under a duty to take reasonable care to ensure that the Keeper does not inadvertently make the register accurate. It is an offence to knowingly or recklessly make a materially false or misleading statement in relation to an application for registration." For liability, see D(2) below.

12 Of course the form is invariably signed by the solicitor, but on behalf of the applicant.

the dismantling, followed by partial replacement, of the pre-2004 rules of implied enforcement rights is another matter altogether, and requires a sound knowledge of some tricky law as well as good judgment and a steady nerve. Hitherto all questions as to real burdens have been questions for Registers of Scotland, albeit assisted by the schedule of burdens which formed part of the application form.[13] Since the end of 2014, these questions too have become subject to "tell me don't show me." It is now for the applicant to list the burdens writs, and for the applicant to decide which burdens, if any, are unenforceable and so should be excluded from the title sheet.[14] None of this, it appears, will normally be checked by the Keeper, so that if the applicant declares, for good reasons or bad, that certain burdens are spent, this will be accepted without inquiry and the title sheet made up accordingly.[15]

In his 2010 article Robert Rennie had complained of the Keeper's "cautious approach to cleansing the Land Register of dead burdens" and worried that burdens left on the Register "will be presumed by solicitors to be valid and enforceable."[16] He continued:[17]

> On the one hand, many burdens would have been extinguished; on the other hand, due to a cautious policy on the part of the Keeper, those very burdens would appear enforceable because they remain on the title sheets. It is to be hoped that this does not occur, but if it does property law will again have been marginalised by registration practice.

With "tell me don't show me" the decision as to which burdens have and have not survived passes from the Keeper to conveyancers. Whether the

---

13   See form 1 question 5(b).

14   See p 6 of the application form. Section 9(1)(a) of the 2012 Act provides that the D section of a title sheet should only contain title conditions which encumber the property.

15   *General Guidance on the One-Shot Rule* (n 11) 2: "When submitting an application over an unregistered plot, the applicant will be asked to identify deeds in which burdens are contained, and to highlight any burdens that he or she considers to be extinguished. The Keeper will rely on the information provided and will not search for other deeds that may affect [*sic*]. However, if the plot is in a research area where the Keeper has already carried out preparatory work and other deeds that contain burdens have been identified, the Keeper will continue to disclose these burdens in the title sheet notwithstanding that the applicant has not included them."

16   Rennie (n 1) at 68-69.

17   Ibid at 69. Of interest in this context is the view of the Reid Committee: "It was suggested in evidence that the Keeper should have the power to omit burdens which were clearly invalid or administratively undesirable to have on the Register. We think that this might give rise to difficulties and disputes and we do not think the Keeper should have any discretion to omit a burden." See Reid Report (n 4) para 108.

latter will be any less cautious than the former is a matter to which we will need to return.[18]

(4) Prescriptive servitudes

Once upon a time the Keeper was open to persuasion that a servitude had been constituted by positive prescription and, if persuaded, would enter the servitude on the A section of the title sheet of the benefited property. The practice was abandoned in 1997, after which prescriptive servitudes were not allowed on the Register unless their constitution was vouched for by court decree.[19] The reason for the change, predictably enough, was the potential partiality and unreliability of affidavit and other evidence:[20]

> Affidavit evidence submitted to the Keeper with respect to a dominant tenement represents a one sided version of events. There is little or no risk for deponents by either being selective or exaggerating the position. There is also scope for more innocent misrepresentation by the deponent of the position on ground. On numerous occasions the Keeper has been the recipient of subsequent contrary evidence from proprietors of putative servient tenements to the effect that no servitude had ever been constituted. The Keeper would then find himself in the middle of a dispute that he had no power to resolve. In addition his indemnity could be at risk should it transpire the affidavit evidence was less than accurate.

But if the new policy was understandable, its results were unfortunate, as Robert Rennie pointed out in his 2010 article. A "purchaser's solicitor will argue that, if the affidavit evidence is not enough for the Keeper, then the title is not safe. Thus the effect of the Keeper's policy, in practical terms at least, is to restrict the methods of creation of servitudes to creation in a deed or an Act of Parliament."[21]

It is not necessary to accept quite such an apocalyptic assessment of the position to see that the Keeper's practice gave rise to certain difficulties. With the introduction of "tell me don't show me," however, that practice has been quietly abandoned. To general surprise,[22] applicants for registration

---

18   See D below.

19   For the implications for claims against solicitors for professional negligence, see Rennie (n 1) at 76-78.

20   I David and A Rennie (eds), *Registration of Title Practice Book*, 2nd edn (2000) para 6.55.

21   Rennie (n 1) at 67.

22   The Scottish Law Commission had endorsed the Keeper's existing practice and given its reasons for so doing at some length: see Report on *Land Registration* (Scot Law Com No 222, 2010) paras 10.7-10.18.

are now invited to state whether a prescriptive servitude exists.[23] If they answer in the affirmative, they are asked for particulars of the servitude and, where possible, its route.[24] No affidavit or other evidence is to be submitted: the distinctly tricky decision as to whether the servitude was properly constituted has been passed from Keeper to applicant, or in practice to the applicant's solicitor.[25] If applicants claim a servitude, then it seems that the Keeper will believe them and enter the servitude on the title sheet accordingly.

C. Some Reasons Why

(1) The 2012 Act

Insofar as Registers of Scotland have sought to justify the change of policy they have done so by reference to the 2012 Act.[26] Yet they are mistaken if by this they mean that the change was required or even implied by the Act. Rather the opposite, indeed, is the case.

Under the 1979 Act the Keeper was given a great deal of discretion as to what might and might not be accepted for registration. A small number of things were forbidden, such as applications which omitted the fee or title number or where the land was insufficiently described; otherwise the Keeper could accept any application if "accompanied by such documents and other evidence as he may require."[27] The 2012 Act, in this as in other matters, is much more prescriptive. Section 21 provides that the Keeper *must* accept an application "to the extent that the applicant satisfies the Keeper" that the "application conditions" are met; if, conversely, the

---

23 Application form p 5. This is a first-registration question only, but a prescriptive servitude can equally be claimed where the application relates to registered property although the details will then have to be given in the further information sheets at the end of the form: see Registers of Scotland, *Guidance Notes on Application for Registration Form* (18 Nov 2014) 12.

24 Application form p 5. The form requires that the route of the servitude be delineated, but I understand that the Keeper overlooks this requirement in the case of underground pipes and, it may be, in other cases where the route in unclear.

25 As the *Guidance Notes* (n 23) 12 observe laconically: "The applicant should satisfy themselves that the servitude has been created by prescription and the right is exempt from challenge."

26 That was the line taken in the series of (excellent) road shows on the new Act given in October and November 2014 and captured on video at www.ros.gov.uk/2012act/.

27 1979 Act s 4(1), (2).

Keeper is not satisfied as to the conditions the application *must* be rejected. The conditions in question are both general conditions which apply to all applications and also particular conditions which apply only to the type of application in question.

Now it is true that the Act does not specify exactly how the Keeper is to be satisfied as to fulfilment of the application conditions; that much, at least, is left to her discretion. But since the difference between being satisfied or not satisfied is the difference between acceptance of an application or its rejection, it must be assumed that the Keeper was expected to do more than simply take the applicant's word for it.[28] Yet in relation to a number of important matters, as we have seen, that is exactly what the Keeper now does.

While, however, the 2012 Act neither requires nor even implies the use of "tell me don't show me," it does at least provide some shelter from the effects of the increase in errors which can be expected to result.[29] For on the one hand, an error on the Register is less serious, and more easily corrected, than under the 1979 Act, where the "Midas touch" gave it immediate legal effect.[30] And on the other, if things go wrong and rights are lost, the Act assists in the transfer of liability from the Keeper to the applicant's solicitor through the solicitor's duty, in section 111, to ensure that the Keeper does not inadvertently make the Register inaccurate.[31] The Keeper's vigilance under the 1979 Act regime, Robert Rennie wrote, reflected "a desire to restrict claims for indemnity;"[32] and if these claims can be deflected elsewhere, the need for vigilance is correspondingly reduced. It is important, however, not to claim too much for the Act in this regard. If the Midas touch has gone it has been replaced with a set of rules which, as we will see, can make the correction of errors even harder than before.[33] And while section 111 certainly assists in the deflection of liability, such

---

28 No doubt it is for this reason that the Keeper is so careful in inspecting the documentation which must accompany applications in respect of an *a non domino* disposition: see Registers of Scotland, *General Guidance on Prescriptive Claimants* (15 Sept 2014).

29 See E below.

30 1979 Act 3(1)(a). For an account of the Midas touch, see Scottish Law Commission, Discussion Paper on *Land Registration: Void and Voidable Titles* (Scot Law Com DP No 125, 2004) paras 5.34-5.39.

31 For s 111, see D(2) below.

32 Rennie (n 1) at 78.

33 See D(1) below.

deflection was often possible under the 1979 Act through its sanctions for the "careless" solicitor.[34]

(2) Other reasons

Nothing said so far explains why so radical a change of policy should have occurred. Two other factors, at least, seem likely to have been important. One is resources. In a development which no one could have foreseen, the Keeper was "invited" in May 2014 to complete the transfer of all land from the Sasine to the Land Register within the startlingly short period of ten years.[35] If resources can be freed up from the processing of applications, this will make that formidable target just a little bit more manageable.[36]

But the change cannot be explained by resources alone. It is not due to resources, for example, that the practice of "tell me don't show me" has been extended to prescriptive servitudes, for they were previously excluded from the Register altogether. To resources must be added attitudinal change. Just as the high level of intervention of the former regime, amounting almost to a nationalisation of conveyancing, was a product of the political and governmental culture of the 1970s,[37] so the withdrawal of state scrutiny is in line with the retreat of government which has been seen across a number of spheres in the recent past. That the Registers should concentrate on registration and leave conveyancers to do the conveyancing is a seductively powerful idea. For if judgments are to be made about titles, why should this not be left to those who, by profession and experience, are best equipped for the task? Freed, then, from the burden of decision-making, the Keeper's staff can concentrate on the efficient registration of the result.

---

34 1979 Act ss 9(3)(a)(iii) 12(3)(n) 13(4). The role of "carelessness" was mentioned briefly at A. above.

35 For the background, see Registers of Scotland, *Completion of the Land Register: Public Consultation* (July 2014). The paper begins with the bland statement that: "The Keeper of the Registers of Scotland has been invited by Scottish Ministers to complete the Land Register over the next ten years."

36 Andy Wightman's assessment is that: "The changes appear to be in response to the Scottish Government's request to meet the ten year target": see "Rethink required on ten year land registration goal" (1 Aug 2014, available at www.andywightman. com/?cat=33).

37 "We are not impressed," wrote the Reid Committee, "by the suggestion that the introduction of a scheme of registration of title is likely to lead to rigidity or bureaucratic control": see Reid Report (n 4) para 150. Yet that was exactly what took place.

Probably the ideal method of processing applications of registration lies somewhere between what we had and what we have. Under the former arrangements, as Robert Rennie noted, staff at the Register took too little notice of the views of conveyancers; now they take too much. What seems to be required is a more nuanced regime in which the Keeper, while making the final decisions, works closely and in a spirit of co-operation with the conveyancer responsible for the application. But even if such a system could be devised, it could not be implemented without a change of mind-set and a substantial increase in public resources. Neither, unfortunately, seems likely to occur in the near future.

F. On a Personal Note

I would like to finish by saying just a little about Robert Rennie, for whom this volume is written. Robert is widely known and admired as a legal practitioner, a scholar, an expert witness, a writer of opinions, and as a lecturer whose wit and wisdom have delighted countless audiences of students and professionals. Less well-known, perhaps, but hardly less important are his many acts of public service. Only one can be mentioned here. Robert was a key figure in the series of legislative reforms which, over the last decade or so, have transformed the law of property in Scotland. As a member of successive advisory committees of the Scottish Law Commission he contributed to the development of policy; as the senior professor of conveyancing[70] in Scotland he then defended and explained the legislative results to many different types of audience. In my role as a Scottish Law Commissioner between 1995 and 2005 I had many occasions to be grateful to Robert for his support, encouragement, and unfailing collegiality.

Of Robert's many important interventions I recall one in particular. When the Bill to abolish the feudal system was going through the new Scottish Parliament in the winter of 1999-2000, it came close to being hijacked by those who argued, inexplicably and incoherently, that the public interest in land was represented by the Crown and that, accordingly,

---

to bring off than before. For example, now that death certificates are no longer to be sent to the Register, a husband could assert that his wife was dead and proceed to sell the matrimonial home. A compliant or careless solicitor might be all too willing to accept that the survivorship clause in the title had been triggered. Also on this point, see Wightman (n 36).

70 Or property law. As Robert has been given to lament, he had become the last professor of "conveyancing" in Scotland.

the feudal link to the Crown must be preserved. Extraordinary as this view was, it gained the support of a number of MSPs on the parliamentary committee, the Justice and Home Affairs Committee, which was charged with considering the Bill. Robert was called by the Committee to give oral evidence. What happened next is captured in the following extract from the Official Report for the morning of Tuesday 9 November 1999:[71]

> **Pauline McNeill:** I presume that you heard the discussion before you came to the table. It was suggested that we spell out the rights that the Crown would retain, particularly in relation to public interest. Do you have a view on that?
>
> **Professor Rennie:** Yes. We are dealing with a bill to abolish – I emphasise that word – the feudal system. It makes no sense to abolish the feudal structure and retain the paramount superiority of the Crown. If that happens, we will not have abolished the feudal system. The bill will have to be radically altered if that is the case ... At the moment, the Crown cannot intervene in a feudal dispute between a vassal and a superior in Bishopbriggs. One cannot appeal to the Crown, as it has no role to play in the current feudal system. As I understood the discussion – I have to say that I might not have understood it all – a new and enhanced role for the Crown was proposed. That role would still be tied to some form of paramount feudal superiority.
>
> **Pauline McNeill:** So you are not interested in retaining any aspect of public interest? Who would represent the public interest in land issues?
>
> **Professor Rennie:** Currently, as feudal superior, the Crown does not represent the public interest.
>
> **The Convener (Roseanna Cunningham):** Are you saying that currently, there is no public interest, in that sense?
>
> **Professor Rennie:** Not in the feudal system. The Crown exercises the public interest through the Government.
>
> **Maureen Macmillan:** Can you see any practical benefits in Robin Callander's proposals?
>
> **Professor Rennie:** Frankly, I cannot see any benefits.

This trenchant defence convinced the doubters. No one could have done it better. When the Committee came to report a month later, it summarised Robert's evidence and added that, while "some members believe that

---

71   Scottish Parliament, Official Report, Justice and Home Affairs Committee, 9 Nov 1999, cols 365-66.

there is – or should be – some sort of public interest in land ... we all agree that retaining the Crown as paramount superior is not the way to address that issue."[72] And so in this way the full abolition of the feudal system – the basis of all the property-law reforms that were to follow – was secured. It was, I fancy, Robert's reference to Bishopbriggs that made the difference.

---

72 Justice and Home Affairs Committee, Stage 1 Report on the *Abolition of Feudal Tenure etc (Scotland) Bill* (SP Paper 44, 1999) vol 1 para 17.

3. A Puzzling Case about Possession

Lord Hope of Craighead

One of Robert Rennie's skills as an academic commentator was to identify cases that were worth drawing attention to because he thought that something might have gone wrong. Not infrequently he did this by means of an article in the *Scots Law Times*. One such case which was the subject of an article which he wrote in 1994 is *Hamilton v McIntosh Donald Ltd*.[1] It was a case about an area of rough peat moss in Aberdeenshire known as the Moss of Balqhuarn, part of a larger area known as Portlethen Moss. There were no buildings on it, and it was not in use for any kind of agriculture. It was just scrub land, which one might have thought was of no real value to anybody. It was also not fenced off, so anyone who wanted to could get access to it. As so often in cases of this kind, nobody paid much attention to what, if anything, was going on there or to whom the land belonged. The landowner was doing nothing to show to anyone who might have had a competing title that the land belonged to him. As far as the defenders who did have a competing title were concerned, there was no reason to think that objection would be taken if they were to make use of the land for their own purposes. That was the situation which, after the expiry of the prescriptive period, gave rise to a dispute about its ownership. On the one hand there was Mr Hamilton, who had a recorded title to the area of land but was making no use of it. On the other were the defenders, whose titles

---

1   1994 SC 304. Professor Rennie's article, "Possession: Nine Tenths of the Law," was published in 1994 *SLT (News)* 261.

    http://dx.doi.org/10.11647/OBP.0056.03

were derived from a disposition which had been granted in favour of one of their predecessors *a non domino*. It was habile to include the *dominium utile* of the disputed area. But the defenders needed to rely on the operation of prescriptive possession under section 1 of the Prescription and Limitation (Scotland) Act 1973 if they were to defeat the claim to ownership of Mr Hamilton.

The defenders succeeded in persuading the Lord Ordinary, Lord Prosser,[2] that various activities which had taken place over the area on their behalf or with their authority during the relevant period were enough to establish that they had a right of ownership. They were also successful in the Inner House, where the Second Division, by a majority (Lord Murray dissenting) held that there was just sufficient evidence of the necessary prescriptive possession to entitle the defenders to succeed, in the absence of any challenge by the pursuer or any adverse possession by him during that period. But, on any view, it was a narrow case. It might have gone either way. Both Lord Justice Clerk Ross and Lord Wylie, who constituted the majority, expressed hesitation in coming to the opinion that the Lord Ordinary had reached the correct conclusion on the evidence that was before him.[3] Lord Murray agreed that the case was a very narrow one. But in his view there was insufficient evidence to enable the necessary inference to be drawn.[4]

There were two features about the case that attracted Professor Rennie's attention. The first was the fact that the evidence about possession which the judges other than Lord Murray accepted was, as he put it,[5] "absolutely minimal." It amounted to little more than some seasonal rough shooting which took place mainly on Saturdays, and some dumping of rubbish which took place on and off throughout the year and on only a small part of the disputed area. Other actions such as three weeks' peat cutting and the carrying out of ground investigation work in relation to proposed road works were not in themselves sufficient because they were localised and transient. But they were held by the majority to point in the same direction as an assertion of ownership rights by the defenders. The second was a point of more general interest. It was about the risks to which the owner of a piece of scrub land of this kind was exposed by a party claiming

2   1994 *SLT* 212.
3   1994 SC 304 at 329H per the Lord Justice Clerk and at 334A per Lord Wylie.
4   Ibid at 333G.
5   1994 *SLT (News)* 261 at 264.

prescriptive possession of it on the basis of a disposition that was granted *a non domino*, if all that was needed to make good that claim were acts of the kind that were regarded as sufficient in this case. Of course, the owner of an estate extending to thousands of acres could not be expected to pace round the estate every week or month looking for evidence of possession by other parties. But the implication of this decision was that a failure to keep an eye on what was going on there, however minimal, could have unfortunate consequences. As Robert Rennie put it at the end of his article, with a characteristic turn of phrase, landowners needed to be vigilant "lest there be a land rush based on all manner of queer goings on in the middle of the night designed to establish possession."[6] He did not, one gathers, approve of the decision.

I was attracted to his article by one other comment that appears at the end of it. There had, it seems, been a suggestion that the case might go to the House of Lords. "If so," said Professor Rennie, "it will be interesting to see what their Lordships will make of it."[7] Remarks of that kind always excite interest. As it happened, the case did not go to the House of Lords after all. So their Lordships never had a chance to deal with the case. There was no further appeal. But the question, what their Lordships would have made of the case, is still worth a second look, even after an interval of more than twenty years.

There are two preliminary points that need to be made before one looks at the substance. The first is that the issue between the parties was, at least at first sight, an issue of fact rather than one of law. As Professor Rennie himself recognised,[8] in such cases there is always a natural reluctance on the part of the appellate court to interfere with a view which has been formed on the evidence by the judge who has heard it. In this case that point is strengthened by the fact that there were concurrent findings of fact both at first instance and in the Inner House. This means that the hurdle that would have had to have been overcome in the House of Lords was that much greater. This leads to the second point. As the decision was always bound to turn on the particular facts and circumstances, it would appear that there was no real principle of law flowing from the decision. In 1994 an appeal to the House of Lords (and now, to the Supreme Court) was available as of right. It would not have been necessary to obtain permission,

---

6   Ibid at 265.
7   Ibid at 265.
8   Ibid at 264.

as will be required when section 117 of the Courts Reform (Scotland) Act 2014 is brought into force.[9] The test for permission is whether the case raises a question of general public importance which is appropriate for further consideration on appeal. Given these two preliminary points it seems to me to be most unlikely that permission would have been given either by the Inner House or the House of Lords, had it been necessary at that time. But, writing as he was in 1994, Robert Rennie did not have to trouble with that point. So the question what their Lordships would have made of the case was not an idle one. There would have been no procedural obstacle in the way of an appeal.

Of course, these two preliminary points would not have disappeared just because the appeal would have to proceed as an appeal as of right. There is no shortage of cases where, both in the House of Lords and in the Supreme Court of the United Kingdom, their Lordships have made it clear that it would be a misuse of the right of appeal to bring cases there which turned purely on their own facts and raised no issue of general public importance at all.[10] But from time to time cases which at first sight seemed to have nothing to be said for them at all have turned out, on further examination, to raise points of real interest.[11] As this was a Scottish case, everything would be likely to have depended on whether the two Scottish Law Lords found something in the appeal that caught their interest. That is especially so as the issue was one about property law, as to which the laws on either side of the border are so different. That having been said, cases about loss of title to land to acts of competing possession through inadvertence are not unknown in the English courts. So, if they had been interested in the case, the Scottish Law Lords would not have found it difficult to carry their colleagues with them to the point of at least listening to the argument and then trying to make something of the case when it come to the point of writing a judgment.

The two Scots Law Lords who were sitting on the Appellate Committee of the House of Lords in 1994 were Lord Keith of Kinkel and Lord Jauncey of Tullichettle. I had not yet reached the House of Lords, so I do not have much of a feeling for what they would have made of the case if they had had to deal with it. It is possible that counsel would have been able to persuade

---

9   Courts Reform (Scotland) Act 2014, section 117.
10   See, e.g., *Wilson v Jaymarke Estates Ltd* [2007] UKHL 29, 2007 SC (HL) 135; *Uprichard v Scottish Ministers* [2013] UKSC 21, 2013 SC (UKSC) 219.
11   See, e.g., *Ritchie v Lloyd* [2007] UKHL 9, 2007 SC (HL) 89.

them that it did raise an issue that was worth further consideration. On the other hand, they might well have felt that there were no grounds on which they could properly interfere with the decision of the Inner House. In that event their judgment would not have added anything of interest to what had already been said by the judges in the Court of Session. It can be assumed that their attention would have been drawn to Professor Rennie's article. But I think that is unlikely that his name would have meant anything to either Lord Keith or Lord Jauncey. They came from a generation of judges who paid little attention to the views of the academic branch of the profession, and it can be assumed that they would have adopted that approach in this case too. Speculation as to what they would have made of his comments is, for this reason, a rather sterile exercise. But my impression, much as I admired and respected both of them, is that they were not inclined to push out the frontiers of the law beyond its established boundaries. So I think that the chances of their reversing the decision of the Inner House must be regarded as rather slim. In that situation Mr Hamilton was probably wise not to take the case any further.

So I would prefer to assume that I would have been sitting on the Appellate Committee when the appeal reached the House, and that my colleague from Scotland on the committee would have been Lord Rodger of Earlsferry. There are several reasons for thinking that this is a happier assumption to make. Like Alan Rodger, I welcomed the opportunity to explore issues of Scottish private law whenever they came our way when we were sitting in London. In our experience, there was not infrequently something in those cases which had not been spotted before, or at least something new about them that was worth saying. For us, the fact that Robert Rennie had thought it worth commenting on the case would at least have attracted our interest. It would also have presented a challenge too, as we would have felt that we could not ignore his comments when we were writing our judgments.

One of the advantages of sitting in London is the opportunity that it gives for comparing the Scots approach to a problem with that which is adopted in similar circumstances in England. As it happens, an appeal which presented a problem not all that distant from that raised by *Hamilton v McIntosh Donald* came before the House of Lords in March 2002. I had been sitting as a member of the Appellate Committee for over five years by then. I had recently been joined by Lord Rodger, although he was not asked to sit with me on this occasion. The appeal was in the case of *J A Pye (Oxford) Ltd v Graham*.[12] It was an English appeal which, like the *Hamilton* case, raised an issue about adverse possession. The landowner, Pye, sought to recover possession of the land, to which it held a paper title, from the defendants who had been using it for over twenty years. The defendants' argument was that inaction of the kind that caused the problem for the landowner in *Hamilton* had resulted in the loss of the right to recover possession by the operation of the Limitation Act 1980. This was because they had been in "adverse possession" of the land within the meaning of paragraph 11 of Schedule 6 to the 1980 Act. The acts which were said to have amounted to adverse possession consisted, to begin with, of using the land for grazing and cutting hay. But as time went on the defendants carried out various other operations such as harrowing and spreading dung on the land to ensure its fitness for grazing in the following season, and later on changed their use of the land to arable. Various witnesses who had observed these activities said that they thought that the defendants were the owners, while it was clear that Pye showed no interest in its agricultural management. The case really turned on what was meant by the expression "adverse possession," not on the extent or quality of the defendants' use of the land. Their use of it was, of course, more than enough to establish a right of ownership by the operation of prescriptive possession if the land had been in Scotland and if they had had a title to it which was habile to include the *dominium utile*. They had been conducting their farming operations there openly, peaceable and without any judicial interruption for more than the prescriptive period. But was this "adverse possession" within the meaning of the English statute?

That was not an uninteresting question. As Lord Browne-Wilkinson observed,[13] the apparently straightforward provisions of the Limitation Act 1980 had given rise to considerable difficulties. The problem was that the expression "adverse possession" had become linked to the idea that a squatter's use of the land had to conflict with the intentions of the paper title owner as to his present or future use of the land. He had to be shown to have acted adversely to the paper title owner, in the sense that his use of the land was inconsistent with any use, present or future, of it by the true owner. The Court of Appeal had found that the problem for the defendants, on this approach, was that they had been using the land in exactly the same fashion as Pye had agreed to their using it under a grazing let in

---

12   [2002] UKHL 30, [2003] 1 AC 419.
13   Ibid at para 31.

the past in the hope that, should this be necessary, they would be able to obtain Pye's agreement to its being used in the future.[14] This analysis of the facts was found not to be entirely sound. The better analysis was that of the trial judge, Neuberger J,[15] who held that the defendants had established title by possession because they had treated the land as their own for the necessary period. So the defendants succeeded in their appeal, and Pye were deprived of their title to it by the operation of the statute. Pye complained that this result was incompatible with their rights under article 1 of the First Protocol to the European Convention on Human Rights, but it was held by a Grand Chamber of the Strasbourg Court that the fair balance required by A1P1 was not upset.[16]

I took the opportunity in my speech in that case to comment on the concept of adverse possession and the apparent injustice of the result.[17] It seemed to me that the concept of possession required both an intention to take or occupy the land (*animus*) and some act of the body (*corpus*) which gives effect to that intention. As for the intention, I said that the animus which was required was the intent to exercise exclusive control over the subjects for oneself.[18] It was not necessary to show that there was a deliberate intention to exclude the paper owner or the registered proprietor. The word "adverse" as used by the statute did not carry that implication. The only intention that had to be demonstrated was an intention to occupy and use the land as one's own. It is worth quoting the way I linked this approach to that taken in Scots law:[19]

> This is a concept which Rankine, *The Law of Land-Ownership in Scotland*, 4th edn (1909), p 4, captured in his use of the Latin phrase *cum animo rem sibi habendi* (see his reference in footnote 1 to Savingy, *Das Recht des Besitzes*, translated by Perry (1848), paras 1-11). It is similar to that which was introduced into the law of Scotland by the Prescription Act 1617, c 12 relating to the acquisition of an interest in land by the operation of positive prescription. The possession that is required for this purpose is possession "openly, peaceably and without any judicial interruption" on a competing title for the requisite period: Prescription and Limitation (Scotland) Act 1973, section 1(1)(a). So I would hold that, if the evidence shows that the person

---

14   [2001] EWCA Civ 107, [2001] Ch 804.
15   [2000] Ch 676.
16   (2008) 46 EHRR 45.
17   *J A Pye (Oxford) Ltd v Graham* [2003] AC 419 at paras 67ff.
18   See Henry Bond, "Possession in the Roman Law" (1890) 6 LQR 259, at p 270.
19   *J A Pye (Oxford) Ltd v Graham* (n 17) at para 71.

was using the land in a way that one would expect him to use it if he were the true owner, that is enough.

I agreed with my colleagues on the Appellate Committee that the only conclusion that could reasonably be drawn from the evidence was that the defendants had occupied and used the disputed land as their own for the necessary period before the action to remove them was brought. I noted that the unfairness in the system laid down by the Limitation Act 1980 lay in the lack of safeguards against oversight or inadvertence on the part of the registered proprietor.

A feature of our system of case law, at least at the appellate level where there is room for the law's development, is that one case tends to feed off another. *Pye v Graham* was an English case which dealt with a different statute. But the examination of the concept of adverse possession in that case might be thought to have some bearing on the points that Robert Rennie was making in his article about the *Hamilton* case. Did the judges in the Court of Session pay sufficient attention to the nature and quality of the possession that was required? As he noted,[20] in Montgomerie Bell's view it had to be of the highest description of which the subject is capable.[21] Neither the Lord Ordinary nor the Judges in the Inner House make any reference to this test. Lord Justice Clerk Ross did, when he was setting out the principles to be applied, say that whether particular acts constitute possession for the purposes of prescription depends upon the nature of the subjects claimed.[22] But two of the authorities to which he referred might have justified a formulation that was closer to that suggested by Montgomerie Bell. In *Buchanan and Geils v Lord Advocate* Lord Mure said that the foreshore was in the occupation of the pursuer "in every way that a foreshore admits of being used."[23] In *Young v North British Railway Co* Lord Watson said that test would be satisfied if the pursuer "has had all the beneficial uses" of the foreshore that a grantee of the Crown would naturally enjoy.[24] In *Aitken's Trustees v The Caledonian Railway and the Lord Advocate* Lord Moncrieff put the matter in much the same way as the Lord Justice Clerk when he said that, when judging the sufficiency of the possession, regard must be had

---

20   1994 *SLT (News)* 261, 264.
21   G J Bell, *Lectures on Conveyancing*, 3rd edn (1882) 707.
22   1994 SC 303 at 332B per Lord Justice Clerk Ross.
23   (1882) 9 R 1218 at 1230.
24   (1887) 14 R (HL) 53 at 54.

to the nature of the subject and the uses to which it can be put."[25] But only a few sentences earlier he had quoted the same words from Lord Watson's speech in *Young*, and the point in *Aitken* was that the possession that had been established by the evidence was of a small portion only of the part of the foreshore over which a right of ownership was being claimed. That was held to be insufficient to establish a prescriptive right to the whole of it. In such a narrow case as *Hamilton* plainly was, small differences matter when the test to be applied is being formulated. Would it have made a difference to the result if the judges had had in the forefront of their minds the test that Montgomerie Bell had suggested instead of the somewhat weaker way of expressing it which, following Lord Moncreiff in *Aitken*, was adopted by the Lord Justice Clerk? Would it have made a difference if reference had been made to my way of putting the point in *Pye*, when I said the question was whether the person was using the land in a way that one would expect him to use it if he were the true owner?

One has, of course, to twist the chronology a bit to bring the speeches in *Pye*, which were delivered in March 2002, into the argument in a supposed appeal to the House of Lords in *Hamilton*. But that would be necessary anyway if one is to assume that Lord Rodger had been sitting with me in the appeal, as he did not become a Lord of Appeal in Ordinary until October 2001. Supposing then that Lord Rodger had been sitting with me sometime after March 2002, one has to ask whether he would have been interested in pursuing the questions which I posed at the end of the preceding paragraph. Would he have thought that something might be gained from looking at an English case which was concerned with a different issue under a different statute when addressing an issue of Scots law in an appeal from Scotland? Without his support I would have been unlikely to have made much progress in persuading my English colleagues that there was something in the point that was worth thinking about. With his support there would have been every chance that I would have been able to do so.

I must move the calendar on quite a bit more to get a feel for what Lord Rodger would have thought of the point if he had been given the opportunity. The answer can be found in a judgment which he delivered in March 2010 in an appeal to the UK Supreme Court on which we both sat. It raised an issue, which has given rise to much litigation in England

---

25   (1906) 6 F 465 at 470.

in recent years, about the test to be applied in determining whether land
is appropriate for registration as a town or village green under section 15
of the Commons Act 2006.[26] This was the case of *R (Lewis) v Redcar and
Cleveland Borough Council*.[27] The question was whether the local inhabitants
had done enough to show that they had made use of the area in question
"as of right" for a period of at least 20 years. One has only to mention this
test to appreciate that the questions that are likely to arise on the evidence
are not dissimilar to those that have to be addressed where a claim to
ownership by the operation of prescription is made under the 1980 Act. In
the *Redcar* case the land in question had been used for many years as a golf
course. The local inhabitants had been using it too, regularly and in large
numbers, for a variety of sports and pastimes including jogging, children's
play and dog-walking which was tolerated and not objected to by those
playing golf on the golf course. The question was whether the inhabitants
were doing these things as of right.

Lord Rodger was sufficiently interested in this issue to add a judgment
of his own based on his own researches,[28] although he agreed with the
leading judgment which was given by Lord Walker. He referred to the
Digest[29] when he was exploring the meaning of the phrase "as of right," in
the light of Lord Hoffmann's observation in an earlier Commons case[30] that
it was to be construed as meaning *nec vi, nec clam, nec precario*. His point
was that it would be wrong to suppose that the Latin word *vi* meant that
some kind of physical force was required. He referred, by way of further
support, to Lord Jauncey's observation in a case about a claim to a public
right of way in Scotland[31] that there is no principle of law which requires
there to be conflict between the interests of users and those of the proprietor,
and to an observation by Lord Sands in another public right of way case
in Scotland[32] in order to make the point that most people who walk their
dogs or play with their children on the disputed land know nothing about
the legal character of their right to do so. The way in which he slipped so

---

26 See *R (Barkas) v North Yorkshire County Council* [2014] UKSC 31 for the most recent in
    this series.

27 *R (Lewis) v Redcar and Cleveland Borough Council (No 2)* [2010] UKSC 11, [2010] 2 AC 70.

28 See ibid (n 27) at paras 79 ff.

29 D 43.24.1.5-9, Ulpian *ad edictum*.

30 *R v Oxfordshire County Council, Ex p Sunningwell Parish Council* [2000] 1 AC 335.

31 *Cumbernauld and Kilsyth District Council v Dollar Land (Cumbernauld) Ltd* 1993 SC (HL) 44
    at 47 per Lord Jauncey.

32 *Rhins District Committee of Wigtownshire County Council v Cuninghame* 1917 2 SLT 169 at
    172 per Lord Sands.

easily to and fro across the border in his use of these authorities suggests quite strongly that he would have been quite happy to do the same if he had been hearing the appeal in *Hamilton*. So it is not an unreasonable assumption that he, like me, would have wanted to look quite closely at the question whether the Inner House really did direct their minds to the correct test as to the nature and quality of the possession that had to be shown to establish the defenders' case when they refused Mr Hamilton's reclaiming motion. If we had been satisfied that this was not so, this would have enabled us to form our own view as to whether the test was satisfied by the evidence.

There, however, my reaction to Robert Rennie's article must stop. There was no appeal, and it would not be fair for me to express a concluded view as to what would have happened if there had been and if, on my rather extended hypothesis, Lord Rodger and I had had the pleasure of hearing it. What I can properly say, however, is that Robert's article did raise a very interesting issue which, although perhaps slightly ahead of its time, focused on a point that was very much in need of attention. The balance between the interests of the landowner and those of the party claiming prescriptive possession needs to be struck in the right place. One is left with an uneasy feeling that in Mr Hamilton's case that was not so. I think that Robert Rennie was quite right to draw attention to this point in the way he did in his article. I confess to a feeling of some regret that I was not given an opportunity to respond to it.

4. "It's in the Post": Distance Contracting in Scotland 1681-1855

Professor Hector L MacQueen

In 1684 the Duke of Gordon engaged Robert Smith to serve him and his family "in chirurgery and physic, and also to supervise his buildings and architecture" – an interesting combination of medical and property services. Smith's salary was to be 200 merks a year plus board when the Duke was at home and a daily subsistence allowance otherwise. Smith and the Duke each signed a copy of their agreement, then exchanged these copies. Some seventeen years later, in 1701, Smith obtained decree from the Sheriff at Edinburgh against the Duke for non-payment of 2,823 pounds Scots due under the contract, representing "so many years board wages, during the years the Duke did not live at home, at the rate of 12 pence per day." Smith's claim suggests that the Duke did not spend much time at home.[1] The Duke sought to suspend the sheriff's decree in the Court of Session in Edinburgh, on the basis that "by the contract produced by the charger himself [i.e. *Smith*], it appears, the clause pursued on is a marginal note, and which, not being subscribed by the Duke, but only by Smith himself, can never oblige the Duke." The court held, however, "that mutual contracts having two doubles need not be subscribed by both parties-contracters, but

---

1   A merk was worth 2/3 of a pound Scots, itself valued in 1707 at one-twelfth of a pound sterling. One shilling Scots exchanged for one penny sterling in 1707, i.e. one penny Scots was 1/12th of a penny sterling.

                    http://dx.doi.org/10.11647/OBP.0056.04

it was sufficient in law if the Duke's principal was signed by Smith and his counterpart by the Duke." An earlier decision said to be to the same effect, *Sinclair of Ossory in Caithness*,[2] was referred to by the court as having settled the question. Smith argued that "there remain some dark vestiges of a subscription [*to the marginal note on his double*], though by the badness of the ink and the wearing of the paper, it is not so legible now." Although this explanation is not implausible, bearing in mind that the documents had been executed seventeen years before the case came into court, the Court of Session seems to have preferred the Duke's claim that "no subscription appeared, nor the least character of letters." But the court "sustained the marginal note, though not signed by the Duke, seeing it was contained in his own double uncancelled." The report summarises the effect of the decision as being that "if a mutual contract is executed by two counterparts, it is sufficient if each party subscribes the paper containing what is prestable on himself."[3] The court thus took a fairly liberal approach to the effect of the Duke's undoubted subscription of the double in Smith's possession as embracing the unsigned marginal note thereon, with perhaps some sort of personal bar arising from the fact that he had not struck out the note in his own double even though that document had indeed been subscribed by Smith. It should however be observed that the court noticed that the clause in the marginal note "seemed materially to differ" in the two copies, and remitted the case for further inquiry on this point before the ordinary judge (presumably the sheriff in Edinburgh).

Smith v Duke of Gordon is a decision which passed virtually unnoticed in cases and legal texts for the next 300 years, apart from a reference in Lord Bankton's *Institute of the Laws of Scotland*, published between 1751 and 1753,[4] and one citation in 1957 in the sheriff court case of *Wilson v Fenton Bros (Glasgow) Ltd*.[5] That case involved the exchange by parties of duplicates of a patent licence agreement, each party signing one copy and then handing that copy over to the other. The sheriff-substitute (J C E Hay) held that the

---

2   No report of this case has been traced.

3   *Smith v Duke of Gordon* (1701) Mor 16987. The case of *Cubbison v Cubbison* (1716) Mor 16988 also involves "doubles of a writ," and in that case there were three such "doubles."

4   Andrew McDouall, Lord Bankton, *An Institute of the Laws of Scotland in Civil Rights with observations upon the agreement or diversity between them and the laws of England*, 2 vols (Edinburgh, 1751-52) 1.11.36 (also available in a reprint as vols 41-43 in the Stair Society series, edited with an introduction by W M Gordon). Note too Bankton's observation on the English law, at 1.11 (*Observations on the Laws of England*) 17.

5   1957 *SLT* (Sh Ct) 3. Note also G Lubbe, "Formation of Contract" in K Reid and R Zimmermann (eds), *A History of Private Law in Scotland* vol 2 (2000) 41-42.

The first Scottish writer to provide us with something like general doctrine on offer and acceptance, in the third (1816-1819) edition of his *Commentaries on the Law of Scotland*, was George Joseph Bell, Hume's successor in the Scots Law Chair at Edinburgh 1822-1839. Perhaps in contrast with Hume and Brown, he introduced the subject in the context of mercantile transactions, as examples of where the formalities of the rules on writing were relaxed:[29]

> Contracts in mercantile dealings are not so frequently formed by solemn deeds, as by letters or correspondence. One merchant gives an order to another at a distance by letter, which that other agrees to perform, or he makes an offer which the other accepts. And although the parties are in the same place, mercantile contracts are most commonly formed in this way. ...

From this point Bell moves into almost two pages on the law of offer and acceptance. In the fifth edition of the *Commentaries* (1826), the last published in his lifetime, he supplemented the passage quoted above with the following:[30]

> It is dangerous to rely on a long correspondence from which to collect the terms of a contract. The engagement should be so distinct and specific, that the party may be enabled at once to put his finger on it and say, "Here is my agreement." And in courts of law nothing short of this can be relied on as the ground of an action.

Bell thus saw the offer-acceptance doctrine as especially conducive to the practice of merchants, helping them to focus on stating their contracts with the minimum of documentation, and also narrowing the field of inquiry for the courts when disputes about the existence of contracts came before them. Two documents were all that was needed: one stating the terms of the bargain, the other acceding to it. Bell distinguished the case of orders in trade:[31]

> If a merchant has sent, not an offer to purchase, but an order for goods, it is so far of the nature of an offer, that it may be rejected; but the person to whom it is addressed binds the bargain, by proceeding with all due diligence to execute the order. Nor is it necessary for him to accept it in order

---

29 G J Bell, *Commentaries on the Mercantile Jurisprudence of Scotland*, 3rd edn (Edinburgh, 1816-19), vol 2, 281. Unless otherwise indicated, as here, references to Bell's *Commentaries* in this paper are to the 5th edition of 1826, the last published in Bell's lifetime (which is also almost entirely reproduced in the 7th and final edition of 1870). The passage quoted above is at vol 1, 325 of the 5th edition.

30 Bell, *Commentaries*, 5th edn vol 1, 326.

31 Ibid, 327.

to bind the bargain. It is an equitable part of this rule, however, that if he do not mean to execute the order, he must instantly communicate his refusal; and should he neglect to do so, he will be held to have engaged himself to the performance of it.

Bell was, however, a little less context-specific in his approach to the subject in the later but more elementary *Principles of the Law of Scotland* (essentially his student lecture notes, first published in 1826). There he simply stated that "a mutual contract, consensus in *idem placitum*, commences by offer and is completed by acceptance."[32] But the detailed discussion occurs almost at the end of his treatment of general contract law, which starts instead with Stair's concept of the conventional obligation which springs from the engagement, or the deliberate and voluntary consent with purpose to engage, of a party. Offer and acceptance is thus still almost a subsidiary topic in this setting rather than the pre-eminent example of formation of contract.

In both *Commentaries* and *Principles* Bell's earliest treatments relied almost entirely on Scottish case authorities. Only in later editions of the *Principles* did much the same text came to be adorned with references to Pothier's treatise on sale, plus the work of Charles Toullier[33] and Jean-Marie Pardessus[34] on French law as well as some English cases.[35] But this does not preclude the possibility that French or English influences were at play in Bell's thinking from his first writings on offer and acceptance. He is known to have been influenced generally by his reading in both systems, in particular by the writings of Pothier, who had been the first fully to articulate offer-acceptance doctrine on the Continent.[36] On the other hand,

---

32   G J Bell, *Principles of the Law of Scotland*, 1st edn (Edinburgh, 1829); 10th edn (Edinburgh, 1899) § 72. Note also §§ 8-9. Unless otherwise indicated, references to Bell's *Principles* in what follows are to the 4th edition of 1838, the last published in his lifetime (reprinted Edinburgh, 2010); the texts under discussion in this paper show virtually no change from 1st to 4th edition.

33   Most probably *Droit civil français suivant l'ordre du Code Napoléon, ouvrage dans lequel on a tâché de réunir la théorie à la pratique*, published in 14 volumes between 1811 and 1831. The Advocates Library in Edinburgh holds the 5th edition, published in 15 volumes between 1830 and 1836. Toullier (1752-1835) was Professor of French Law at Rennes from 1778.

34   The references appear to be to multi-volume works and may therefore be to either *Traité du contrat et des lettres de change*, 2 vols (1809) or *Cours de droit commercial*, 4 vols (1813-1817). Both works appear in the catalogue of the Advocates Library. Pardessus (1772-1853) was Professor of Commercial Law at Paris from 1810.

35   Bell, *Principles*, 4th edn 1839, §§ 72-79.

36   R J Pothier, *Traité des obligations* (first published 1761) [4]; idem, *Traité du contrat de vente* (first published 1762), 31-33; R Zimmermann, *The Law of Obligations: Roman Foundations*

supported it.[66] There was also the principle of delivery, without which a writing was not binding. But handing a letter to the post office was not delivery to the addressee; even if the letter could not be reclaimed from the post office, that was a matter of public regulation only, and in any event various misadventures could befall the communication while it was in the post that would prevent delivery to the actual addressee. The argument from equity was also challenged:[67]

> But it is said that, according to modern writers, the definition of strict law is to be sacrificed, and the principles of equity are to be introduced. That may be true as to the common law of England, but not so as to the law of any other civilised country in Europe. Besides, what is meant in this sense by principle of equity but consuetude making law? It is not that equity is to be allowed to control the law, and there is no ground for equity to be brought in here.

The basic rule was that the offeror had the right to retract until the acceptance was known to him. The fundamental differences between the two sides were thus about whether or not there was a right to revoke an offer once made, and about whether or not an acceptance had to be communicated to the offeror to conclude a contract between the parties. On the revocation point, Lord President M'Neill was clear that "a simple, unconditional offer may be recalled at any time before acceptance, and that it may be so recalled by a letter transmitted by post," and cited Stair as authority on the point.[68] On the communication point the Lord President said that "an offer is nothing until it is communicated to the party to whom it is made" and that "the recall or withdrawal of an offer that has been communicated can have no effect until the recall or withdrawal has been communicated, or may be assumed to have been communicated, to the party holding the offer."[69] But this principle of communication did not apply to an acceptance, which was different in nature from a revocation:[70]

> The one consists in effectually undoing something that the party himself already done, and which binds him, unless it is effectually undone; the other consists in merely acceding to a proposal made.

---

66 Perhaps surprisingly the printed argument for James does not refer to Stair on the offerer's power to withdraw the offer or on the general need for consent to be manifested by external signs.

67 (1855) 18 D 8.

68 Ibid D 10, 12.

69 Ibid D 10 (see also ibid, 11).

70 Ibid D 11 (see also ibid, 13).

What the acceptor had to do varied according to the circumstances. Where, as in this case, writing was required, it was not enough to create the writing and then keep it; but personal delivery was also not necessary:[71]

> Where an offer is made by letter from a distance through the medium of the post, the offeror selecting that medium of transmission authorises and invites the offeree to communicate his acceptance through the same medium. … By putting the letter of acceptance into the post-office, the offeree did just what he was invited to do, and all that it was incumbent on him or possible for him to do by way of acceptance, by the mode of communication which he was authorised, if not invited by the offeror to adopt.

Hence, the Lord President reasoned, "the act of acceptance was completed by the putting of the letter into the post-office; and … a letter of recall, which did not arrive till after that act, cannot be held to have interrupted the completion of the contract."[72] He found this supported by the Scottish authorities of Bell's *Commentaries* and *Higgins v Dunlop*. His position was also reinforced by his view that the requirement of delivery in relation to the formal writing was satisfied by putting the acceptance in the hands of the post office.[73] At no point did he cite *Adams v Lindsell* or any other English or other authority.

The second member of the majority in *Thomson*, Lord Ivory, agreed in substance with the Lord President's view of the law and its application; but the third member, Lord Deas, while reaching the same result, did so more on the basis which had been actually argued by the pursuers, *viz* that the offer was binding if the act of acceptance was made within a reasonable time. An express stipulation to the contrary in the offer was needed to make the result otherwise. Accordingly:[74]

> It is enough that the offeror has said, or is held to have said, that if the offer be accepted *debito tempore*, he shall be bound. This being the nature of his offer, whether expressly or by implication, he cannot resile from it if the party to whom it is addressed, having the offer, and nothing but the offer, before him, has, by duly posting his acceptance *bona fide*, done all in his power to comply with the only condition in the offer to make it absolutely binding on the offeror.

---

71   (1855) 18 D 11.
72   Ibid.
73   Ibid D 12-13.
74   Ibid D 24.

Lord Deas also observed that in mercantile cases "a reasonable time would, by the usage of trade, have meant in course of post."[75] "It follows," he added,[76]

> that, if posting the answer were not acceptance here, posting the answer, even in due course of post, never could be acceptance in any mercantile transaction. This would be a great impediment to mercantile dealings, where the party who receives an offer of goods, or for goods, and duly posts his acceptance, naturally goes into the market and deals with other persons upon the footing that this particular bargain has been concluded.

The Deas view of the case was thus essentially the one that had been articulated first by Bell, justified by the perception that the commercial marketplace demanded both speed and certainty, and resting more on the irrevocability of offers than on the view that postal acceptances created a contract. He noted (but without committing to) Lord Fullerton's view in *Dunlop v Higgins* that the posting of the acceptance only barred the offer's revocation, while also reserving his opinion on the soundness of *Dunmore v Alexander* and its apparent ruling that a postal acceptance could be revoked by a further communication from the offeree catching up with or even over-taking the first letter.

Lord Curriehill's powerful dissent started from Stair's statement that offers, being non-obligatory, could be withdrawn before acceptance. It was not necessary for the offer to state as much. On this point he was therefore in agreement with the Lord President and Lord Ivory. The question for him was, which of two powers was exercised first: the offeror's power to revoke, or the offeree's power to accept? In his view, the answer depended on which of the communications was first to be delivered to its addressee or a person acting for that addressee, and the evidence showed that it was the revocation. He could see no reason in either principle or authority for distinguishing between the communications as to when they took effect. Stair's distinction between desire, resolution and engagement was again referred to in support of the argument that a communication had to be brought to the notice of the party whom it was intended to affect. That was reinforced by the requirement of delivery in relation to obligatory documents. Posting a letter was not to be treated as such delivery. The post-office was not an agent or mandatory of either party, nor was it a common

---

75   (1855) 18 D 24.
76   Ibid.

carrier; the inability of a sender to recover a letter from the post-office was a matter of public regulation which equally prevented the addressee from demanding it until it reached its address. The writer of a letter might have lost control of the document but he had "no more lost his control over the act of his will which he therein expresses, than if that document were still in the hands of his own servant or messenger."[77] This was the explanation of *Dunmore v Alexander*, the ground of the judgement being that stated by Lord Newton in the Outer House.[78] Neither *Dunlop v Higgins* nor *Adams v Lindsell* had involved revocations, while both had proceeded upon what was held to be a usage of trade in such commercial cases. Neither could be authority in a case about the sale of land in Scotland which was not alleged to be subject to any such usage of trade. Bell's statement that "in the common case it is not necessary that the acceptance shall have reached the person who makes the offer" was supported by no authority, had not been fully accepted in *Higgins*, and was only correct in certain cases, such as that of the unconditional promise or that of the order in trade.

What then could be said of the law of offer and acceptance after *Thomson v James*? First, it was now plainly a doctrine of the general law of contract. Even though all the judges emphasised the importance of the fact that this was a case about the sale of land, with its concomitant of formal writing requirements, there was little doubt of its bearing on other situations, above all commercial transactions. Second, three of the four judges were clear that offers could be freely revoked by the offeror prior to acceptance unless there was an express statement or implication to the contrary. Next, the same three were also clear that such revocation required communication to the offeree to be effective. The judges all further agreed that an offer also required communication before it could be accepted. But only Lord Curriehill was of the view that acceptance too needed communication, indeed, in the case of the written acceptance, delivery, to the offeror or his representative to take legal effect and conclude a contract. The majority view seems to have been that, not just postal acceptances, but acceptances in general did not need communication to have this effect. While more than a mental decision to accept, or the preparation of a written acceptance without sending it, was

---

77 (1855) 18 D 21.

78 Lord Curriehill also commented: "[M]y confidence in the general principle, stated by Lord Newton as the ground of the judgment in the case of Lady Dunmore, is much strengthened by the circumstance that that eminent judge was for a considerable time professor of civil law in the University of Edinburgh." ((1855) 18 D 23). As Alexander Irving, Lord Newton held the Edinburgh Civil Law Chair from 1800-1827.

5. Assignations of All Sums Securities

Dr Ross G Anderson

No appointment was ever more successful and none illustrates more clearly the desirability of having as a professor one who is conversant with the practice of the branch of the law he is called on to teach. To set a man to teach conveyancing who is not engaged in large practice, and who only knows the subject from books or historically, is like making a man professor of surgery who has only read about it and who never performed an operation.[1]

A. The Chair of Conveyancing

(1) Introduction

Robert Rennie was appointed the Professor of Conveyancing in 1993. During a tenure marked by indefatigable industry, Robert's chair became, in the eyes of the profession, the face of the Glasgow Law School. With Robert's retirement, there comes the opportunity to reflect not just on Robert's contributions, but also on the place of the Chair he has held with such distinction in the Scottish legal profession, in legal education and in legal scholarship. So before addressing the technical topic I have chosen for my contribution, it is first to the history and context of the Chair that I turn.

---

1   D Murray, *Memories of the Old College of Glasgow* (1927) 236, describing the first holder of the Chair of Conveyancing, Professor Anderson Kirkwood.

     http://dx.doi.org/10.11647/OBP.0056.05

(2) The first Conveyancing Chairs

2014 saw the Tercentenary of the appointment of the first holder of the Regius Chair in Civil Law in the University of Glasgow, William Forbes in 1714. But it was in the nineteenth century that the Universities of Glasgow and Edinburgh founded chairs of Conveyancing. If the word "conveyancing" is considered to be a word for which Scots lawyers have peculiar affinity, it may be because University Chairs in Conveyancing is a peculiarly Scottish phenomenon (although the basic idea which underlies these Chairs has a modern appeal in the United States, where all self-respecting law schools must have a Professor of "clinical legal education"). The creation of the Chair of Conveyancing in the University of Edinburgh marked a significant break with the effective monopoly exercised by the Faculty of Advocates on the chairs in law in that University, since the appointment to the Chair of Conveyancing would come from the ranks of the Society of Writers to Her Majesty's Signet. The notion of the "lower branch" of the legal profession – solicitors – being remotely qualified to found a University Chair was a source of considerable invective from members of the Faculty of Advocates, the politically conservative members of which found the appointment of the leading Whig, and future editor of the *Edinburgh Review*, Macvey Napier, as the first holder, almost too much to bear.[2] One of the most prolific contributors to the contemporary conservative periodical, *Blackwood's Edinburgh Magazine*, himself an advocate, pointedly observed how, in England, conveyancing was in the hands of the bar:[3] the English, he ventured, would "laugh" even to hear even of a *lectureship*, never mind a *Professorship*, of conveyancing in a University.[4] The "abstruse science" of

---

2 "Francisculus Funk," "The Pluckless School of Politics, No 1" (1823) 14 *Blackwood's Edinburgh Magazine* 139-44. Funk was the pseudonym of John Cay, Advocate: see A L Strout, *A Bibliography of Articles in Blackwood's Magazine: volumes I through XVIII, 1817-1825* (1959) 110. Cay was sheriff at Linlithgow from 1825 to 1865. Cay was one of the oldest friends of John Gibson Lockhart (for whom see n 4): D Douglas (ed), *The Journal of Sir Walter Scott, from the original manuscript at Abbotsford* (1890) (reprinted 2013) I, 22, n 1. For the background to the Edinburgh Conveyancing chair in the WS Society's lectures, first given by Robert Bell, brother of George Joseph, see my "Introduction" to G Watson (ed), *Bell's Dictionary and Digest of the Law of Scotland*, 7th edn (1890) (reprinted 2012) xviii-xxxi.

3 As it remains to this day: see, for instance, the references to "conveyancing counsel" in the English Civil Procedure Rules, r 40.18 and 40.19 and Practice Direction 40D.

4 "C.N.," "Tail-Piece" (1823) 14 *Blackwood's Edinburgh Magazine* 144. "C. N." = Christopher North, the pseudonym of a number of contributors, often John Wilson, Advocate and Professor of Moral Philosophy in the University of Edinburgh, but in this case Strout (n 200) attributes this tail-piece to John Gibson Lockhart, Advocate, but best known as a satirist and as the biographer of his father-in-law, Sir Walter Scott.

conveyancing,[5] in so far as it related to deeds, according to this disaffected and "nearly fee-less advocate" was insufficiently learned to justify the erection of a University Chair; and *esto* there was a need for such a chair – as advocates say – only a member of the Faculty of Advocates would be sufficiently respectable to hold it.[6]

The background to the Glasgow Conveyancing chair is no less without human interest. As in Edinburgh, the local professional association – of which a good proportion of Glasgow's law graduates have become members – the Faculty of Procurators in Glasgow,[7] finding the instruction of the University Professors out of touch with the needs of aspiring writers,[8] took matters into its own hands. The Faculty of Procurators appointed, in 1816, one of its own, James Galloway, to give a series of lectures on Conveyancing. Galloway's lively lectures, though now largely forgotten,[9] display considerable learning and a palpable enthusiasm for the subject.[10] Eventually, the Faculty of Procurators agreed to endow a chair in the University, on the Edinburgh model, in 1861.[11] The first holder was Anderson Kirkwood, of whom David Murray – someone well placed to judge[12] – wrote the words which introduce this contribution. The central importance to the University of a Professor with the invaluable experience of the law in action, as well as law in the books, is evident in the roles of the first two holders of the Chair, whose efforts were instrumental in organising the practicalities – funding, contractual negotiations and dealing

---

5   Cf G L Gretton, "Sharp Cases make Good Law" 1994 *SLT (News)* 313-14: "Feudal law is hardly a popular subject. Indeed, together with 'mediaeval' and 'Dickensian' it is an all purpose term used for condemning the grubby and unwanted survivals of an obscure and barbarous past. Of course, most feudal law has long since been abolished. But some parts remain, perhaps unloved, and perhaps unloveable, but law."

6   "Pluckless School of Politics" (n 2) 139 ff.

7   See D Murray, "The Faculty of Procurators in Glasgow" (1897) 13 *Scottish Law Review* 36. The Faculty received its royal patronage from His Majesty in 1950. For Murray, see n 12 below.

8   Compare the French '*écrivain*' and David Murray, "The Term 'Writer' as used in Scotland," *Glasgow Herald*, 15 March 1884.

9   D M Walker, *A History of the School of Law: The University of Glasgow* (1990) 41.

10 J Galloway, *Lectures in Conveyancing* (1838).

11 Ordinance of the Scottish Universities Commission, 15 June 1861, signed by John Inglis (then Lord Advocate): *Edinburgh Gazette* June 18, 1861, 792-93.

12 A remarkable lawyer, scholar (not just in law) and bibliophile, Murray was himself a conveyancer: see e.g. J Rankine, J L Mounsey and D Murray (eds) *The Scots Style Book* (1902-1905) 7 vols. A founding partner of Maclay Murray & Spens LLP, he was arguably the foremost Scottish legal scholar of the generations his long life spanned. He donated 24,000 items of this 40,000 volume library to the University of Glasgow. To this day, that collection, too little recognised, remains one of Glasgow's greatest resources. For Murray, see M S Moss, "Murray, David" *Oxford DNB* (2004-).

with the small matter of acquiring the site – for Sir George Gilbert Scott's unmistakable building at Gilmorehill.[13]

(3) The 1916 election to the Conveyancing Chair

The Emeritus Professor of Comparative Law at Oxford, Bernard Rudden, himself a qualified solicitor, once pointed out that academics are, from the nature of their position, risk averse, sometimes unsuited, and often little grounded, in the realities of commercial life.[14] And it is difficult to imagine any Professor, insulated from the pressures of daily practice, and whose knowledge of the law was derived only from the books, being able to offer to students Galloway's lively, if portentous, admonition that:[15]

> One single blunder in a deed, by which it may be rendered invalid and ineffectual – whether this may have arisen from ignorance, or carelessness – might have the effect to subject the unfortunate conveyancer by whom the deed had been framed, in damages, to such a ruinous extent, as might blast all his future prospects, and involve him in penury and misery during the remainder of his life…

But practical experience and scholarly achievement are not mutually exclusive: a point perhaps never better demonstrated in the 1916 election to the Chair of Conveyancing. The election would mark the first appointment of a professional academic in the modern sense to a law chair at a Scottish university. David Murray, whose words open the present contribution, was a colossus not just in the west of Scotland but of the Scottish legal profession as a whole. A former Dean of the Faculty of Procurators, he was a member of the Council of the Faculty of Procurators that made the appointment to the 1916 Chair. All of the applicants wrote to Murray personally and, characteristically, Murray has meticulously preserved each application for posterity.[16] The other members of Council who would have been eligible to vote were William Gillies (Dean), David Murray (Ex-Dean), James Mackenzie (Ex-Dean), Peter Lindsay Miller, John Mair, William

---

13   Murray (n 1).

14   B Rudden, "Selecting Minds: An Afterword" (1993) 41 *American Journal of Comparative Law* 481 at 486.

15   J Galloway, *Lectures on Conveyancing* (1838) 9. The student or academic reader who considers the warning overblown should reflect on *Lonedale Ltd v Scottish Motor Auctions (Holdings) Ltd* [2011] CSOH 4.

16   *Applications for Chair of Conveyancing* (1916) [GUL Sp Coll Mu21-a.3].

George Black, Thomas Alexander Fyfe, Andrew Mackay, James Graham, Daniel Munro Alexander, and Allan Maclean.[17]

(4) The candidates

In the election there were 13 candidates, all drawn from the local profession. For present purposes, historical interest immediately focuses on three of those candidates: Hugh Reid Buchanan, John Richard Cunliffe, and William Sharp McKechnie.

John Richard Cunliffe, a local writer with long experience, submitted a modest letter of application focussing on his practical experience and eschewing testimonials. Almost as an afterthought, Cunliffe mentions in passing that, since he was applying for a University Chair, it might be "not irrelevant to mention that I have done a good deal of literary work," referring to his editorial work on a number of English classics and his *New Shakespearean Dictionary* (1910). Having been spared the responsibilities of the Conveyancing Chair, Cunliffe would go on to produce *Blackie's Compact Etymological Dictionary* (1922) and the standard student text, *A Lexicon of the Homeric Dialect* (1924). To put the merit of that work in modern context, it was republished in the United States by the University of Oklahoma, in 1963, with paperback editions following in 1977 and, again, as recently as 2012.[18]

Hugh Reid Buchanan,[19] a prize-winning MA philosophy graduate, had proceeded to Germany, to study at Jena and Berlin, where he had spent two years studying philosophy and jurisprudence, before returning to take an LLB with distinction. He had been the University's lecturer in Roman law before becoming the solicitor to the Caledonian Railway Company and, at the time of his application, a partner with M'Grigor Donald & Co. His time at the Railway Company had made him valuable contacts with establishment figures: Buchanan's testimonials for the chair contained references from the Dean of the Faculty of Advocates (and future Lord President) James Avon Clyde, KC MP; a future Dean of the Faculty of Advocates and Court of Session judge, J Condie S Sandeman KC; and two

---

17 *Minute Book of the Royal Faculty of Procurators.*
18 In addition, Cunliffe compiled *Blackie's Compact English Dictionary of Current English* (1969) and the *Secondary School English Dictionary* (1969).
19 See 1912 *SLT (News)* 85 for a portrait. Walker, *School of Law* (n 9) 85 described Buchanan as a "vigorous and scholarly man."

future Lords of Appeal in Ordinary: H P Macmillan KC (Lord Macmillan) and William Watson KC MP (Lord Thankerton).

William S McKechnie[20] was one of Glasgow's limited number of DPhil graduates,[21] who had received his doctorate for his published work, *The State and the Individual*.[22] With that solid scholarly background, McKechnie, after working for a time as a writer,[23] took his first academic post at Glasgow University as the Lecturer on Constitutional Law and History. He was, during his time as a lecturer, extraordinarily productive: producing what, a century on, is still considered to be a fundamental study of the sources for *Magna Carta*;[24] a critique of Parliament's second chamber in *Reform of the House of Lords*[25] (which heavily influenced the Parliament Act 1911); and a monograph setting out the constitutional consequences of that far-reaching measure, *The New Democracy and the New Constitution*, in 1912.

As a professional academic, McKechnie had applied for a University Chair before. In 1909, McKechnie had applied for the Chair of Constitutional Law and Constitutional History in the University of Edinburgh. McKechnie submitted what were probably (at least at that time)[26] the most impressive

---

20 See J S Medley (revd J C Holt) "McKechnie, William Sharp (1863-1930), historian" *Oxford DNB* (2004-); 1911 *SLT (News)* 9 for a portrait; and 1916 *SLT (News)* 89.

21 Glasgow, like Edinburgh, St Andrews and Aberdeen, awarded the DPhil, as the arts and humanities research degree, until at least 1917 with the regulations being finally amended in 1919 to introduce the PhD as the higher research degree: *Regulations for the Degree of Doctor of Philosophy (University Court Ordinance No LXXIV (Glasgow No 21))*, *as approved by Order in Council, dated 18th August 1919*. The Ordinance is reproduced in A Clapperton (ed) *University Court Ordinances 1915-1924* (1925) 66-67. Ironically it was in 1917, just as the Scottish universities introduced the PhD as its standard "lower" doctorate, that the DPhil became the standard Oxford doctorate: R Simpson, *The Development of the PhD Degree in Britain, 1917-1959 and since: An Evolutionary and Statistical History in Higher Education* (2009).

22 W S McKechnie, *The State and the Individual: an introduction to political science, with special reference to socialistic and individualistic theories* (Glasgow, 1896). W Innes Addison, *A Roll of the Graduates of the University of Glasgow, 31st December 1727 to 31st December 1897* (1898) 674 and 681 records that 2 DPhils were awarded in 1896.

23 McKechnie had been admitted as a member of the Faculty of Procurators in 1890 after serving his apprenticeship with Roberton, Low, Roberton and Cross. He appears to have practised full-time until 1894.

24 W S McKechnie, *Magna Carta: A Commentary on the Great Charter of King John, with an Historical Introduction* (1905) (2nd edn 1914) (reprinted 1958); R H Helmholz, "Magna Carta and the Ius Commune" (1999) 66 *University of Chicago Law Review* 297 at 303. The full text of McKechnie's study has now been made available online by the Liberty Fund as one of the classic text's on liberty, available at http://oll.libertyfund.org/titles/338

25 W S McKechnie, *The Reform of the House of Lords* (1909).

26 Hector MacQueen has suggested that "the most distinguished field of candidates ever for a law chair in a British university" were received by the University of Edinburgh

set of testimonials ever compiled for a Professorial appointment to a Scottish law chair:[27] with a printed booklet containing glowing testimonials from scholars in Scotland, England, France, Germany, Austria and the United States, together with reviews from the *Times Literary Supplement*, *The Daily Telegraph*, *The Manchester Guardian*, some US newspapers, reviews in French and German journals, as well as the Scottish newspapers. But to no avail: the election to the Edinburgh constitutional Chair too was in the gift of the Faculty of Advocates and the Faculty, true to form, appointed one of their own, Hepburn Miller.[28]

An academic background, however, was no guarantee of election to the Glasgow Conveyancing Chair in 1916. For although his talents as a legal scholar were beyond question, some members of the Council wondered how McKechnie would manage to discharge the duties of the chair – which, after all, required the teaching not of constitutional theory, but the intricacies of feudal conveyancing; and, moreover, placed a heavy demand on the Professor for opinions and appointment in many title deeds as arbiter ("a kind of official referee," the English authors of his *Dictionary of National Biography* entry record). McKechnie did have conveyancing experience: he had practised full-time for four years after he qualified as a partner in the firm of McKechnie and Gray. And although, for the best part of twenty-five years, he had worked in the University, he had continued to practise and the firm remained in existence until 1915.

David Murray, for his part, though well qualified to judge McKechnie's scholarship, was of the view that McKechnie was not the man for the Chair, instead considering Buchanan "the best of all the candidates, followed by Cunliffe." The implication is that Murray placed

---

in 1938 for the Edinburgh Chair of Civil Law, which attracted Fritz Schulz, Fritz Pringsheim Adolf Berger, David Daube and F H Lawson: see H L MacQueen, "Two Toms and an Ideology for Scots Law" in E C Reid and D L Carey Miller (eds), *A Mixed Legal System in Transition: T B Smith and the Progress of Scots Law* (2005) 44 at 56. The Chair was in the gift of the Faculty of Advocates who nonetheless managed to elect one of their own, the "atrabilious" Matthew G Fisher KC (who had studied in Göttingen), for whom, see Sir Nicholas Fairbairn QC, *A Life is too Short, autobiography*, vol I (1987) 61 and A F Rodger, "David Daube 1909-1999" (2001) 118 ZSS (RA) xxi-xxii. Fisher's entire scholarly output appears to have been a single article mid-way through his two-decade tenure.

27 *Application and testimonials of William Sharp McKechnie, M.A., LL.B., D.Phil., Lecturer on Constitutional Law and History in the University of Glasgow, for the Chair of Constitutional Law and Constitutional History in the University of Edinburgh* [GUL Sp Coll MacLehose 688].

28 His father was a Lord of Session, Lord Craighill.

McKechnie third. But Murray's was not the majority view. For the end result, recorded by Murray, placed Buchanan only fourth; McKillop, third; and Cunliffe, second. "Leaving Dr McKechnie," Murray tersely noted, "as elected."[29] Murray's dissatisfaction may be reflected in his recording of contemporary professional gossip. "After McKechnie had been elected, it was remarked," Murray pointedly noted on the front of Alexander Donaldson's application (Donaldson came seventh), "that, as he [McKechnie] knew nothing about Conveyancing he should take a six month course with Mr Donaldson, so as to qualify himself."[30]

(5) Wider significance of McKechnie's appointment

It is a modern phenomenon that University Law Schools are often conspicuous for the absence of academic staff with experience of legal practice. It has long been suggested that there is much to be gained for legal scholars from obtaining at least the minimum experience of legal practice. But McKechnie's appointment is a rare example of a professional academic being elected by a professional body for a coveted post. He was, indeed, the first professionally trained academic – published doctorate and all – to be appointed to a chair of law in a Scottish university. He voluntarily created honours courses for advanced study. With his scholarly background, and his own experience of professional practice, it is near certain that McKechnie would have been intimately familiar with the history and tradition of the Chairs of Conveyancing in Glasgow and Edinburgh. There was thus an obvious subject for his inaugural lecture. So, in the autumn of 1916, McKechnie chose to address the matter of professional pride that had hung over the lecturers and professors of Conveyancing – members, to a man, of the lower branch of the profession – for over a century: "Conveyancing as a University Study."[31] It may be, in no small part, due to the stature of men like McKechnie in the twentieth century that the Chairs of Conveynacing have maintained, until now, such a central role in the Scottish Universities. But McKechnie's appointment was of wider significance still: McKechnie's career set the mould for the full-time professional legal academic in Scotland.[32]

---

29 The election took place on 2 March 1916: *Glasgow Herald*, 3 March 1916.

30 Murray noted this on the front of Donaldson's application. Donaldson, on the vote, was placed seventh.

31 Murray's collection (n 16) preserves a flyer for the lecture: Wednesday 18th October 1916 at 4.30pm.

32 W S McKechnie's son, Sheriff Hector McKechnie KC too would make a significant

(6) The end of an era

In 1970, the holder of the Chair was J M Halliday.[33] Amongst many other works, Halliday published a commentary on the Conveyancing and Feudal Reform (Scotland) Act 1970. The preface records that he was indebted to Mr Robert Rennie for being "largely responsible for preparation of the index."[34] I suspect this invaluable contribution to a standard text was what may have been, in University language, Robert's first "scholarly collaboration" (Robert, with characteristic modesty, described to me his input to that commentary more prosaically: "that's all you were allowed to do in those days"!) But however that may be, I have chosen to honour Robert's service as a worthy holder of a Chair which has had many worthy holders by delving into areas surrounding the practical operations of the assignation of rights in security.

B. Two Aspects of Standard Securities

The "accessory principle" is a well-known principle common to most European legal systems. The accessory principle applies, in particular, to securities, whether real securities (such as the landlord's hypothec) or personal securities (such as cautionary obligations). The accessory principle has a number of aspects. One is that the accessory, the security, cannot exist in the abstract, for it is parasitic to the principal. Discharge of the principal debt thus extinguishes, *ex lege*, the accessory security. Another aspect is transfer: where the principal goes, so too must the accessory security follow (*accessorium sequitur principale*).[35] Cautionary obligations and floating charges – the subject of Robert's PhD[36] – are good examples of where assignation may occur automatically.[37]

---

contribution to the study of Scots law in his work as the first Literary Director of the Stair Society.

33 Halliday himself was honoured with a valuable *Festschrift:* D J Cusine (ed) *A Scots Conveyancing Miscellany: Essays in Honour of J M Halliday* (1987).

34 J M Halliday, *The Conveyancing and Feudal Reform (Scotland) Act 1970* (1970) v.

35 *Selby v Brough* (1794) 2 Ross LC 661 at 666 per Lord President Campbell; *Watson v Bogue (No.1)* 2000 SLT (Sh Ct) 125 and *Trotter v Trotter* 2001 SLT (Sh Ct) 42.

36 R Rennie, *Floating Charges: A Treatise from the Standpoint of Scots Law* (PhD, University of Glasgow, 1971).

37 Assignation of standard securities, as will be seen, is covered by an express statutory provision: Conveyacing and Feudal Reform (Scotland) Act 1970, s 14, which innovates on the common law *accessorium sequitur principale* rule. The assignation of floating charges, in contrast, is regulated by the ordinary law of assignation and thus more easily effected.

As Andrew Steven has demonstrated, however, the Scottish standard security pays little heed to such fundamental doctrines as the accessory principle.[38] On Steven's examination the standard security proves not to be much of an accessory security at all.[39] But the problems to which the accessory principle seeks to provide answers often relate not to questions of property law – who holds the security – but to questions of debt:[40] which debts, incurred to which creditor, are covered? It is this general issue I wish to address in this contribution in the context of the assignation of all sums securities.

C. Further Advances

(1) Heritable securities pre-1970

Prior to the introduction of the standard security with the Conveyancing and Feudal Reform (Scotland) Act 1970, there were three ways of constituting a heritable security: (i) the pecuniary real burden; (ii) the bond and disposition in security and (iii) the *ex facie* absolute disposition qualified by back letter.[41] For present purposes, suffice it to say that one of the drawbacks of the bond and disposition in security was that it was security only for the sums advanced by the creditor on or around[42] the time the security was taken – further advances made after the security had been taken were liable to founder on the Bankruptcy Act 1696 which struck at "debts contracted for thereafter."[43] All sums securities could not therefore be effectually created over real rights in

---

38 A J M Steven, "Accessoriness and Security over Land" (2009) 13 *Edinburgh Law Review* 387.

39 Steven (n 38).

40 For the statutory definition of which, see n 55 below.

41 A pecuniary real burden, such as a ground annual, could also be used to create a *debitum fundi*, but normally only in favour of a predecessor in the feudal chain. It could not generally be used in order to secure a loan from a bank not already a party to the feudal relationship. It was accepted that the money need not be advanced until after the debtor had signed.

42 It was accepted that the money need not be advanced until after the debtor had signed the bond for the money: *Dunbar v Abercromby* (1789) 2 Ross LC 638 at 644 *per* Lord Eskgrove. "The limits of this rule," Gloag conceded, "are not very easy to define": Gloag and Irvine, *Rights in Security* (1897) 67. Today the issues often arise under the Insolvency Act 1986, s 245, for which, see *Re Shoe Lace Ltd* [1992] BCC 367 at 369-70 *per* Hoffmann J, affd [1993] BCC 609.

43 RPS 1696/9/57. It is necessary to appreciate the distinction between sasine and infeftment which, until the Infeftment Act 1845, were two separate procedures: see *Burnett's Tr v Grainger* 2004 SC (HL) 19 at para [91] *per* Lord Rodger of Earlsferry.

land;[44] moreover, according to Lord Justice Clerk Braxfield, an agreement to provide credit was not, for the purposes of the 1696 Act, a debt.[45]

But the law developed. From 1814, the creation of a revolving facility was permitted by way of the cash credit bond and disposition in security where credit to a certain sum was committed up to which limit the borrower could redraw even after the granting of the security.[46] Another development was the recognition that the security conferred on a holder of an *ex facie* absolute disposition was such as to cover further advances. The borrower under such a security was not the owner of the lands secured: the security holder became the owner and the borrower had a reversionary personal right to reconveyance of his property on repayment of the indebtedness to the security holder. And this right to reconveyance could itself be used as a security. So suppose Brian granted to the Bank of Scotland for "all sums due or which hereafter may become due" an *ex facie* absolute disposition to the Bank of Scotland. Having borrowed £1,000 from the Bank of Scotland at 8%, the Bank of Ireland offers him credit for a second ranking security at 7%. Brian assigns his reversionary right in security to the Bank of Ireland. Intimation of that security to the Bank of Scotland has the effect of limiting the existing security for the sums already advanced. Although not spelled out in the speeches of the House of Lords in *Union Bank of Scotland Ltd v National Bank of Scotland Ltd*,[47] the rationale for the rule where a second ranking security is constituted, was stated by Lord Chelmsford in *Hopkinson v Rolt* to be to ensure that no "perpetual curb is imposed on the mortgagor's right to encumber his equity of redemption."[48] The rationale is similar to that underlying the doctrine of catholic and secondary creditors: the catholic

---

44 *M'Lellan's Creditors* (1734) House of Lords, unreported: see Erskine, 2.3.50 and Bell, *Commentaries* (7th edn 1870) II, 730.

45 *Stein's Creditors v Newnham, Everett & Co* (1794) 2 Ross LC 648 at 650 (in which the Lord President sat as Lord President Probationer). See too Lord Braxfield in *Pickering v Smith* (1788) 2 Ross LC 645 at 647: "An infeftment is not to dance backward and forward; if extinguished today, it cannot revive tomorrow." Braxfield's view is not modern Scots law.

46 Payment of Creditors (Scotland) Act 1814 (54 Geo III, c 37) s 14. Statutory authority for such a revolving facility remains in the form of the Debts Securities (Scotland) Act 1856 (19 & 20 Vict, c 91), s 7 and, in addition, 1970 Act, s 9(6): "The Bankruptcy Act 1696, in so far as it renders a heritable security of no effect in relation to a debt contracted after the recording of that security, and any rule of law which required that a real burden for money may only be created in respect of a sum specified at the date of creation, shall not apply in relation to a standard security."

47 (1886) 14 R (HL) 1, following the decision of the House in an English appeal, *Hopkinson v Rolt* (1861) ER 829.

48 *Hopkinson* (n 47) 845.

creditor cannot be allowed to (ab)use his position to destroy the security of subsequent creditors. In modern terms, the policy could be stated to be to encourage competitive lending and to ensure that any attempts by the first creditor, in contract, to monopolise his position as lender to the borrower, is not supported by the general law.

(2) Clayton's case issues

In a case where there are two separate securities – one ranking after the other – the effect of notice of the subsequent security crystallises the sum due. Crystallisation is also important in order to apply the rule in *Clayton's case*,[49] that the earliest debit is extinguished by the earliest credit. In the event that the first creditor does not rule off the crystallised sum, and ensure any further advances (such as cheques honoured after the crystallisation date) are recorded in a separate account: otherwise any repayments made by the debtor will automatically reduce the secured (pre-crystallisation sum) rather than the unsecured sum (post-crystallisation advances).

(3) The modern law

But the modern statutory provisions allow the first ranking security holder to maintain his priority for "any future debt which, under the contract to which the security relates, he is required to allow the debtor in the security to incur."[50] The scope of the rule on further advances is thus much reduced under s 13. Moreover, with the abolition of the ranking preference afforded by an inhibition,[51] many of the issues surrounding further advances and which Robert explored in detail,[52] no longer arise. There is also the curious discrepancy between the provisions of the Conveyancing and Feudal Reform (Scotland) Act 1970 and the Companies Act 1985 on the case of further advances by second ranking security holder. Originally both acts contained the wording still found in the Companies Acts: where a second ranking security is taken which is intimated to the first ranking security

---

49   *Devaynes v Noble (Clayton's Case)* (1816) 35 ER 767 at 793. See further P Hood, "Clayton's Case and Connected Matters" 2013 *Juridical Review* 501-39.

50   1970 Act, s 13(1)(b). Unlike under Land Registration Act 2002, s 49 there is no need for the obligation to make further advances to appear on the register. For floating charges, see Companies Act 1985, s 464(5)(b): "future advances which he may be required to make under the instrument creating the floating charge or under any ancillary document."

51   Bankruptcy and Diligence (Scotland) Act etc 2007, s 154.

52   R Rennie, "Inhibitions, Standard Securities and Further Advances" (1994) 39 *JLSS* 52.

holder, the effect of intimation is to restrict the first-ranking security to the "advances" presently made or which he may be required to make.[53] The 1970 Act was, however, amended in 2003 in the course of the *Entfeudalisierung* of Scottish immoveable property law,[54] as a result of which "advances" was replaced in s 13 of the 1970 Act with the more readily intelligible "debts." "Debts" is defined in the 1970 Act to include any obligation, whether or not it is an obligation to pay money.[55] "Advance," in contrast, is limited to money claims. How the s 13 notice works in a case where there is a standard security in respect of a continuing obligation by the debtor to do something other than to pay money is obscure.

(4) Relevance to assignation cases

The point about further advances is that the authorities referred to relate always to the situation where there are two separate security rights. The modern legislation – s 13 of the 1970 Act and s 464(5) of the 1985 Act – now expressly sanctions the situation where the first ranking security holder (subject to the law of catholic and secondary creditors) can maintain his priority for further advances. That this position has been reached in the context of two securities is important when we turn to consider the policy and principle that should apply in the case of an assignation of a single security.

D. Assignation of All Sums Securities

(1) Gretton's article on all sums securities

Another contributor to this *Festschrift* in Robert's honour is himself an honoured member of that most exclusive club, dwindling – with Robert's retirement – to three members *ordinarius*, and known to Lords of Appeal in

---

53 Companies Act 1985, s 464(5).
54 Title Conditions (Scotland) Act 2003, s 111. The operation of s 13 of the 1970 is excluded in relation to the issue of perpetual debentures under s 736 of the Companies Act 2006: Redemption of Standard Securities (Scotland) Act 1971, s 2. Section 4 of the 1971 Act provides that the 1970 Act and the 1971 Act may be cited together as the "Conveyancing and Feudal Reform (Scotland) Acts 1970 and 1971."
55 1970 Act, s 9(8)(c): "'debt' means any obligation due, or which will or may become due, to repay or pay money, including such obligation arising from a transaction or part of transaction in the course of any trade, business or profession, and any obligation to pay an annuity or *ad factum praestandum*, but does not include an obligation to pay any ... rent or other periodical sum payable in respect of land, and 'creditor' and 'debtor' shall be construed accordingly."

Ordinary as "the Professors of Conveyancing:"[56] Professor George Gretton. It was Gretton who first recognised the importance of Lord Dunpark's decision in *Sanderson's Trs v Ambion Scotland Ltd*.[57] Judgment was given in 1977 and, until it was belatedly reported in 1994, was not widely known.

(2) Sanderson's Trs

The case was unusual. S Ltd granted to H Ltd a standard security over development land. H Ltd then assigned its standard security to the trustees of a discretionary trust, in security, for a loan of £28,000. The standard security was granted for all sums due or to become due by S Ltd to H Ltd. The standard security and the assignation of it were recorded, in the order of standard security followed by assignation, on the same day. Following registration, the trustees made further advances to S Ltd. S Ltd then went into receivership. The trustees claimed that the further advances were covered by the standard security which they held as assignees. The trustees raised an action to enforce.

Assignations of standard securities are permitted by s 14 of the Conveyancing and Feudal Reform (Scotland) Act 1970. That section provides:

> Any standard security duly registered or recorded may be transferred in whole or in part, by the creditor by an assignation in conformity with Form A or B of schedule 4 to this Act, and upon such an assignation being duly registered or recorded, the security, or, as the case may be, part thereof, shall be vested in the assignee as effectually as if the security or the part had been granted in his favour.

Form A appeared to require specification of either (a) the certain sum for which a security is granted; (b) a maximum sum of £X, to the extent of £Y being the amount now due thereunder; or (c) other cases described in terms of a Note to the form.[58] In *Sanderson's Trs*, because the standard security

---

56   Lord Rodger of Earlsferry, *The Church, the Courts and the Constitution* (2008) 95: "That feudal law, which has a strong claim to being the real intellectual achievement of the Scottish judges, was unceremoniously binned by the Scottish Parliament, unmourned even by its supposed acolytes, the Professors of Conveyancing." Although, as Robert has pointed out, he is the last Professor to hold a titular Chair of Conveyancing: R Rennie, "The End of Conveyancing as we know it" (2003) 48(11) *JLSS* 15 and "A Tale of Two Systems" (2014) 59(11) *JLSS* 13.

57   1994 *SLT* 645 OH.

58   The Note is in these terms: "In an assignation, discharge or deed of restriction (1) a standard security in respect of an uncertain amount may be described by specifying

assigned was in "all sums" terms, it was argued that the assignation was not in Form A terms and thus ineffectual. That argument was shortly disposed of on the basis that "sufficient compliance" with the forms and procedure contained in the 1970 Act, provided that the assignation "so conforms as closely as may be."[59] But Lord Dunpark also provided a number of powerful rationales for why specification of the sum should not be necessary.

His Lordship did not find the pre-1970 law of much assistance. The Bankruptcy Act 1696, as we have seen, rendered invalid any attempt to extend a heritable security to a debt contracted after the recording of the heritable security.[60] The *ex facie* absolute disposition in security, Lord Dunpark recognised, "was the only pre-1970 method of creating a real security for future, as well as for past, loans, without limit of amount."[61] And where the creditor in such a case – the infeft owner – sought to transfer his position, by assignation (of the debt) and disposition (of ownership of the land), there was no requirement to specify the debt assigned.[62]

The next rationale identified by Lord Dunpark was that, in a case where the only party who has an obligation to make further advances is the cedent (the creditor of the outstanding sums) it makes sense for any assignation to crystallise the sums assigned. In such a case, where a creditor seeks to assign the claim presently owed to him with the security, it is necessary to specify the sum assigned. Cedent and assignee need to know what is being assigned. Suppose a facility of £1000 of which £500 is outstanding. Any assignation by the creditor has to specify the sum because the creditor as cedent. For having agreed to a facility of £1000, the cedent has an obligation to extend credit to that sum. The obligation to make further advances cannot be assigned. The case of further advances by a cedent, following assignation of an existing claim plus the security, is the inverse situation of further advances on a

---

shortly the nature of the debt or obligation (e.g. all sums due or to become due) for which the security was granted, adding in the case of an assignation, *to the extent of £X being the amount now due thereunder* and (2) a standard security in respect of a personal obligation constituted in an instrument or instruments other than the standard security itself may be described by specifying shortly the nature of the debt or obligation and referring to the other instrument or instruments by which it is constituted in such manner as will be sufficient identification thereof."

59   1970 Act, s 53(1).

60   Ibid, s 9(6).

61   1994 *SLT* 645 at 649H.

62   This form of security – *fiducia cum creditore* – suffers from the disadvantage that the creditor becomes the owner of the collateral. As a result, the creditor can transfer good title to a third party. The borrower, who pays back the debt, may not then be able to acquire a re-transfer of the property from the creditor, not least in the situation where the creditor has become insolvent.

second security being taken. With assignation, the cedent transfers away the first-ranking position. In a case where there are two securities, one ranking behind the other, the s 13 notice may crystallise the sum for which the first-ranking security holder maintains his first ranking security.

(3) The problems

It was Professor Gretton who highlighted the great practical difficulties which may arise on the assignation of all sums securities, in an article which accompanied the reporting of the *Sanderson's Trs* decision.[63] He used this example: a debtor grants an all-sums security to the Bank of Pictavia. Suppose the loan was originally for £100,000 but the indebtedness is now down to £1,000. The same debtor has unsecured indebtedness to the Bank of Dalriada for £100,000. As Professor Gretton pointed out, were the Bank of Dalriada to take an assignation of the security the debtor would now find himself with £101,000 of secured debt. Suppose, then, Professor Gretton asked, the debtor had concluded missives to sell his property, on the basis that the £1,000 would be discharged from the purchase price. Prior to settlement, the debtor learns that the Bank has assigned its security and that he will need to come up with a redemption figure that is now in six figures. Such a result, Professor Gretton argued, would be "absurd," for it could place the debtor in breach of his missives. Similarly, if the debtor were to be sequestrated shortly after the assignation of the security, the result would be that the Bank of Dalriada had managed to jump the unsecured creditors' queue, without being subject to the law of unfair preferences. For the law of unfair preferences applies only to acts of the debtor.[64] An onerous assignation by one creditor to another, in contrast, like a ranking agreement concluded between creditors, is challengeable neither under statute nor, probably, at common law.[65]

Nonetheless, I suggest that Lord Dunpark's decision was correct and that assignations of all sums securities are permitted. The result, I would suggest, is not absurd, for the following reasons:

---

63   G L Gretton, "Assignation of All Sums Standard Securities" 1994 *SLT (News)* 207.
64   Bankruptcy (Scotland) Act 1985, s 36(1).
65   Of course, there may be questions about the extent to which an assignation is valid. An assignation of an all sums security for £1,000 (the outstanding indebtedness) could be said to be valid only to the extent of £1,000 of debt.

(i)   The debtor seeking to sell his heritable property is, *ex hypothesi*, doing so for a price. That price can be used to pay, in Gretton's example, the Bank of Dalriada (the assignee of the security) at settlement;

(ii)   Even in the absence of assignation of the security, the Bank of Dalriada could use diligence by inhibition, the effect of which would cause the same problems as an undischarged standard security (diligence may, of course, not be possible if there has been no default on the unsecured loan to Bank of Dalriada, but if there has been no default somewhere, it is less likely that the BofD would be in the market for a security).[66]

(iii)   The argument that the debtor's land "cannot be burdened by the extra £100,000 without his consent,"[67] ignores the fact that the debtor has already expressly, by his own deed, granted an all-sums security.

(iv)   The effect of assignation of an all sums standard security is contained, as Gretton observes, in s 14 of the 1970 Act. Section 14 provides that, "upon such an assignation being duly registered or recorded, the security, or, as the case may be, part thereof, shall be vested in the assignee as effectually as if the security or the part had been granted in his favour." The effect of the assignation, therefore, curiously, is *ex tunc*: the security is deemed to have been granted to the assignee from day one.

(v)   The assignation of the security would not breach a pre-existing negative pledge clause granted by the debtor: as Gretton himself perceptively observes, the assignation is not an act *of the debtor*. Moreover, the effect of s 14 is to deem the security to have been granted by the debtor to the assignee. If the security, as granted by the debtor, was not a breach of the negative pledge clause, neither is the assignation.

(vi)   The assignation forms contained in Schedule 4 to the 1970 Act cannot supply a requirement not mentioned in s 14, namely that any all sum standard security is immediately converted into a security for a fixed sum. The wording of the style assignation in Schedule 4 does appear to envisage specification of a maximum sum for which the security is assigned. That may be for a fixed sum. But there is no good reason why the assignation may not be expressed to mirror the terms of the security itself: for "all sums due and to become due." As the Lord Ordinary held in *Sanderson's Trs v Ambion Scotland Ltd*, an assignation of a standard security is not necessarily disconform to the Act if it does not state the sum due to the cedent at the date of the assignation. The

---

66 The loan agreement between the debtor and the Bank of Dalriada – assuming the unsecured indebtedness arose under a loan – may contain a consent to preservation and execution clause, although, if the debtor is a consumer, Consumer Credit Act 1974, s 93A may prevent summary diligence.

67 Gretton (n 63) at 209.

Lord Ordinary in *Liquidator of Letham Grange Development Co Ltd v Foxworth Investments Ltd*,[68] also held that it is possible to have a hybrid Form A/Form B security. Strict conformity, with either the security or the assignation forms, does not appear to be required, providing the security is consistent with the operative terms of the Act.

(vii) Assignations of personal rights to payment occur without the consent of the debtor. At common law, accessory securities (in the wide sense, including personal securities, such as cautionary obligations) are transferred with an assignation of the claim even if there is no mention of the accessory securities. The debtor's consent to assignation of either the underlying debt or a security granted in respect of that debt is not therefore required.[69]

(viii) Indeed, under the law of catholic and secondary creditors (which applies admittedly as between two or more secured creditors) the law sometimes implies a transfer of securities between creditors, where the creditors, as well as the debtor, do not expressly consent.[70]

(ix)   As Gretton observed, it was Professor Halliday's view that in order for an assigned standard security to cover further advances by the assignee, a formal variation of the security would be required.[71] The rationale is that such a variation would supply the debtor's express consent to the security covering post-assignation further advances by the assignee of the security to the debtor. But is the best evidence of the debtor's consent to those further advances being covered not, in fact, the debtor's consent to the acceptance of those further advances? It might be argued that, at the stage any such advances have been made, the debtor would not necessarily know that the security has been assigned, since s 14 envisages registration rather than intimation. But that point is an argument for requiring, as under the general law of assignation, intimation to the debtor in order to interpel the debtor with the effects of the assignation. Further advances by an assignee of the security is yet another situation where it is intimation that could

---

68   2011 *SLT* 1152 at para [101], *per* Lord Glennie (revd on a different point, [2013] CSIH 13; 2013 *SLT* 445, itself revd [2014] UKSC 41, 2014 *SLT* 775).

69   Even claims arising out of regulated consumer credit agreements which are not secured on land may be freely assigned by the creditor although may be assigned without the debtor's consent (although, between 1 February 2011 until 30 March 2014), Consumer Credit Act 1974, s 82A required the creditor to notify the debtor. The purpose s 82A, and Art 17 of the Consumer Credit Directive 2008/48/EC, was obscure given existing EU members states' private laws on the question.

70   *Littlejohn v Black* (1855) 18 D 207 referred to with approval by Lord Reed in *Szepietowski v National Crime Agency* [2014] UKSC 65, [2014] AC 338 at paras [81]-[84].

71   J M Halliday, *Conveyancing and Feudal Reform (Scotland) Act 1970*, 2nd edn (1977) para 9-07; *Conveyancing Law and Practice* (1987) vol III, para 40-19.

be said to play a central role: until the assignee has intimated the assignation to the debtor, any advances by the assignee will not be covered by the security.[72]

(x) Finally, and perhaps most tellingly, the permissibility of assignation of all-sums securities, in policy terms, can be tested by the mirror-image situation. Take the example of the Bank of Pictavia and the Bank of Dalriada referred to above. The Bank of Pictavia has an all sums security but only £1,000 of indebtedness, while the Bank of Dalriada has unsecured claims for £100,000. There is nothing wrong with the Bank of Pictavia taking an assignation of the Bank of Dalriada's unsecured claim. The effect would be that the all-sums security now covered the £101,000. The effect on any proposed sale by the debtor would be the same.

E. Practicalities

(1) The debtor who has granted an all sums security

All this having been said, however, the practical difficulties highlighted by Professor Gretton remain. Suppose the debtor has concluded missives to sell in the knowledge, in our example, that he has only £1,000 of debt outstanding to the Bank of Pictavia. After conclusion of the missives, he learns that the Bank of Dalriada, to whom he is already indebted to the extent of £100,000 now holds the security. Does this assignation render him in breach of the missives? Any breach of the missives relates to the warranty of "good and marketable title" not to acts of the seller, for, in our example, the seller has done nothing. The assignation is not an act of the seller. How then can the debtor under an all sums security protect himself? There are two practical responses: the first by transactional lawyers, the second by the courts.

(2) The need for intimation

Transactional lawyers seeking redemption statements from a heritable creditor that holds an all sums security need to seek an undertaking that no assignation of the security has taken place or will take place prior to

---

72 Cf Land Registration (Scotland) Act 2012, s 41. But that applies only to applications under s 21 or 29. An application to register the assignation of a registered standard security would fall under s 26.

settlement. The response of the courts must be to apply by analogy the traditional Scottish approach to intimation: although the assignation of the security may take place only on registration, that registration cannot affect the debtor, even with respect to existing indebtedness, unless and until the assignee of the security has interpelled the debtor by intimating the assignation of the all sums security to him. For because assignation takes place without the debtor's consent, the debtor cannot be prejudiced by that about which he does not know and about which he has no obligation to inquire. The result is that if a debtor concludes missives to sell, without having received intimation of the assignation of the security, the security, in any question with the debtor, cannot cover more than was due to the original creditor. The debtor, *qua* seller, has no obligation to run searches to check that the holder of his all sums security has not changed. That this is the correct analysis can be tested by asking the question of what would happen in the mirror-image situation where the creditors agree between themselves to assign not the security but the claim: the unsecured creditor assigns the claim to the holder of the all sums security. That assignation has effect against the debtor only from the date of intimation. If the debtor has entered into missives to sell the property, but between missives and settlement there has been a registration of an assignation of the security,[73] the seller cannot be prejudiced until the assignation has been intimated to him: he need redeem only to the extent of £1,000.[74] As a result of that payment, he is entitled to a discharge of the security from the assignee who, in turn, may have a claim against the cedent. The assignee *may* have a breach of warrandice claim against the cedent, but probably not. For the warrandice in an assignation of a claim plus security is only *debitum subesse*: the debt is due and owing. But for warrandice purposes, as for others, that warranty can be given only at the date of the assignation. Take again the example of £1,000 owed by the seller under a standard security, which is assigned to another creditor who has unsecured indebtedness

---

73 Of course, in most cases involving a sale, a registration of an assignation of the security prior to settlement will be picked up in the searches, alerting the buyer to the need for a discharge from the assignee.

74 The Scottish Law Commission is likely to recommend superseding intimation as a constitutive requirement for completing an assignation with registration: Scottish Law Commission, Discussion Paper on Moveable Transactions (2011) ch 11. But intimation will remain, as it does in other legal systems which allow for effective assignation without intimation, for practical purposes to "interpel" the debtor.

after he had received the purchase price and had delivered the disposition to the purchaser?

Reading the judgments of the House of Lords in *Burnett's Trustee* one can gain the impression that the case was concerned solely with personal insolvency legislation. In a sense that is true because the central rules of the Scots law of personal insolvency are statutory. But in reality it concerned the building blocks of Scots property law. In particular, the judgment of the House of Lords supported the clear distinction between the law of property and the law of obligations which is common to many legal systems which have been strongly influenced in their structure by Roman law. It reaffirmed the decision of the whole bench of the Court of Session in *Young v Leith* that:[5]

> [A] completed real right, good in a question between granter and grantee, and bad against all the rest of the world, is an absolute legal contradiction in terms.

I believe that the exercise of clarification, which the insolvency profession initiated, will bring lasting benefits to Scots law. The distinction between real rights and personal rights, which is the hallmark of civilian legal systems, gives a simple and principled framework to property law. It can readily be understood by the non-specialist lawyer and provide a simple template for legal analysis. But that does not mean that we should become obsessed about real rights and personal rights and treat as heretical or unprincipled any reform proposal which creates an exception to general rules. The effect of *Sharp v Thomson* is that a floating charge will not attach property for which a disponee has paid the purchase price and of which the disposition has been delivered. It is an exception to the general rule in insolvency that priority in insolvency is determined by the prior acquisition of the real right. That exception can be justified by the unusual nature of the floating charge, both in its origin as an equitable charge in English law and also in the way it creates a real right in security over land without registration in the Land Register. To deny the ability of the law to create exceptions to general rules would be to introduce inflexibility. It would risk consigning Scots property law and commercial law to an ossuary. In my view the real value of the clarification which *Sharp* and *Burnett's Trustee*

---

5   (1847) 9 D 932 at 945.

have provided is that there is a clear structure which law reformers can use to develop our law.

B. Exceptions to the General Principles

The effect of the floating charge in *Burnett's Trustee* is not the only departure from the general rules of insolvency law. There are also special rules for transactions specifically induced by the debtor's fraud and also for trusts.

The title of a debtor which has been acquired through fraud is voidable in the hands of an attaching creditor and thus also in the debtor's insolvency.[6] In such cases fraud passes against creditors. But the scope of the doctrine is not clear; fraud in a contract is not a *vitium reale*. Professor Thomson suggests that it is only where the insolvent's fraud specifically induced the transfer of the ownership of the property, which would not otherwise have passed, that the property will not fall to the trustee in sequestration.[7]

It is well established in our law that property which a debtor holds in trust for another does not fall within the sequestration of the debtor's estate. That rule extends to land and to latent trusts,[8] and since 1985 has been the subject of a statutory provision.[9] Until recently, Scots lawyers and South African lawyers have analysed the right of the beneficiary as an unusual personal right against the trustee which prevails in the latter's insolvency – the protected personal right. Recently, it has become more fashionable to analyse trust rights in terms of a separate patrimony. The trustee has separate patrimonies. He has his own patrimony, which comprises his personal assets and liabilities, and a separate trust patrimony which comprises the assets and liabilities of the trust.[10]

It is also well settled in Scots law that an obligation to assign a security over property or an obligation to grant a conveyance does not create

---

6   Bell, *Comm* I, 309-10; *Mansfield v Walker's Trustees* (1835) 1 Sh & Macl 203; *A W Gamage Ltd v Charlesworth's Trustee* 1910 SC 257.

7   J M Thomson, "Fraud," in *The Laws of Scotland: Stair Memorial Encyclopaedia*, vol 11 (1990) para 778; K G C Reid, "Property" in *The Laws of Scotland: Stair Memorial Encyclopaedia*, vol 18 (1993) para 694.

8   *Heritable Reversionary Co Ltd v Millar* (1892) 19 R (HL) 43.

9   Bankruptcy (Scotland) Act 1985, s 33(1)(b).

10   Lord Malcolm has recently supported this analysis: *Glasgow City Council v The Board of Managers of Springboig St John's School* [2014] CSOH 76 at paras 16 and 17. So also has Lord Drummond Young in *Ted Jacob Engineering Group Inc v RMJM* 2014 SC 579 at para 90. See also Scottish Law Commission, Report on *Trust Law* (Scot Law Com No 239, 2014) para 3.4.

a trust in respect of that property.[11] This rule is of central importance to the Scots law of property and distinguishes it from English property law in a fundamental way. In *Mansfield v Walker's Trustees*,[12] Lord Brougham pointed out the absence of equitable estates in Scotland and described English equitable titles thus:[13]

> An agreement to convey an estate for a valuable consideration executed is with us, to all substantial purposes, a conveyance which vests the property in the purchaser. ... Whatever is covenanted to be done is held in equity as done, so that a title by mere agreement is quite as paramount to any subsequent incumbrance, or other *puisne* title, as a legal conveyance. This is not the law of Scotland.

The last sentence is of central importance. The absence in Scots law of that rule of equity has generated academic controversy as to the scope of a constructive trust to confer rights which would prevail in a debtor's insolvency. In the rest of this essay I consider that question in the context of a recent decision of the UK Supreme Court on the English law of constructive trust: *FHR European Ventures LLP v Cedar Capital Partners LLC*.[14]

C. The Constructive Trust in Scots Law

(1) *FHR European Ventures LLP v Cedar Capital Partners LLC*

FHR was a joint venture vehicle for the purchase of the issued share capital of Monte Carlo Grand Hotel SAM, for which the joint venture paid €211.5 million. Cedar acted as FHR's agents in negotiating the purchase and owed fiduciary duties to FHR. Unknown to FHR, Cedar also entered into an exclusive brokerage agreement with the vendors by which it became entitled to a fee of €10 million following the successful conclusion of the sale and purchase. The sale went ahead and the vendors paid Cedar that fee. FHR on learning of the payment sought to recover it from Cedar.

---

11   *Bank of Scotland v Liquidators of Hutchison, Main & Co Ltd* 1914 SC (HL) 1; *Gibson v Hunter Home Designs Ltd* 1976 SC 23.
12   (1835) 1 Sh & Macl 203.
13   *Mansfield* (n 6) at 338-39.
14   [2014] UKSC 45. I had the pleasure of sitting on the panel for the case and also prepared a briefing note for my colleagues on what might be the approach of Scots law in such circumstances.

The practical issue in *FHR* was whether a principal of an agent who had breached his fiduciary duty by taking an undisclosed commission could assert a proprietary remedy against a third party to which, it was asserted, the agent had transferred the money. The legal question was whether a bribe or secret commission received by an agent was held by the agent on trust for his principal; or did the principal merely have a claim against the agent for equitable compensation in a sum equal to the bribe or commission?

Lord Neuberger delivered the unanimous judgement of the court, holding that Cedar held the secret commission on trust for FHR. He set out three principles from the judgment of Millett LJ in *Bristol and West Building Society v Mothew*,[15] namely:

(i) an agent owes a fiduciary duty to his principal because he has undertaken to act for or on behalf of the principal in circumstances which give rise to a relationship of trust and confidence;

(ii) an agent must not place himself in a position in which his duty and his interest may conflict, and as part of this rule, the agent must not make a profit out of his trust; and

(iii) a fiduciary who acts for two principals with potentially conflicting interests breaches his obligation of undivided loyalty unless he has obtained the informed consent of both following full disclosure.

A Scots jurist can readily assent to those principles.[16] So also can he or she agree with the well-established principle that where an agent receives a benefit in breach of his fiduciary duty, the agent is obliged to account to the principal for such a benefit: *Regal (Hastings) Ltd v Gulliver*[17] has frequently been relied on in commercial cases in Scotland. In English law the agent must pay a sum equal to the profit by way of equitable compensation; Scots law does not speak of equitable compensation but the obligation to account and pay is clear.

In English law, where an agent acquires a benefit, which came to his notice as a result of his fiduciary position, he is treated in equity as having

---

15 [1998] Ch 1 at 18.

16 See, in relation to (ii), for example *Hamilton v Wright* (1839) 1 D 668 (Lord Cockburn at first instance) (1842) 1 Bell's App Cas 574; *Aberdeen Railway Co v Blaikie Brothers* (1853) 1 Macq 461; *Magistrates of Aberdeen v University of Aberdeen* (1877) 4 R (HL) 48. See also Laura Macgregor's discussion of fiduciary duty in chapter 6 of her admirable book, *The Law of Agency in Scotland* (2013), including her discussion of the constructive trust at para 6.38ff.

17 [1967] 2 AC 134 (Note).

acquired the benefit on behalf of the principal. Thus the thing acquired is beneficially owned by the principal because the general rule is that equity treats as done that which ought to have been done. This rule is strictly applied in favour of the principal so that the agent must disgorge a benefit even if the principal could not otherwise have acquired it.[18]

But what is the legal basis of the principal's claim when a bribe or secret commission, unlike an emerging business opportunity which an agent wrongfully diverts from his principal, is something which the principal would not have received if the agent had complied with his fiduciary duty? In the past English case law has not spoken with one voice on whether a principal enjoys a proprietary remedy in relation to bribes and secret commissions, as Lord Neuberger's judgment in *FHR* shows.[19] More recently the Privy Council in *Attorney General for Hong Kong v Reid*[20] held that bribes which had been paid to a corrupt police officer were held on trust for his principal and could therefore be traced into properties which the policeman had acquired in New Zealand. There has also been a very learned academic debate with powerful jurists on each side. On the one hand Professor Sir Roy Goode[21] and Professor Sarah Worthington[22] among others have argued that the principal has no proprietary interest in such a bribe or commission while Lord Millett[23] and Professor Lionel Smith[24] among others have argued that an agent who obtains any benefit in breach of his fiduciary duty holds that benefit on trust for his principal.[25] Many other articles have been published in what Sir Terence Etherton described as "this relentless and seemingly endless debate."[26]

---

18   *Keech v Sandford* (1726) Sel Cas Ch 61; *Cook v Deeks* [1916] 1 AC 554; *Phipps v Boardman* [1967] 2 AC 46; *Bhullar v Bhullar* [2003] 2 BCLC 241.

19   *FHR* (n 14) at paras 15-28.

20   [1994] 1 AC 324.

21   R Goode, "Proprietary Restitutionary Claims" in W R Cornish and G Virgo (eds) *Restitution: Past, Present and Future* (1998), ch 5; R Goode, "Property and Unjust Enrichment" in A Burrows (ed), *Essays on the Law of Restitution* (1991) ch 9; R Goode, "Proprietary Liability for Secret Profits – A Reply" (2011) 127 LQR 493-95.

22   S Worthington, "Fiduciary Duties and Proprietary Remedies: Addressing the Failure of Equitable Formulae" [2013] CLJ 720-52.

23   P Millett, "Bribes and Secret Commissions" [1993] RLR 7-30; P Millett, "Bribes and Secret Commissions Again" [2012] CLJ 583-614.

24   L Smith, "Constructive Trusts and the No-profit Rule" (2013) 72 CLJ 260-63.

25   Further valuable contributions to the debate include G Virgo, "Profits Obtained in Breach of Fiduciary Duty: Personal or Proprietary Claim?" (2011) 70 CLJ 502-04 and D Hayton, "Proprietary Liability for Secret Profits" (2011) 127 LQR 487-93.

26   T Etherton, "The Legitimacy of Proprietary Relief" (2014) 2(1) *Birkbeck Law Review* 59-86, 62.

FHR gives an answer to this debate for the purposes of English law. A principal enjoys a proprietary remedy against his agent in relation to benefits such as bribes which were not derived from the principal's assets or from assets which should have been the property of the principal. In the case of *FHR* one might readily assume that the vendor would have accepted a lower price for the shares in the hotel company if it had not had to pay the commission; but the rule did not turn on evidence that the purchaser had suffered any loss. The rule is simple: "any benefit acquired by an agent as a result of his agency and in breach of his fiduciary duty is held on trust for his principal."[27] Thus the principal can require the agent to account for any such benefit or he can claim the beneficial ownership of the funds or assets which the agent has obtained. The principal may also trace or follow in equity the proceeds of the bribe or commission in the hands of knowing recipients, a remedy which would not be available unless he had a proprietary claim. Lord Neuberger observed that this view was consistent with other common law jurisdictions, notably Australia, New Zealand, Singapore and the United States of America.

(2) Remedies for breach of fiduciary duty in Scots law

Where does Scots law stand on this issue?

Agency plays a central role in our commercial life. Company directors, solicitors, financial advisers, commercial representatives and many others operate through the law of agency. While James LJ may have been guilty of overstatement when he suggested that the "safety of mankind" required the enforcement of the no profit rule without any inquiry as to whether the principal had suffered loss,[28] the strict enforcement of an agent's duty of loyalty plays a vital role in our commercial law. The "no conflict" and "no profit" rules are essential components of the law of agency and are well vouched in Scots law. An agent who profits from his agency in breach of his fiduciary duty must disgorge his profits to his principal. That is not in doubt. But there is uncertainty in Scots law as to the legal mechanisms by which a principal can obtain a remedy for a breach of fiduciary duty.

---

27 *FHR* (n 14) at para 35.
28 *Parker v McKenna* (1874) 10 Ch App 96 at p 124.

The discussion in the English case of *FHR* is useful as it focused on three different circumstances in which an agent may act in breach of his fiduciary duty. They were:

(i)   Where the agent has used the principal's property – including property which the agent holds on trust for his principal – to make a profit for himself;

(ii)   Where the agent uses his position or knowledge as an agent to divert from his principal an emerging business opportunity; and

(iii)   Where the agent takes a bribe or secret commission from another party.

The Supreme Court has ruled that in each case English law allows the principal a proprietary remedy which prevails in the agent's insolvency and also allows equitable tracing.

A Scots lawyer may have difficulty in seeing a basis for a proprietary claim in the second and third circumstances because Scots law has no equitable rule treating as done that which ought to have been done.[29] Nonetheless, there are several statements in Scots cases[30] and in textbooks[31] that suggest that a constructive trust may arise where a person in a fiduciary position breaches his duty to his principal. Thus in volume 24 of the Stair Memorial Encyclopaedia the learned authors state:[32]

> A constructive trust arises from circumstances where a person in a fiduciary position derives a benefit from that position or a trustee makes a profit from carrying on the truster's business.

But, as those authors acknowledge, it is not clear what is meant by "constructive trust;" and they refer to McLaren's comment that a constructive trust is "merely another name for the duty of restitution, which may be

---

29   *Mansfield* (n 6).

30   *York Buildings Co v MacKenzie* 13 May 1795, 3 Pat 378, Lord Thurlow at 393; *Hamilton v Wright* (1839) 1 D 668, Lord Cockburn at 673 (an obiter dictum as Wright was a trustee under an express trust); *Laird v Laird* (1858) 20 D 972, Lord President McNeill at 981 (again obiter); *Aberdeen Railway Co v Blaikie Brothers* (1853) 1 Macq 461 in which it was suggested by the Lord Chancellor and Lord Brougham that the laws of Scotland and England were essentially the same in relation to fiduciary relationships.

31   J McLaren, *Wills and Succession*, 3rd edn (1894) para 1926f; A Mackenzie Stuart, *The Law of Trusts* (1932) 37-38; W A Wilson and A G M Duncan, *Trusts, Trustees and Executors*, 2nd edn (1995) para 6.5-6.81.

32   D M Ross et al, "Trusts, Trustees and Judicial Factors," in *The Laws of Scotland: Stair Memorial Encyclopaedia*, vol 24 (1990) para 30.

enforced against a party acquiring property dishonestly or in breach of trust."[33]

In this essay I do not use the term "constructive trust" in that wider sense. Nor do I discuss the remedial constructive trust, which some common law jurisdictions recognise but English law does not. Rather, I concentrate on the institutional constructive trust in English law which arises by operation of law and which may exclude the assets held on trust from the insolvency of the fiduciary and the third party recipient. Does Scots law have such a trust arising from a fiduciary relationship? If so, what is its scope?

Before examining authorities which address directly the existence of such an institutional constructive trust, it may be useful to look at other remedies which Scots law provides in order to provide context for that examination. It is an established principle of Scots law that no man may profit from another's fraud;[34] and that has been extended to a principle that no man may profit from another's breach of fiduciary duty.[35] Professor Niall Whitty has discussed this in some detail in his powerful and convincing critique[36] of the First Division's novel reliance on the English doctrine of "knowing receipt" in *Commonwealth Oil & Gas Co Ltd v Baxter*.[37] In short, if a trustee or other fiduciary profits from his office without the informed consent of the beneficiary or principal, the latter can demand an accounting and insist upon the performance of the trust or fiduciary obligation by transfer of the profit or asset to the trust patrimony or to the principal. This is a personal claim which is part of the law of obligations rather than a proprietary claim. Where the property in question is transferred to a third party, the beneficiary or principal will in many cases have a personal claim against the third party recipient where the third party has received the property (i) gratuitously or (ii) in bad faith with notice of the fraud or breach of fiduciary duty. In the first case (gratuitous transfer) the beneficiary or principal has a claim for restitution in our law of unjustified enrichment;[38] in the second case (bad faith) he can rely on the "no profit from another's

---

33 Ross et al, "Trusts" (n 33) para 30, fn 1, referring to McLaren, *Wills* (n 31) para 1517.
34 *Clydesdale Banking Co v Paul* (1877) 4 R 626; *Thomson v Clydesdale Bank* (1893) 20 R (HL) 59; *New Mining and Exploring Syndicate Ltd v Chalmers and Hunter* 1912 SC 126.
35 *Style Financial Services Ltd v Bank of Scotland* 1996 SLT 421; *Bank of Scotland v Macleod Paxton Woolard & Co* 1998 SLT 258; *Macadam v Grandison* [2008] CSOH 53.
36 N R Whitty, "The 'No Profit from Another's Fraud' Rule and the 'Knowing Receipt' Muddle" 2013 *Edin LR* 37-62.
37 2010 SC 156.
38 *New Mining* (n 34).

breach of fiduciary duty" principle.[39] Thus where no claim is being made to recover an asset in the insolvency of the fiduciary or of the third party recipient, Scots law has remedies in its law of obligations which do not depend on the concept of the constructive trust.

That has not prevented judges and jurists from using language that suggests that personal remedies against the fiduciary and a third party recipient arise as a result of a constructive trust. Professor George has demonstrated in his article, "Constructive Trusts" that most of the cases cited in connection with constructive trusts concern other aspects of fiduciary relations.[40] Even the comparatively recent case of *Huisman v Soepboer*,[41] could be said not to be concerned with an institutional constructive trust which had effect on insolvency. The case concerned a claim by a partner for a profit share of a joint venture to purchase and resell a farm. Huisman sued one of his co-venturers, Soepboer, and also a company controlled by the first defender. Soepboer had taken title to the farm in the name of the company contrary to the terms of the joint venture agreement. Huisman sought a joint and several decree against Soepboer and the company for payment of the profit share on the sale of the farm on the basis that the company obtained its title in bad faith. Lord Penrose upheld the relevancy of the claim and, relying on the English case of *Soar v Ashwell*[42] and Scottish textbooks, held that there might be a constructive trust and that the company might be liable jointly and severally with Soepboer. In my view it was not necessary to attribute that liability to the existence of a constructive trust, as Lord Penrose did. The joint and several liability of the defenders could rest on the principle of no profit from a breach of fiduciary duty.

There are other cases where the Scottish courts have asserted the existence of a trust but have not analysed the meaning of the deemed trust or its effect, if any on the insolvency of the deemed trustee. For example, there is a suggestion in *United Horse Shoe and Nail Co Ltd v Stewart & Co*[43] that a claim for the profits arising from an infringement of a patent is based on treating the infringer as if he were a trustee for the patentee. In *Stevenson v Wilson*[44] the trustee in sequestration of a partnership sold

---

39 The giving of valuable consideration is no defence if the third party is in bad faith: *Clydesdale Banking Co v Paul* (n 34) and *Bank of Scotland v Macleod Paxton Woolard* (n 35).
40 G L Gretton, "Constructive Trusts" 1997 *Edin LR* 281-316 and 408-19.
41 1994 *SLT* 682.
42 [1893] 2 QB 390.
43 (1886) 14 R 266, Lord Kinnear at 270; (1886) 15 R (HL) 45, Lord Watson at 48.
44 1907 SC 445.

shares in a private company, the purchaser paid the price but the directors refused to register him as the proprietor of the shares and the vendor declined either to rescind the sale and repay the price or to receive the dividends on the purchaser's behalf. The First Division treated the vendor as a quasi-trustee and upheld a declarator that the purchaser had the sole beneficial right, title and interest in the shares and dividends. The opinions in the Outer House and Inner House contained no detailed discussion of relevant authorities and the decision seems a pragmatic way of forcing the trustee in sequestration to annul the contract if he wished to wind up his administration of the bankrupt estate. I agree with Lord Hope's view[45] that the circumstances of that case were special and they do not ground any general rule.

But there is also clear authority in Scots law for the existence of an institutional constructive trust as an incident of a fiduciary relationship.[46] In my view the cases where the court has treated money or assets which a solicitor or factor has received from his client for a specific purpose as belonging to a separate patrimony and thus excluded from the former's insolvency are consistent with an implied trust or an institutional constructive trust.

Thus in *Macadam v Martin's Trustee*[47] a solicitor received funds for investment in a heritable security but died before making the investment. The First Division excluded the funds from the solicitor's insolvency because they had been acquired for a specific purpose and had to be applied for that purpose or returned to the owner.

In *Colquhoun's Trustee v Campbell's Trustees*[48] the court was faced with an insolvency. A solicitor was instructed by two clients to obtain securities over land for advances which the clients made to a third party. The solicitor received bonds and dispositions in security from the third party borrower in favour of his clients but did not record them. Instead, shortly before his and his firm's insolvency, he obtained an *ex facie* absolute disposition in favour of his firm and recorded it. The estates of the solicitors' partnership and the partners were sequestrated; prior bondholders sold the security subjects and there was a competition in a multiplepoinding between the

---

45   *Sharp* (n 2) at 480H-481B.
46   Professor George Gretton (n 40) argued for the abolition of the constructive trust but did not dispute its existence.
47   (1872) 11 M 33. See also *Blyth v Maberley's Assignees* (1832) 10 S 796.
48   (1902) 4 F 739.

trustee in sequestration and the clients for the balance of the sale price. The Lord Ordinary, Lord Kyllachy, held that the bankrupt firm and the trustee in sequestration were both disabled from taking the benefit of the solicitor's breach of trust. His reasoning was that there was a constructive trust. He stated:[49]

> For it being once conceded that as between a law-agent and his client there is a fiduciary relation, the result of what took place here was in law really this: The bankrupts being bound under their trust to complete their clients' security by recording the bonds, must be held in law to have taken and recorded the subsequent absolute disposition primarily for their clients, and only in reversion for themselves. In short they must be held to have done in the matter what it was their duty to do. In that view, the absolute disposition was at the date of their sequestration held primarily in trust for the two competing claimants.

The First Division upheld his judgment. The Lord President (Kinross), with whom Lord McLaren concurred, adopted the Lord Ordinary's reasoning: the solicitor was guilty of a fraudulent breach of trust and the trustee in sequestration was in no better position; accordingly the absolute disposition was held on trust primarily for the clients. Lord Kinnear also agreed with the judgment of the Lord Ordinary but relied on the principle that the creditors of the bankrupt and thus the trustee in sequestration could not take advantage of his fraud.

Jopp v Johnston's Trustee[50] is perhaps the best known of these cases. A solicitor who had been granted a factory and commission, sold shares on behalf of his client and deposited the proceeds in his personal account. The funds were mixed with his private money in the bank account. He later withdrew funds and placed them on deposit receipt. Later he died insolvent. The Second Division treated the deceased solicitor as having been in the position of a trustee in relation to his client's funds, which did not form part of his sequestrated estate. The client was therefore able to follow the funds into the deposit receipts and recover the sums that remained on deposit.

In *Newton's Executrix v Meiklejohn's Judicial Factor*[51] a stockbroker, who had purchased shares on behalf of his client pledged those and other shares to a bank under a general letter of hypothecation in security for advances

---

49   *Colquhoun's Trustee* (n 48) at 742.
50   (1904) 6 F 1028.
51   1959 *SLT* 71.

which he received. After his death a judicial factor was appointed under s 163 of the Bankruptcy (Scotland) Act 1913. Lord Guest held that the client's executrix was entitled to a preferred ranking on the sale proceeds in the insolvency.[52]

In *Southern Cross Commodities Property Ltd v Martin*[53] Lord Milligan held that the pursuers were entitled to a declaration that a heritable property, which had been purchased with the pursuers' funds which two of its directors had misappropriated and whose title was in the name of another company under the directors' control, was held on a constructive trust. It is true, as Professor Gretton has argued,[54] that the court was concerned solely with the obligational issue of the transfer of the property to the pursuer company and not any claim against the unsecured creditors of the title-holding company which was not insolvent. But both counsel and the judge proceeded on the basis that the directors' fiduciary position and their breach of fiduciary duty could make the title holding company, which was their creature, a constructive trustee.

In *Sutman International Inc v Herbage*[55] the directors of a company, who were a husband and wife, misappropriated funds of their company and invested them in heritable property. The husband became insolvent and his estates were sequestrated. The company and its liquidator sought a declarator against the couple and the husband's trustee in sequestration that the company was the true beneficial owner of the property. Lord Cullen held that the directors had misappropriated the company's funds and that made the declaration.

In those cases the Scottish courts have recognised an institutional constructive trust, as I have described it, in contexts where persons who were under fiduciary obligations, held property of their clients or company.

In *Ted Jacob Engineering Group Inc v RMJM*[56] Lord Drummond Young, in a careful judgment which focused on comparative law, explained the different approaches of Scots law and English law to the law of trusts and highlighted their functional equivalence. He discussed remedies for breach

---

52 He referred to Bell, *Comm* I, 286 (in which Bell relied on English authorities for the principle that where a factor, who was entrusted with his principal's funds for investment, misapplied them, the produce of his misapplication, if distinguishable, remained the principal's), *Macadam* (n 47) and *Jopp* (n 50).

53 1991 *SLT* 83. Dr Parker Hood commented on the case in 1994 *SLT (News)* 265-68.

54 Gretton (n 40) 296-97.

55 Unreported, 2 August 1991; summarised 1991 GWD 30-1772.

56 2014 SC 579.

7. The Offside Goals Rule and Fraud on Creditors

Dr John MacLeod

I understand that, as a student, Professor Rennie was known to miss the occasional conveyancing class in order to play football. This siren call is not the only danger that the beautiful game has posed for Scots property law. It also gave us a name, and a dubious metaphor, for the so-called offside goals rule.

Few areas of Scots property law have attracted as much modern scholarly interest.[1] One of the reasons why the rule might appear unworthy of the fuss is the simplicity with which the core case may be stated. The classic instance is double sale: Alfred concludes a contract for the sale of his field to Betty; before Betty has obtained her real right, Alfred sells it a second time to Cecil, who registers first. The offside goals rule says that, if Cecil was in bad faith, the transfer to him is voidable at Betty's instance. Betty can also set aside a gratuitous transfer to Cecil even if he is in good faith.

---

1 D Carey Miller, "A Centenary Offering: The Double Sale Dilemma – Time to be Laid to Rest" in M Kidd and S Hoctor (eds), *Stella Iuris: Celebrating 100 years of the teaching of law in Pietermaritzburg* (2010) 96; R G Anderson, *Assignation* (2008) paras 11-04-30; D L Carey Miller with D Miller. *Corporeal Moveables in Scots Law*, 2nd edn (2005) paras 8.28-32; D A Brand, A J M Steven and S Wortley, *Professor McDonald's Conveyancing Manual*, 7th edn (2004) paras 32.52-62; S Wortley, "Double Sales and the Offside Trap: Some Thoughts on the Rule Penalising Private Knowledge of a Prior Right" 2002 JR 291; K G C Reid, *The Law of Property in Scotland* (1996) paras 695-700. Professor Rennie has perhaps been a little sceptical about the attention lavished on it, observing that "the rule against offside goals has become quite fashionable recently." R Rennie "Land Registration and the Decline of Property Law" (2010) 14 *Edin LR* 62 at 74.

  http://dx.doi.org/10.11647/OBP.0056.07

There is broad consensus on the basic elements. A grant is voidable under the offside goals rule if:

(i)   the granter was under a prior obligation to grant a real right to the avoiding party, which obligation gave rise to a concomitant obligation not to alienate or burden the property;

(ii)   the grant was made in breach of the prior obligation;

(iii)   the grantee knew of the obligation or the grant was not for value.[2]

If the rule can be briefly stated and there is agreement about its content, why are Scots property lawyers so concerned about it? One reason is that it bears on the discussion of the relationship between real and personal rights which was at the centre of Scots property law discourse at the turn of the 21st century. In particular, it threatens to undermine the clear distinction between real and personal rights established in *Burnett's Trustee v Grainger*.[3] The rule appears to run contrary to the maxim *prior tempore potior iure est*.[4] The puzzle is to explain how a party with a real right can be vulnerable to a challenge brought by someone with a mere personal right.

A. *Mala Fides*, Personal Bar and the Publicity Principle

Although the topic was addressed during the foundational period in the seventeenth and eighteenth centuries,[5] modern discussion begins with *Rodger (Builders) Ltd v Fawdry*[6] which offers little consideration of the basis of the rule. Lord Jamieson, giving the leading judgment, was content to rely on three nineteenth-century cases where the rule had been applied and to observe that the purchaser was in bad faith.[7]

In the first of these, *Marshall v Hynd*,[8] the judges' primary concern was the level of knowledge needed to put the second purchaser in bad faith.

---

2   Reid *Property* para 695, approved in *Advice Centre for Mortgages v McNicoll* 2006 SLT 591 at para 46.

3   2004 SC (HL) 19. For a summary of this debate, see the Scottish Law Commission *Report on Sharp v Thomson* (SLC No 208, December 2007) Part 1.

4   For a very forceful statement of this view, see Anderson *Assignation* paras 11-05 and 11-30.

5   Anderson *Assignation* paras 11-06-23.

6   1950 SC 483.

7   1950 SC 483 at 500, citing *Marshall v Hynd* (1828) 6 S 384, *Petrie v Forsyth* (1874) 2 R 214 and *Stodart v Dalzell* (1876) 4 R 236.

8   (1828) 6 S 384.

If knowledge is to constitute bad faith, there must be some rule which explains why the party with the knowledge should have acted differently. This issue was addressed in the third case mentioned in *Rodger (Builders)*, *Stodart v Dalzell*, where Lords Ormidale and Gifford suggested that the second purchaser's knowledge of the prior right meant that he was not entitled to rely on the faith of the records regarding his seller's right.[9]

These authorities make Lord Gifford's characterisation of the rule as a species of personal bar in the second of the three cases, *Petrie v Forsyth*, understandable.[10] On this model the first buyer has acquired a right, albeit not one which has been published. Under normal circumstances, that right could not be invoked against second buyer who had registered because the latter could invoke the faith of the records. However, the second buyer's knowledge of the right means that he is barred from making this argument since he knew better. As Reid and Blackie point out, however, personal bar is difficult to maintain in this context because of the absence of inconsistent conduct by the second buyer.[11]

Even if the language of personal bar is eschewed, a rule which restricts reliance on the register to those who are in good faith is conceivable. Indeed such rules exist in the Land Registration (Scotland) Act 2012.[12] Wortley makes tentative moves towards such an analysis with his suggestion that the basis of the offside goals rule might lie in an aspect of the publicity principle: "the publicity principle is not merely there to protect third parties: in certain circumstances, it can also be used to penalise them."[13]

The difficulty with this approach is that the act of publicity (be it registration, intimation or delivery) is not merely a mechanism for making a transfer known. It is constitutive of the transfer. Until that act is completed, ownership remains with the seller and the first buyer's right is merely personal. The first buyer has no proprietary interest of which third parties could have notice. This stands in contrast to the good faith requirements

---

9   (1876) 4 R 236 both at 242. Similar comments were made by Lord Kinloch in *Morrison v Somerville* (1860) 22 D 1082 at 1089 and by Lord Jamieson in *Rodger Builders* 1950 SC 483 at 500.

10   (1874) 2 R 214 at 223.

11   E C Reid and J W G Blackie, *Personal Bar* (2006) para 2-08. See further J W G Blackie, "Good Faith and the Doctrine of Personal Bar" in ADM Forte (ed) *Good Faith in Contract and Property Law* (1999) 129 at 147-60.

12   E.g. Land Registration (Scotland) Act 2012 s 86, particularly paragraph (3)(c).

13   Wortley (n 1) at 314.

in the 2012 Act,[14] which cover cases where the Land Register misstates the relevant real rights.

In that context, an argument based on the faith of the records or the publicity principle might have difficulty answering Lord Low's objection: "Assuming that they knew of the obligation, they knew also that it did not affect the lands."[15] Like its correlative right, the seller's duty is personal. The second buyer might argue that his knowledge of it was irrelevant because the obligation of which he knew did not bind him. Further, arguments about publicity or personal bar offer little in the way of an explanation for why a gratuitous transferee who was ignorant of the earlier transfer should be vulnerable.[16]

B. *Mala Fides* and the Transfer Agreement

Carey Miller suggests that the import of the second buyer's bad faith can be explained, not by reference to the publicity principle but by invoking the principle of separation of contract and conveyance.[17] This principle recognises transfer as a distinct juridical act requiring intention on the part of transferor and transferee. Carey Miller argues that the second buyer's bad faith means he has a defective intention to acquire, which renders his right voidable.[18]

Carey Miller employs an unusual understanding of intention. Both seller and second buyer wish the transfer to take place and, on a conventional view of intention, that would be enough. At the time of the transfer their wills are directed to that end. The fact that they know it to be wrong does not affect this intention. A poacher has a sufficient *animus acquirendi*, although he knows that he is committing a crime.[19] Further,

---

14   Land Registration (Scotland) Act 2012 ss 86-93.

15   *Morier v Brownlie & Watson* (1895) 23 R 67 at 74.

16   E.g. *Alexander v Lundies* (1675) Mor 940.

17   Wortley describes Carey Miller's analysis as an "abstract system approach" (Wortley (n 1) at 312), a characterisation which Carey Miller accepts ("A Centenary Offering" at 96). However, the analysis turns on the need for a real or transfer agreement. A transfer agreement might be necessary even in a system which also requires a valid *causa* for the transfer. Therefore, it seems marginally preferable to see the analysis as resting on the principle of separation.

18   Carey Miller *Corporeal Moveables* para 8.28. See also para 8.30 and Carey Miller (n 1) at 114.

19   Erskine, *Inst* 2.1.10.

the vices of consent, such as fraud and force and fear, operate for the protection of one of the parties to a transaction where his consent has been improperly obtained. What is being suggested here is something completely different: both parties give free and informed consent and it is a third party who needs the protection.

A second problem with Carey Miller's analysis is a variant of the problem with the publicity principle argument. Even if bad faith can affect intention to acquire, some explanation of why the knowledge amounts to bad faith is needed. As noted above, knowledge only constitutes bad faith when coupled with a rule explaining why the knowledge should have made you act differently.

As for the gratuity case, Carey Miller addresses this in straightforward policy terms, suggesting that the reason is simply that "a party who fails to give value should not trump a competing party with an earlier right."[20] This approach has intuitive appeal. The law of transfer is primarily geared towards the needs of commerce and thus of onerous transferees. Donees are not worthy of this protection.

Once again, however, a little more seems necessary. Suppose Donna makes a written promise to David that she will convey a field to him. The next day, she concludes a contract with Betty for the sale of the same field. Foolishly, Betty pays up front. On the third day, Donna delivers the disposition to David who duly registers it. Betty clearly has a right against Donna for breach of contract but David is safe. The story would be different if Betty's missives had been concluded on Day 1 and the promise to David made on Day 2. If the basic idea behind the vulnerability of donees under the offside goals rule is that they are less worthy of protection than onerous transferees, it is difficult to see why Betty should be worse off because the promise happened to come first. To say that David has the earlier right is to fall into the error which underlies the personal bar analysis: the idea that some kind of proto-property right is acquired before completion of the transfer of which the act of transfer merely gives notice. All David has on Day 1 is a personal right against Donna. Similarly, if the gratuity case is explained by lack of sympathy for donees, why can a promisee invoke the rule against later donee?[21]

---

20 Carey Miller *Corporeal Moveables* para 8.32.
21 E.g. *Alexander v Lundies* (1675) Mor 940.

C. *Mala Fides* and Fraud

The difficulties with the publicity principle and the transfer agreement as bases for the offside goals rule drive analysis back to an earlier approach. The nineteenth-century cases cited in *Rodger (Builders)* marked a shift in the analysis of the rule. Up to that point, it was thought to rest on fraud.

Seatoun v Copburnes,[22] decided in 1549, is probably the first recorded case which can be understood in terms of the offside goals rule. Lady Seatoun sought to reduce an infeftment given to James Copburne by his father. She argued that, prior to that sasine, she and the priests and college of the Kirk of Seatoun had bought an annualrent[23] of the lands from the father. Lady Seatoun alleged that infeftment on the annualrent had been completed, so she might have relied on her prior real right but she chose not to do so. Instead she suggested that "the said laird in manifest defraud of the said lady and preistis *dolose infeodavit suum filium in suis terris,* and sua, said scho [i.e. she], that that alienatioun *in dolo et fraude (ut predicitur) facta de iure erat retractanda.*" In other words, she sought reduction of the infeftment on the basis that it was granted in fraud of her right to the lands.

Fraud also played a key role in the first major scholarly discussion of the offside goals rule: Stair's treatment of resolutive conditions in contracts of sale. A resolutive condition is a term which purports to make the property revert to the transferor in given circumstances. Stair's view was that such conditions had no proprietary effect. The transferee merely had an obligation to reconvey if the condition occurred. This raised the question of the effect of the obligation on third parties who obtained the property from the transferee. Although the origin of the obligation to convey differs from double sale, the end result is the same: an alienation in breach of an obligation to grant a real right to someone else.

As with *Seatoun v Copburnes,* Stair analyses the situation in terms of fraud:[24]

> ...though there may be fraud in the acquirer, which raiseth an obligation of reparation to the party damnified by that delinquence, yet that is but personal;

---

22   (1549) Sinclair *Practicks* n 459.

23   I.e. a subordinate real right, giving the holder a right to an annual payment from the owner of the burdened property.

24   Stair, *Inst* 1.14.5. He does go on to consider whether the 1621 Act might apply to gratuitous alienations of property subject to a resolutive condition but concludes that the law is not clear. It would later become firmly established that insolvency at the time of the grant was a prerequisite of such a challenge.

and another party acquiring *bona fide* or necessarily, and not partaking of that fraud, is *in tuto*. But certain knowledge, by intimation, citation, or the like, inducing *malam fidem*, whereby any prior disposition or assignation made to another party is certainly known, or at least interruption made in acquiring by arrestment or citation of the acquirer, such rights acquired, not being of necessity to satisfy prior engagements, are reducible *ex capite fraudis*, and the acquirer is partaker of the fraud of his author, who thereby becomes a granter of double rights; but this will not hinder legal diligence to proceed and be completed and become effectual, though the user thereof did certainly know of any inchoate or incomplete right of another.

Certain elements of the analysis are worthy of particular note: the idea that the primary wrong is done by the granter (referred to as the acquirer because of the context of a resolutive condition); that the successor is only vulnerable if the prior right is known of and that the basis of this is not his own fraud but participation in the granter's fraud. As with his general analysis of fraud,[25] Stair characterises the vulnerability of a transaction affected by fraud in terms of a personal right to reparation from the wrongdoer.

D. Is Fraud a Broad Enough Concept to Account for the Offside Goals Rule?

As Anderson and Reid show,[26] the fraud analysis persisted until the nineteenth century. Indeed references to it can also be found in the later cases, existing alongside arguments based on publicity or personal bar. Thus, in *Morrison v Sommerville*, Lord Kinloch gives a classic fraud-based analysis:[27]

> In granting a second right, the seller is guilty of fraud on the first purchaser. Against the seller himself the transactions would be clearly reducible. But, in taking the second right in the knowledge of the first, the second disponee becomes an accomplice in the fraud, and the transactions is reducible against both alike.

---

25 Stair, *Inst* 1.9.9-15.

26 Reid *Property* para 695; Anderson *Assignation* 11-06-23.

27 (1860) 22 D 1082 at 1089. This analysis is reflected in the issue which the Inner House appointed to be put to the jury: "whether, in violation of a previous minute of agreement, dated 7th October 1850, No 8 of the process, the said disposition was granted fraudulently by the said George Somerville, and was taken fraudulently by the said John Craig Waddell, in the knowledge of the said previous agreement, and in defraud of the pursuer's rights under the same." (1860) 22 D 1082 at 1090.

In *Petrie v Forsyth*, Lord Neaves proceeded on the basis that the second purchaser's conduct was fraudulent.[28] However, Lord Gifford took a different approach, distinguishing between fraud, *mala fides* and "mere knowledge."[29] He concluded that what was needed was knowledge sufficient to put the second purchaser under a duty to contact the first. Lord Gifford clearly considered this to fall short of fraud. On such a model it is difficult to see how fraud can form the basis for the doctrine.

A similar line of reasoning is articulated by Lord Drummond Young in *Advice Centre for Mortgages*:[30]

> The theoretical basis for the foregoing principle is not discussed in any detail in the decided cases, perhaps because its practical application is very obvious, at least in simpler cases. The origins of the principle seem to lie in the concept of fraud in its older sense. This is not the modern sense, involving a false representation made knowingly, but rather consists of actings designed to defeat another person's legal right. Nevertheless, the law has moved away from the concept of fraud. In *Rodger* Lord Jamieson said: "[F]raud in the sense of moral delinquency does not enter into the matter. It is sufficient if the intending purchaser fails to make the inquiry which he is bound to do. If he fails he is no longer *in bona fide* but *in mala fide*." Thus implied or constructive knowledge, just as much as actual knowledge, will bring the principle into operation and render the second purchaser *in mala fide*.

The discomfort with fraud as a rationale is also evident in academic analysis: Kenneth Reid is careful to specify that "the original analysis based on 'fraud' remains correct, provided that 'fraud' is not confined to its narrow modern meaning."[31] Wortley goes further, seeming to regard the second purchaser's liability in cases of mere knowledge of the prior right as being more than a fraud-based justification can support.[32] Dot Reid views offside goals as part of the law of fraud, specifically of secondary fraud, but suggests that this is a survival of the older, broader view which was heavily dependent on the concept of inequality derived ultimately from scholastic thinking. This leaves the offside goals rule in the law of obligations but outside the established categories of enrichment or delict.[33]

---

28   (1874) 2 R 214 at 221.
29   Ibid at 223.
30   2006 *SLT* 591 at para 44.
31   Reid *Property* para 695.
32   Wortley (n 1) at 301.
33   D Reid "Fraud in Scots Law" (PhD Thesis, University of Edinburgh, 2012) ch 7, esp pp 243-44 and 250-51.

The doubt stems from the interaction of two developments. First, there is the sense that while Scots law took a broad view of fraud in the early-modern period, later developments saw it narrow considerably. This process, particularly the influence of *Derry v Peek*,[34] is thought to have limited fraud to deceit.[35] Secondly, there appears to be a relaxation in the level of knowledge required for offside goals in some of the dicta in the nineteenth-century cases. This broadened the scope of the rule and can appear to move it away from a category of intentional wrongdoing.

Is it possible to address these concerns and thus to continue to rely on fraud as a basis which can guide future development?

(1) Fraud on creditors rather than fraud as deceit

In response to the objection that the meaning of fraud has narrowed, reference may be made to a species of fraud which is recognised by the modern law but which does not involve deception: fraud on creditors. It is worthy of note that mere knowledge of what is going on is sufficient to render the debtor's counterparty a participant in the fraud in that context.

The best known example of fraud on creditors is the transfer or burdening of assets by an insolvent debtor. The classic examples are well-known. A debtor recognises that he is irrecoverably insolvent. Knowing that his assets will be sold to pay his debts, he decides that he would rather see them go to his friends, so he gives them away. In some cases the transfer might be intended to allow the debtor continued use of the property, as where a businessman in embarrassed circumstances transfers the family home to his wife. Whatever the purpose, the result is the same: a pool of assets which was already insufficient to meet the debtor's obligations is further diminished. Creditors' interests are thus prejudiced. Both common law and statute allow for the reversal of such transfers or grants at the instance of creditors or the insolvency official. These grants are usually gratuitous but an onerous grantee who colludes with the debtor in his attempt to frustrate his creditors is also liable to have his grant reduced.[36]

It is clear that the basis of this rule at common law is that the transactions are fraudulent.[37] This rule is very widely recognised in both the Common

---

34 (1889) 14 App Cas 337.

35 This development is discussed in detail in Reid "Fraud in Scots Law" ch 4 and 5.

36 J MacLeod "Fraud and Voidable Transfer: Scots Law in European Context" (PhD thesis, University of Edinburgh, 2013) ch 4 esp pp 83-92 and 113-24.

37 W W McBryde *Bankruptcy*, 2nd edn (1995) ch 12 esp paras 12-11-48; MacLeod "Fraud and Voidable Transfer" ch 4.

Law and Civilian tradition.[38] In the latter it is commonly referred to as the *actio Pauliana*, a term which betrays the rule's origins in Roman law.

The debtor may have contracted the debts in good faith with the full intention of paying them. In such a case, the creditors have not been deceived into giving credit but they are nonetheless said to be defrauded. As with the offside goals rule, this provokes a degree of discomfort in the modern sources, leading McBryde to suggest that fraud in this context is anomalous and to caution against use of authorities on fraud in the general sense.[39]

The striking thing is that the anomalous fraud looks very similar to the offside goals rule. Both rules involve actions by a debtor which render him incapable of fulfilling his obligation and thus frustrate the creditor's hopes of recovery. As with the offside goals rule, the grantee may find himself liable either because he knew what the debtor was doing or because his grant was gratuitous. Furthermore, as with Stair's account of the offside goals situation, the primary fraud is that of the debtor while the grantee is liable as a participant in the debtor's fraud.[40]

Anderson notes the parallel between the offside goals rule and the *actio Pauliana*, but points to two differences: in the *actio Pauliana* having given good consideration is usually a defence and the relevant *mala fides* is knowledge of insolvency rather than knowledge of a prior right.[41] However, these differences reflect a different context rather than a fundamental conceptual division. The reason that payment is usually a good defence to the *actio Pauliana* is that such payment renders the transaction neutral in its effect on the patrimony. There is no prejudice to ordinary creditors. It makes no difference to them whether the debtor has a piece of machinery worth £5,000 or £5,000 in his bank account. Both are assets which are

---

38   B M Goodman, "The Revocatory Action" (1934-35) 9 *Tulane Law Review* 422; A Boraine "Towards Codifying the *actio Pauliana*" (1996) *South African Mercantile Law Journal* 213; A Vaquer, "Traces of Paulian Action in Community Law" in R Schulze (ed), *New Features in Contract Law* (2007) 421; J J Forner Delaygua *La protección del crédito en Europa: La acción pauliana* (2000); P R Wood, *Law and Practice of International Finance* (University edn, 2008) 79-85; C von Bar and E Clive, *Principles, Definitions and Model Rules of European Private Law: Draft Common Frame of Reference Full Edition* (2009) Vol 5 2634ff and R J de Weijs "Towards an Objective Rule on Transaction Avoidance in Insolvencies" (2011) *International Insolvency Review*. http://dx.doi.org/10.1002/iir.196

39   McBryde *Bankruptcy* para 12-13.

40   E.g. *M'Cowan v Wright* (1853) 15 D 494 at 500 per Lord Hope. See further MacLeod "Fraud and Voidable Transfer" 82-87.

41   Anderson *Assignation* para 11-17.

available to them for the satisfaction of their rights. Things are different in the offside goals situation because what matters for the creditor is not the value of the patrimony as a whole but the presence in it of the particular asset to which he is entitled.

This line of thought leads to an explanation of why the relevant *mala fides* is knowledge of the insolvency in an *actio Pauliana* situation and knowledge of the competing right in an offside goals situation. Knowledge that someone is insolvent implies knowledge of personal rights against his patrimony: if you know someone is insolvent you know that he has creditors whom he cannot pay. Specific knowledge of the creditors' rights is not necessary because the counterparty knows enough to understand that the transaction will frustrate the creditors' hopes of recovery. Conversely, if a buyer knows that someone else has a personal right to a particular asset, the general solvency of the seller is not relevant. Even if the seller is generally solvent, the competitor will still be frustrated.

The *actio Pauliana* and the offside goals rule can both be seen as protecting creditors whose debtors act to frustrate their hopes of satisfaction, the difference in the detail of the two rules results from differences in context and thus in the nature of the protection necessary.

Insolvency fraud is not the only instance of fraud on creditors recognised by Scots law, although the other instance is less obvious at first sight. A creditor who intends to do diligence can use an inhibition to render the debtor's heritable property litigious.[42] As with the *actio Pauliana*, the concern is that the creditor's recourse (in this case by means of diligence) against the debtor's assets will be frustrated by voluntary acts of the debtor. The point is made most clearly by reference to the historic terms of letters of inhibition. Prior to their abolition,[43] letters of inhibition were the means by which the Court of Session, acting in the name of king or queen sanctioned the inhibition of the debtor. The letters instructed messengers at arms to make two prohibitions. First, they were to "inhibit and discharge" the debtor, prohibiting any dealing with his property whether heritable or moveable and any act pursuant to which diligence might be done against his assets. Secondly, "all our lieges of this realm, and all others whom it

---

42 *Burnett's Tr v Grainger* 2004 SC (HL) 19 at para 22 per Lord Hope. Inhibition is not the only instance of litigiosity in Scots law for the others, and for more extensive discussion of inhibition, see MacLeod "Fraud and Voidable Transfer" ch 5 and 6.

43 Bankruptcy and Diligence etc (Scotland) Act 2007 s 146.

effeirs" were to be inhibited and discharged from concluding any of the prohibited transactions with the debtor. The former prohibition required to be by personal service on the debtor, the latter by proclamation at the market cross. The reason for this drastic action was also narrated in the letters: namely that the king is informed that the debtor intends to diminish his estate "in defraud and prejudice of the complainer."[44]

Again, the fraud in this case is not deception. The problem facing the creditor is assets leaving the debtor's patrimony meaning that there is not enough there to satisfy the former's right. Letters of inhibition are no longer issued but the new schedule of inhibition reflects the old thinking. To take the example of an inhibition by a creditor suing to enforce a debt in the Court of Session:[45]

> ...In Her Majesty's name and authority, I [name], Messenger at Arms, by virtue of [document which warrants the inhibition] inhibit you from selling, disposing of, burdening or otherwise affecting all land and heritable property in which you have an interest to the prejudice of [the inhibitor].

Again, inhibition has its own special characteristics, notably the absence of any need to prove bad faith on the part of those dealing with the debtor but that is because registration of the inhibition operates to put everyone on notice that the debtor has been so restricted.

Another speciality of inhibition illustrates the fact that inhibition operates to protect satisfaction of a personal right. A general creditor's inhibition covers the heritable property of the debtor because any of it could be subject to an adjudication for enforcement of the debt. Where, however, the creditor inhibits with a view to enforcing a personal right to a particular plot, the effect of the inhibition is restricted to that asset.[46] The general state of the patrimony is irrelevant to the creditor, provided that his access to that plot is secured.

Fraud in the sense of deception and fraud on creditors may well have been part of a broader concept of fraud which has since fallen away but both survive in the modern law. Therefore, a narrowing of the concept of fraud is not a reason to doubt its appropriateness as a grounding concept for the offside goals rule.

---

44   Stair, *Inst* 4.1.4.
45   Diligence (Scotland) Regulations 2009 Sch 1.
46   Bankruptcy and Diligence etc (Scotland) Act 2007 ss 150(1) and 153.

limitation to the rule has been doubted in light of *Trade Development Bank v Warriner & Mason (Scotland) Ltd.*[60] In that case, a condition against leasing in a standard security was given effect against a tenant on the basis of the tenant's bad faith *vis-à-vis* the prohibition. This led Kenneth Reid to suggest that the personal-right-to-a-real-right requirement had fallen away and that the scope of the rule was instead controlled by the requirement that the granter was in breach of an antecedent obligation in making the grant.[61]

As Webster has pointed out,[62] framing the rule's application in these terms is difficult to reconcile with the earlier decision of the Inner House in *Wallace v Simmers.*[63] There the court declined to apply the rule to protect a licensee against an action for ejection by a third party purchaser on the basis that this was not a personal right to a real right. Sale by one who has granted an irrevocable licence is a breach of an antecedent obligation (since it renders the licensor unable to fulfil his obligation), but *Wallace* means that the rule will not apply even if the third party is in bad faith.

The view that not every grant in breach of a prior obligation is challengeable as an offside goal is supported by recent authority.[64] In *Gibson v Royal Bank of Scotland Plc*, however, Lord Emslie expressed some doubts about whether the "personal right to a real right" test was appropriately expressed.[65] Nonetheless, his alternative formulation: that the right be capable of "affecting the records" seems to come to much the same thing for heritable property. The records are only affected in any meaningful way by transfer, extinction or grant of a real right.

Lord Emslie's formulation has the disadvantage of not being apposite to cover moveable property. On the other hand it usefully raises the question of the holder of a real right who is contractually bound to grant a discharge transferring that right before the discharge is granted. For instance, Dominic may own a plot which has the benefit of a right of way over Serena's land. She pays him for a discharge because she wants to develop the land. Before the discharge is granted, Dominic gifts the plot to Gary, who refuses to grant the discharge. Should Serena be able to invoke the offside goals

---

60 1980 SC 74, approved in *Trade Development Bank v Crittall Windows Ltd* 1983 SLT 510.
61 Reid *Property* paras 695-96.
62 P Webster "The Relationship of Tenant and Successor Landlord in Scots Law" (PhD thesis, University of Edinburgh, 2008) 211-13.
63 1960 SC 255.
64 *Optical Express (Gyle) Ltd v Marks & Spencer plc* 2000 SLT 644 and *Gibson v Royal Bank of Scotland Plc* 2009 SLT 444.
65 2009 *SLT* 444 at paras 43-50, esp para 44.

rule? On Lord Emslie's formulation, she can. On the traditional model, the picture is less clear but protecting her seems to be the correct result. Had Dominic contracted to grant a servitude to her, Serena would have been able to rely on it and there is no obvious reason why one type of transaction with a servitude should be favoured over another.

Therefore, the requirement might be better rephrased as a personal right to the grant, transfer, variation or discharge of a real right. This is rather cumbersome. The basic point expressed by the "personal-right-to-real-right" formulation appears to be widely accepted and the phrase remains a useful (if slightly imprecise) handle for the concept. The question remains, however, of how this idea sits with the rationale for the offside goals rule presented here.

Personal rights to subordinate real rights

One implication of the suggestion that the offside goals rule protects personal rights to the grant, transfer or discharge of real rights is that the rule extends beyond double sale. Someone with a personal right to the grant of a servitude or a lease should be able to invoke the rule too.[66] So, if Bert contracts to grant a right of way to Sally but transfers the property to Ernie before Sally is able to register the grant, Sally can invoke the offside goals rule against Ernie if he was in bad faith or the transfer was gratuitous.

Subordinate real rights present difficulties in terms of remedies. If, the holder of the prior personal right hears of the wrongful grant before it is completed, he may be able to obtain an interdict against completion.[67] What of the case where the prior rightholder only discovers the grant after the fact? Where the first grantee was entitled to transfer of the asset, there is no difficulty in returning the property to the seller. That is only a short term step, after which it will pass to the first grantee. Where, on the other hand, the first grantee is merely entitled to a subordinate right, setting a transfer aside seems to go too far. If the first grantee is entitled to a servitude, all he needs is an opportunity to complete his real right. He has no interest in the seller being the owner instead of the second buyer.

---

66   There is express authority to this effect in South Africa *Grant v Stonestreet* 1968 (4) SA 1 (A). A similar result was reached in *Greig v Brown and Nicholson* (1829) 7 S 274, although the court's reasoning is not very clearly expressed.

67   *Spurway, Petr* (10 December 1986, unreported), OH, available on LexisNexis.

The South African solution is to allow the personal right to be enforced directly against the successor.[68] This result has been explained in terms of a broad, equitable approach.[69] It seems to come close to collapsing the distinction between real and personal rights and may explain the tendency in South Africa to suggest that the doctrine of notice (their equivalent of the offside goals rule) affords "limited real effect" to personal rights.[70] Such an approach is not particularly attractive for Scots law. How then can the problem of the offside goal against a right to a servitude be solved?

One answer is suggested by reflecting on the fact that reduction of a deed granted in breach of inhibition is *ad hunc effectum*. Everyone also knows that reduction *ad hunc effectum* means that only the inhibitor is entitled to treat the reduced deed as null. Familiarity with the rule and lack of familiarity with Latin are apt to mask how strange this is. The words *ad hunc effectum* simply mean "to this effect." Why should those words have come to signify that the reduction only benefits the inhibitor?

To answer this question, we need to make brief mention of seventeenth-century decisions concerning fraud on creditors by an insolvent debtor. In many of those cases, reduction was granted but the Lords specified the effect of reduction. In some cases this was to allow the reducing creditor to rank *pari passu* with other creditors;[71] in others, the reduction only benefited certain classes of creditor.[72] The particular scope was determined by what was necessary to reverse the prejudice caused by the debtor's fraudulent actions and the rationale is fairly clear. To go further would be to go beyond the purpose of the rule: which is to secure creditors against the debtor's attempts to frustrate their claims. The limitation was typically introduced by the phrase "to the effect that" or some variation thereon.

---

68 1968 (4) SA 1 at 20 per Ogilvie JA. The reasoning of the court in *Greig v Brown and Nicholson* (n 65) in Shaw's report is limited to the brief and rather surprising suggestion that since both rights were personal "the common owner is divested by the conveyance" without the need to complete the grant of servitude by taking possession. This analysis would be difficult to maintain light of the clarification of the relationship between real and personal rights and of the race to completion in *Sharp v Thomson* 1995 SC 455 and *Burnett's Trustee v Grainger* 2004 SC (HL) 19.

69 *Meridian Bay Restaurant (Pty) Ltd v Mitchell* 2011 (4) SA 1 (SCA) at paras 30-1 per Ponnan JA.

70 "Die juiste siening na my mening is dat vanweë die kennisleer aan 'n persoonlike reg beperkte saaklike werking verleen word": *Associate South African Bakeries (Pty) Ltd v Oryx & Vereinigte Bäckerien (Pty) Ltd* 1982 (3) SA 893 (A) at 910 per Van Heerden JA.

71 E.g. *Kinloch v Blair* (1678) Mor 889 and *Brown v Murray* (1754) Mor 886.

72 E.g. *Cunninghame v Hamilton* (1682) Mor 1064 and *Bateman & Chaplane v Hamilton* (1686) Mor 1076. For further discussion of these cases, see MacLeod "Fraud and Voidable Transfer" 124-26.

Turning back to inhibitions, the import of the phrase *ad hunc effectum* is readily explicable. The prohibition on dealing was imposed to protect the inhibiting creditor and no one else. Therefore, to allow the reduction to have effect in relation to anyone else would go beyond the purpose of the rule. We can surmise that there was an initial period when the words *ad hunc effectum* merely introduced the statement of the reduction's operation and that later the specification was dropped as the Latin tag became detached from its meaning.

What this shows us is that limitation of the effect of reductions is not limited to inhibitions, which raises the possibility of applying it in the third class of fraud on creditors: offside goals.

Reduction of deeds granted in fraud of creditors is about putting assets back in a patrimony so that creditors can obtain rights in them. This is obviously the case with inhibition, or fraud by an insolvent debtor, but it is also the case in a classic double sale of land. Reduction is not an end in itself. Rather, it puts the fraudulent granter in a position to perform by granting a real right affecting the asset. Alternatively, it allows the creditors to get the court to make the grant for the debtor by means of diligence. This endgame is what justifies the reduction.

Where reduction is *ad hunc effectum*, its effect is specified so it goes no further than necessary to secure the protected interest. Thus reduction *ex capite inhibitionis* merely operates to render an adjudication against the former owner competent. That being achieved, it has no further value.

In some cases, the practical distinction between *ad hunc effectum* and catholic reduction is a minor one: if a transfer to Billy is reduced to allow Dan to register his disposition, Dan's registration will deprive Billy of any right that he has. However, it makes a big difference where an offside goal has been scored and there is a personal right to a servitude. The reduction would be *ad hunc effectum* to enable a deed of servitude granted by the seller to be registered and constituted a real right, but it would go no further. For all other purposes Billy would remain owner.

Of course, the net result of this approach is very similar to the South African rule. A transferee who was faced with a valid offside goals challenge in these circumstances could save everyone a lot of time and money simply by agreeing to grant the relevant subordinate real right. In doing so, he would be in no worse a position than if reduction *ad hunc effectum* had been obtained and the grant had been made from his author. The courts might even be justified in allowing the procedure to be short-circuited and compelling the transferee to make such a grant. Nonetheless, for the sake of a proper understanding of the relationship between real and personal rights, it is important to grasp why such a short cut might be permitted.

Does the fraud-on-creditors analysis prove too much?

The fraud-on-creditors analysis can account for one implication of the view that the offside goals rule is a mechanism for protecting personal rights to real rights rather than being restricted to the case of double sale. However, it appears to struggle with a more fundamental aspect. If the basis of the offside goals rule is fraud on creditors and some general duty not to participate in the breach of personal rights owed to others, why should it be restricted to creditors holding a particular class of personal rights? After all, any kind of creditor can challenge a fraudulent grant by an insolvent debtor or protect his right with an inhibition. Why then, should the offside goals rule be restricted to a particular class of personal right?

The first point to note is that the offside goals rule is not the only mechanism which gives external effect to personal rights. Scots law also recognises that inducing breach of contract and the personal-right-to-a-real-right restriction do not apply to it. Therefore, the fact that a right is not a personal right to a real right does not necessarily mean that the third party is safe. Rather, it is likely to mean that he is liable in damages but safe from reduction of the transfer (as there is no offside goal). So the consequences of the personal-right-to-a-real-right restriction are not as sharp as first appears.

This argument depends on the mental element of inducing breach of contract being substantially the same as that for offside goals. This is broadly the case: the test for the mental element of inducing breach of contract is likely to be met in most bad-faith offside goals cases. If the second purchaser knows of the prior right, then breach of its correlative obligation is a necessary means to the end sought by the second purchaser: obtaining the property for himself.

The difficulty arises in those cases where the second purchaser is put on notice but has something which falls short of clear and certain knowledge of the prior right. This is a divergence between inducing breach of contract and offside goals. However, it is not as big a gap as may appear at first. In *OBG v Allan*, Lord Hoffmann made it clear that wilful blindness, where someone decides not to inquire for fear of what they might find, was as good as knowledge.[73] That is sufficient to cover a lot of the offside goals

---

73   [2008] 1 AC 1 at paras 40-41.

cases and a reining in of the mental element to match that for inducing breach of contract would be desirable since the present approach creates too much uncertainty for potential purchasers.[74]

Even under the present law, there will be few cases where the mental element for the offside goals rule is fulfilled but that for inducing breach of contract is not. Where both are fulfilled, the restriction of the offside goals rule to personal rights to real rights affects which remedies are available rather than whether any remedy is available.

This brings the analysis back to the nature of the remedy under the offside goals rule. As suggested above, avoidance for fraud on creditors is aimed at putting an asset back in a patrimony so that a creditor can obtain a real right in it. It operates *ad hunc effectum* and goes no further. It gives the fraudulent transferor no right to possess the property.

That, in turn, provides a rationale for the result in *Wallace v Simmers*.[75] Miss Simmers had a licence (a personal right) against her brother which entitled her to occupy a house on his property. He sold the property in breach of that licence. Suppose that she had obtained a reduction of the transfer from her brother to the buyer. What would the effect of that reduction have been? Her brother had no obligation to grant her any real right and, since reduction would not have given him any right to possess the property, he would not be in a position to secure her possession and thus to fulfil his obligation under the licence. The *hunc* in *ad hunc effectum* in this case would have no content. Therefore the reduction would have been pointless.

Restricting offside goals to personal rights to the grant of real rights is therefore consistent with the fraud rationale because it reflects the nature of avoidance for fraud on creditors.

(3) Gratuitous acquirers

An analysis based on the wrongful nature of the second purchaser's conduct faces obvious challenges in dealing with the case of gratuitous acquisition.[76] Yet recognition that the seller's conduct amounts to fraud means that the "no profit from fraud" rule and the law of unjustified enrichment can be

---

74 See further MacLeod and Anderson "Offside Goals and Interfering with Play" at 94-95 and MacLeod "Offside Goals and Induced Breaches of Contract" 278 at 281-82.

75 1960 SC 255.

76 For examples of an offside goals challenge by a gratuitous acquirer, see *Alexander v Lundies* (1675) Mor 940 and *Anderson v Lows* (1863) 2 M 100.

invoked to explain the vulnerability.[77] This rule presents its own challenges because of the indirect nature of the enrichment. However, this exception to the normal rule against recovering indirect enrichment can be explained as an extension of the fraud rule: had the donee known what was being done, he would have been bound to refuse the property. That being the case, it might be argued that he would act wrongfully in seeking to hold onto the property when he finds out the facts.[78] The voidability of the grant enables the party who would be so-wronged to prevent this wrong from being done. Therefore, an obligation to reverse the enrichment is justified although the enrichment is indirect.

Of course, an onerous transferee in good faith may also discover later that he was an unwitting accomplice in the seller's wrong, but in such a case the balance of policy is a little different. Such a transferee is not seeking to retain a pure enrichment but rather the benefit of a lawful bargain. Were it to be forfeited, he would be left with a claim for money and so exposed to the risk of the seller's insolvency. Given the personal rights do not rank according to the rule *prior tempore potior iure*, there is no obvious reason why that burden should be shifted from the first buyer to the second when both were duped by the seller.

This analysis draws on the point made by Carey Miller regarding the relative lack of favour which the law shows to donees, but it gives a reason for allowing a donee whose personal right predates a right under an onerous contract to keep the property if he got his real right first. In that case, the donee was not an unwitting accomplice in any fraud because his author was perfectly entitled to make the promise at the time when he made it.

E. Implications of Fraud on Creditors as a Rationale

On the analysis suggested above, avoidance of the transfer gives effect to the first creditor's delictual right to reparation against a second purchaser who acquired in bad faith. It does that by putting the second purchaser in the position he would have been in had the wrongful act not taken place. The voidability of gratuitous grants is based on an analogous rule in the

---

77 Reid "Fraud in Scots Law" 243-49 and 256-58.
78 This idea of "incomplete *dolus*" which is completed at the time of enforcement has been deployed in the context of innocent misrepresentation: MacLeod "Fraud and Voidable Transfer" 48-50.

law of enrichment, which can be viewed as an extension of the fraud rule. One advantage of this view is that it allows the offside goals rule to be set alongside the other instances of fraud on creditors. Once that is established, they can offer guidance on some of the contested issues surrounding the offside goals rule.

The implications for the relationship between offside goals and subordinate real rights have already been discussed but the fraud-on-creditors analysis also casts light on another point of contention: the time at which the grantee must be put in bad faith for the offside goals rule to apply. It was suggested *obiter* in *Rodger (Builders)* that a buyer who was in good faith when missives were concluded but who discovered the prior right before registration of the disposition would be vulnerable.[79] This view was followed by Lord Eassie in *Alex Brewster & Sons v Caughey*,[80] whose decision was, in turn, endorsed by Lord Rodger in *Burnett's Trustee v Grainger*.[81] Lord Rodger took pains to explain why the position of the trustee in sequestration was distinguishable from that of a second buyer in an offside goals case. That was necessary because of his view that a second buyer who hears of a prior right must stand aside for the first purchaser whereas there is no such obligation on the trustee.

Despite its high authority this seems to be wrong in principle and has rightly been subject to academic criticism.[82] A clue as to why it is wrong can be found in the extract from Stair which Lord Rodger gave to distinguish between the position of the trustee or the creditor doing diligence and the second purchaser:

But certain knowledge, by intimation, citation, or the like, inducing *malam fidem*, whereby any prior disposition or assignation made to another party is certainly known, or at least interruption made in acquiring by arrestment or citation of the acquirer, such rights acquired, not being of necessity to satisfy prior engagements, are reducible *ex capite fraudis*, and the acquirer is partaker of the fraud of his author, who thereby becomes a granter of double rights.[83]

While the general rule is that a bad faith acquirer will be vulnerable as a partaker in his author's fraud, the rule does not apply to those who

79   1950 SC 483 at 500 per Lord Jamieson.
80   Unreported, 2 May 2002. Available at http://www.scotcourts.gov.uk/opinions/EAS0904. html
81   2004 SC (HL) 19 at para 142.
82   Anderson *Assignation* paras 11-24-31.
83   Stair, *Inst* 1.14.5, cited 2004 SC (HL) 19 para 142.

acquire "of necessity to satisfy prior engagements." As Lord Rodger rightly observed, the trustee in sequestration and creditors doing diligence may readily be considered to fall into this class.

However, Lord Rodger neglects the fact that, once a purchaser has concluded his contract with the seller, he too is a creditor[84] and takes "of necessity" because, like other creditors, taking an asset is the only way that he can ensure that his right is fulfilled. Indeed, it might be argued that the necessity affecting a purchaser is more pressing than that affecting a creditor who is owed money. It makes no difference to the latter which of the debtor's assets is sold provided that it raises sufficient funds to pay the debt. A purchaser's right, on the other hand, can only be satisfied by transfer of the asset he contracted to buy.

The point becomes clearer after reflection on other cases for fraud on creditors in the context of insolvency and of inhibition. It is no fraud to accept what you are owed and that is all that a buyer who registers with supervening knowledge of a prior contract does. There is an unavoidable conflict of rights and, in such a situation, each person is entitled to look to his own interests. The purchaser who knows of the prior contract before he concludes his own contract is in a different position because he can avoid the conflict of rights by not agreeing to buy the property.

F. Summary

The analysis in this chapter has suggested that the offside goals rule is best understood as an instance of the law's response to fraud on creditors. Avoidance is natural restitution, giving the defrauded creditor reparation for the wrong. Like the other instances of fraud on creditors, grantees may be liable as participants in the fraud (where they are in bad faith) or on the basis of an enrichment rule which prevents the completion of an incomplete *dolus* (where the grant is gratuitous).

Categorisation of the rule as an instance of fraud on creditors suggests that avoidance on the basis of the offside goals rule is *ad hunc effectum*, with the scope of the reversal being defined by what is necessary to allow the defrauded creditor satisfaction by obtaining a real right in the relevant property. This factor explains both how the offside goals rule can protect

---

84 R G Anderson "Fraud and Transfer on Insolvency: ta … ta… *tantum et tale*" (2004) 11 *Edin LR* 187 at 202.

a personal right to a subordinate real right and why the rule is limited to personal rights to real rights. The fraud-on-creditors rationale also implies that a creditor who was in good faith when he acquired his personal right is entitled to pursue satisfaction of that right even if he discovers a conflicting personal right before he gets his real right.

Painful though it is for an academic to admit it, skipping those conveyancing classes does not appear to have done any harm to Professor Rennie's grasp of Scots property law. The Scots lawyer can handle a little football and, it appears, Scots law can handle the offside goals rule too.

8. A New Era in Conveyancing: Advance Notices and the Land Registration etc. (Scotland) Act 2012

Ann Stewart

For decades, property lawyers in jurisdictions other than Scotland expressed astonishment that Scottish solicitors effectively underwrote their seller client's obligation to a purchaser to provide, after settlement, records in the property and personal registers that would be clear of any entry, deed, decree or diligence, which was either prejudicial to the validity of, or was an encumbrance on, the seller's title to the property. Solicitors did this by granting to the purchaser, by way of formal letter to the purchaser's solicitor, a firm's undertaking either that the records would be clear, or to clear them if they were not. The "letter of obligation," the document by which this apparently reckless practice was effected, was an invariable feature of the Scottish conveyancing landscape.

But that has all now changed. The Land Registration etc. (Scotland) Act 2012 introduced a new concept to Scottish conveyancing – the advance notice procedure – which has transformed the way in which property transactions are conducted, and in the vast majority of cases has eliminated the requirement for any letter of obligation.

http://dx.doi.org/10.11647/OBP.0056.08

A. Letters of Obligation

(1) Historical background

The origin of the practice of granting a letter of obligation at settlement may be said to be lost in the mists of time. As early as 1900 James Sturrock,[1] in an annotation to a lecture by Professor Allan Menzies on searches in conveyancing transactions, refers to a case in 1896[2] in which Mr Gordon, the law agent, sold the property "and granted the usual obligation to produce a search showing a clear record." Although in that case, the law agents themselves had had an interest in the property and signed the disposition as consenters, the fact that, four years later, Sturrock describes the granting of a letter of obligation as "usual" indicates that this was already standard practice. This is in spite of the fact that there is no legal obligation on a seller's solicitor to give a letter of obligation.

Is it necessary to delve back further to identify the origins of this practice? Arguably, over a century of practice must be compelling enough evidence that this was firmly embedded in Scottish conveyancing tradition. Later conveyancing manuals allude to this practice as being "general and almost universal"[3] and "usual practice."[4]

(2) What is the function of a letter of obligation?

Until recently, the letter of obligation was a "little understood, but vital, part of any transaction."[5] There is an intrinsic weakness in the conveyancing process, for which the letter of obligation was the plaster cast. The weakness arises because of a hiatus in the succession of steps in the conveyancing process around settlement.[6]

---

1   J S Sturrock, *Conveyancing According to the Law of Scotland* (1900) 935, based on the Lectures of Allan Menzies, Professor of Conveyancing at the University of Edinburgh between 1847 and 1856.
2   *Dryburgh v Gordon* [1896] 24 R 1.
3   J Burns, *Conveyancing Practice According to the Law of Scotland*, 4th edn (1957) 302.
4   J M Halliday, *Conveyancing Law and Practice in Scotland*, 2nd edn (1997) 515.
5   J H Sinclair and E Sinclair, *Handbook of Conveyancing Practice in Scotland*, 5th edn (2006) 181.
6   "Settlement" is the term used for the steps that take place on the date of entry when the price is paid by, and the disposition is delivered to, the purchaser and (usually) entry is taken by him. In commercial property transactions this is often referred to as "completion."

The "gap" period

A seller is required to exhibit clear searches in the property and personal registers before settlement of the purchase takes place. The existence of any adverse deed, or an inhibition against the seller that predates the missives, will be disclosed in such searches, and usually steps have to be taken to discharge such entries before the purchaser will proceed to completion and pay the price. Those searches must be ordered up and exhibited to the purchaser's solicitors as close as possible to the date of entry, but before settlement takes place. Such searches can only disclose the state of play of the registers at a date that pre-dates settlement. The date to which the searches are certified may also pre-date the date of settlement, perhaps by two or more days. So there is a gap between the date to which the Registers have been searched, and the date on which the purchaser hands over the price.

There is another, consecutive gap that occurs between settlement and the date on which the purchaser registers his title and obtains a real right to the property. While it is possible, immediately following completion of the transaction, to take the delivered deed to the Land Register and present it in person (and this does happen reasonably frequently), in the majority of cases, following completion there is a delay, perhaps only of a day or two, while the post completion formalities are dealt with, any stamp duty land tax[7] paid, and registration forms completed, before the disposition in favour of the purchaser arrives at the Registers and is entered onto the records. Professional practice guidance permits a period of up to fourteen days after settlement within which to present the purchaser's application for registration.[8] Solicitors whose offices are not located in Glasgow or Edinburgh usually have no choice but to submit applications by post or through legal document exchange arrangements, or resort to the expense of a courier.

During this gap, or invisibility period, there are risks. A competing deed could be presented for registration before the purchaser's disposition is presented. Until comparatively recently, the possibility of the seller being sequestrated or going into liquidation or administration during the

---

7 To be replaced in Scotland on 1 April 2015, by land and buildings transaction tax.
8 Law Society of Scotland, Rules and Guidance, Section F, Division C – Letters of obligation and advance notices, para 3, available at http://www.lawscot.org.uk/rules-and-guidance/section-f-guidance-relating-to-particular-types-of-work/division-c-conveyancing/guidance/letters-of-obligation-and-advance-notices/

gap period also posed a serious risk. To provide protection against the occurrence of these risks – particularly insolvency or the emergence of a rival deed – the letter of obligation historically stepped into the breach.

The guarantee of clear records

It is unusual for a solicitor to bind himself personally, and thus be liable to incur personal liability, in respect of the obligations of his client. Generally when conducting a transaction, it will be beyond any doubt that the solicitor is acting as the agent for a disclosed principal. Missives are entered into by solicitors "for and on behalf of our client." The letter of obligation was a clear exception to this general rule.

The letter of obligation was, in effect, a guarantee that the registers would be clear of any competing deeds or decrees and diligences affecting the seller. Although the styles of wording used varied slightly depending on whether the transaction involved recording in the General Register of Sasines (now unlikely, since all transfers of property[9] will induce a first registration in the Land Register, where the seller's title is in the Sasine Register), or in the Land Register, the effect was the same: if any deed, decree or diligence appeared on the records that would prejudice the purchaser's title, then provided these had not been created by or against the purchaser, the firm was obliged to remove them. The firm's exposure under a typical letter of obligation was a maximum of fourteen days, or until the purchaser's deed was registered, if earlier.

The undertaking

The undertaking given in a typical letter of obligation (for a sale of registered property) would say:

> With reference to the settlement of this transaction today, we undertake to clear the records of any deed, decree or diligence (other than such as may be created by, or against, the Purchaser) which may be recorded in the Personal Registers or to which effect may be given in the Land Register in the period from [date of certification of Form 12 or 13 Report (search)] to fourteen days after today's date inclusive (or to the earlier date of registration of the

---

9   Following the introduction of the 2012 Act on 8 December 2014, all conveyances, whether for valuable consideration or not, induce a first registration in the Land Register, if the title to the property is still in the Sasine Register.

Purchaser's interest in the Property) and which would cause the Keeper[10] to make an entry on, or qualify her indemnity in, [the Title Sheet to be updated] [the Land Certificate to be issued] in respect of that interest.

(3) Minimising risk to the seller's solicitor

Professional indemnity insurance

That the solution to the gap period, and the underwriting of these risks, was taken on by the solicitor profession in Scotland (which appears to be the only jurisdiction in which such a mechanism was used) seems, on the face of it, perverse. If there is a risk associated with a process, then the obvious solution is to arrange insurance to protect against that risk. In fact, title indemnity insurance cover was available in situations where no letter of obligation was to be granted, although it was not routinely obtained.

However, insurance cover was and remains available, albeit indirectly, for the gap period risks. It takes the form of the professional indemnity insurance that all firms of solicitors have to take out to be able to practice. The Master Policy is arranged by the Law Society of Scotland, to provide indemnity for solicitors against a variety of types of professional liability, arising out of business which is customarily carried on or transacted by solicitors in Scotland. This includes claims arising out of letters of obligation. Solicitors make a contribution annually to the Law Society for the cost of this insurance which sets a mandatory limit of indemnity, currently £2 million, for each firm. Individual firms can, and do, arrange their own top-up cover for protection in the case of claims of higher amounts. Since letters of obligation were given in commercial property transactions involving tens or hundreds of millions of pounds, such top-up cover was essential for firms with a commercial property practice.

Professional indemnity insurance cover was and remains available for a letter of obligation or other undertaking by the firm in any circumstances. However the letter of obligation was given a benign treatment under Special Conditions that apply to the Master Policy if it is "classic."[11]

---

10 The Keeper of the Registers of Scotland.
11 That "benign" treatment continues beyond 8 December 2014, at least for the PI insurance year 2014/2015. Whether it will continue beyond November 2015 is up to the insurers.

The classic letter of obligation

The wording of the classic letter of obligation had to contain the components of the style wording above, including the fourteen day time limit, although there was no mandatory style. Before granting the letter of obligation, the seller's solicitor had to comply with certain conditions, designed to ensure that any risk of a claim was minimised.

The conditions were:

- A search in the property and personal registers must have been obtained immediately before settlement. What was meant by "immediately before" was not always clear, but Law Society Guidance indicated that the searches in both registers could be up to seven days' old (equivalent to five working days), counting back from the date of settlement to the date to which the search was certified as being correct.[12] In residential property transactions there was a requirement under the Council of Mortgage Lenders Scottish Solicitors' Handbook[13] for the search in the personal registers to be no more than three working days old.

- The client had to be asked to confirm whether or not there were any outstanding securities.

- The solicitor issuing the letter of obligation had to be unaware of any other security; and

- Where the undertaking was a firm's undertaking to deliver a discharge of a standard security, the solicitor granting the obligation had to have sufficient funds to pay off the loan.

Provided these conditions were complied with for a letter of obligation, then even in the case of a claim which had to be met from professional indemnity insurance, the excess that the firm in question was required to pay in the event of any claim (the "self-insured amount") was nil, and there was no adverse impact on any premium loading or discount for that firm. If a letter of obligation was given in classic terms, but the conditions had not been complied with (known as a "failed classic"), then the normal self-insured amount applied. Obligations which fell outside the "classic"

---

12   Law Society of Scotland, Rules and Guidance, Section F, Division C – Letters of obligation, para 4, available at http://www.lawscot.org.uk/rules-and-guidance/section-f-guidance-relating-to-particular-types-of-work/division-c-conveyancing/guidance/letters-of-obligation-and-advance-notices/

13   Available at http://www.cml.org.uk/cml/handbook/scotland. No changes have been made to the CML Handbook to reflect any changes in practice relating to the coming into force of the provisions of the Land Registration (Scotland) Act 2012, although individual lenders are left to make whatever arrangements they consider are required.

obligations to clear the records or deliver an executed discharge (known as "non-classic") resulted in the application of a double excess if a claim was made and met[14] as well being taken into account for any discount or loading to Master Policy premiums for the firm in question.[15]

An unpopular arrangement

It probably goes almost without saying that the letter of obligation was extremely unpopular with solicitors in Scotland, but it had for many years been an unavoidable evil, due in large part to the effect of professional custom and tradition, and it is a not an understatement to say that, without the letter of obligation as an integral part of the settlement procedure, the conveyancing process as we knew it would have collapsed.

While, as already noted, a solicitor had no legal obligation to grant a letter of obligation, Law Society guidance had moved from the position held several decades ago that no letter of obligation had to be given unless the missives expressly provide for it, to the recent view of the Conveyancing Committee of the Law Society that "conveyancing transactions should be settled with a letter of obligation being granted by the solicitor personally" and "[w]hile there is no legal obligation to give a letter of obligation where missives are silent, there is a professional duty on a solicitor to grant a letter of obligation unless the solicitor advises to the contrary at the earliest possible opportunity."[16]

In recent years there had been increasing unwillingness on the part of solicitors to grant letters of obligation in certain circumstances. In transactions where the solicitor acted for an insolvency practitioner in a sale, for example, the practice had evolved of flatly refusing to give any letter of obligation. This was in part due to the refusal by insolvency practitioners to accept any personal liability. The letter of obligation was equally unpopular with insurers, and this was exacerbated in the late 1980s and early 1990s by the increased incidence of second standard securities over residential properties which were granted unknowingly by home owners. These securities were usually granted at the time of making home improvements, such as installation of double glazing

---

14 Known as a "double deductible."
15 But see n 11
16 Law Society of Scotland, Rules and Guidance, Section F, Division C – Letters of obligation.

or replacement kitchens, with the owner being under the impression that they were being asked to sign some credit agreement, unaware that the "agreement" would then be registered against their title. The preponderance of such second standard securities led to the requirement to make proper enquiry of the client as to the granting of other securities, and the prudent conveyancer would include an enquiry about carrying out any home improvements.

Against a background of increasing concern, it was clear that something would need to be done. One only needs to look at the legal systems of other countries and jurisdictions, including our closest neighbour, England, and to certain advance warning systems that were already operating in Scotland – the most obvious being the notice of letters of inhibitions procedure[17] – to see the prospects of a solution in some form of priority notification procedure, linked to the registration of deeds and documents in the Registers of Scotland.

B. The New System of Advance Notices

(1) The genesis of the Scottish Advance Notice

The Scottish Law Commission, always innovative in bringing forward new approaches to old problems, had already decided to include the thorny topic of land registration reform in its Sixth Programme of Law Reform,[18] at the request of the Keeper of the Registers of Scotland. There then followed a series of Discussion Papers[19] on a wide range of aspects of land registration, which had been introduced in Scotland by the Land Registration (Scotland) Act 1979. The third of these Discussion Papers, which dealt with a miscellaneous collection of issues, first flagged the prospect of a priority notice scheme.[20]

That early consideration of how a priority notice procedure in Scotland could work drew from a number of other jurisdictions for inspiration, both selecting and rejecting elements of other systems to consider how best to

---

17 Introduced by the Titles to Land Consolidation (Scotland) Act 1868, s155.
18 (Scot Law Com No 176, 2000).
19 Discussion Paper on *Land Registration: Void and Voidable Titles* (Scot Law Com DP No 125, 2004), Discussion Paper on *Land Registration: Registration, Rectification and Indemnity* (Scot Law Com DP No 128, 2005) and Discussion Paper on *Land Registration: Miscellaneous Issues* (Scot Law Com DP No 130, 2005).
20 DP on *LR: Miscellaneous Issues* (n 19) part 7.

tailor the system for Scotland. The DP identified the key advantages of a scheme of advance notices.[21] Uppermost is the certainty of success against the threat of a competing title (or the comfort that there are no competing titles) that a priority notice system would bring,[22] coupled with the reduction of exposure to risk from letters of obligation that would follow as a consequence.[23]

However the DP also identified disadvantages to such a system, citing arguments that it could be regarded as unnecessary[24] – the imminent introduction of ARTL[25] would enable the instantaneous signing, payment for and delivery of conveyancing documents, removing the risk from a competing deed. It was, however, recognised in the DP that ARTL would not necessarily be suitable for all types of transaction, and might not therefore be a sufficient solution.[26] It has proved to be the case that, although there have been many transactions completed under ARTL, it can only cope with transactions that are a dealing of the whole of an already registered interest, and its application, since introduction, has been largely confined to residential transactions and remortgages.

Another criticism of a priority notice system identified in the DP was that it would be disproportionate.[27] The level of risk from insolvency has in any event decreased, since a trustee in sequestration is no longer able immediately to complete a title to property in the bankrupt's estate following on appointment, but must wait for a period of 28 days to elapse.[28] While there may be risks attendant with the liquidation or administration of a company, the Scottish Law Commission did not consider these to be either considerable or insurmountable.

The original proposal for priority notices in the DP suggested backdating the effective date of registration of the protected deed to

---

21   DP on *LR: Miscellaneous Issues* (n 19) para 7.21-7.28.

22   Ibid para 7.22-7.24.

23   Ibid para 7.25-7.27.

24   Ibid para 7.29-7.30.

25   Automated Registration of Title to Land, a system by which the transfer document (disposition) is created within an electronic system, digitally signed and electronically delivered, thus eliminating the gap period. ARTL was subsequently introduced, but it is (currently) limited in the types of deeds and transactions that it can facilitate.

26   DP on *LR: Miscellaneous Issues* (n 19) para 7.30.

27   Ibid para 7.31-7.33.

28   Bankruptcy and Diligence etc. (Scotland) Act 2007, s 17.

the date of registration of the notice.[29] This would be similar to the way inhibitions work: a notice of letters of inhibition is registered,[30] which provides a period of twenty one days in which the inhibition itself can be registered on condition that the schedule of inhibition is served on the debtor after registration of the notice.[31] If registration takes place within this period, the effective date of the inhibition is backdated to the date of service of the schedule of inhibition. If registration does not take place, the notice lapses.

Applying this backdating effect to priority notices would mean that a real right in the property could, retrospectively, be obtained prematurely.[32] The priority notice would always be registered before the date of entry, and sometimes could be registered before conclusion of missives. To adopt this model would mean that ownership) would pass to the purchaser before settlement, but so too would liabilities incidental to ownership. It is easy to see why these proposals were not generally supported at the time.

However pressure on, and dislike of, the system of letters of obligation continued to grow. By the time the Scottish Law Commission was preparing its Report on Land Registration[33] it had already received representations, including from the Law Society of Scotland, to look again at a priority procedure for land registration. The Report proposed a much more straightforward system of advance notices,[34] that this time received a considerable degree of support from the profession.

The Report also contained a draft Land Registration Bill,[35] which was the starting point for the Land Registration etc. (Scotland) Act 2012. The Bill introduced to the Scottish Parliament on 1 December 2011[36] differed in some material (and minor) respects from the draft Bill prepared by the Scottish Law Commission, but the proposals for a system of advance notice were largely intact.

---

29   DP on *LR: Miscellaneous Issues* (n 19) para 7.19-7.20.
30   Titles to Land (Consolidation) (Scotland) Act 1868, s 155.
31   Ibid. The addition of service of the schedule of inhibition on the debtor was amended by the Bankruptcy and Diligence etc. (Scotland) Act 2007, s 149, after the publication of the DP.
32   DP on *LR: Miscellaneous Issues* (n 19) para 7.34.
33   Scot Law Com No 222, 2010.
34   Report on *Land Registration* (n 33) part 14.
35   Ibid vol 2.
36   Available at http://www.scottish.parliament.uk/parliamentarybusiness/Bills/44469.aspx

(2) The statutory system of Advance Notices

The principles of Advance Notices

The statutory structure for advance notices in conveyancing transactions adopts the principles for providing a period of priority protection for deeds that are intended to be granted and intended for registration in the Land Register.[37] The key elements of the advance notice procedure are:

(i)   An advance notice relates to a specific deed that a granter intends to grant to another person.

(ii)   An advance notice has to be applied for by the person who intends to grant the deed, and who may validly grant the deed, or by a person who has the consent of the person who may validly grant the deed.[38]

(iii)   Once registered, the advance notice provides a period of thirty-five days' protection to the grantee, from any competing deeds, or other subsequent advance notices, that are registered against the property during that period, or an inhibition registered against the granter during the protected period.

(iv)   The protected period starts the day after the date of registration of the advance notice.

(v)   A second advance notice (and third (and potentially an unlimited number of advance notices))[39] can be applied for, but subsequent advance notices provide a separate, not a continuous, period of protection.

The detail of the Advance Notice protection

The introduction of Advance Notices is a major transformation for conveyancing practice in Scotland, and one that many in the profession would regard as long overdue.

The Advance Notice concept is similar to, but not exactly the same as, the priority period which currently exists for registration of documents in the Land Registry of England and Wales. In England and Wales it is tied in with a register search. The system that now applies in Scotland

---

37   See generally Land Registration etc. (Scotland) Act 2012, Part 4. Specific provisions are discussed in detail below.

38   There is something of a conceptual non sequitur in the way the legislation has been drafted, discussed further below.

39   There is nothing in the legislation about multiple consecutive advance notices for the same deed, but in theory this is technically possible although, in practice, unlikely.

borrows from both the English system[40] and the system that applies in Germany.[41]

It should be borne in mind that the advance notice procedure is voluntary. There is no compulsion to use it, but the advantages of it over the flawed and precarious letter of obligation alternative are compelling.

Under the provisions of the 2012 Act, it is possible to apply to the Keeper for an advance notice in respect of a deed that a person intends to grant.[42] For a fee of £10,[43] an advance notice application can be submitted,[44] for example when a seller has agreed to sell a piece of his land, and consequently will be granting a disposition in favour of the purchaser.

The advance notice application is submitted to the relevant register in advance of the completion date for the transaction, and once it is registered, it provides a period of protection of thirty-five days (beginning with the day after the advance notice is registered in the relevant register)[45] in which any competing deed, or another advance notice, would not have priority.[46]

So, for example, if the seller registers an advance notice for a disposition over his property that he intends to grant in favour of the purchaser, and then some other person presents a competing disposition for registration in respect of the property in question, although the competing disposition would be entered onto the Register initially, the existence of the earlier advance notice would prevent the competing disposition from prevailing, provided always that the purchaser with the benefit of the advance notice submits his disposition for registration within the thirty-five day period of protection.

However, if the purchaser fails to submit his disposition within the thirty-five day period, in that case, the earlier registered disposition will take effect at the expiry of the thirty-five day period.

Advance notices apply to other types of deed, such as a standard security or deed of servitude, and also to a registrable lease or sub-lease,

---

40   The Land Registration Act 2002 and Land Registration Rules 2003.
41   German Civil Code BGB, Articles 883 to 888.
42   Land Registration etc. (Scotland) Act 2012, s 56.
43   The Registers of Scotland (Fees) Order 2014, SSI 2014/188, sched 1, para 3(b).
44   Land Registration etc. (Scotland) Act 2012, s 57.
45   Ibid, s 58.
46   Ibid, ss 59-61.

date of entry in residential offers. The PSG approach proceeds on the basis that the more of the protected period that continues after settlement will mean that if the application for registration were to be rejected for some reason, there would be a good chance that the presenting solicitor could correct whatever was wrong with the application and re-submit it, all still within the protected period of the advance notice.

Compulsory or optional?

The approach recommended by the PSG is that the seller should be bound to apply for an advance notice. The advantages to a purchaser of the advance notice protection are obvious, but some sellers might question why they should have to make this application, which they may not consider to be of any benefit to them. However, while the protection is principally for the purchaser against any competing deeds, it also brings certainty for the seller, since, once a search has been obtained disclosing the advance notice, the seller can relax for the rest of the protected period too, and the protection provides greater certainty around settlement, compared to the step into the unknown that the gap period presented.

The form of the advance notice should be adjusted with the purchaser, since the advance notice will only protect the specific deed to be granted by that seller to that purchaser. The purchaser will want to be sure that the purchaser's details on the application are correct. Practitioners will need to bear this in mind, in case of a last minute substitution of a nominee to take title to the property. An advance notice that does not refer to that nominee will not protect a deed in its favour.

The requirement for consent

Only the seller can apply for an advance notice for the disposition to the purchaser, because of the requirement in the 2012 Act that only a person who intends to grant, and may validly grant the deed can make the application.[64] So, if there is a requirement for an advance notice for a standard security that the purchaser intends to grant, or for any other deeds that the purchaser intends to grant – for example, where the purchaser is planning a back-to-back sub-sale – the consent of the seller will be needed

---

64   Land Registration etc. (Scotland) Act 2012, s 57(1).

to make that application. To avoid the requirement in each transaction for specific consent to be sought each time (with the possibility that it is then withheld by the seller) the PSG wording builds in automatic consent of the seller to any application for an advance notice that the purchaser wants to submit. This allows these applications to go ahead at a time to suit the purchaser, without further reference to the seller.

One aspect of the procedure that a purchaser intending a back-to-back (i.e. simultaneous) sub-sale needs to consider is the approach to take where the purchaser does not want the seller to know about the sub-sale. Care would need to be taken in relation to applying for an advance notice for the proposed sub-sale disposition, because that advance notice will show up in any search obtained by the seller after the advance notice has been registered, alerting the seller to its existence. The alternative would have to be either that that no advance notice application can be made, or that the timing of the application for the sub-sale deed advance notice will need to be later than the period covered by the search, meaning that it would need to be a last minute application.

The automatic consent of the purchaser to the discharge of the advance notice, should this ever be required, has also been built in to the PSG offer. If the advance notice has to be discharged, this is likely to be because the original purchaser has withdrawn or failed to complete the transaction, so obtaining consent at that time could be problematic, although there may be a need to discharge an advance notice if it transpires that the purchaser's name is incorrectly stated, or, as anticipated above, a last minute substitution of a nominee is made. A discharge in the case of a failed purchase may only be necessary if there is an immediate requirement to apply for another advance notice in favour of a new purchaser, with an imminent settlement date. The second purchaser will want to have the first advance notice removed, as otherwise it would have priority over any advance notice registered for the second purchaser. In most cases, however, it will simply be a case of allowing the first advance notice to expire at the end of its thirty-five day period.

Additional advance notices

The PSG wording provides for a seller to obtain a second advance notice in a transaction, if the purchaser requests it. This could be necessary, if the first advance notice has been obtained too soon, or if there is a delay in completing the transaction and the protected period is due to expire in only a few days after the postponed settlement date.

Who pays?

The cost of the advance notice should be met by the seller. The application is made by the seller, so the seller is responsible for paying the fee for the application to the Registers. The cost is only £10, and it would cost much more than that in administrative time to recover that sum from the purchaser and process it. While the advance notice provides the purchaser with protection, it is protection against the possible acts of, and deeds granted by, the seller, or decrees or diligence done against the seller, so it seems a fair arrangement in all the circumstances.

If the purchaser wants to submit an advance notice application for any deeds it intends to grant, it should meet the cost of those, and of any discharge of such advance notices, if the seller requires it in cases where the transaction does not proceed.

If a second advance notice is required in the transaction, it should be paid for by whichever of the seller or the purchaser is responsible for the delay. Although there can be disagreement sometimes about the party to which any delay is attributable, this provision will cater for most circumstances, where the position is usually clear.

(4) Timing issues for advance notices

The PSG wording proposes submitting the application for an advance notice not earlier than five working days before completion. In terms of transactional timing, this also really means not *later* than five working days before completion as well. This timescale pre-supposes that a search (now called a legal report) in the property and personal registers has already been obtained, and the parties have seen and dealt with anything relevant that it discloses. As soon as the advance notice application has been made, a continuation legal report can be ordered, immediately before completion. That continuation report will disclose the advance notice,[65] and the purchaser can complete the transaction in the knowledge that protection is in place.

Timing will also be important if there is a delay in settlement, or if the purchaser's application for registration is rejected immediately. If the parties have allowed as much of the protected period as possible to

---

65 The advance notice can also be viewed on Registers Direct (an online system allowing viewing access to information in the Registers of Scotland).

be extant after completion, then this may be sufficient to turn around a rejected application and submit it again before the expiry of the protected period. Correctly counting the number of days could become important: the thirty-five day period does not start until the day after the day the notice is entered in the application record, or recorded in the Sasine Register, where applicable.

(5) The application process

Application types

Applications for an advance notice are created electronically, within a system built by the Registers of Scotland, access to which is by secure login.[66]

The online form is simple and easy to complete. It requires details of:

(i)   the granter of the deed,

(ii)   the grantee of the deed,

(iii)   the type of transaction (first registration, dealing of whole, transfer of part),

(iv)   the type of deed, and

(v)   details of the property (including the title number if it is registered, or an adequate conveyancing description (sufficient to identify the boundaries of the property concerned) if it is not).

However not all advance notice applications can be submitted electronically – some have to be printed out.

The advance notice system will accept four types of application:[67]

(i)   A first registration – this is where the advance notice is in respect of the grant of a deed that will take the property out of the Sasine Register, and transfer it to the Land Register. However the advance notice has to be recorded in the Sasine Register, as the title to the property is not yet in the Land Register – that will only happen when the intended deed is actually presented for registration.

(ii)   An intended deed that applies to the whole of a registered interest.

(iii)   An intended deed that applies to part only of a registered interest, and

---

66   Registers of Scotland, *Guidance* (n 51).
67   Ibid.

(iv) Where an extant advance notice requires to be discharged. This will only be necessary if it needs to be removed from the application record, or its discharge needs to be shown in the Sasine Register during the currency of the thirty-five day period.

It has transpired that the online system for creation of advance notices does not have the ability to save drafts of advance notice applications, meaning that it is not possible for the purchaser to approve the seller's electronically created draft. As such approval is recommended, so that the purchaser's solicitor can ensure that his client's details are correct, Word version drafts of the advance notice forms have been created by the PSG, to allow adjustment of the terms of the application to be made between the parties, then copied and pasted directly into the online form. As an immediate solution to the shortcomings of the online system, these draft forms have helped to maintain transactional momentum in the early days of adjusting to the 2012 Act. However, it would be just as acceptable, as the profession becomes more familiar with the content of advance notice applications, for these details to be adjusted by email.

Submission of advance notice applications

Where an advance notice is sought for a deed relating to a property to which title is still in the Sasine Register, in which case the deed will, when presented for registration, induce a first registration, it is necessary to print the advance notice form, sign and date it and submit it in paper form.[68] This is because the advance notice has to be recorded in the Sasine Register, and every writ to be recorded in the Sasine Register has to be "impressed with a stamp or seal,"[69] which can only be done in hard copy. Electronic submission would not be competent, since a hard copy print of that submission would not be the original. An application for discharge of an advance notice that is recorded in the Sasine Register must also be printed, signed, dated and submitted in hard copy.[70]

If the advance notice relates to a deed which will transfer part of a registered interest, then a plan to identify that part has to accompany

---

68 Registers of Scotland, *Guidance* (n 51)
69 Land Registers (Scotland) Act 1868, s14.
70 Registers of Scotland, *Guidance* (n 51).

the application (unless the part is a flat in a flatted building, where it is the whole building that is shown as a single unit on the cadastral map).[71] The plan must sufficiently identify the property to allow it to be plotted immediately onto the cadastral map. Submission of a plan can be done by way of uploading an electronic plan, including a plan in pdf format, to the advance notice system, or by providing co-ordinates for the plot, or, if the part to be transferred is a plot in a development that has Development Plan Approval,[72] then all that is required is the Development Plan number and the relevant plot number in the development. If the plan is not available in some electronic format, then the advance notice application has to be printed, signed, dated and submitted in hard copy, with a suitable paper plan, signed and docqueted as relative to the advance notice application.[73]

An advance notice application for a deed that relates to the whole of a registered title, and an application for a discharge of an advance notice in the Land Register, can be submitted electronically.[74] An application for a discharge must refer to the allocated advance notice number for the advance notice to be discharged, which will then enable automatic pre-population of the discharge application form with other details from the original advance notice.[75] Exceptions to electronic submission of these types of advance notice application are only permitted in certain circumstances: where the online submission system is "down" for a forty eight hour period, or longer; where the person applying for the advance notice is the applicant who is not using a solicitor (it is expected that such applications will be rare); or if the applicant does not have access to a computer (possible in remote areas of Scotland where internet access is unavailable).

Where the property affected by the advance notice application is partly Sasine Registered and partly Land Registered, two advance notice applications are required, one for each register.[76] However if the title to

---

71 Land Registration etc. (Scotland) Act 2012, s 56(d)(iii).The cadastral map is the name given to the map, maintained by the Registers of Scotland showing the extent of all registered titles. See the 2012 Act, s 11.

72 Development Plan Approval is a service offered by Registers of Scotland to developers (e.g. house builders), that will identify and resolve any title extent issues in advance of the sale of individual houses (or plots) from the development. The development is approved and allocated a reference number and the location of each plot in the development is allocated a plot number.

73 Registers of Scotland, *Guidance* (n 51).

74 Ibid.

75 Ibid.

76 Ibid.

the property is in the Land Register and encompasses more than one title number, only one application is required, and can be submitted electronically, referring to each title number affected, unless the transfer relates to part only of one or more of the titles, and a plan showing the extent to be transferred cannot be uploaded electronically (or Development Plan Approval, or co-ordinates are not available).

Acknowledgement of advance notice applications

Electronic submissions of advance notice applications receive an email acknowledgement confirming that submission has been successful.[77] Once the advance notice has been entered on the application record, which should be the same day as submission, provided the application record is still open (meaning usually receipt of the application before 4pm), a second email is sent, confirming that it has been registered.

Paper submissions to the Land Register receive an email acknowledgement, whereas submissions to the Sasine Register are acknowledged by letter.[78]

Email acknowledgements include a pdf of the completed advance notice form, together with an application number and an advance notice number, and, where the advance notice relates to part of a registered plot, a pdf plan showing the extent that has been delineated on the cadastral map is included with the acknowledgement.

The thirty-five day period starts the day after registration. The acknowledgement notifies the applicant of the start and finish dates of the protected period.

C. The Future is Here

A new era of conveyancing started on 8 December 2014. But the fun doesn't stop here. The appetite for land reform at the Scottish Parliament appears to be unabated, with a Bill currently progressing through the Parliament that will see the community right to buy extended to the whole of Scotland,

---

77 Registers of Scotland, *Guidance* (n 51).
78 Ibid. The logic of this is unclear. Acknowledgement by letter is stated to be "in accordance with usual Sasine practice." It is to be hoped that in practice email acknowledgement will be adopted, with the letter is sent as an email attachment.

not just rural areas,[79] and the passing of a Bill that enables counterpart execution of deeds and effective delivery by electronic means.[80]

The Law Society of Scotland has set up a Working Party on the Future of Conveyancing, with a remit to take forward a variety of initiatives to ensure that conveyancing procedures in Scotland keep pace with modern practice, as well as harnessing the benefits of technology. The Working Party will be looking at standards, processes and standardisation, to make the sale and purchase of property a better experience for the consumer and for the practitioner. There is plenty of scope for improvement and, in most quarters, an appetite for change for the better.

With the advent of the advance notice system, will the traditional letter of obligation become a thing of the past? Early experiences of advance notice applications have not been entirely trouble free. Rejection of applications, with greater frequency than the profession anticipated, or delays in processing applications, has produced situations where recourse has had to be made to a hybrid form of letter of obligation – the gap now being the date of last search or settlement and the start of the protected period – admittedly a much shorter gap, usually no more than a day or two. But this, like all new procedures should settle down with time, and the profession cannot count on the benign treatment of letters of obligation under the Master Policy continuing indefinitely.[81]

And there will still be circumstances anyway, in which a letter of undertaking will have to be given in conveyancing transactions. The advance notice procedure will not cover the situation where a discharge of the seller's standard security is not available at settlement (an increasingly common occurrence, in both commercial and residential transactions). While the default position in commercial property transactions is to insist on delivery of a discharge at completion, undertakings to deliver a discharge are routinely given at residential settlements. How long that can continue, and whether the Working Party can find a way to tackle that issue are challenges for the future.

It is clear that the ghost of Mr Gordon[82] would have considerable difficulty in recognising the post-designated-day conveyancing landscape, but there can be no doubt that more change, and for the better, awaits us all.

---

79 The Community Empowerment (Scotland) Bill.
80 The Legal Writings (Counterparts and Delivery) (Scotland) Bill.
81 See n 11.
82 The solicitor who gave the undertaking in *Dryburgh* (n 2).

9. *Bona Fide* Acquisition: New in Scottish Land Law?

Professor David Carey Miller[1]

A. Introduction

It is a privilege and a pleasure to write in recognition of the outstanding contribution of Professor Robert Rennie. The law and legal education of Scotland has traditionally recognized the subject of conveyancing as one demanding acute legal skills directed to matters of obvious social utility. Robert Rennie has been a standard-bearer in the field.

The Land Registration etc. (Scotland) Act 2012 ("2012 Act") has been described as a "bold step forward" by Scottish conveyancing specialists Professors Robert Rennie and Stewart Brymer.[2] The primary purpose of the 2012 Act is to provide a new legislative base for the Land Register and reform and restate the law on the registration of rights to land.[3] The limited focus of this paper is on a provision making possible acquisition

---

1   Thanks to 2014 Aberdeen LLB Hons graduate Katriona Dunn for her invaluable contribution as a research assistant. I am also grateful to Dr Craig Anderson, Mr Malcolm Combe, Dr Simon Cooper, Professor Roderick Paisley, Professor Kenneth Reid, Dr Andrew Simpson and Dr Andrew Steven for commenting on my drafts or discussing the paper's subject with me; but the flaws and failings are mine alone.

2   R Rennie, S Brymer, "A Bold Step Forward" (2012) 57(3) *The Journal of the Law Society of Scotland* 32, available at http://www.journalonline.co.uk/Magazine/57-3/1010910.aspx

3   Registers of Scotland, *Consultation on Implementation of the Land Registration etc. (Scotland) Act 2012 – Post Consultation Report* (March 2014) 2.

    http://dx.doi.org/10.11647/OBP.0056.09

by a good faith party from a disponer (i.e. transferor) who does not have a valid title.

The 2012 Act will replace much of the Land Registration (Scotland) Act 1979 ("1979 Act") and the Land Registration (Scotland) Rules 2006 ("2006 Rules"). The 1979 Act has come under considerable criticism. It was some twenty years old when Lord Jauncey of Tullichettle said: "Nobody could accuse the [1979] Act of being well drafted."[4] The context of this paper is the 2012 Act's policy departure from the "registration of title" system under the 1979 Act which provided a comprehensive guarantee of title linked to possible compensation. The Scottish Law Commission Report ("SLC Report"), from which the 2012 Act derives, recommended a departure from the Keeper's 'Midas touch' under the 1979 Act with, instead, the effect of registration "determined by the relevant legislation and the general principles of property law."[5] This short paper cannot deal with the differences between the 1979 and 2012 statutes in any detail; after a brief overview comment on the apparent change of direction, the focus will be on a provision – section 86, in Part 9 of the 2012 Act – dealing with invalid titles including the situation of what might be called a "registered fraud" – i.e. the situation of a transaction void on account of fraud – therefore invalid – which gets on to the register. Under this section, provided there has been a total period of one year's possession, a good faith party registered as proprietor acquires ownership) through a process of 'realignment' even though his or her transferor's title was invalid – and may have been obtained by fraud.

In permitting *bona fide* acquisition, section 86 is notable in a number of respects and the provision also raises certain questions. It appears to be a novel form of acquisition in Scottish land law. But is it positive or negative prescription, or, rather, is it simply a statutory form of original acquisition? It is necessary to examine the role and functioning of section 86, as well as the context from which it arose and that in which it applies, in order to reach a conclusion as to its novelty and nature. This contribution will also seek to comment on the form of acquisition the provision represents and, perhaps more importantly, its policy position.

---

4   *Short's Trustee v Keeper of the Registers of Scotland* 1996 SC (HL) 14 at 26.
5   Scottish Law Commission, Report on *Land Registration* (Scot Law Com No 222, 2010) recommendation 62(b).

B. Context of Section 86

The Registration Act 1617 introduced land registration into Scotland by establishing the Register of Sasines, a register of deeds subservient to ruling property law. A full and viable land law and conveyancing developed albeit on a model initially overtly feudal. Over time, the feudal factor came to be more relevant in terms of form than substance. Its final demise[6] – following a Scottish Law Commission reform project with Edinburgh University property specialist Professor Kenneth Reid as lead Commissioner[7] – was the immediate predecessor, in terms of land law development milestones,[8] of the reform of the 1979 registration system, the focus of this paper. Unrelated to the feudal factor, the Register of Sasines was beginning to show its age by the latter half of the twentieth century.[9] The 1979 Act introduced the Land Register to Scotland, which became operational on a limited area basis in 1981 and gradually extended to the entire country as a register controlling the state of title in respect of all new property transactions. The 1979 Act, largely reflecting an English model[10], came to be subject to criticism, not least for its curative effect which put the emphasis on compensation from public funds rather than rectification of the register. One commentator described the 1979 Act as "both badly drafted and conceptually lacking."[11]

In 2002 the SLC commenced an examination of the law. Three extensive Discussion Papers were issued[12] and the SLC Report with a draft new Act was published in February 2010.[13] The Bill received Royal Assent on 10

---

6   In the Abolition of Feudal Tenure etc (Scotland) Act 2000, s 1.

7   Scottish Law Commission, Report on *Abolition of the Feudal System* (Scot Law Com No 168, 1999).

8   On this and other major legislative developments in land law see R Rennie, *Land Tenure in Scotland* (2004).

9   See A J M Steven "Scottish Land Law in a State of Reform" 2002 *Journal of Business Law* 177, 193.

10   See SLC Discussion Paper on *Land Registration: Void and Voidable Titles* (DP No 125, 2004) para 1.22, n 54: "The Reid Committee saw the English system as its main model, and in important respects the 1979 Act is a copy of the English Land Registration Act of 1925."

11   Steven (n 8) 179.

12   (1) Discussion Paper on *Land Registration: Void and Voidable Titles* (DP No 125, 2004); (2) Discussion Paper on *Land Registration: Registration, Rectification and Indemnity* (DP No 128, 2005); (3) Discussion Paper on *Land Registration: Miscellaneous Issues* (DP No 130, 2005).

13   Report on *Land Registration* (n 4).

July 2012 and a designated day of 8 December 2014 was later announced.[14] Professors Rennie and Brymer commented positively, stating that "[t]he Registers of Scotland and the Scottish Law Commission are to be congratulated for undertaking such a much-needed and comprehensive review of our land registration system."[15]

Under section 3(1) of the 1979 Act the registered proprietor is owner of the land. Upon the registration of an invalid transaction, the register may be rectified but not to the prejudice of the registered proprietor in possession unless that party caused the inaccuracy by fraud or carelessness.[16] If, by B's act of fraud, the land of registered proprietor A is transferred to C as proprietor, under the 1979 system, C is owner.[17] Of course, according to the ordinary rule of property law, A ought to remain owner regardless because he did not intend any transfer of his property and, quite obviously, the right of disposal is key to ownership. That said, the 1979 Act represents the position of a positive system of registration of title in which a conveyance "forged or granted *a non domino* confers ownership in just the same way as registration of a conveyance which was granted by the true owner and properly executed."[18] The extent to which this position changes under the 2012 Act is the essential subject of this paper.

Section 86 being concerned with acquisition from one without a valid title is pertinent to the situation of a title deed void on the basis of fraud. Of course, the case of a void (i.e. invalid) title is distinguishable from that of a voidable title (i.e. "a subsistent title subject to the possibility of future challenge"[19]). A measure of the position of a system of registration is, arguably, its treatment of the fraud situation. It is submitted that the extent to which the registration factor has priority over the defect of a fraudulent act is a telling one in assessing the position of the system on the scale between, on the one hand, the position of the principles of property law being controlling and, on the other, that of the overriding primacy of registration.

---

14   Land Registration etc. (Scotland) Act 2012 (Designated Day) Order, 2014/127, art 2.

15   Rennie and Brymer, "A Bold Step" (n 1), 32.

16   1979 Act, s 9(3)(a)(iii).

17   See this discussion in Part C below.

18   See DP on *LR: Void and Voidable* (n 9), para 1.9. See also E Cooke "Land Registration: Void and Voidable Titles" 2004 *Edin LR* 401-405, 402.

19   K G C Reid, "Property," in *The Laws of Scotland: Stair Memorial Encyclopaedia* vol 18 (1993) para 601.

C. Outline of Section 86

Part 9 of the 2012 Act is headed "Rights of persons acquiring etc in good faith." The "etc" refers to provisions relevant to servitudes and encumbrances, not concerned with acquisition as such. This paper is concerned only with acquisition of ownership from a "disponer without valid title"[20] in terms of section 86. Part 9 also deals with the good faith acquisition of leases.[21]

The role of section 86 is provided for in section 50 concerned with transfer by disposition; the requirement that ownership of land is transferred by a valid disposition is stated in section 50(2) in the form of a rule, i.e. that "[r]egistration of a valid disposition transfers ownership." This positive proposition is fortified by being stated in the negative in the following subsection: "[a]n unregistered disposition does not transfer ownership."[22] The prerequisite of registration provided for in section 50 is stated to be subject to the provisions of "(a) sections 43 and 86 and (b) any other enactment or rule of law by or under which ownership of land may pass."[23] Section 43, concerned with "prescriptive claimants," provides for a provisional form of registration by the Keeper which remains provisional until the normal ten year prescription is completed.[24] It may be noted that sections 43 and 86 are complimentary in providing for *a non domino* transfers in the respective situations of, on the one hand, that fact being known to the Keeper and, on the other hand, it being unknown. Section 43 represents a new application of positive prescription in its familiar role providing for the obtaining of title to land through the passage of time on the basis of an ex facie valid deed; no more will be said of it.

The sphere of application of section 86 is defined in subsection 1: a non-owner ("A") registered as proprietor and in possession of the land purports to dispone the land to a good faith party ("B"). This follows the SLC Report which states that "[t]he first condition for the realignment of rights is that the granter of the disposition in question is not the owner but is registered as owner."[25] The following conditions – continuing the usage of "A" as non-owner registered as proprietor and "B" as good faith acquirer – set out in section 86(3) must be met:

---

20 s 86 subheading.
21 Under ss 88 and 89.
22 s 50(3).
23 s 50(4).
24 See D Johnston, *Prescription and Limitation of Actions*, 2nd edn (2012) para 17.18.
25 Report on *Land Registration* (n 4), para 23.4.

(i)   the land has been in the possession, openly, peaceably and without judicial interruption –

    (a)   of A for a continuous period of at least 1 year, or

    (b)   of A and then of B for periods which together constitute such a period,

(ii)   at no time during that period did the Keeper become aware that the register was inaccurate as a result of A (or B) not being the proprietor,

(iii)   B is in good faith,

(iv)   the disposition would have conferred ownership on B had A been proprietor when the land was disponed,

(v)   at no time during the period mentioned in paragraph (a) –

    (a)   was the title sheet subject, by virtue of section 67, to a *caveat* relevant to the acquisition by B,

    (b)   did the title sheet contain a statement under section 30(5), and

(vi)   the Keeper warrants (or is to be taken to warrant) A's title.

Section 86 is the most important part of Part 9 of the 2012 Act dealing with the "realignment" of rights.[26] In the Consultation on Implementation of the 2012 Act, Professor George Gretton comments as follows on realignment:[27]

> The basic rule in the 2012 Act is that where an entry in the LR is not justified by the deeds, the LR is inaccurate and ought to be rectified. But the Act specifies an exception, in certain types of case where the rule is that the LR is not to be rectified, but instead, the parties should have the rights (or lack thereof) that the LR says they have (or that they lack). This is realignment. It is the converse of rectification. Where there is realignment, the effect is that the entries in the LR are deemed accurate. Accordingly, where there is realignment, no question of rectification can arise.

The reference to realignment as the converse of rectification is, it would appear, on the basis that realignment provided for in the 2012 Act represent an opposite policy to the general one insofar as, in realignment, the incorrect

---

26   The label "realignment principle" seems more appropriate than "integrity principle" which features as an alternative in the SLC papers: see Report on *Land Registration* (n 4), paras 13.12 and 23.4.

27   RoS, *Post Consultation Report* (n 2), part 9, para 9.3.

position prevails and is not open to rectification. It may be noted that the Registers of Scotland describe Part 9 as "an exception to the rule that if there is an inaccuracy in the Land Register it is to be rectified."[28]

Under section 86(3)(b), the fact that the person named as proprietor in the register is not actually the true proprietor must not be known to the Keeper or the acquirer. The acquirer will be in bad faith if he or she knows. The Keeper, knowing that the grantee cannot acquire because the party purporting to be grantor in fact has no right to the property, should obviously not register on a final basis.[29] Consistent with recognition of this is the prerequisite of section 86(3)(b) that at no time during the one year period did the Keeper become aware of the ownership issue. The Explanatory Notes[30] state that: "[i]n the absence of evidence to the contrary, the awareness of the Keeper referred to in subsection (3)(b) can be deduced from the information on the register."[31] In other words, the Keeper's state of knowledge is assumed to be consistent with what appears to be the position as reflected on the register and any contrary allegation must be established by reference to the actual knowledge of the Keeper.

David Johnston QC, in the second (2012) edition of his definitive work on prescription in Scots law, distinguishes the section 86 scenario as "entirely distinct"[32] from the provisions that apply to "normal" prescriptive claimants under the 2012 Act's revised position,[33] where the Keeper marks the entry provisional because he or she knows that the applicant named on the register is not the owner. The question whether acquisition in terms of section 86 is a form of prescription will be considered in a subsequent section of this paper.

Turning to the Explanatory Notes, the effect of section 86(1)-(3) is stated to be that:[34]

> if the register shows someone as proprietor, but that person's title is in fact void, then when that person dispones the title to another (and that second person is duly registered as owner), if the requirements in subsection (3)

---

28 Registers of Scotland, *Consultation on Implementation of the Land Registration etc. (Scotland) Act 2012* (2013) para 9.01.
29 But may do so on a "provisional" basis; see, below, n 32.
30 Prepared by the Scottish Government to assist the reader of the 2012 Act but not forming part of the Act and not endorsed by Parliament.
31 Explanatory Notes (n 29), para 201.
32 Johnston, *Prescription* (n 23), para 17.21.
33 Set out in Land Registration (Scotland) Act 2012, s 43.
34 Explanatory Notes (n 29), para 201.

(including regarding good faith and possession for one year) are met, then that second person acquires ownership.

This highlights the importance of the good faith and possession requirements, both of which are examined in more detail below.

Responding to an invitation by the writer to comment on section 86 and its application to a problem scenario – drafted for teaching purposes and presented later in this paper – Professor Kenneth Reid noted that the section's solution was less radical than the "Midas touch" of the 1979 Act and provided the following example:[35]

> Suppose that land belongs to A. Forging A's signature, B dispones the land to C, whose title is registered in the Land Register. Under the 1979 Act, C becomes owner on registration and, if C is in possession, A cannot get the land back but must make do with indemnity from the Keeper. Under the 2012 Act, C's registration has no effect and A remains owner throughout. C then has a claim for indemnity against the Keeper.

Taking the same situation, but adding that C has disponed the land to D, under the 1979 Act he or she would, of course, be in the same protected position as C. D's position, like C's would be secure provided possession was retained. The Register would be inaccurate in showing C or D as owner and could, in principle, be rectified in the event of a loss of possession by the registered owner. Under section 86 of the 2012 Act, provided D's acquisition was in good faith and the other requirements of the section are complied with, he or she will be owner. In this situation there would be no question of an inaccuracy in the register.

Section 86 appears to be an exception to the principle of *nemo dat quod non habet*.[36] Indeed, Johnston notes that section 86-89 are exceptions to the *nemo dat* principle.[37] Of course, the notion of registration as a guarantee of title necessarily involves some compromise in terms of adherence to *nemo dat*.[38] For Johnston the justification is the importance that the public

---

35   Email message of 20 March 2014 from Kenneth Reid to David Carey Miller. I am grateful to Professor Reid for agreeing to my reference in this paper to this and subsequent comments made by him.

36   Or, perhaps strictly correctly in terms of the sources of Scots law: *"nemo plus juris ad alienum transferre potest, quam ipse haberet"*: see Reid, *Property* (n 18), para 669, n 1. See also Report on *Land Registration* (n 4), para 19.2, n 2.

37   Johnston, *Prescription* (n 23), para 17.21.

38   See Report on *Land Registration* (n 4), para 21.21.

should be able to place reliance on the register, and it is essential to the land registration system that a registered title is guaranteed.[39]

Before examining the possession and good faith aspects of section 86 in more detail, the position regarding the date of acquiring ownership may be noted. This is provided for in section 86(4)-(6). Where the land has been in the possession openly, peaceably and without judicial interruption of A for a continuous period of at least one year or of A and then of B – the good faith disponee – and their possession together constitutes a period of at least one year, ownership is acquired on the date on which the disposition in favour of B is registered.[40] Alternatively, where a continuous period of the requisite possession commences before registration in B's name, but does not expire until a date later than the date of registration, ownership is acquired on the date on which the period of possession is completed.[41]

D. Section 86(3) Conditions

(1) Possessory Requirement

Under section 86(3)(a), there must have been a period of at least one year of continuous possession, "openly, peaceably and without judicial interruption." The SLC Report notes that this definition "ties in with the concept of possession in the prescription legislation."[42] This is a reference to the Prescription and Limitation (Scotland) Act 1973[43] which gives title on the basis of an *ex facie* valid deed where there is possession for "a continuous period of ten years openly, peaceably and without any judicial interruption." But does this affinity mean that section 86 is a form of prescription? The role of positive prescription in the context of Scottish land law and conveyancing practice is a most significant one and one might be forgiven for identifying section 86 as another form of prescription. As already mentioned, David Johnston covers the provision in a chapter dealing with the positive prescription of interests in land.[44] But, of course, that could be said to be justified on the basis that section 86 provides for

---

39 Johnston, *Prescription* (n 23), para 17.21.
40 ss 86(4), (5).
41 ss 86(4), (6).
42 Report on *Land Registration* (n 4), para 23.7.
43 s 1(1)(a).
44 Johnston, *Prescription* (n 23), para 17.21.

a form of acquisition involving possession for a stipulated period of time. The passage of time factor in the required period of one year's possession is, of course, the reason why the provision is thought, by some, to be prescription. But a one year prescription of heritable property? Turning back to the Prescription Act 1594, the original period in Scotland was 40 years. This was reduced by the Conveyancing (Scotland) Act 1874, s 34 to 20 years and then to ten in the 1973 Prescription and Limitation (Scotland) Act. The requirement of only one year's possession would be exceptional but is a comparison appropriate? Section 86 requires registration in good faith whereas positive prescription is about possession *animus domini* – possession on the basis of an intention to hold as owner evidenced by an *ex facie* valid deed in favour of the possessor. The 1973 Prescription and Limitation (Scotland) Act does not allow prescription where possession is on the basis of a registered forged deed where the party appearing as grantee was aware of the forgery at the time of registration in his or her favour.[45] The starting point here is the position of the common law that forgery cannot be a basis for acquisition.[46]

In commenting on the Draft Prescription and Title to Moveable Property (Scotland) Bill,[47] one writer notes that "[t]he fact that the entire period of possession would have to be completed in good faith is a major distinction when viewed in comparison to positive prescription of land."[48] The better view, it is submitted, is that the established form of prescription in land law reflects an approach incompatible with, or at least distinct from, acquisition in terms of section 86 on the basis of a passage of time factor subject to a controlling good faith requirement. The important good faith requirement will be looked at in more detail in the next section.

Against identification as prescription, acquisition can only be by B who does not necessarily have to have possessed but must always take transfer by registration in good faith. This, it may be argued, points to a form of original acquisition distinct from positive prescription.[49] Indeed,

---

45   s 1(2)(b). See Johnston, *Prescription* (n 23), para 17.19. See also n 10, DP No 125, 2004, paras 3.4-11.

46   Hence s 1(2)(a) ruling out prescription based on possession founded on the recording in the General Register of Sasines of a forged deed; see Johnston, *Prescription* (n 23), para 17.30.

47   See Scottish Law Commission, Report on *Prescription and Title to Moveable Property* (Scot Law Com n 228, 2012).

48   C M Campbell "Prescription and Title to Moveables" (2012) 16 Edin L R 426-430.

49   In my continuing interchange with Professor Kenneth Reid (n 34), on 24 March 2014, he rejected the "form of prescription" suggestion on the basis of the possessory aspect. Explaining that the reason for the possession requirement is to give notice to the true

title could be said to arise by registration. Certainly, in acquiring a title under section 86, more than just the possessory requirements have to be fulfilled. In terms of section 86(3) six separate requirements must be met. In essence, in addition to the possession and good faith requirements, derivative acquisition must be competent in terms of the system of the 2012 Act with the Keeper unaware of the invalidity and, of course, no *caveat*[50] or statement of uncertainty regarding registration.[51] As the SLC Report puts it, "the disposition should be such that, were it not for that defect, the disponee would acquire a good title."[52]

A counter to any suggestion that a form of prescription was intended by the drafters of section 86 is the fact that their thinking appears to have been influenced by section 25 of the Sale of Goods Act 1979 (SOGA).[53] With regard to the general issue of a choice between the protection of an owner's interest and recognition of the interest of an innocent good faith acquirer, the SLC Report notes that there are exceptions to the general position that an acquirer's good faith is irrelevant to the problem of a void title.[54]

> The general law says that good faith does not protect…against such nullities. But there are exceptions. One of these is section 25 of the Sale of Goods Act 1979 which in some cases enables a good faith buyer to acquire a valid title from a non-owning seller. We mention this particular exception because, as will be seen, it has had an influence on our thinking about land registration.

While a mutual feature of section 86 and section 25 of the SOGA is the priority accorded to a good faith purchaser, it does seem that the notion of a SOGA provision pointing the way for a land registry property issue

---

owner that there is a threat to his title, Professor Reid observes, "unlike true prescription, the disponee is rewarded with a good title, not because he has possession for a period … but because he relied on the Register in good faith."

50 In terms of s 67.

51 In terms of s 30(5).

52 Report on *Land Registration* (n 4), para 23.5.

53 SOGA, s 25 provides: "Where a person having bought or agreed to buy goods obtains, with the consent of the seller, possession of the goods or the documents of title to the goods, the delivery or transfer by that person, or by a mercantile agent acting for him, of the goods or documents of title, under any sale, pledge, or other disposition thereof, to any person receiving the same in good faith and without notice of any lien or other right of the original seller in respect of the goods, has the same effect as if the person making the delivery or transfer were a mercantile agent in possession of the goods or documents of title with the consent of the owner."

54 Report on *Land Registration* (n 4), para 19.3; see also para 13.21: "Assuming good faith … a third party … would receive a good title, rather as under section 25(1) of the Sale of Goods Act 1979."

needs to be justified in view of the policy distinction between, on the one hand, title to corporeal moveable property and, on the other, title to land.

The affinity between section 86 of the 2012 Act and section 25 of the SOGA is referred to by Professor Reid in his email correspondence with the writer. Noting that "there are comparable provisions to protect *bona fide* acquirers…in other countries" he observes that the provisions concerned have "no effect on voidable titles, because a *bona fide* acquirer already gets… title under the common law; so [the] purpose is to give protection where the registered title of the transferor is void."[55] The void/voidable distinction is, indeed, an important one in terms of defining section 86 with reference to the principles of the common law. On the basis that control over disposal is fundamental to the right of ownership, there is an important difference between, on the one hand, a complete absence of the owner's intention to transfer property in the circumstances of an act of fraud and, on the other hand, the owner's sufficient consent obtained in a way which makes it challengeable as an act of intention. Section 86 – applying to "acquisition from disponer without valid title" – is, of course, concerned only with the former situation. It may be noted that in the case of a voidable deed which is reduced by court decree, the decree is registered to reflect the correct position.[56] In a subsequent section defining 'inaccuracy' it is stated that a voidable deed reduced does not produce an inaccuracy.[57] Observing that this is not the rectification of an inaccuracy but "simply a later registration that changes the register" the Explanatory Notes go on to note that "[t]his applies only to voidable deeds" because where an entry proceeds from a void deed the register is "inaccurate from the outset, and should be rectified."[58]

Moving from characterisation to substance, as regards the period of "at least"[59] one year of possession, it suffices that there is "straddling possession," that is possession of A and then of B for periods which together constitute at least one year, or indeed that A possesses for such a continuous period.[60]

---

55 See message of 20 March 2014 (n 34).
56 See s 54 inserting a new provision (s 46A) in the Conveyancing (Scotland) Act 1924.
57 s 65(4)(a).
58 Explanatory Notes (n 29), para 170.
59 Why "at least"? Whether acquisition in favour of B obtaining registration in good faith is on the basis of A's possession (s.86(5)(a)) or A's and B's combined (s.86(5)(b)) a minimum period of one year must have passed, hence "at least."
60 Report on *Land Registration* (n 4), para 23.6; Recommendation 105.

If the section 86 one year passage of time requirement is not in direct support of B's acquisition why is it there? Primarily, it seems, as an appropriate window within which the party potentially affected by the invalid register entry may intervene and assert his or her position in terms of the principles of property law. This is accepted in relevant comments on section 86. In the Annotations provided to the Bill, the Committee note that "in the majority of circumstances, one year's possession is sufficient."[61] Yet this does not cover every single circumstance, and the Committee go on to further note that "we feel that it may not be long enough in all circumstances, especially where large amounts of land or pieces of land spread out across the country are owned, for example by utility companies..."[62] However, in the SLC Report, it is noted that no clear view was held as to what the length of the period should be,[63] however one year is "enough time for a person to become aware of the problem, seek legal advice and, if necessary, raise an action in court."[64] Does this suggest that the provision is in fact a form of negative prescription? One way of looking at the device is in terms of its protection of the affected party in requiring a period of "at least one year" in which it is open to him or her to challenge the position as reflected in the Register and apparently confirmed by the circumstances of possession. But, that said, the true owner is not deprived by the lapse of time but remains owner until conveyance to an innocent third party or, if that does not happen, until the normal ten year prescription has effect.

(2) Good Faith Requirement

The SLC Report notes that the aim of the good faith requirement is "to protect the innocent, but only the innocent,"[65] something the Report feels that the 1979 Act falls short on in its "fraud or carelessness" test[66] – "[e]xperience has exposed the shortcomings of this test."[67] It may be noted that

---

61 Economy, Energy and Tourism Committee, *Stage 1 Report on the Land Registration etc. Scotland Bill* (2012), 213.
62 *Stage 1 Report* (n 61), 213.
63 See DP on *LR: Void and Voidable* (n 9), para 4.52 (proposal 7(e)) – as to whether one year, two or some other period.
64 Report on *Land Registration* (n 4), para 21.32.
65 Ibid, para 23.8.
66 Land Registration (Scotland) Act 1979, s 9(3).
67 Report on *Land Registration* (n 4), para 23.8.

the SLC's preference for a good faith control over the problem of title from a void basis was first presented in a 2004 Discussion Paper.[68]

From the point of view of the position of the 1979 Act *vis-à-vis* an act of fraud it is significant that only the proprietor's "fraud or carelessness" gives an exception to the central rule that the Register cannot be rectified if this would prejudice a proprietor in possession. The possibility of this formulation leading to an undesirable outcome is shown in the case of *Kaur v Singh*[69] where an estranged husband forged his wife's signature and disposed of their flat; the innocent purchaser in possession was protected against rectification until the defrauded wife was able to retake possession. Under section 86 the innocent – i.e. good faith – registering purchaser would be protected, regardless of the present circumstances of possession, provided there had been one year's possession by the fraudulent seller or one year made up by that party's possession combined with that of the innocent purchaser. Both the 1979 and 2012 approaches give title despite a basis invalid for fraud. Whereas under the 1979 Act the critical factor is the innocent party's maintenance of possession[70], under the new legislation it is the factor of good faith at the time of registration – if necessary continuing until the required one year period is complete.

The concept of *bona fides* has a well-established general role in Scottish property law.[71] The SLC Report indeed notes that in Scots law, "good faith is the traditional and well-understood test."[72] Certainly Scots law has a long history of penalising bad faith; in a case in 1781, Lord Braxfield noted that "[a]s to *bona fides*, although *male fides* may cut down a right, *bona fides* cannot establish a right."[73] But while *bona fides* has a long-standing general role in Scottish property law, until the 2012 Act it does appear to have been used as a control device in the law regulating the acquisition of land. In contrast,

---

68   See DP on *LR: Void and Voidable* (n 9); for a succinct review see Cooke, *Void and Voidable* (n 18).

69   1999 SC 180.

70   Report on *Land Registration* (n 4) is critical of the uncertainty of a wronged party's right to rectification being suspended in the circumstances of an innocent party's possession, see para 17.23-27, noting, at para 17.27, that the notion that the law requires "the Register to remain in error" causes the public to be "incredulous and sometimes irate."

71   See "Bona Fide Possession" in Reid, Property (n 18), paras 131-37; see also my "Good Faith in Scots Property Law" in Forte (ed) Good Faith in Contract and Property Law (1999) 103.

72   Report on *Land Registration* (n 4), para 23.9.

73   *Mitchells v Ferguson* (1781) Ross's Leading Cases 120 at 127, per Lord Braxfield.

in the Victorian statutory development of commercial law applying to moveable property good faith came to have an important role.[74]

In land law *bona fide* possession gives entitlement to the fruits and benefits of property but the good faith factor does not have a key role – perhaps no role – in any translation of possession into title. This has been noted above in respect of positive prescription. Historically, in the context of a basic system of registration, possession supported by a colourable title had a certain role but this declined with the development of registration.[75] The common law possessory judgment protecting seven years possession on the basis of a written title[76] is of limited relevance in modern law and, in any event, the better view is that it did not require good faith.[77] From the point of view of the novelty of section 86, the position of the common law was clear, in principle – regardless of the grantee's good faith in being innocent of any defect – there could not be acquisition on the basis of an invalid deed. In modern law the controlling limit – and the clear indication of applicable policy – is the ten year period of possession on the basis of an *ex facie* valid deed required for positive prescription.

This generalized background survey suggests that good faith did not play any significant part in the process of acquisition of ownership of land. The paramount *nemo plus* (or *nemo dat*)[78] principle ruled. But for present purposes the main point is that although "fraud or carelessness" could be relevant in the case of a bad faith acquirer, good faith has no role under the 1979 Act but has an important one in the new system. As already noted, the 1979 Act does not apply the good faith factor in determining the priority issue which may arise as a consequence of the register being guaranteed.[79] For the purposes of section 86 the registering grantee's good faith must be subjective in the sense of actual belief in the Register. The SLC Discussion Paper explains the position:[80]

---

74 Perhaps most significantly, as part of the Sale of Goods Act 1979 (first passed in 1893); See Carey Miller, "Good Faith" (n 70) 120.

75 Reid, *Property* (n 18), para 134.

76 See Craig Anderson, "The Protection of Possession in Scots Law" in E Descheemaeker (ed) *The Consequences of Possession* (2014) 111.

77 Reid, *Property* (n 18), para 146.

78 See message of 20 March 2014 (n 34).

79 See Report on *Land Registration* (n 4), para 23.8-14 concluding that a good faith test would be preferable to the "fraud or carelessness" one of the 1979 Act.

80 See DP on *LR: Void and Voidable* (n 9), para 7.11.

It seems self-evident that only subjective good faith can be relevant for Register error. To lose the statutory protection the acquirer must know, as a positive fact, that the Register is wrong… If mere suspicion were enough, an acquirer, alerted to the possible error, would have no choice but to go behind the Register and inspect the prior deeds, in disregard of the curtain principle and consequently of one of the main purposes of registration of title.

E. Possible Section 86 Application Scenario

This possible working example of the application of section 86 was drafted for the Aberdeen University Conveyancing (Honours) class of 2013/2014.[81]

Mr and Mrs Grabbie have looked after their aged neighbour John Kindness at Kinmuck in Aberdeenshire, for almost ten years. Mr Kindness's only relation is his son Bruce who lives in Australia. In addition to his house property Mr Kindness owns, under a separate title, a three acre field where he keeps a pair of Shetland ponies. The Grabbies have a Welsh cob which shares the field with the Shetland ponies. Mrs Grabbie looks after the land and the three ponies. In January 2014, in declining health, going blind and showing signs of dementia, Mr Kindness gave Mr Grabbie a full power of attorney. At the same time he says that he wants to talk to his son about the Grabbies getting a liferent over the pony field when he dies. Kindness's solicitor, who drew up the power of attorney, is present at the signing and hears his client's statement about the field. In October Mr Grabbie gets Mr Kindness to sign a paper telling him, untruthfully, that it is a council tax exemption document. In fact, it is a letter from Kindness to his solicitor stating that he has decided that the Grabbie's should get the field outright and instructing that it be transferred to Mrs Grabbie as soon as possible, with all necessary formalities dealt with by Mr Grabbie in terms of the power of attorney he holds. This deception is only possible because of Mr Kindness's eyesight and there is no question of his lacking capacity. Mr Grabbie takes the letter to Kindness's solicitor who draws up missives and a disposition transferring the field to Mrs Grabbie. The disposition is signed by Grabbie acting on the basis of his authority under the power of attorney. In January 2015 the field property is registered in Mrs Grabbie's name in terms of the Land Registration (Scotland) Act 2012. She informs the Council that she is owner and arranges for payment of the council tax from her bank account. Mrs Grabbie continues to attend to the ponies in the field on a daily basis but also has the property re-fenced. In February 2016, after moving the ponies to her daughter's farm, she sells the field to property developer Phil Marbles who knows nothing of the circumstances of Mrs Grabbie's

---

81   For further examples of the working of the 2012 Act, see Report on *Land Registration* (n 4), Part 25.

acquisition. The field is sold for £9,000. Mr Marbles obtains possession of the field and commences a market gardening operation pending his intended application for a change of use for development. In March 2016 the field is registered in Mr Marbles' name. In August he obtains planning permission to erect fifteen houses and the field is now valued at £180,000. Prior to that, in May 2016, John Kindness died. After the funeral his son from Australia goes drinking with the Grabbies and tells them that he has inherited the entire estate of his father who died intestate. At the end of a long evening Mr Grabbie tells Bruce Kindness what he did with the field. In the sober light of day Kindness reports the transgression to his dad's solicitor and asks if the transfer to Mrs Grabbie and the subsequent one to Phil Marbles can be reduced because of Mr Grabbie's fraud.

An Edinburgh QC gives the Kindness solicitor an opinion to the effect that: (i) in terms of section 86 Marbles got a good title to the field on registration in his name in March 2016, and; (ii) that the John Kindness estate is entitled to compensation from the Keeper on the basis of sections 94 and 95. The opinion adds that, applying section 95(1), the increase in value is not a consequential loss which the Kindness Estate can recover because it was solely due to Mr Marbles' efforts and, for this reason, the compensation payable will be quantified on the basis of value of the field at the time the right was lost – i.e. £9000.

F. Conclusion

The SLC Report, progenitor of the 2012 Act, in a part on the "[e]ffect of registration," says that there are two types of inaccuracy under the 1979 Act "which we call in the discussion papers 'actual' inaccuracy and 'bijural' inaccuracy." The Report goes on to explain:[82]

> An inaccuracy is actual if what the Register says in simply untrue. An inaccuracy is 'bijural' if what the Register says is false in terms of general law, but true for the purposes of the Act.

In a subsequent part on "[i]naccuracy in the register" the Report says that "as a result of the new scheme bijural inaccuracies[83] will disappear" for which "there will be few mourners."[84] One takes this to mean that the

---

82 Report on *Land Registration* (n 4), para 13.7.
83 On this see P O'Connor "Deferred and immediate indefeasibility: bijural ambiguity in registered land title systems" (2009) 13 *Edin LR* 194-223.
84 Report on *Land Registration* (n 4), para 17.33.

revised registration system of the 2012 Act will square more with general property law than the 1979 Act's system did. As the Explanatory Notes state: "[t]he Act seeks to re-align registration law with property law by, for example, adjusting the circumstances in which a person can recover their property rather than only receive compensation under the state guarantee of title from the Keeper."[85] But all that said, section 86 represents a compromise – involving the 'integrity' or 'realignment' principle – in terms of which "in certain cases the registration of an invalid deed will confer on the good faith grantee an unchallengeable right."[86]

Without acknowledging the utility of the bijural analysis, section 86 does seem to be a departure from the general position of the 2012 Act insofar as this seeks to bring the registration system closer to the general law. The section imports a corporeal moveables exception to *nemo dat* in the justification for recognising the entitlement of a good faith acquirer in circumstances in which there is nothing to suggest that the disponer does not have a right of disposal. The position of section 86 is seen to be analogous to that of section 25 of the Sale of Goods Act 1979 and, to that extent – as the SLC position seems to be – this is not an alternative regime but, rather, a realignment providing a new statutory answer to a particular question, if not deriving from, at least with some relationship to existing law.

An alternative perspective is that the 2012 Act's treatment of fraud gives a reduction window to the defrauded party and, to that extent, eases the extreme position of the 1979 legislation. This, combined with the justification for benefitting an honest acquirer in circumstances which raise no doubt, is part of a new registration law system. To that extent, if there is any utility in the bijural analysis, one might say that this is a replacement of the bijural content rather than a departure from the bifurcated approach implicit in bijuralism.

What may be seen as the extreme – but, of course, widely subscribed to – idea of registration wiping the fraud slate clean is replaced but the statute, nonetheless, retains a system allowing what amounts to relatively easy condoning of the wronging of an owner of land deprived by fraud. The scenario produced for the 2013/14 Aberdeen Conveyancing Honours class seems to me to demonstrate that.

Seeing the one year period of the 2012 Act as a form of negative prescription could be contrasted with the twenty year period applying to

---

85 Explanatory Notes (n 29), para 3.
86 Report on *Land Registration* (n 4), para 13.36.

an owner's right to recover stolen moveables from a party innocent of the theft.[87] But, of course, the real right of ownership in land is imprescriptible[88] and, on that basis, we probably cannot see section 86 as a form of negative prescription. That would, in any event, be problematic because it is not an external challenge to the registration system[89] but integral to it.

This rather leads to the conclusion that section 86 is consistent with the SLC's conceptual system in the 2012 Act. The section provides for a "realignment" of general property law in bringing recognition of the good faith purchaser's interest into the equation. The radical extent of this "realignment" is demonstrated by the policy borrowing from moveable property. Whoever would have thought of *"mobilia non habent sequelam"* applying to land?

Conceptual structure and system apart, is the policy position of section 86 a good one? That, it is suggested, comes down to the question how far the security of a registered deed, in giving priority to the property, should go. Of course, one needs to address the effects of policy to be in a position to make an informed choice. In a recent contribution focussing on registered land titles in English law Dr Simon Cooper, referring to the solution route of "correction power... controlled by a clearly defined and hard edged rule," observes that:[90]

> [t]he quality of predictability inherent in such a rule would avert potential costs of policing and enforcing property claims, it would allow better forecasting of the occasions for correction and ensure improved information about risk, thus removing a potential deterrent to entering the land market.

Prima facie, it seems that section 86 scores relatively well on these criteria.

While section 86 is an innovative solution which much to commend it this writer is not convinced that the position of good faith should give priority over an act of fraud after only one year. From the point of view of the common law of Scotland that would be a radical concession and it is difficult to see why such a position should be adopted in the context of a shift from positive registration to a system intended to be generally closer to the common law.

---

87   Prescription and Limitation (Scotland) Act 1973, Schedule 3 (g).

88   Ibid, Schedule 3 (a).

89   See Johnston, *Prescription* (n 23), para 3.02, arguing that if negative prescription were allowed to extinguish rights "the standing of the property registers would soon become very dubious."

90   Simon Cooper "Regulating Fallibility in Registered Land Titles" (2013) 72 *CLJ* 341-68, 346.

10. *Res Merae Facultatis:* Through a Glass Darkly

Sheriff Douglas J Cusine

A. Introduction

When Robert and I went to study Law at the University of Glasgow in 1964, one of the entrance requirements was a pass in what was then called "Lower" Latin, later an "O" level and now a Standard Grade. In the class on Civil (Roman) Law, there were frequent mentions of Latin, without any translation, and in it and the other classes such as Scots Law, there was an assumption that the audience had some idea of what the various Latin terms meant. At present, any such assumption would be misplaced. I do not know when the requirement for Latin was dropped, but in more recent times, because the language is taught in only a few schools, law lecturers will either continue to use Latin terms, but translate them, or perhaps avoid using them.

When I was an academic lawyer, I benefited enormously from Robert's knowledge of the law and his experience of practice. We rarely conversed in Latin, but it might have seemed to so a bystander!

While a knowledge of Latin is no longer required of law students, Latin survives in at least one Scottish statute – the Prescription and Limitation (Scotland) Act 1973 ("the 1973 Act"). In Schedule 3, the Act gives a list of things to which the rules on prescription do not apply and one of these is something which is "exerciseable as a *res merae facultatis*." One assumes that the term was used in the legislation simply because a translation

　　　http://dx.doi.org/10.11647/OBP.0056.10

would not assist in understanding what is comprehended by it. There is no discussion of the concept in the Scottish Law Commission documentation which led up to the Act, beyond the description "rights of such a character that their exercise would be expected only periodically or irregularly,"[1] nor in the Parliamentary debates which preceded the 1973 Act,[2] except that during the Second Reading on the Bill, the Minister described the right as one "which the proprietor may assert or not as he pleases, without the risk of losing the right by failure to assert it."[3] As the expression is not defined in the 1973 Act, its meaning must be the common law meaning.[4]

Res merae facultatis means a thing or right which is a mere faculty, but it is clear that the right being discussed is something which the holder can exercise or not,[5] and if it exercised, it can be done at any time. As the Extra Division in *Peart v Legge*[6] observed, that is "correct (up to a point) because the possessor of any right may choose to exercise it or not."[7] Thus every right could be described as *res merae facultatis*. However, that leads to confusion and it is clear that *res merae facultatis* is narrower than other rights, if only because it is exempt from prescription. An example of the confusion which could arise can be seen in the following example. If I own a piece of ground, I am at liberty at any time to build on it (title and planning considerations apart), or to refrain from building. The right of ownership never prescribes, unless there has been prescriptive possession for 10 years on a competing title. Assuming that there is no such adverse possession, my rights as owner are *res merae facultatis*. However, if I have an express grant of a servitude of access, it is entirely up to me whether I use it or not, but if I do not use the servitude right, it will be lost in 20 years, and so the choice whether to exercise it or not also goes. If that right were categorised as *res merae facultatis*, it would be a subsidiary right, and as such, would remain valid only if the principal right remained. If I have the right to use a piece of ground for the construction of a road, that is a principal right, and it never prescribes. *Res merae facultatis*, therefore, has to be confined to that narrower class of rights which do not prescribe, unless

---

1   Memorandum on *Prescription and Limitation of Actions* (SLC Memo n 9, 1968) p 12.
2   HL Deb 5 April 1973, cols 418-25; HL Deb 17 April 1973, cols 1050-51; HL Deb 8 May 1973, cols 257-58; HL Deb 10 May 1973 cols 513-14.
3   HL Deb 5 April 1973, col 422 (Lord Polwarth).
4   *Peart v Legge* 2008 SC 93 at 101.
5   D Johnston, *Prescription and Limitation of Actions*, 2nd edn (2012) para 3.07.
6   2008 SC 93.
7   *Peart* (n 4) at 101, citing W M Gloag, *The Law of Contract*, 2nd edn (1929) 738.

lost in some other way. If I have a right which is *res merae facultatis*, I could discharge it expressly, or by my abandoning it, or it could be discharged by my acquiescing in something done by another which is inconsistent with the exercise of my right, e.g. by permitting a wall to be built over a passageway which I could, at some time, make into a road.

I intend to look at Institutional and other writings, and some of the reported cases, not with a view to trying to categorise rights which are *res merae facultatis*, but rather to challenge the view that a right which is *res merae facultatis* does not impose any obligation on any other party.

B. Institutional and other Writers

The customary place to begin is with Stair, but I have not been able to trace any mention of *res merae facultatis*, except in More's *Notes*: "But rights *merae facultatis* are not liable to be cut off by prescription."[8]

The first mention I have been able to trace is in Bankton:[9]

> It is a general rule, that *res merae facultatis numquam praescribitur*. A mere faculty, or power of using a thing cannot prescribe. A faculty is either a Liberty granted by the public law ... or Private, competent to one in the exercise of his right, as to build on his own ground at his pleasure.... One, by forbearing the exercise of a faculty during the course of prescription will not be hindered to use it, which is the import of the foresaid maxim: thus the proprietor may raise his building to the prejudice of his neighbour.

Erskine states:[10]

> Certain rights are *ex sua natura* incapable of the negative prescription, at least where statute does not interpose. First, powers which one may exercise or not at his pleasure *ex gr.* a power or faculty to burden lands with a certain sum, or to revoke a right granted.... Hence also the right inherent in every proprietor of building or using any other act of property on his grounds, cannot prescribe by any length of time, though a neighbouring landholder should suffer ever so much by the exercise of it.

Bell in his *Principles* says no more than "negative prescription will not affect *res merae facultatis*."[11]

---

8   Stair, *Inst* (5th edn) notes pcclxvi.

9   Ibid 2.12.22-23.

10   Ibid 3.7.10.

11   Bell, *Principles*, 10th edn §2017.

Turning to other writers, Kames mention the notion:[12]

> But there is here a remarkable Limitation, which makes a considerable
> further Restriction upon Rights prescribable; which is, That personal Powers
> or Faculties, such as Faculties to burden, to alter or innovate, to revoke, &c.
> though inferring a Burden upon others, are not lost *non utendo*. The true
> and adequate Reason whereof is this, that it being involved in the very Idea
> of a Faculty, to be exercised *quandocunque* at the arbitrary Pleasure of the
> Possessor, as well now as afterwards, as well afterwards as now, Neglect
> or Desertion, the Causes operative of Prescription, can never be inferred
> simply from Forbearance. In Rights the very Design of which is to be made
> effectual *quam primum*, such as Obligations for Money, or other Prestation,
> Forbearance to act upon these, implies Neglect and Dereliction. But where
> it is the very Intention of the Thing, that the Matter should lie over, where
> it is entirely arbitrary, whether the Power be exercised this Day or hereafter,
> the forbearing to act at present cannot infer in the Nature of Things Neglect
> or Dereliction. These Limitations upon the negative Prescription, *viz.* Acts of
> personal Liberty, that imply but one Person, and Faculties of the Nature to
> be exercised *quandocunque*, are both of them generally comprehended under
> the Expression of, though very different in their Natures and carefully to be
> distinguished. As for the positive Prescription, all Rights may be acquired
> thereby that are capable of Possession.

In Kames' *Elucidations*, commenting on the Prescription Act, he states:[13]

> The statutes of this island are not illustrious for profound knowledge. The
> exceptions are few, and this present act 1672 is one of the most illustrious
> ... *Res merae Facultatis*. Where a man provides to himself a power to exercise
> the faculty or not, as he finds it convenient and where therefore delay is no
> evidence of dereliction, nor even of negligence.

Further on in the same Article, he says:[14]

> (T)here is another species of rights and privileges more properly termed *res
> merae facultatis*, because they concern the privileged person only and affect
> not others; such as my choosing a spot for a kitchen-garden, planting a tree,
> or building a house at my March.

In his *Lectures*, while not specifically mentioning *res merae*, Hume states:[15]

---

12   H H Kames, *Essays Upon Several Subjects in Law* (1732) 108.
13   H H Kames, *Elucidations Respecting the Common and Statute Law of Scotland* (1777) 275.
14   Kames, *Elucidations* (n 13) 248.
15   G Campbell H Paton (ed), *Baron David Hume's Lectures 1786-1822: Volume 3* (1952) 65.

Prescription shall not apply to those claims which by their kind, do not seem destined to be used at any particular season, but are in their very nature arbitrary or discretionary to be used at any time – sooner or later – according to the convenience of the person concerned; so that his silence is no sufficient ground of inference of a purpose to abandon, nor can any particular day or term be fixed on, at which, more than another, prescription should begin to run against him.

Slightly further on, he makes this point:[16]

Beside, in some of those instances the right, ... is effectual, to the party concerned, and yet does not encroach on or shall impair the interest of any other person, does not operate in the shape of a call or claim on any one, does not result in any demand against any one, to yield anything, or donor perform anything, for the benefit of the party who uses the right.

In *Lectures on the Law of Scotland*, J S More has this to say:[17]

Rights which are *mere facultatis*, as they are called – that is rights which a party may or may not exercise at pleasure, and by the non-exercise of which no right is enjoyed or conferred on any other party, are not liable to be cut off by prescription. Thus the right of a proprietor to erect a mill or any other building on his lands, though not exercised for a hundred years, will never prescribe, however desirable it might be for his neighbour that no such building be erected.

Napier observes:[18]

Negative prescription involves the idea of opposing interests; a party debtor being thereby understood to be relieved from his obligation by the neglect, inferring dereliction, of the party creditor. So all rights and uses of property which imply no claim against another may be exercised *quandocunque*; [citing Kames and a case][19] These, and the like Imprescriptible rights, have come under the denomination of *res merae facultatis*.... Besides the *res merae facultatis* which involve no idea of any opposing interests, there are certain personal powers and faculties which, from their nature, come under the same demomination, although the patrimonial interests of another be concerned in the exercise or non exercise of such powers. It is involved in the very idea of a *faculty* that it may or may not be exercised, according to the will of the party in whose favour it is constituted.

---

16   Paton, *Hume's Lectures* (n 15), 65.
17   J S More, *Lectures on the Law of Scotland* (1864) vol 1, 419.
18   M Napier, *Commentaries on the Law of Prescription in Scotland* (1839) 645-47.
19   Kames, *Elucidations* (n 13) 248; *Haig v Haliburton* (1707) M 10727.

Millar on *Prescription* comments:[20]

> The solum of a public footpath belongs to the proprietor of the land through
> which it runs; and his right to erect gates across the path ... is consequently
> a right to make a certain use of his property at his own pleasure, is *res merae
> facultatis*, and is not liable to be extinguished by failure to exercise it.[21]

Trayner's Latin Maxims defines *res mere facultatis* in this way:[22]

> A matter of mere power; a mere faculty.... It is a right which may or may
> not be exercised at the pleasure of him who holds it; and such rights are
> never lost by their non-exercise for any length of time, because it is of their
> essential character that they may be used or exercised at any time.

Gloag:[23]

> [I]n certain cases the negative prescription is excluded on the ground that
> the right against which it is pleaded is one *res mere facultatis*, a right which
> the creditor may exact or not at pleasure. In one sense this is obviously
> true of every right, and it is difficult to frame a general canon of distinction.
> According to Pothier (*Vente*, v391), the principle of *res merae facultatis* applies
> where the right in question is one Implied by law, e.g. the right to increase
> the height of a building; or where it is *inter naturalia* of a contract e.g. the
> right, in pledge, to recover the article.

In his book on *Prescription and Limitation*, David Johnston looks at the
notion of *res merae facultatis* against the background of some of the reported
cases and then states:[24]

> It seems reasonable to conclude that *res merae facultatis* is a property right
> which cannot be lost by negative prescription either: (1) because it is a right
> whose exercise implies no claim on anyone else or against their rights; or (2)
> because it is a (normal) incident of ownership) which can be lost only as a
> consequence of the fortification in some other person of a right inconsistent
> with it. The common ground between these two categories is that they are
> rights which are lost only by the establishment of any adverse right, and that
> can happen, if at all, only by positive prescription. But so long as there is no
> adverse right there is no question of their prescribing.

---

20 J H Millar, *A Handbook of Prescription According to the Law of Scotland* (1893) 87.
21 He cites *Sutherland v Thomson* (1876) 3 R 485 and *Galbreath v Armour* (1845) 4 Bell App
374.
22 J Trayner, *Trayner's Latin Maxims*, 4 edn (1993) 554.
23 Gloag, *Contract* (n 7), 738.
24 Johnston, *Prescription* (n 5), para 3.16.

He also observes that there has been recent academic discussion of the concept, principally against the background of *Peart v Legge*.[25]

In A S Brett's *Liberty, Right and Nature*,[26] in a chapter entitled "The language of natural liberty: Fernando Vazquez de Menchaca,"[27] the author says:

> Within the prescription literature in general, prominent among those *imprescriptibilia* is *facultas*, where by a *facultas* is understood a power of free choice of doing something or not, at will.... A faculty is, in this connection, expressly contrasted with a right (*ius*): *if* I have right of doing something which I do not exercise, then after thirty years another person may claim to have prescribed that *ius*, to the extent that I no longer have it. But a faculty, which lies within my own free will, can never enter the sphere of civil law.

While there may be some merit in drawing a distinction between a right and a faculty, it does not advance our understanding of what rights are comprehended within *res merae facultatis* and which are not. It may be that while an elephant is difficult to describe, but is easily recognised, a *res merae facultatis* is neither easy to describe, nor to recognise. In the end, what is or is not *res merae facultatis* may come within that well-known jurisprudential notion that each case turns on its own facts.

C. Cases

Morison's Dictionary has a separate heading of *Res Merae Facultatis* and reports a number of cases on it,[28] but they do not greatly assist in defining or categorising those rights which are *res merae*, and some of the cases relate to issues which are no longer of any moment.

In *Crawford v Bethune*,[29] the right to work minerals was regarded as *res merae facultatis* and in *Agnew v Magistrates of Stranraer*[30] a right of oyster fishing was also so regarded. These are examples of incidents of ownership and, as has been noted, the right of ownership of land never prescribes,

---

25 *Peart* (n 4).
26 A S Brett, *Liberty, Right and Nature* (1997) 192-93.
27 Author of *Controveriarum illustrum usuque frequentium libri tres* (1564), born 1512.
28 10728-32.
29 (1822) 1 S 111.
30 Ibid 2 S 42.

except against an adverse title followed by prescription.[31] In *Gardner v Scott*,[32] Lord Fullerton stated:[33]

> [I]t is true that where a party grants a disposition with a double manner of holding ... the disponee has the option of holding by a base or a public infeftment. It is with him to choose either, so long as no other completed right intervenes. In any question with the grantee of such a right, the grantee is bound to throw no obstacle in the way of completing the right granted by himself.

This will be a mystery to those unfamiliar with the feudal system of landholding. In *Swan's Trs v The Muirkirk Iron Co*[34] the right to use a watercourse as a navigable canal was *res merae*.

Leck v Charmers[35] involved a dispute about the use of a common stair. In 1812 a tenement of land in Trongate, Glasgow was disponed and the deed provided that the disposers and disponees intended to erect an outside staircase to access the upper storeys. The ground on which the staircase was to be erected was held *pro indiviso*, maintained at mutual expense and it was foreseen that both parties would use the stair. The defenders averred that they had had exclusive use of the stair for 40 years and sought to exclude the pursuers from using it. The court held that one co-proprietor could not exclude the other from the use of such a stair. In his decision, Lord Cowan said:[36]

> Mere discontinuance to use and enjoy his property or its consequent for a hundred years, or any period, could not prevent the right being asserted at any time, so long as no adverse right has been reared up to its prejudice.... The joint right of the pursuers to use this staircase ... was, in truth, capable, at any distance of time, to be resumed and asserted.... The precise character of the legal right thus contended to have been acquired by the defenders is not very clearly stated in the record, but was explained by their senior counsel to be that of servitude. What kind of servitude could thus be raised up I am at some loss to understand.... [His Lordship notes that property cannot be lost simply by non use, but mentions another title followed by prescriptive possession] The right of the pursuers was, in truth, *res merae facultatis* capable at any distance of time to be resumed and asserted.

---

31   See also *Mackenzie v Davidson* (1841) 3D 646 on the right of salmon fishing, especially the opinion of Lord Moncreiff at 657.

32   (1840) 2 D 185.

33   *Gardner* (n 32) at 201.

34   (1847) 12 D 622.

35   (1859) 21 D 408.

36   *Leck* (n 35) at 417.

In *Gellatly v Arrol*[37] a tenement was conveyed in different storeys. The upper storeys were reached by a common stair, but the titles reserved the right in the proprietor of the ground storey to open up and use a door which already existed from the common stair and this right was *res merae*. Some of the judicial observations are useful. Lord Benholme:[38]

> Now I think that a right thus originally vested in the proprietor of this lower storey is, and can never be held as derelinquished; but that he should be held at any time entitled, in terms of the titles of both parties, to revert to the exercise of the original right of access.

Lord Neaves:[39]

> It is certain that the rugby of a party to make operations *in suo* never can be lost *non utendo*; and the question here is, strictly speaking, as to operation of that kind. It regards the right of the pursuer to open a door in his own wall, so as to give him physical access to the common stair.... This seems to me clearly to be *res merae facultatis*. It has been kept up in the titles, and still belongs to him as an accessory of his property.

Finally, Lord Justice-Clerk Inglis:[40]

> [A]ssuming that there is a door-way, the reserved right to open it is *res marae facultatis*, to which negative prescription is inapplicable.

In *Sutherland v Thomson*[41] the proprietor of land through which there was a right of way was held entitled to erect gates over the route provided they did not constitute an obstruction.[42]

In *Smith v Stewart*[43] the litigation arose out of the terms of a document described as a "Bond of Servitude" dated 1825 which was related to a piece of ground between two properties. The Bond contained the following provisions:

> [R]estricting us and our assignees ... from building nearer to the garden wall belonging to the said John Baxter ... than twenty feet ... hereby grant to the said John Baxter ... full power and liberty to use the said space of twenty feet

---

37 (1863) 1 M 592.
38 *Gellatly* (n 37) at 602.
39 Ibid.
40 *Gellatly* (n 37) at 599.
41 (1876) 3 R 485.
42 *Sutherland* (41) at 490 (Lord Neaves).
43 (1884) 11 R 921.

as a road or entry ... and to open up a passage or entry not exceeding ten feet wide in [said] dyke.

The litigation arose more than 40 years later (which at that time was the period of the long negative prescription). The pursuers argued that the right had prescribed, but this was rejected by the First Division. Lord President Inglis, with whom the other judges agreed, said:[44]

> It appears to me that the provision in Mr Baxter's favour entitled him to use the strip ... as an entry ... whether it was to be made into a street or not. There was no restriction as to the time within which the privilege was to be exercised.... But how is it possible to say that such a right ... can be lost by negative prescription? The right is clearly of the nature of a *res merae facultatis* – a right which is to be used in the future when occasion arises and is of such a nature as has never been held to fall under the negative prescription.

Rankine describes the decision as "narrow."[45] Two sheriff court decisions applied *Smith v Stewart, – Mitchell v Brown*[46] and *Crumley v Lawson*.[47] In *Mitchell*, Sheriff Guthrie (the editor of the 10th edition of Bell *Principles*) commented on *res merae*, saying, "It may be thought that the doctrine has been borrowed from some civilians without sufficient consideration or definition."[48]

The final case prior to *Peart v Legge*[49] is *Anderson v Robertson*[50] in which it was held that a lower proprietor whose land was damaged by surface water coming from the land of an upper proprietor because that proprietor had filled in a ditch had no ground of action as the right to fill in the ditch was *res merae*.[51] There is a list of cases on *res merae* in Walker on *Prescription and Limitation of Actions*.[52] A South African case is mentioned in Voet[53] and in that case, it was submitted by counsel that the right to have a veranda over a public road was *res merae*.[54]

---

44   *Smith* (43) at 924-25.
45   J Rankine, *Law of Land-ownership in Scotland*, 4th edn (1909) 87, n 5.
46   (1888) 5 Sh Ct Rep 9.
47   (1892) 8 Sh Ct Rep 307.
48   5 Sh Ct Rep at 13.
49   2008 SC 93.
50   1958 SC 367.
51   Lord Mackintosh in *Anderson* (n 50) at 375.
52   D M Walker, *Prescription and Limitation of Actions*, 6th edn (2002) 78.
53   Voet, *Commentaries on the Pandects*, 13, 7, 7 (ed Percival Vane).
54   *Jones v Town Council of Cape Town* 12 SC 19 at 25 (1895) C J de Villierv.

In *Peart v Legge*,[55] the parties owned neighbouring irregularly-shaped pieces of ground. There was a dispute about access. In 1981, the defender's father acquired ground from the Marquis of Lothian, and that ground was separated by a stone wall from a track owned by the Marquis. The 1981 deed included an express right of access over ground owned by the Marquis and a right to breach the wall, subject to certain conditions. In 1997, the Marquis sold the ground to the pursuer, but that was subject to the right of access in the 1981 deed. No attempt had been made since 1981 to take access, nor had the wall been breached. The court rejected an argument that the right to breach the wall was *res merae*.

Having examined some of the cases cited above, Johnston concludes that *res merae* is a property right and it does not impose any obligation on any other party,[56] a comment with which David Carey Miller agrees.[57] However, both Kames and Hume mention that, in some cases, there is an obligation on others. Thus Kames in the passage cited above says, "that personal Powers or Faculties, such as Faculties to burden, to alter or innovate, to revoke, &c. though inferring a Burden upon others, are not lost *non utendo*."[58] Hume's position is that, "in some instances,"[59] the right does not impose any obligation on others. Furthermore, having quoted the passage from Johnston, the court in *Peart* observed, "the present case (like *Smith v Stewart*) cannot be said to involve a right whose exercise implies no claim against the rights of another; any right of access over the property of another implies such a claim."[60] If one considers cases such as *Gellatly*,[61] *Leck*[62] and *Smith v Stewart*,[63] while the issue was whether the rights had prescribed, I submit that in *Gellatly* and *Leck*, it would not have been open to the other co-proprietor to do something to frustrate the right of access to the common stair and in *Smith*, the adjoining proprietor would not have been entitled to dig up the route over which the road might have gone, or to build over it.

---

55 2008 SC 93.
56 Johnston, *Prescription* (n 5), para 3.16.
57 D Carey Miller, "Res Merae Facultatis: Mysterious or Misunderstood" (2008) *Edin LR* 451-55.
58 Kames, *Essays* (n 12) 108.
59 Paton, *Hume's Lectures* (n 15), 65.
60 *Peart* (n 4) at 102.
61 (1863) 1 M 592.
62 (1859) 21 D 408.
63 (1884) 11 R 921.

Against that background, the purpose of this article is to give examples of rights which, in my view, are *res merae facultatis* and *do* impose an obligation on someone else. There are, to my mind a number of rights which look like servitudes, but are not. In *Servitudes and Rights of Way,*[64] we mention some of these rights and have a question mark against them, largely because at the time of writing in 1998 there were no reported cases settling matters one way or another. The two main rights which I want to address are access to a neighbour's property and fire escape. I will also suggest some further possible examples of *res merae.*

D. Examples of *Res Merae Facultatis* Imposing Obligations

(1) Access to a neighbour's property

I have been unable to find any reported Scottish case where the issue of whether one has a right to access a neighbour's property was decided. That may be because in most instances, neighbours will be accommodating to reasonable requests. That said, in April 2014, *The Times* reported the results of a survey carried out by Yale, the home security company, which revealed that one in three stated that they did not get on with their neighbours, and for one in seven, things were so bad that they had decided to move house.[65] However, for whatever reason, the matter, if litigated in Scotland, has not been reported. There is a plethora of cases, reported and not, about ownership of, or access over tiny strips of ground. (The lengths to which neighbours are prepared to go (as a matter of principle) over such matters brings only joy to a lawyer's heart, provided always that funds for payment are available.)

To start, here is a simple example. During high winds, A's dustbin lid is blown into the neighbour's garden. It would seem strange to say that A does not have the right to enter the garden to recover the bin lid. Should the neighbour seek to prevent recovery, that would be theft, and so I would suggest that there is an obligation on the neighbour either to assist recovery, or least not to obstruct it. In Roman law, a neighbour could be interdicted from refusing to allow A to recover fruits which had

---

64   D J Cusine and R R M Paisley, *Servitudes and Rights of Way* (1998) Ch 3.
65   *The Times*, 2 April 2014, 3.

fallen from A's tree into the neighbour B's property.[66] It also permitted a person to access a neighbour's property to recover trees which had blown down.[67] The access required in such cases is for a limited purpose and a limited period. Removing the football from the remains of the glasshouse is another example.

However, access to a neighbour's property might be required in circumstances where the access might have to be combined with some form of "parking" as the following example shows. Let us assume that in the high winds, the roof of A's garden shed is blown into the neighbour's garden. Whether the roof is intact or not, it is unlikely that A will manage to remove the roof without using, for example, a wheelbarrow or a trailer to transport the roof back to A's premises. Other help may also be needed. In these examples, the neighbour will probably be keen for A to remove the items as quickly as possible.

There must be a large numbers of properties where the boundaries are so close together that it would be highly desirable, or in some instances essential, to get access to the adjoining property to carry out inspection and, more important, repair, or perhaps demolition. For example, there might not be sufficient room on a property to put up scaffolding, or use a cherry-picker which may be essential for inspecting, and if necessary repair, say, the pointing. Another situation where access to a neighbouring property would be needed would be where branches of a tree overhang a neighbouring property, and the owner of the tree wishes to cut the tree back, rather than entrust this to the neighbour.

The right, I suggest, can be exercised not only by A, but also by contractors instructed by A. A might not be able to paint the eaves of his house, or do the pointing. Furthermore, I would suggest that A's contractor would be entitled to leave materials on the neighbour's property pending completion of the work. For example, it would be unreasonable to argue that scaffolding would have to be dismantled and removed each day. By contrast, it might not be unreasonable to argue that a ladder be removed each day.

A "servitude" of scaffolding erection to repair a wall has been recognised in the Civilian authorities.[68] It has long been recognised in mixed legal

---

66 Dig. 43/8.1 pr; Ulpian 71 *Ad Edictum.*
67 Dig. 43, 27.
68 Voet, *Commentaries on the Pandects*, 8, 2, 14 (ed Percival Vane).

systems similar to Scotland, e.g. Sri Lanka.[69] The right is implied where the location cannot be accessed by other means and the repair is necessary. That is broadly the principle in *Moncrieff v Jamieson*[70] which decided that foreseeability is also needed.

The right of "laddergang" would entitle the owner of one property to rest a ladder on the property of another in order to carry out repairs, maintenance, or renewal of parts of the "dominant" subjects. In the title on Conveyancing in the *Stair Memorial Encyclopaedia*,[71] mention is made of a letter in the Workshop section of the *The Journal of the Law Society of Scotland* which mentions this "servitude."[72] It is stated to be common in the Dumfries area to find a provision in the titles of buildings which are divided horizontally to the effect that the owner of one property may rest a ladder on another in order to paint or clean windows. As the author of the title observes, there is no reported case on the point and he also suggests that the true test of whether a right exists would arise in a situation in which there was no provision in the titles of the "servient" tenement and the right required to be established by means other than express grant. Such a right might be constituted as a real condition in the titles of the servient tenement.[73] The only reported case which is close to one involving laddergang is *Finlay & Co Ltd v Bain*[74] where the right claimed became necessary only upon severance of the properties which had originally been in single ownership. Among other things, the defender claimed a right of access over the pursuer's property in order to inspect and repair the back of his property which, as the report discloses, abutted on to that of the pursuer. The properties were too close to allow this to be done without obtaining access to the other property. Sheriff Principal Cameron (later Lord Cameron) refused interdict and was prepared to recognise the existence of a right of access for these limited purposes. It seems to follow that the limited right might entail the need for a ladder to be placed on the "servient" tenement or, in the case of repointing, scaffolding, moveable or

---

69   *VC Cooray v U P Samarasinghe* (1959) 60 NLR 389. I am grateful to Roddy Paisley for this reference.

70   2001 SC (HL) 1.

71   R Rennie, "Conveyancing," in *The Laws of Scotland: Stair Memorial Encyclopaedia*, Reissue (2005) para 515, n 4.

72   (1979) 24 *JLSS* (Workshop) xliv.

73   K G C Reid, "Property," in *The Laws of Scotland: Stair Memorial Encyclopaedia* vol 18 (1993) paras 344 and 375.

74   1949 *SLT* (Sh Ct) 2. See also *Murray or Brydon v Lewis* Unreported, 1957, Edinburgh Sheriff Court (Scottish Record Office ref. A1522/1957, SC 39/17, Box No 1141).

otherwise, might have to be "parked" on the adjoining property. As a matter of principle I would argue that Sheriff Principal Cameron was correct in his opinion, but the principle he laid down would have to be extended in order to make the right to repair the adjoining property effectual.

Other examples would involve subjects such as railway lines where the operator of the track, currently Network Rail, is required by statute to carry out repairs.[75] The obligation to carry out repairs includes an obligation to maintain, in good order, fences alongside railway tracks. Network Rail has a right of way over accommodation/occupation roads provided under the Railways Clauses Consolidation (Scotland) Act 1845, s 60. The Railway Regulation Act 1842, s 14 enables Network Rail to apply to the Department for Transport for permission to go on to land near to the railway to make good after an accident or slip has happened, or to take preventive measures if an accident or slip is anticipated. Access can be taken without the Department's prior consent in cases of necessity.

Another example is a similar obligation imposed on the operators of airports. The Civil Aviation Authority has a right of access at all times to aerodromes.[76] The definition of "aerodrome" includes not only the airport buildings, but the surrounding ground.[77] Prison walls would be in the same category, as would electricity sub-stations, nuclear power plants and the like. In these examples, the same issue arises about an obligation on the neighbour not to impede this right. In each case, if access was impeded, the operator of the railway, aerodrome etc. would be in breach of a statutory obligation.

A right of access to a neighbouring property to effect repairs is recognised in English law,[78] but the matter is now regulated by the Access to Neighbouring Land Act 1972 as amended.[79] Under this Act, the court must be satisfied that the proposed works are "reasonably necessary for the preservation of the whole or any part of the dominant land; and that they cannot be carried out, or would be substantially more difficult to carry out, without entry upon the servient land."[80] That said, the court will not make an order for access if the servient proprietor or any other person "would

---

75   Railways Clauses Consolidation (Scotland) Act 1845, ss 57-69.

76   Air Navigation Order 2005. SI2005/1970, art 145(1)(c).

77   Civil Aviation Act 1982, s 105(1); Transport Act 2000, ss 40 and 84.

78   *Ward v Kirkland* [1967] Ch 194.

79   For details, see C J Gale, *Easements*, 19th edn by J Gaunt (2012) paras 11-60 and 11-84; C Sara, *Boundaries and Easements*, 5th edn (2011) 116-20.

80   1972 Act, s 1(2).

suffer interference with, or disturbance of, his use and enjoyment of the servient land, or that proprietor, or any other person in occupation of the land would suffer hardship." It is not the purpose of this article to examine this Act in detail, but it is obvious that access will be granted under it only in very limited circumstances. It is, however, equally obvious that the need for such access can be broader than that which the 1992 Act permits, which is access for (a) maintenance, repair or renewal of buildings, (b) the clearance, repair or renewal of drains, sewers, pipes or cables, or (c) the treatment, cutting back, felling, removal or replacement of any hedge, tree shrub which is, or is in danger of becoming, damaged, diseased, dangerous, insecurely rooted or dead. There have been very few cases under the Act.[81]

In these examples of repairs, there must be some doubt about whether there is any obligation on the neighbour to do anything more than facilitate the work. It may be that scaffolding can rest on a relatively flat part of the neighbour's ground, but does that prevent the neighbour changing the landscape, with the result that it is more difficult, or even impossible to put scaffolding up? It is one of the features of ownership) that, subject for example to title conditions, planning etc., one can do with one's property as one wishes. The other proprietor might not be pleased, but on what basis could the neighbour be prevented from doing as he or she wishes?

This right to access a neighbouring property cannot, in my view, be a servitude. It is a right to be exercised only when required. It would be somewhat odd to argue that one would need to point or repair one's property at least once in 20 years to prevent the right prescribing.

(2) The right of fire-escape

Assume that I own premises which require a fire-escape, but the boundary of my property is so close to the neighbour's that my fire escape rests thereon. The Fire Regulations require the occupiers of some premises to conduct regular fire alarm tests and "mock" evacuations. Not all occupiers are required to do so and, accordingly, there will be a large number of properties with fire escapes which will be used only when required. Again, it would be absurd to suggest that there would need to be a fire at least every twenty years to stop the right prescribing. The right therefore is *res*

---

81 E.g. *Dean v Walker* (1997) 73 P & CR 366 in which it was argued, unsuccessfully, that because a wall was owned in common, the Act did not apply.

merae facultatis and so it would not prescribe. So far, this is not so different from the other examples of access to neighbouring properties. However! I would suggest that, in this example, there is an obligation on the adjoining proprietor not to interfere with the fire escape, for example by undermining the foundations. Interference would have the consequence of putting the owner of the premises with the fire escape in breach of the Planning and Building Regulations. In the most recent case involving a fire escape,[82] the Court held that a servitude of projection and support existed in Scots Law. It is submitted that these rights are *res merae facultatis* in that it would not be open to the "affected" proprietor to remove the projection, or support, even if the fire-escape had not been used for 20 years.

(3) Other examples

Three other examples will be suggested here. One example is a "servitude" which is used only occasionally. In *Durham v Briggs*,[83] the court held that a servitude to water cattle in time of "great frost or drought" had been established by usage. While it is unlikely in Scotland that either weather condition would not be seen for 20 years, such a right is, without doubt, a servitude, as would be a right of pasturage used, say, only in summer. Nevertheless, the following example may be one where the right is res *merae*, rather than a servitude. Assume that I have the right to draw water from A's well, but also a right to draw from B's well, but only if the supply from A's well is either not available or not adequate. Twenty years might pass, during which time A's well has proved to be fit for purpose. If, however, in year 22, there is a severe drought, my right to draw from B's well, I would submit, cannot have prescribed despite its not having been required up to that point. A right to make up title to a property, I would suggest, is *res merae*. Finally, a right to access a property. In *Bowers v Kennedy*[84] it was argued that the right of access in that case was *res merae*, but the Court did not accept that and held that the access right had prescribed. Nevertheless, it did say that access to a property is an incident of ownership[85] and I would submit that the right is also *res merae*.

---

82 *Compugraphics International Ltd v Nikolic* 2011 SC 744.
83 (1793) Hume 735.
84 2000 SC 555.
85 *Bowers* (n 84) 564 C-D per Lord President Rodger delivering the Opinion of the Court.

E. Conclusions

(i)   A *res merae facultatis* is a property right which does not prescribe.

(ii)   It can be a right in respect of one's own property, or over another property.

(iii)   Like a servitude, it can be constituted expressly or by Act of Parliament, but it cannot be constituted by other methods by which a servitude may be, such as implied grant or acquiescence. In the case of neighbouring properties, it can be created by implication.

(iv)   It is not open to parties to provide that a right is *res merae* (because it is not possible to contract out of ss 6-8 of the 1973 Act),[86] but a right which is described, say, as a servitude, may nevertheless be *res merae*.

(v)   Where the right is in respect of another property, the proprietor of that property is under an obligation not to impede the exercise of that right, in the parlance of servitudes *"patiendo."*

(vi)   While a right which is *res merae* does not prescribe, it can be discharged expressly, or lost in other ways, such as abandonment, or acquiescence, or where another person acquires by positive prescription a right which is inconsistent with the continued existence of the *res merae*.

---

86   1973 Act, s 13.

dominant proprietor to fence off the dominant tenement so that the taking of access into adjacent land from the dominant tenement is impossible. In Scotland such a positive obligation could be imposed by a real burden or possibly by a servitude condition. Such a provision is not unknown in practice[18] but appears to be rare. In one modern English case[19] it was observed that it is acceptable for a dominant proprietor, a farmer, to transport his sheep up an easement of access over the servient tenement onto the dominant tenement so that they might graze on the dominant tenement and, having grazed on that tenement, if the sheep spread out onto the adjacent land outwith the dominant tenement, the servient proprietor could have no objection. Although no time period as regards the sheep grazing on the dominant tenement was judicially specified, one would expect this observation would relate to a situation in which the sheep are allowed to move naturally as they graze. A different situation might arise if the dominant farmer used devices giving encouragement to the sheep to move quickly from the dominant tenement onto the adjacent land such as the storage on the adjacent land of particularly attractive food for the sheep. This sort of nutritional inducement to directed movement of the livestock may well be restricted by the negative restraint imposed by the *Irvine Knitters* rule. Difficult cases may arise if a shop has been built on a composite site comprising and extending beyond the dominant tenement in a servitude of access. It is undecided what sort of devices, presumably employed as part of what is now termed "the overall retail experience," would be regarded as unacceptable inducements to the potential customers to move from the dominant tenement into the remainder of the shop.

B. Minerals Rights

The Scottish case law decided in relation to the *Irvine Knitters* rule invariably relates to the use of the surface of land on both the servient and dominant tenements. However, given Professor Rennie's longstanding interest in

---

18 In *Magistrates of Dunbar v Sawers* (1829) 7 S 672, the magistrates granted a servitude of drainage. There was an express reservation of the magistrates (who were the servient proprietors) as a counter stipulation to the servitude of the right to enter the dominant tenement and put up works to ensure that the dominant proprietor did not use drain for adjacent land. The exact nature of that reservation is unclear. It may have been a real burden or a servitude condition.

19 *Giles v Tarry* [2012] EWCA Civ 837.

minerals rights and areas below the surface of land,[20] a brief comment on that particular matter is required.

Minerals rights are regarded in Scotland as capable of being conveyed as geographic separate tenements (i.e. slices of land) and there is no reason in principle why the *Irvine Knitters* rule should not apply to minerals rights just as it applies to slices of land such as storeys of property above first floor level, airspace above land[21] or land at ground level. Some Scottish cases[22] have been decided in which one of the parties has attempted to apply the *Irvine Knitters* rule so as to limit the other party's activity (usually access) in what the first party believed was his own land. However, this body of Scottish case law relating to minerals has typically dodged the application of the *Irvine Knitters* rule by deciding that the rule did not apply because the area where the activity was carried out was also owned as a property right by the owner of the minerals. Put another way, it was decided that the area in question was not owned by the party objecting to the activity and was not subject only to a servitude in favour of the minerals proprietor. These cases relate to the proper construction of the wording employed in particular grants or reservations of minerals. They in no way suggest that the *Irvine Knitters* rule does not apply to servitudes benefiting minerals held as a property right.

Two early English cases confirm that the analogous English rule does indeed apply to such minerals held as property rights.[23] Both of these cases were considered and distinguished in a Scottish case[24] but only on the basis that the Scottish court was not dealing with a servitude benefiting a

---

20   R Rennie, *Minerals and the Law of Scotland* (2001).

21   In this regard see the terms of the Tenements (Scotland) Act 2004 s 2(7). It is unstated whether this section carries with it a servitude of access to obtain access to the additional triangular area of airspace but, it is submitted, such a servitude is likely to be implied by statutory expansion of the dominant tenement of any servitude benefiting the sector including the roof failing which the taking of access to the triangular area may breach the *Irvine Knitters* rule.

22   See e.g. *Duke of Hamilton v Graham* (1871) 9 M (HL) 98; *W Davidson v Duke of Hamilton and W Walker* (1822) 1 S 411; *Turner (Tait's Trustee) v Ballandene and Husband* (1832) 10 S 415 at 418 per Lord Craigie.

23   *Dand v Kingscote* (1840) 6 M & W 174, 151 ER 370; *Durham and Sunderland Rail Co v Walker* [1842] 2 QB 940.

24   *Hamilton v Graham* (1871) 9 M (HL) 98. The rule in *Irvine Knitters* would also be inapplicable if the access were taken over an area held in common property by the owner of the benefited property: *Gavin v Junor* 2009 SLT (Sh Ct) 158; *MacKay v Gaylor* 2014 SLT (Sh Ct) 131. An issue of construction sometimes arises as to whether a right expressed in loose terms is a servitude of access or a right of common property: *Willemse v French* 2011 SC 576.

property right. It seems clear that the *Irvine Knitters* rule would be applied in a Scottish case to a servitude benefiting minerals held as a property right if the issue ever came up for decision in a pure and unavoidable form. That did occur in the two English cases just noticed. At that time the minerals working and processing appear to have been a relatively simple affair of the minerals being dug out by miners at a particular coal or mineral face in manageable amounts and immediately loaded into bogies. The material was then transported across the dominant tenement and onto the servient tenement. There was no issue of a manufacturing complex or any processing of the minerals within the dominant tenement. This is an issue that will be considered later in this essay.

C. Qualified Nature of the Rule

Absolute though the rule in *Irvine Knitters* appears to be at first blush, further examination shows that this is not so nor is it applied in a wholly inflexible way. Common law jurisdictions such as England, certain Canadian Provinces and some Australian States have attempted to mitigate the rigours of their own native version of the *Irvine Knitters* rule by developing a number of judicially created qualifications to permit extension of an easement of access to benefit additional land in several situations. These are not yet fully worked out in reported Scottish case law but, in principle, they all appear compatible with Scots law. These will be set out below as the first and second exceptions. In addition, there are a couple of exceptions that are better established in "native" Scottish authority. These are set out below as the third and fourth exceptions.

The qualifications permit the servitude to be used to benefit land outwith the dominant tenement where one or more of the following exceptions apply. In very brief summary they are:

(i)   First exception – ancillary use.

(ii)   Second exception – anticipated additional land.

(iii)   Third exception – personal bar.

(iv)   Fourth exception – separate journeys.

These will be examined in turn.

(1) The first exception

This applies where the use of the additional land outside the dominant tenement is ancillary to a permissible use of the dominant tenement.

The main body of case law illustrating this exception relates to English easements of access.[25] This indicates that access will be allowed to and from relatively small areas of land adjacent to the dominant tenement where access to such areas is required for the proper enjoyment of the dominant tenement. A similar notion of a servitude benefiting the dominant tenement being capable of facilitating access to an adjacent area of land where the use of that area is ancillary to the dominant tenement is seen in only one Scottish case.[26] In that Scottish case a stable originally built on the dominant tenement had been redeveloped and a new stable serving the house on the dominant tenement had been built so that it was located on a small plot of land adjacent to the dominant tenement. In a decision that has never properly been reported, the Sheriff took the view:[27]

> I am disposed to think that the subjects benefited in this case was [sic] still the same, the stable being really an adjunct to the dwellinghouse.

This case was appealed to the Court of Session and the Sheriff's interlocutor reversed in part but the judgement is not reported.[28] Albeit the records that remain are unclear, the Court of Session appears to have restricted the dominant proprietor's access to his house only and to have excluded access to the stable.[29] By reference to authority, therefore, one cannot therefore

---

25 The English cases comprise *National Trust v White* [1987] 1 WLR 907; *Macepark (Wittlebury) Ltd v Sargeant* [2003] 1 WLR 2284; *Das v Linden Mews Ltd* [2002] 2 EGLR 76; *Peacock v Custins* [2002] 1 WLR 1815; *Massey v Boulden* [2003] 1 WLR 1792; *Martin Wilkins and Wendy Wilkins v Thomas William Lewis* [2005] EWHC 1710 (Ch).

26 *Blair v Strachan*, 20 Jun 1889, Sheriff Guthrie Smith. See *Aberdeen Weekly Journal*, 25 Jun 1889. There is other material relevant to the case in the *Aberdeen Journal*, 13 Mar 1889 at 7; *Aberdeen Evening Express* 13 Mar 1889 at 3. The property was at 124 Hadden Street, Woodside, Aberdeen.

27 The use of "was" in the quoted text follows from the odd Scottish conveyancing convention that regards "the subjects" as singular.

28 There was further litigation on a matter of obstruction of the same servitude of access reported as *Blair v Strachan* (1894) 21 R 661. For material in the National Archives of Scotland relative to both actions see CS46/1890/6/56 and CS46/1894/6/65.

29 See the note of the terms of the interlocutor in that appeal at (1894) 31 SLR 548 at 549. There is similar authority in Canada excluding the possibility of taking access via an easement of access to a plot adjacent to the dominant tenement even though the use of that plot benefited the dominant tenement: *Gordon v Regan* (1985) 15 DLR (4th) 641 at paras 28-37 per Griffiths J.

argue with any assurance that the "ancillary use" exception has been judicially recognised as part of Scots law.

However, albeit seemingly rejected in this one Scottish case, there still appears to be room for development of the exception in cases with more suitable circumstances. What then might those circumstances be and how can one circumscribe them? Clearly this exception relating to "ancillary use" cannot be used to undermine the entire *Irvine Knitters* rule although it has been applied enthusiastically in some English cases. For example, in one case[30] where an easement of way benefitted a cottage it was held the easement could be used even where the cottage was extended with two rooms on adjacent land not part of the dominant tenement. By contrast, in a case decided only two years later,[31] it was held inadmissible to take access over an easement of way to some 800 acres of farm land outwith the dominant tenement which itself consisted of about 1,200 acres of agricultural land. Albeit some of the decisions are somewhat difficult to reconcile,[32] for this exception to the *Irvine Knitters* rule to operate, it remains the case that there must be some element of the use of the adjoining land being "ancillary" to the use of the dominant tenement. Consequently, a dominant proprietor cannot take access to adjacent land of whatever extent and whatever the slimness of the connection with the proper use of the dominant tenement. Furthermore, the use of the adjacent land must be ancillary to some use of the dominant tenement that was not expressly excluded by the terms of the servitude itself. For example, where a servitude of access is granted to a plot of land expressly on the basis that it may be used as an access to a house but not as an access to a vehicle garage, the owner of the house on the dominant tenement cannot build a garage on the adjacent land and claim to take access to the garage over the servitude route on the basis that the use of the garage is ancillary to the house.

A clear example of ancillary use as an exception to the *Irvine Knitters* rule that is recognised daily in Scotland is a servitude of access over a lane leading to a house on the dominant tenement that is also benefited by a servitude of drain and septic tank over a field in the ownership of a third party. If the owner of the house wishes to repair the drain and septic tank it is manifestly clear that he, together with his contractors and employees,

---

30   *Massey v Boulden* [2002] EWCA Civ 1634, [2003] 2 All ER 87.

31   *Martin Wilkins and Wendy Wilkins v Thomas William Lewis* [2005] EWHC 1710 (Ch).

32   As noted in *Macepark (Wittlebury) Ltd v Sargeant* [2003] 1 WLR 2284 by Gabriel Moss QC, who attempted to provide some guidance as to the meaning of "ancillary."

may take access from the public road, up the servitude lane, across his own property and into the land of the third party located outside the dominant tenement in the access servitude. It does not matter at all that the servitude of drainage and septic tank is first acquired long after the creation of the servitude of access and was not clearly envisaged by the parties to that original servitude of access. So too, can the owner of a dominant tenement use a servitude of way to take access to his property and then proceed to leave his property by another servitude of way leading over an entirely different servient tenement. Both such examples of ancillary use, however, could be regarded as being in excess of the servitude of access if the terms of the grant or reservation of that servitude of access expressly prohibit such use. That, however, would not be a breach of the *Irvine Knitters* rule but a transgression of an express servitude condition restricting the purpose of the servitude.

Another example would be where a person purchases a field with a servitude of access out to the public road along a private lane. The dominant field benefits from rights of lateral support, most likely in the form of servitudes or rights of common interest, owed to it by adjacent land in the ownership of third parties. The dominant proprietor may acquire rights of access to the adjacent land to carry out works to enhance that lateral support. The owner of the dominant tenement, together with his contractors and employees, may use the servitude of access and pass across his own property into the land of the third party to carry out the works to enhance lateral support. Again, this ancillary use could be excluded by express provision in the terms of the servitude of access.

So too, one may consider part of an underground tunnel used for passage based on a servitude of access where the next part of the same tunnel is also used for passage but this time based on a property right held by the person taking passage. The servitude of access over the first part of the tunnel may be regarded as benefiting, *inter alia*, the second part of the tunnel. It may happen that the owner of the second part of the tunnel may require to drive large pins into the roof and walls of that part of the tunnel to stop that roof and those walls falling in. Those pins will penetrate into the surrounding strata which are outside the dominant tenement and are owned by a third party.[33] So too, if the pins are insufficient, may the owner of the second part of the tunnel require to excavate part of the surrounding

---

33 For this a servitude *tigni inmittendi* would be needed.

rock outside the dominant tenement to stop the rock falling into the part of the tunnel comprising the dominant tenement. Additional rights from the third party may require to be obtained. In both of these cases, however, additional rights do not have to be acquired by the owner of the second part of the tunnel from the owner of the first part of the tunnel (the servient tenement) to enter or use the land of the latter. The owner of the second part of the tunnel may use the existing servitude of access over the first part of the tunnel to go into the dominant tenement and then enter the lands of the third party to carry out these works as they are ancillary to, and necessary for, the proper use of the dominant tenement comprising the second part of the tunnel.

A further example may be seen where a servitude of access benefits a dominant tenement consisting of a quarry. If the quarry is dug out of the ground so that it forms an open basin, the quarry walls cannot safely be dug in such a way that would leave a cliff face existing at ninety degrees to the remaining surrounding surface of the land. Instead, for safety sake, the walls of the quarry must be stepped at an angle so that there is a reduced danger of collapse or rockfall. If the stepping takes place entirely within the dominant tenement so that the top of the stepping, which is at the level of the surface of the land, is located inside or on the very boundary line this will inevitably result in a measure of rock within the dominant tenement remaining unexploited. This could be avoided if the dominant proprietor stepped the sides of the quarry by digging out some of the minerals on the neighbouring land owned by a third party leaving the bottom of the stepping on the boundary line between the dominant tenement and the third party land. Of course, the dominant proprietor would require to obtain rights from the third party to encroach in this way into the neighbouring land. However, as regards the servitude of access into the quarry, the stepping of the sides of the quarry may be regarded as ancillary to the originally envisaged and proper use of the dominant tenement to the extent that such digging and stepping is required to extract all of the minerals from the dominant tenement.

In all of the examples indicated above, the additional rights in the land adjacent to the dominant tenement may be obtained by means of a positive servitude benefiting the same dominant tenement served by the servitude of access. On one view, the very form of the additional rights as servitudes could be argued as fitting well with the "ancillary" use exception as a positive servitude, by definition, is ancillary to the relevant dominant tenement. The positive servitude over the adjacent land may exist only if it confers a benefit on the land which is also the dominant tenement in the servitude of access. However, it would be too much to suggest that the servient tenement in any positive servitude benefiting land which is also the dominant tenement in a servitude of access can be accessed by that servitude of access. Consider, for instance, a servitude of access benefiting a farm extending to 100 hectares. If the owner of the farm subsequently obtains a grant of a servitude of pasturage over 10,000 hectares of adjacent hill pasture benefiting the farm, it seems somewhat extravagant to suggest that he may use the existing servitude to take access to the extensive hill pasture. It seems likely that the "ancillary" use exception to the *Irvine Knitters* rule will be more tightly drawn but it is not at all clear upon what basis that will be done. Perhaps recourse could be had to an element of "reasonable foreseeability." That, however, is to speculate far beyond any decided authority.

Lastly, one should notice that other doctrines may assist the law to overcome some of the conceptual limitations and uncertainties of the "ancillary" use exception to the *Irvine Knitters* rule. Where the owner of the servient tenement in a proposed route of passage grants a servitude of access to a 100 hectare farm which is then already benefited by a servitude of pasturage over the adjacent 10,000 hectares of hill grazing, the access in favour of the farm is clearly a positive servitude. The access to the hill grazing cannot be a servitude unless separately granted in favour of the owner of the hill grazing over which the servitude of pasturage is exercised. If constituted in this way the owner of the hill grazing can then communicate the benefit of enjoyment of his servitude of access to the dominant proprietor in the servitude of pasturage as the latter has a lawful right to be on the dominant tenement in that servitude. Such a method of creation, however, requires the co-operation of the owner of the hill grazing and he is entitled to refuse to accept the benefit of a servitude of access. Alternatively, the party owning the servient tenement in the proposed servitude of access to the farm may simultaneously grant two rights. First, a servitude of access to that farm and, secondly, a right of access which, although not a separate servitude in its own right, is a right ancillary to the servitude of pasturage over the hill grazing.[34] There is no requirement, either at the time of grant of the ancillary access right

---

34 The possibility of the implied grant of such ancillary rights was recognised in *Moncrieff v Jamieson* 2008 SC (HL) 1. It is *a fortiori* the case that such rights may be granted expressly.

or at any time thereafter, that the servient tenement in the servitude of pasturage must be owned by the same person who owns the land subject to the right of access ancillary to that servitude of pasturage. So too there is no requirement that the servient tenement in the servitude of pasturage and the land subject to the ancillary right of access be contiguous and not separated by the dominant tenement in the servitude of access. This double grant is useful in two situations. First, where the grant of access is made when the farm is already benefited by the servitude of hill grazing. Second, where the owner of the route in the proposed servitude of access is also the owner of the hill grazing.

(2) The second exception

The second exception exists where, although there is no express provision to that effect,[35] it is clear by reasonably implication from the terms of the deed or the surrounding circumstances that it was always intended by both parties to the servitude that the dominant tenement would be extended to incorporate the additional land or, at least, this possibility was contemplated and left open by both parties to the servitude when the servitude was created.

The authority for this rule is contained in a number of English[36] and Australian cases.[37] For example, if a servitude is expressly created in favour of the front door and entrance hall of a house, it is reasonable to accept that the servitude benefits the entire house as the front door and access hall are merely means of access to the house itself. Another example is where the deed itself defines as the dominant tenement "Plot A" but contemplates access to Plot B even though the definition of the dominant tenement does not expressly extend to it. Involved in this exception are elements of the function of the dominant tenement and the adjacent land. The exception could be regarded as relating to situations in which it is reasonably

---

35 Express provision would expressly bring the additional land within the dominant tenement and thus access to that additional land would comply with the *Irvine Knitters* rule. However, there are difficulties in the drafting and registering of deeds with such express provision: Cusine and Paisley, *Servitudes and Rights of Way* (n 3) paras 2.41-2.43; Title Conditions (Scotland) Act 2003 s 75.

36 See e.g. *Thorpe v Brumfitt* (1872-73) LR 8 Ch App 650; *Callard v Beeney* [1930] 1 KB 353.

37 See e.g. *Shean Pty Ltd v Owners of Corinne Court* [2001] WASCA 311; *Owners Corporation – Strata Plan no 8450 v Owners Corporation – Strata Plan No 54547* [2002] NSWSC 780; *Perpetual Trustee Company Limited v Westfield Management Ltd* [2006] NSWCA 337; *Westfield Management Ltd v Perpetual Trustee Co Ltd* [2007] 233 CLR 528.

foreseeable that the dominant tenement, by design or natural topography, is to perform function ancillary to the adjacent land. It perhaps must perform a role benefiting the adjacent land similar to that performed by the servient tenement in relation to the dominant tenement. This seems to be the case in servitudes of access where the dominant tenement's only function is as a route of access to the adjacent property. If such be the case, when one considers the benefit to the adjacent land, the dominant tenement in the servitude of access operates functionally as part of a servient tenement. If indeed that is so, the elements of this function or design must exist as at the date of the grant or reservation of the servitude of access so that they are reasonably evident to the parties to that juristic act. Years after the grant of a servitude of access the dominant proprietor cannot so design a house so that the sole means of entry is located on Plot A and the remainder of the property on Plot B.

The argument is perhaps easiest to make where the servitude is one of drain or other service media. Consider the case where the servitude is phrased that a property owner is entitled to join a particular drain on his property into the main drain on the servient property and thereafter use it. It seems to be overly strict to argue that the dominant tenement is only the particular drain within the property owner's land. It seems manifestly obvious that it would always have been intended that this particular drain should be connected to a house or other structure on the land to which it provides a benefit and that that house or structure would be comprised within the dominant tenement for the servitude of drainage. Again, it is the function of the drain that strongly suggests the existence of a more extensive dominant tenement.

(3) The third exception

This applies where the owner of the servient tenement personally bars himself as regards objection to an extension of the benefit of the servitude to adjoining land. This is truly not a special exception to the *Irvine Knitters* rule but an application of a general principle. The basis of this line of authority is perhaps to be seen in Roman Dutch and Roman law. The Roman Dutch writer Johannes Voet (1647-1713) illustrates this by reference to a servitude of leading water:[38]

---

38   Voet, *Pandects*, 8 4 13.

Et aquae ductum habens, inde rursus aquam alteri nequit praedio concedere, nisi id nominatim pacto praeter ordinariam servitutum naturam actum sit. Nec ad alium fundum proprium postea forte acquisitum ducere: imo, ne ad aliam quidem eiusdem fundi partem, quam ad quam servitus ab initio acquisita fuit.	And one who has a right of water-leading cannot in turn grant water out of it to another tenement, unless that has been specially arranged by agreement apart from the ordinary nature of servitudes. Nor can he lead to another farm of his own which perhaps he has later acquired. Nay he cannot do so even to another part of the same farm than that for which the servitude was originally acquired.[1]

This, in turn, is derived from the writings of the Roman jurists Pomponius and Africanus collected in the *Digest* of Justinian.[39] They wrote respectively as follows:

Ex meo aquae ductu Labeo scribit cuilibet posse me vicino commodare: Proculus contra, ut ne in meam partem fundi aliam, quam ad quam servitus adquisita sit, uti ea possit. Proculi sententia verior est.	Labeo states that if I have a right to channel water, I can oblige any neighbour I chose with the use of the watercourse. Proculus, on the other hand, holds that I cannot even use it for the benefit of any part of my estate other than that for which the servitude was acquired.
Per plurium praedia aquam ducis quoquo modo imposita servitute: nisi pactum vel stipulatio etiam de hoc subsecuta est, neque eorum cuiuis neque alii vicino poteris haustum ex rivo cedere: pacto enim vel stipulatio intervenientibus et hoc concedi solet, ...	You are channelling water across the estates of a number of owners by virtue of a servitude, however created. You cannot grant the right to draw water from the channel to any of these owners whom you chose or to another neighbouring proprietor, unless a pact or stipulation was added to this effect. Such a right is normally granted by the addition of a pact or stipulation....

---

39 D 8.3.24 (Pomponius) and D 8.3.33 (Africanus).

This reference to a special arrangement in the passage from Voet, quoted above, was considered in the South African Courts as having the potential to permit the recognition of a new servitude in addition to the primary servitude.[40] In the case in hand that was regarded as an additional personal servitude but, on different facts, could potentially be a praedial servitude benefitting the additional land. Scots law has some difficulty in recognising that servitudes are created by personal bar alone.[41] The better analysis appears to be that the doctrine precludes the Erskine, John of Carnock enforcement of the *Irvine Knitters* rule by the person concerned, the present servient proprietor, but that this bar remains personal and would not bind his singular successors. They, of course, could bar themselves by their own acts. This personal bar preventing the servient proprietor's objection to an extension of the use of the servitude to benefit land adjacent to the dominant tenement has been recently applied in the Scottish case.[42] A broadly similar principle is known in England[43] albeit in the most recent case relating to the matter sufficient facts were not proved to apply the doctrine.[44]

To give rise to personal bar the actings of the dominant proprietor must be known to the servient proprietor or at least reasonably ascertainable by him. Similar actings, even if unknown to the servient proprietor, if not hidden could be regarded as being "open" as that term is recognised in the context of the Scottish doctrine of positive prescription and may, in due course of time give rise to a prescriptive servitude in respect of which

---

40   *Van der Merwe v Wiese* 1948 (4) SA 8 (C) at 14 per Fagan J and discussed in R J P Jordan, "Praedial servitudes: the imposition of positive duties upon the servient owner" (1958) 75 SALJ 181 at 186.

41   See Cusine and Paisley, *Servitudes and Rights of Way* (n 3) 377-85, para 11.37-11.46; E C Reid and J Blackie, *Personal Bar* (2006) paras 6.56 and 6.63; *Moncrieff v Jamieson* 2005 1 SC 281 at paras 25-29 per Lord Marnoch and paras 80-86 per Lord Hamilton; *Moncrieff v Jamieson* 2007 SC (HL) 1 at para 46 per Lord Scott of Foscote; *Robson v Chalmers Property Investment Co Ltd* 2008 SLT 1069; *George Jobson Forbes Fyvie v J Ross Morrison and Yvonne Morrison*, Arbroath Sheriff Court, case ref A155/98, decision of Sheriff Principal R A Dunlop QC and decision of the Sheriff on 10 Dec 1999. For more general application see *MacGregor v Balfour* (1899) 2 F 345 per Lord President Balfour at 352; *Munro v Jervey* (1821) 1 S 161; cf *Winans v Lord Tweedmouth* (1888) 15 R 540.

42   *Ben Henderson and Mrs M A (otherwise Rita) Henderson and Michael John Walker and Mrs Gail Mather Walker and Andrew Connor and Linda Connor v William Irvine and Mrs Gillian Irvine*, Alloa Sheriff Court, case ref A314/08 (hearing 20 Apr 2010), note of Sheriff D N Mackie. See K G C Reid and G L Gretton, *Conveyancing 2010* (2011) 13.

43   *Price and another v Nunn* [2013] EWCA Civ 1002.

44   At para 32.

the dominant tenement comprises an area outwith the dominant tenement in the original servitude.[45] The principle in all of this is clear. The servient proprietor, by doing nothing to prevent excessive use of a servitude, could contribute to the eventual creation of a second real right of servitude that entitles the dominant proprietor use the route of the original servitude to benefit an area outwith the dominant tenement in that original servitude.

(4) The fourth exception

This exception may be best illustrated in a servitude of access. It applies where the activity on the additional land does not lead to a direct and single journey from that land across the dominant tenement and down the servitude road but there are actually two journeys interspersed by an intervening legitimate act of "processing," "storage" or something similar.

This exception is truly a way of saying that the basic rule in *Irvine Knitters* is not engaged at all. Put another way, there is no breach of the *Irvine Knitters* rule where someone using the servitude to access the dominant tenement does so in connection with a legitimate and genuine purpose on that dominant tenement before passing through to the additional land and there are substantially two separate journeys. This applies equally in reverse when someone leaves the adjoining land via the dominant tenement and then passes out to the public road over the servient tenement. There is no need in this case to show the use of the adjoining land is "ancillary" to the proper use of the dominant tenement. There is no need to show that the access to adjacent land was envisaged when the servitude was originally constituted. There is no need to show that the servient proprietor is personally barred from objecting. This is an entirely different exception with a different justification. All that needs to be shown is that the journey to/from the adjoining land from/to the dominant tenement is genuinely separate from a genuine journey to/from the dominant tenement over the servitude access. To explain why this is so requires a detailed examination of the general *Irvine Knitters* rule.

---

45 Prescription and Limitation (Scotland) Act 1973 s 3(2); See also the observations in the English case of *Smiths v Muller and Fowlers* [2008] EWCA Civ 1425 at para 10 per Rimer LJ; *CDC2020 Plc v Ferreira* [2005] EWCA Civ 611 per Lloyd LJ at para 21; *Mills v Silver* [1991] Ch 271.

D. The Formulation of the General *Irvine Knitters* Rule with Specific Reference to the Fourth Exception

In the context of a servitude of access it is a convenient shorthand to express the *Irvine Knitters* rule to the effect that a servitude of access is to be used only for the purpose of taking access to the dominant tenement. However, this abbreviation does tend to mislead somewhat. The rule is not that the servitude of access can be used only to take access to the dominant tenement but that the servitude of access may be used only for the legitimate and genuine purposes of the dominant tenement. It is worth confirming that this formulation relating to the purposes of the dominant tenement is indeed the position of both Scots and English law. In one of the leading English cases[46] the various judges emphasised the easement of access could be used for the reasonable and honest use of the dominant tenement, a formulation which can be construed to open the door to consideration of the purposes of the dominant tenement. In *Irvine Knitters* the wording used was even more explicit in this regard in that Lord President Emslie spoke of the link of the servitude to the genuine "purposes of the dominant tenement."[47] This distinction between the servitude linked not to the dominant tenement but the purposes of the dominant tenement is subtle but very important. The distinction may immediately be illustrated by reference to simple examples with the underlying principle then being drawn out.

(1) Examples

A rule which limits the exercise of a servitude of way to the geographic bounds of the dominant tenement is a rule that seeks a red line to be drawn round a dominant tenement and this is to be regarded as the *ne plus ultra* of anyone properly using the servitude. It would preclude anyone using the servitude of access to access the dominant tenement and then moving outside the boundary to conduct a simple operation such as painting the outside face of the fence on the boundaries of the dominant tenement. It would preclude the taking of access into the dominant tenement by means of a servitude of way and leaving the dominant tenement by means of a second servitude of way as the *solum* of the second servitude would be

---

46   *Williams v James* (1867) LR 2 CP 577 at 580-81 per Bovill CJ, at 581-82 per Willes J and at 583 per Montague Smith J.
47   1978 SC 109 at 119.

outside the dominant tenement. It would preclude the receipt of water in a plot of land by means of a contract or lease or other right enabling aqueduct into the dominant tenement and then the transport of that same water in tankers down a servitude road where the dominant tenement in that servitude road comprised the plot of land but not the source of the water. It would prevent a plot of land being used as a distribution centre for goods that need to be carted to other lands operated as part of the same business group. None of these examples fall foul of the Scottish rule that is to the effect that a servitude must be used for the legitimate and genuine purposes of the dominant tenement.

In addition to these examples some further applications have been judicially noticed. If the rule were to the effect that the servitude may be used only to gain access to the dominant tenement (and not for the legitimate and genuine purposes of the dominant tenement) then the dominant proprietor taking access to the dominant tenement via the access servitude would have to retrace his steps if he wished to proceed to anywhere else. He clearly does not have to do so because this is not the rule. In the Canadian case of *Miller v Tipling*, Mulock CJ, sitting in the Ontario Court of Appeal, stated the matter thus:[48]

> The law is well established that a right-of-way appurtenant to a particular close must not be used colourably or for the real purpose of reaching a different close. This does not mean that where the way has been used in accordance with the terms of the grant for the benefit of the land to which it is appurtenant, the party having thus used it must retrace his steps. Having lawfully reached the dominant tenement, he may proceed therefrom to adjoining premises to which the way is not appurtenant; but, if his object is merely to pass over the dominant tenement in order to reach the other premises, that would be an unlawful user of the way...

One consequence of what is observed in this *dictum* is this. Having used the servitude and having reached the dominant tenement the dominant proprietor (and anyone else entitled to use the servitude as his invitee) is not wholly precluded from passing onto adjacent lands even if these adjacent lands are outside the dominant tenement. The point was re-emphasised in another Canadian case in which a passage from Gale on *Easements* was quoted. This is *Gamble v Birch Island Estates Ltd*, decided in the Ontario High Court.[49]

---

48   (1918) 43 DLR 469 at para 31.
49   (1970) 13 DLR (3d) 657 at para 23 per Stark J.

It now remains to consider whether the law will permit the extension of the user of the right of way to additional property acquired by the grantee or its successors in title. This branch of the law appears to be well established. In *Gale on Easements*, 13th ed. (1959), p. 265, one finds this language:

"If a right of way be granted for the enjoyment of close A, the grantee, because he owns or acquires close B, cannot use the way in substance for passing over close A to close B. Romer L.J., *Harris v. Flower & Sons* (1905) 74 L.J.Ch. 127. It need hardly be said that the mere fact that the grantee uses the way to enter close A does not make close B incapable of access from A; the question must always be whether the ostensible use of the way for the purposes of the dominant tenement is genuine or colourable."

This is slightly reworded in later editions as may be illustrated by the nineteenth edition of Gale on *Easements* published in 2012:[50]

"It does not, of course, follow that the mere fact that the grantee uses the way to enter close A makes close B incapable of access from close A. The question must always be whether the ostensible use of the way for the purposes of the dominant tenement is genuine or colourable: "the true point to be considered ... should seem to be, *quo animo* the party went to the close; whether really and *bona fide* to do business there, or merely in his way to some more distant place."

The quotation within this passage from the sixteenth edition of Gale is from the seventeenth-century English case of *Lawton v Ward*.[51] This indicates the longstanding nature of this form of the rule related to the legitimate purposes of the dominant tenement. In Scotland we are not dealing with a variant of or exception to the rule established for the first time in *Irvine Knitters* but with the true nature of the rule itself.

It is clear that a dominant proprietor may not use the servitude of access to the dominant tenement merely for the purpose of taking access to lands outwith the dominant tenement. A number of Australian,[52] English[53]

---

50 Para 9.56. This same passage also appears in earlier editions such as the 16th (1997) at para 9.31.

51 (1697) 1 Ld Raym 75 at 76 note (a); 91 ER 946 at 947.

52 See e.g. *Westfield Management Ltd v Perpetual Trustee Co Ltd* [2007] 233 CLR 528.

53 See e.g. *Skull v Glenister* (1864) 16 CBNS 81; 143 ER 1055; *Finch v Great Western R Co* (1879) 5 Ex D 254; *Harris v Flower & Sons Limited* [1904] WN 106; *Ackroyd v Smith* (1850) 10 CB 164, 138 ER 68.

Canadian[54] and South African[55] cases illustrate this. It is little surprise that Scots law is to similar effect.[56] The rule may now be regarded as well established and is expressed in the phrase – the dominant tenement may not be used as a "bridge." A clear cut case is where the dominant proprietor uses the servitude merely for the purpose of taking access to property outwith the dominant tenement and the servitude is used merely for the "colourable" purpose of taking access to those premises.[57] Such a taking of access to property outwith the dominant tenement without any reference to the use of the dominant tenement itself is not part of the legitimate purposes of the dominant tenement.

(2) "Legitimate and genuine purpose"

What then distinguishes the "legitimate and genuine" purposes of the dominant tenement from a mere "colourable purpose"? This is a simple question with a multifaceted answer. The following discussion may be helpful in making the distinction.

(3) Single journeys

Single unbroken journeys, particularly if repeated, are likely to fall foul of the *Irvine Knitters* rule and be regarded as using the dominant tenement as a "bridge." If the taking of access involves a single, unbroken journey over the servient tenement through the dominant tenement to the land outside the dominant tenement that is likely to be regarded as an improper use of the servitude. This would apply *mutatis mutandis* to egress out to the public road from land outwith the dominant tenement.

---

54 See e.g. *Telfer v Jacobs* (1888) 16 OR 35; *Purdom v Robinson*, [1899] 30 Can SCR 64 at 71 per Sir Henry Strong CJ; *Friedman v Murray* [1953] 3 DLR 313; *Pearsall v Power Supermarkets* [1957] 8 DLR (2d) 270; *Gordon v Regan* (1985) 15 DLR (4th) 641 at paras 28-37 per Griffiths J; *Eastern Contractors v Gamble* (1970) 13 DLR (3d) 657; *Graham v Kucera* 2009 BCSC 1508.

55 See e.g. *Berdur Properties (Pty) Ltd v 76 Commercial Road (Pty) Ltd* 1998 (4) SA 62 (D) examined in R R M Paisley, "The demon drink and the straight and narrow way: the expansion and limitation of praedial servitudes," in H Mostert and M J de Waal (eds), *Essays in Honour of CG van der Merwe* (2011) 193.

56 There is a discussion of the authorities in Cusine and Paisley, *Servitudes and Rights of Way* (n 3), paras 12.64 *et seq.*

57 See, once again, the Canadian case of *Miller v Tipling* (1918) 43 DLR 469 at para 31 per Mulock CJ.

However, this is not an absolute rule because, quite apart from the ancillary uses examples noticed above, it may be possible to construct an argument that there may be instances where a journey to a point outwith the dominant tenement could be regarded as genuinely for the purposes of the dominant tenement itself. For example, if a dominant proprietor is approached by a neighbour who requests a one off permission to use the servitude access and then to cross the dominant tenement to carry out some small task on the neighbouring property, it would appear to be good neighbourliness on the part of the dominant proprietor to allow such a journey. It seems at least arguable that such a good neighbourly act would be within the genuine purpose of the use of the dominant tenement and would not be regarded as using the dominant tenement as a bridge. However, such acts may require to be relatively small and this particular example does appear to stretch the point a little. The better view seems to be that such access may simply constitute a *de minimis* breach which is not truly an exception but is simply not worth litigating. It is most unlikely that this neighbourly behaviour example could be extrapolated to allow a journey for major engineering or building works (even on a one off basis) on the adjacent land or activities such as the widespread planting of trees on, or removal of trees from, the adjacent land if that was not also related to the legitimate and genuine purposes of the dominant tenement. On balance, it seems best to seek to justify single journeys to a point outwith the dominant tenement by reference to the "ancillary use" exception.

(4) Separate journeys

Separate journeys (a) over the servient tenement to the dominant tenement and (b) from the dominant tenement to the adjacent land comply with the *Irvine Knitters* rule in that they do not use the dominant tenement as a "bridge." Where the dominant proprietor takes access over the servitude road into the dominant tenement for legitimate and genuine purposes within the dominant tenement, this, if there were to be nothing else, clearly complies with the rule. If he should then make an entirely separate journey from the dominant tenement into the adjacent land, this will comply with the rule because he is not in any way exercising the servitude in respect of this second journey. So too if he returns to the dominant tenement and then makes a separate journey out through the servient tenement this is not in any way an exercise of the servitude and will not breach the *Irvine v Knitters* rule. The key issue is that the journey to the dominant tenement over the servient tenement and the journey from the dominant tenement to the servient tenement are "separate." It is not enough to preclude the journeys from being separate to show that the second journey into the adjacent lands could be made only after making the first journey. So too it is not enough to preclude the journeys from being regarded as separate to show the dominant proprietor has put himself into the position to make the second journey by making the first.

(5) How to distinguish separate journeys

The separate nature of the journeys (a) across the servient tenement to the dominant tenement ("the first journey") and (b) from the dominant tenement to adjacent land ("the second journey") can be observed from certain circumstances. It is important to note that none of the factors identified below will be determinative in its own right. They will all be assessed together to determine whether the servitude is being exercised for the genuine purposes of the dominant tenement.

(6) A gap in time between journeys

A gap in time between the various journeys assists in showing they are separate and thereby in complying with the *Irvine Knitters* rule. Let us look at an extreme case which illustrates the matter beyond all doubt and then move onto more usual situations. In the extreme case a person who has entered the dominant tenement a year ago may leave that dominant tenement and pass into adjacent land as he pleases. The gap of a year is more than sufficient to show the second journey has no connection with the first. More usual day to day cases involves a lesser period of time but this does not preclude a shorter period being a sufficient gap between the journeys. If a lorry or van leaves the public road, using the servitude of access to cross the servient land and enters a factory on the dominant tenement and stops there for a legitimate reason, that amounts to a genuine self-contained journey to the dominant tenement over the servitude road. If, later in the same day, for some legitimate reason that lorry or van then moves to another part of the factory complex on land adjacent to the dominant tenement that may be regarded as a separate self-contained journey from the dominant tenement to adjacent land and not an abuse of the servitude of access to the dominant tenement because it does not involve any exercise of the servitude. The fact that there is a gap in time between the two journeys assists in demonstrating the separate and legitimate nature of the journeys.

Certainly, it may be that the longer this intervening time gap is, the easier it may be to demonstrate two separate journeys. For example, in one nineteenth century English case, *Williams v James*,[58] the period of time between moving hay from adjacent fields onto the dominant tenement and the transport of the hay down the servient road was rather vaguely stated as the period between summer and September.[59] That might have been as little as a few weeks but also it could have been a month or so. The period was a factor in determining that the dominant proprietor's use of the easement of access to the dominant tenement was consistent with the proper exercise of that right. Another example of a time period of what is probably about a week or a fortnight may be observed in a Scottish case.[60] The exact time period is uncertain but, as will become clear from the *dictum* quoted below, may be calculated with reasonable certainty by reference to the time between repeat municipal bin collections. In the Scottish litigation in question the Lands Tribunal considered an expressly constituted servitude of passage in the following terms:

> ...a right of access over the footpath lying to the side and rear of the adjoining subjects known as number Six Maxwell Crescent, aforesaid which footpath is shown delineated and hatched in black on the plan Declaring that the right of access hereby granted is for the purpose of gaining access to and egress from the rear garden ground pertaining to the subjects disponed and for no other purpose whatsoever...

In their comments the Lands Tribunal observed:[61]

> We do not accept that the use of a wheelie bin is an improper use of the right of access. Use of a garden for storage of a wheelie bin must now be accepted as a reasonable garden use. That the refuse in the wheelie bin may come from the house rather than the garden does not affect the means for access and egress to and from the garden by someone using a wheelie bin.

In the *Irvine Knitters* case itself, a small shop on the original dominant tenement (84-90 High Street) and property on additional adjacent land on either side of the original dominant tenement were demolished and rebuilt

---

58   (1867) LR 2 CP 577.
59   Ibid.
60   *Forrester & Fleetham v Sharp*, 6 Mar 2001, unreported, LTS/LO/2000/45.
61   Page 5 of the written decision.

as a single larger shop on a composite site (78-106 High Street) including the original dominant tenement and the additional land.[62] It was during the construction phase that the servient proprietors first raised objections to construction traffic using the servitude over their land. Presumably the route of access had been a quiet back lane and then, without their agreement, it became an access to a construction site and was traversed by lorries carrying materials and equipment. One wonders if a degree of sensitivity and diplomacy on the part of the dominant proprietors or their contractors might have avoided any problem. However, that was not to be. What then followed was a little surprising, at least at first blush. Instead of litigating the matter on the basis of *inciviliter* use (the first legally implied servitude condition) or by reference to an asserted unwarranted increase in the burden on the servient tenement (the second legally implied servitude condition), the servient proprietors took a different approach. They argued that the proposed access to the new shop would breach the third legally implied servitude condition in that the dominant proprietor sought to take access to land outwith the dominant tenement. This approach had tactical advantages in that it avoided a difficult examination of matters of fact and law regarding the conduct of the dominant proprietors (or their contractors) within the servient tenement and concentrated attention on interpretation of titles where one might anticipate an answer might be more clear-cut particularly where a plan is attached to the title deeds. It also allowed the servient proprietors to seek the remedy of interdict even after the construction traffic had ceased and enabled them to object to the future commercial use of the composite shop. So, the commercial pressure could be maintained on the dominant proprietors even if they were to rush through the construction phase and claim the offending conduct had already ceased.

Consequently, it was not until the development was complete that litigation actually started as regards the proper use of the existing servitude of passage. That servitude was exercisable over a private lane and originally gave access only to the rear of the original shop on the dominant tenement but not to the property on the additional adjacent land on either side. Lord President Emslie and Lord Cameron considered that the dominant proprietor could comply with the rule limiting the exercise of the servitude to original dominant tenement by converting the part of

---

62 *Irvine Knitters Ltd v North Ayrshire Co-operative Society Ltd* 1978 SC 109.

the new shop within the footprint of the old shop into a distribution centre. Lord President Emslie observed:[63]

> ... the access may unquestionably be used for all purposes to which the [dominant proprietors] choose to devote the dominant tenement and it is easy to figure that some rearrangement of the [dominant proprietors'] use of their new building, even if they choose to devote that part of it built on the dominant tenement exclusively to the function of a genuine distribution centre or store in connection with all their retail enterprises, will result in their being able to use the right of access for purposes which can be identified as the purposes of the dominant tenement. That a proprietor may use his dominant subjects for a genuine purpose which serves the interests of his business enterprise, as a whole, carried on in those subjects and elsewhere, cannot be doubted and the case of *Williams v James* is a good example of circumstances in which a proprietor's use of a right of access to one of three fields on which he grew hay all of which he stacked on the dominant field, was held to be unexceptionable.

Lord Cameron set out a similar view, albeit his observations as regards distribution appear to me more limited to distribution not to all other retail outlets but to distribution within the greater retail outlet on the composite site:[64]

> I do not doubt that if the [dominant proprietors] decided to designate and to use the whole of the subjects 84-90 High Street as a store or distribution centre for the whole of their supermarket compound within the range of 78-106 High Street, they could legitimately do so, but equally I am of opinion that if they were to claim a right to import through the access or accesses giving on to 84-90, goods of any kind which immediately were delivered or transported to other parts of 78-106 High Street then they were acting beyond the legal limits of the right of way in favour of the subjects identified as 84-90 High Street. The proof appears to me to yield an inference beyond doubt that this is precisely what the [dominant proprietors] have been doing to a material degree. What the [dominant proprietors] are not entitled, in my opinion, to claim a right to do in virtue of this servitude right, is to use the subjects Nos. 84-90 as a "bridge" over which passengers or goods can pass as of right to the subjects Nos. 78-82. That the [dominant proprietors] might legitimately "ferry" such goods once properly received by this right of access into the subjects Nos. 84-90, used as a storage and distribution centre, by way of the public highway to other subjects in the same ownership is a very separate issue, and one in which other considerations might operate and I expressly reserve my opinion on that matter.

---

63   At 119.
64   At 122.

There probably is an element of time delay suggested in these judicial references to the legitimate use of the dominant tenement as a storage or distribution centre in the context of a single retail unit straddling the dominant tenement and adjoining land. The process of storage or distribution usually takes some time. However, it would be fair to say that one would not expect material to rest in a store for months or even for weeks. It is worth remembering that the entire premises in *Irvine Knitters* were developed as a supermarket. It is reasonable to assume that perishables and fresh food would be delivered. It is equally reasonable to assume that when delivered to a distribution centre within the dominant tenement it would be a legitimate use of the dominant tenement to distribute this sort of material within a very short period of time, certainly within the same day, probably within hours if not minutes of its delivery to the distribution centre.

Albeit Lord Cameron observed that materials could not be "immediately" delivered from the storage centre forming the dominant tenement to other parts of the building outside that tenement, the gap in time to constitute legitimate "storage" or "distribution" may be very short – possibly extending to a few minutes in appropriate commercial cases. One might surmise that the courts might be tempted to allow a party conducting a genuine business on the dominant tenement the opportunity to make a genuine business choice as to how long this period should be. If good commercial practice indicates that the storage period should be a certain period of time, it is to be doubted if the courts will take the view that this is wrong and impose some arbitrary period divorced from commercial reality. For example, it seems unlikely that the Courts would require fresh milk to be stored for days in order to qualify as the legitimate and genuine use of the area to which the milk was delivered as a storage facility. Similarly, where stone is extracted from a quarry face on the land outwith a dominant tenement and conveyed to places within the dominant tenement for processing and storage, it seems unlikely that the courts would require that process to be extended to some arbitrary minimum of time so that it might be regarded as sufficiently stored or processed to form part of the legitimate purposes of the dominant tenement. The important issue is that the material has gone through a genuine commercial process within the dominant tenement. Although foreseeability is not required, this seems all the more acceptable where the process is one which was within the contemplation of the parties when the servitude right of access and egress to and from that dominant tenement was granted.

Indeed, it may be possible with regard to some journeys, that a gap in time is not essential to show that they are separate. A gap in time is just one factor in the identification of a gap between two legitimate journeys. For example, if a postman enters a factory on the dominant tenement via the servitude road and hands in a letter at the factory office, an employee in the office who picks up the same letter may wish to deliver it immediately to the addressee in another part of the factory complex which is located outside the dominant tenement. On the face of it there appear to be two separate legitimate journeys. The first enables access to the dominant tenement via the servient tenement. The second is undertaken as part of the purposes of the dominant tenement.

(7) Different transport for the two journeys

A factor in showing the distinction between the two journeys may be the method of transport. Where different vehicles are used for the two journeys this may assist in showing the journeys are separate and thus in complying with the *Irvine Knitters* rule. This is particularly so where the vehicles carrying out the second journey never enter the servient tenement but are specialised vehicles adapted for the second journey. The access over the servient tenement to the dominant tenement is a general access for all purposes but the access taken to the adjacent land from the dominant tenement is for certain defined, limited purposes. For example, let us consider a dominant tenement operated as a quarry and containing rock crushing machinery, quarry offices and a weighbridge. Assume that the source of the rock is outside the dominant tenement and the dominant tenement is accessed via a single servitude of access from the main public road. If workmen employed at the quarry travel along the public road and up the servitude road and arrive in their own private cars they may park them in a safe area within the quarry (the dominant tenement). Following modern work practices, we may assume, typically, they will then dismount from their vehicles and sign into work in some way and not use their private cars until they leave at the end of the day. That entry into the quarry on the dominant tenement represents a single journey. It is separate and distinct from any journeys they might make within the quarry. Even if these same employees drive quarry trucks, vans or lorries back and forth all day between the dominant tenement and the rock face within the adjoining land, this is arguably not a misuse of the servitude of access. These journeys made during the working day are all separate journeys between the dominant tenement and the adjacent land and the workmen do not use the servitude route at all. These journeys are all legitimate uses of the dominant tenement. Even if the initial journey of the employee in the morning and his last journey at night both require him or her to cross the servient tenement, and even though this initial and last journey is carried out to enable the workmen to carry out their jobs (which necessarily involves repeatedly passing into land adjacent to the dominant tenement), arguably this would not be a misuse of the servitude of access. In addition, the position appears to be no different even if a workman had a role in the quarry that required him to spend most of his working day at the quarry face in the adjacent land. His private car, presumably, is parked at a safe place in the quarry (the dominant tenement).

This applies *mutatis mutandis* to journeys out of the adjacent land and into the dominant tenement. For example, where material is ferried into the dominant tenement from the quarry face on the adjacent land by special vehicles (such as large quarry trucks unsuited or un-licenced for the public road) and deposited in the dominant tenement and, at some later stage, is taken out of the quarry on the dominant tenement over the servitude in different vehicles licenced for public road use, this will be a factor in demonstrating two separate journeys.

An example in a domestic setting could be as follows. A house with attendant garage is built on a dominant tenement benefited by a vehicular servitude of access. A part of the garden to the house, comprising the lawn, is held on a separate title not benefited by the servitude of access. If the owner of the house comes home from work in her car she will park it in the garage. After entering the house to change clothing she may take a mower from the same garage and proceed to the lawn to cut the grass. The second journey to the lawn outside the dominant tenement is made on foot. An additional factor favourable to regarding this journey as separate from the one taken over the servient tenement is the fact that the second journey is not taken every time the first journey is completed. Normally, a person does not mow his or her lawn every evening in the year. In this regard it is possible to argue there is a distinction with the quarry example given above. It may be a factor adverse to showing the journey to the quarry face is indeed separate journey if the workmen invariably make the second journey every time they complete the first journey.

(8) Nature of the activity between the journeys

The *dicta* quoted above from the *Irvine Knitters* case contemplated involved storage and distribution on the dominant tenement. It is important to note that this is not a closed list of the activities that may be taken into account in determining if there are two separate journeys. These two activities identified in *Irvine Knitters* are largely "passive" in their nature, albeit distribution infers the activity of sorting and taking away. If such passive activities are sufficient to distinguish one journey from another, it seems likely that a more "active" manufacturing process between journeys would lead to a stronger case.

At the lower end of the spectrum of "active" behaviour one could cite the instance of employees reporting for work at a site hut on the dominant tenement and then passing to a point of work on the adjacent land outwith the dominant tenement whether that land is owned or leased by the employer. The fact that signs are placed on the dominant tenement which expressly require such reporting of employees and members of the public could be argued to indicate, in a modest way, the policy of complying with a two separate journey requirement. Further across the spectrum one may refer to a process of manufacture of some sort on the dominant tenement which is a much more active "activity." For example, where a source of sand or particular clay in an adjacent field facilitates a cement making business on a dominant tenement, the servitude of egress from that dominant tenement may be used to ferry out the finished product of cement even though it contains sand that had its origins in the land outwith the dominant tenement. This seems to hold good whether the sand is dug out of the adjacent land by vehicular diggers driven by men or by some sort or automated machine with conveyor belts. A multitude of other variants, of even more intense activity and duration, can be imagined.

(9) No artificial expedients to mark a distinction

It is clear that the Courts will be alert to artificial expedients intended to exaggerate a distinction between the two journeys. Such artificial expedients will be discounted entirely. This approach is clear from the highly significant nineteenth century English case of *Williams v James*[65] *which was relied on in Irvine Knitters*. This English case involved the owner of the *solum* of the route of an easement of access seeking a declaration for

---

65   (1867) LR 2 CP 577.

trespass to land. The easement benefited a field known as the Nine acre field. The owner of that field also owned two adjoining fields known as Parrott's land. Those two fields had no easement over the plaintiff's land. In the summer of 1866 the tenant of all three fields mowed all three fields and stacked the hay on the Nine acre field. In September the tenant sold the hay to the defendant who extracted it via the route of the easement. The jury found that the stacking of the hay was done "honestly."[66] All the judges opining considered this significant. Bovill, C.J. indicated that there must be a *bona fide* and not a mere colourable use of the right of way.[67] The stacking of the hay was in the ordinary and reasonable uses of the dominant tenement and therefore complied with this. So too was carriage of the hay out within the "ordinary and reasonable" uses of the servitude itself. Similar sentiments were expressed by Montague Smith J[68] and Willes J. The latter of these judges expressed himself as follows:[69]

> The finding of the jury was, that the land was used honestly, and not in order to get a right of way further on. This is equivalent to finding that the stacking of hay on the Nine acre field was in the reasonable and ordinary use of it as a field; and also that the carting was from the Nine acre field and not from Parrott's land.

There was no issue of using the ground as a distribution centre to commercial retail centres in this English case although, it seems reasonable to surmise that the hay would be used on other farms or perhaps even sold at market.

In the passage of his opinion in *Irvine Knitters* quoted earlier, Lord Cameron expressly reserved his view as to whether goods could be taken over the servient tenement by means of the servitude into the part of the new shop located on the dominant tenement, then immediately out onto the public road and then directly into the remainder of the shop outside the dominant tenement. If this indeed were to be possible it would amount to a neat trick in the particular location of the shop to enable circumvention of the *Irvine Knitters* rule. The very same device came up for consideration in a more recent English case involving an agricultural operation.[70] A farmer owned two separate but adjacent fields only the first of which was benefited by an easement of access. The first field also benefited from a gate leading directly out to the public highway. The easement could not be used by the

---

66 At 577.
67 At 580.
68 At 582-83.
69 At 582.
70 *Giles v Tarry* [2012] EWCA Civ 837.

famer to bring his sheep directly to the second field. So, to circumvent this limitation, he led them over the easement of access into the first field and out onto the public road. Following a brief pause on the public road, he led them back into the dominant tenement and across into the adjacent land. In the Court of Appeal it was held this was an artificial device or expedient and the farmer, in substance and intention, was using the easement to access property outwith the dominant tenement.[71] From this it is clear that in applying the *Irvine Knitters* rule that the law will give no regard to commercially pointless and self cancelling manoeuvres intended to give an impression that there are two separate journeys.

(10) Servitude conditions in the servitude excluding the activity

In some situations the servient proprietor may be able to preclude the activity which the dominant proprietor wishes to carry out on the dominant tenement to justify the distinction between the first and second journeys. For example, if a servitude of access is granted with the express servitude condition that the servitude will not be used to facilitate storage or a distribution centre on the dominant tenement, the servient proprietor will be entitled to seek interdict of any traffic purporting to use the servitude where that traffic is bringing material into the dominant tenement for storage or distribution even to adjacent property owned by the dominant proprietor. An example of this occurred in a recent English case.[72] In that case the storage of agricultural materials on the dominant tenement where those materials had been grown outside the dominant tenement was held to be in breach of the title conditions (imposing a servitude condition) requiring it to be used for the business of running an agricultural and forestry estate.[73] Consequently, it was not permissible to seek to use the easement to facilitate such storage.

E. Conclusion

In all of the above it is important to recognise that the potential existence of various exceptions does not empty the *Irvine Knitters* rule against use of the dominant tenement as a bridge of all substance. There remain

---

71   At paras 10-23 per Norris J.

72   *Wilkins and Wilkins v Lewis* [2005] EWHC 1710 (Ch).

73   See *Wilkins* at paras 31 and 37 et seq, especially at 50.

cases, chiefly involving a building or a business in a building straddling the dominant tenement and adjacent land, where it does operate – indeed this is illustrated by the actual decision in *Irvine Knitters*.[74] However, the various exceptions outlined above are yet to be fully judicially explored and developed. If this is done the rigid use of the rule to cause injustice will be avoided and Scottish property law will operate better for both the dominant and servient proprietors.

---

74 See also the South African case of *Berdur Properties (Pty) Ltd v 76 Commercial Road (Pty) Ltd* 1998 (4) SA 62 (D).

12. Enforcing Repairing Obligations by Specific Implement

Professor Angus McAllister

A. Repairing Obligations

Repairing obligations in leases may either be owed by the landlord to the tenant or vice versa, depending upon which of them has responsibility for the repair in question. Which party owes the obligation is likely to vary according to the type of lease. At common law, all landlords of urban leases have an obligation to provide subjects in a tenantable or habitable condition, and to maintain them in a like condition throughout the let.[1] However, most commercial leases are granted on a full repairing and insuring (FRI) basis, contracting out of the common law and making repairs the responsibility of the tenant.

The opposite is true in the case of residential leases: it is not normally possible to contract out of the landlord's common law obligation because it has been strengthened and considerably reinforced by statute.[2] In all residential tenancies, the landlord has a duty to provide a house that is

---

1   J Rankine, *A Treatise on the Law of Leases in Scotland*, 3rd edn (1916) 241; for other references, including the institutional writers, see A McAllister *Scottish Law of Leases*, 4th edn (2013) paras 3.12 and 3.40.

2   There may be a partial exception to this in the case of private sector residential tenancies under s 18 of the Housing (Scotland) Act 2006, which allows limited contracting out of statutory repairing obligations.

   http://dx.doi.org/10.11647/OBP.0056.12

wind and watertight and in all other respects reasonably fit for human habitation at the commencement of the tenancy and to keep it that way throughout its currency.[3] The slight discrepancy in wording between the common law and statutory wording is probably due to the fact that the latter is taken from the equivalent English provision; however, it has been held that there is no significant difference between the common law and the statutory formulations.[4]

The repairing obligations of private sector residential landlords (collectively known as "the repairing standard") extend much further and are spelled out in greater detail, beyond the basic habitability requirement, which mirrors the common law obligation and applies to social tenancies.[5]

In agricultural leases, both the landlord and the tenant have repairing obligations, e.g. their respective obligations regarding the maintenance of fixed equipment.[6]

B. Enforcement by Specific Implement

In principle, it ought to be possible for either party to enforce a repairing obligation by specific implement, by means of a decree *ad factum praestandum*, compelling the other party to fulfil the broken obligation. Specific implement is a primary breach of contract remedy in Scotland.[7] There are a number of situations where it cannot be used (e.g. for the payment of money), but where it is competent it is a right which the court has the discretion to refuse only in exceptional circumstances; these include situations where it would be impossible to enforce, or where its imposition would cause exceptional hardship to the recipient. Damages would then be the appropriate alternative remedy. In such cases the onus is on the defender to aver and prove that it would be inequitable for implement to be granted.[8]

---

3   Housing (Scotland) Act 2006 ss 13(1)(a) and 14(1) (private sector tenancies); Housing (Scotland) Act 2001, Sch 4, para 1 (social tenancies).
4   *Galloway v Glasgow City Council* 2001 HousLR 59; *Todd v Clapperton* [2009] CSOH 112, 2009 *SLT* 837.
5   Housing (Scotland) Act 2006 s 13(1)(b)-(f).
6   Agricultural Holdings (Scotland) Act 1991, s 5; Agricultural Holdings (Scotland) Act 2003 s 16.
7   For a general discussion of specific implement, see WW McBryde *The Law of Contract in Scotland*, 3rd edn (2007) para 23-01 to 23-37.
8   *Salaried Staff London Loan Co Ltd v Swears & Wells Ltd* 1985 SC 189; 1985 *SLT* 326.

in which both remedies are likely to be denied, and those where they may be granted tend to be similar. A notable exception is keep-open obligations, where the landlords' remedy is still confined to damages, a position confirmed by the House of Lords in *Co-operative Insurance Society Ltd v Argyll Stores (Holdings) Ltd.*[19] Interestingly, however, the court made a distinction between court orders requiring a defendant to carry on an activity, such as running a business, and orders which require him to achieve a result, such as the enforcement by specific performance of building contracts and repairing obligations.[20]

The English action is therefore supposedly more restricted in scope than the Scottish one, but can, nevertheless, encompass the enforcement of repairing obligations. Admittedly, English house tenants are given statutory assistance by section 17 of the Landlord and Tenant Act 1985 which specifically facilitates the use of specific performance to enforce repairing obligations against residential landlords. There is no statutory equivalent of this in Scotland. Nevertheless, given the wider scope of the Scottish remedy indicated in the keep-open cases, it would seem strange if it could not be successfully used to enforce repairing obligations.

F. Keep-open Decrees

If we look at the actual wording of the decrees granted in keep-open cases, we find a degree of generality and even vagueness that would never have been contemplated under the old law. In *Retail Parks Investments* the Royal Bank was ordered *inter alia* "to use and occupy the premises as bank offices" and to keep them open for business during "all normal business hours." In *Co-operative Wholesale Society Ltd v Saxone Ltd*[21] the defenders were ordered "to keep the subjects open as a high class shop" for the sale of "footwear, hosiery, and handbags of all descriptions." In Lord Hamilton's view the expression "high class shop" was "a familiar commercial expression readily capable of objective assessment."[22] In *Highland and Universal Ltd v Safeway Properties Ltd (No 2)*[23] the expressions "high class retail store" and "normal

---

19 [1998] AC 1; [1997] 2WLR 898.
20 1998 AC 1 at 13 per Lord Hoffmann. For a general discussion regarding the competence of specific performance to enforce repairing obligations in England, see *Rainbow Estates Ltd v Tokenhold Ltd and Another* [1999] Ch 64.
21 1997 *SLT* 1052; 1997 SCLR 835.
22 1997 *SLT* 1052 at 1055.
23 2000 SC 297; 2000 *SLT* 414

hours of business" were again held, for the purposes of a decree *ad factum praestandum*, to be sufficiently precise phrases with an easily ascertainable meaning. And in *Oak Mall Greenock Ltd v McDonald's Restaurants Ltd*[24] decree was granted ordaining McDonald's to keep the restaurant in question open as "a quick service restaurant for the consumption of food and non-alcoholic drink both on and off the Leased Premises." In applying the guidelines laid down in *Retail Parks*, Lord Drummond Young observed:[25]

> In framing an order for specific implement of a lease or other contract, commercial realities must be taken into account. In particular, it must be presumed that, when they agreed on the terms of their contract, the parties considered the expressions used by them to be sufficiently precise to let them know what had to be done. Consequently, if the order for implement essentially repeats the provisions of the contract, it is inherently likely that the parties will know what [it] means and what must be done to comply with its terms.

Unmoved by the hardship that would be experienced by the McDonald's organisation by having to keep open a restaurant that had been trading at a loss for almost four years, his lordship decided that this was not an exceptional case where the court should exercise its discretion to refuse specific implement.

As already noted in relation to Lord McCluskey's comments in *Retail Parks*, Lord Drummond Young's observation could equally apply to the repairing obligations owed by many social and private landlords.

G. *Pik Facilitites v Shell UK*

In *Pik Facilities Ltd v Shell UK Ltd and Another*[26] a specific implement action to enforce a commercial tenant's repairing obligation failed because the lease had ended. However, the case did not fail because of lack of specification or precision. Lord Kingarth concluded, though without any great enthusiasm, that the pursuers' pleadings were adequate in this respect. This case is significant as it is an isolated example following in the wake of the keep open decisions in which an action of specific implement almost succeeded.

---

24 2003 GWD 17-540.
25 Ibid at para 6.
26 2005 SCLR 958.

H. Third Party References

Rule 29(2) of the Ordinary Cause Rules for the Sheriff Court provides as follows:[27]

> 29.2 – Remit to person of skill.
>
> (1) The sheriff may, on a motion by any party or on a joint motion, remit to any person of skill, or other person, to report on any matter of fact.
>
> (2) Where a remit under paragraph (1) is made by joint motion or of consent of all parties, the report of such person shall be final and conclusive with respect to the subject-matter of the remit.

The remit of technical detail to a person of skill has a long history at common law, and has been used in the past in order to determine the detailed measures required to fulfil repairing obligations in leases. In *Barclay v Neilson*[28] the Inner House, finding that the landlord of a farm was obliged to carry out such repairs and make such additions as were necessary to enable the tenant properly to cultivate the farm according to the terms and conditions of the lease, ordered:

> Of consent remit to Mr John Dickson, Saughton Mains, to visit the said farm, and report to the Court what additions and repairs are necessary for that purpose...

In the words of the Lord President:[29]

> I do not think that this is a case for a proof at large, and I take the liberty of suggesting that, if neither of the parties have anything to say against it, the proper course will be to have the amount of additions and repairs which are necessary to enable the tenant to cultivate the farm in a proper manner settled by a remit to a man of skill.

This procedure would therefore appear to have the potential to help get round some of the problems of specification involved in framing an action *ad factum praestandum*. However, two difficulties immediately arise, both inherent in what was said above.

---

27 Act of Sederunt (Sheriff Court Ordinary Cause Rules) 1993, SI 1956. For a discussion of this procedure see T Welsh (ed), *Macphail's Sheriff Court Practice*, 3rd edn (2006) para 13.27-13.34.

28 (1878) 5 R 909; see also *Brock v Buchanan* (1851) 13 D 1069.

29 (1878) 5 R 909 at 911 per the Lord President.

(1) Rule 29(1) makes it absolutely clear that such a remit can only be made on matters of fact, and not on questions of law. This principle is also long established at common law. In *Quin v Gardner & Sons Ltd*[30] it was held that a remit requiring construction of the contract in question was incompetent because it involved a question of law. In the context of repairing obligations in leases, in was held in *McFarlane v Crawford*,[31] applying *Quin*, that a crave framed in the following terms was incompetent:

> to remit to a person of skill (a) to inspect the premises at 19 Duncan Street; (b) to report to the Court the present condition thereof, and whether the premises are wind and water tight and in good repair and in a proper tenantable and habitable state; and (c) if not, what repairs are necessary to make the premises thoroughly wind and water tight, and otherwise put them into good repair and a proper tenantable and habitable condition...

In the words of Sheriff Welsh:[32]

> [T]he lease being silent as to the obligation of the defenders for the upkeep of the premises, the reporter would require to inform himself what the common law implied in such circumstances; that is to say, he would require to apply his mind to a question of law at the outset of his investigations. Having informed himself upon this matter, he would then require to find out the state of the facts. He would next require to apply his mind to the construction of the defenders' legal obligation for upkeep, and consider whether that obligation applied to each or all of the matters of fact which he so found. In short, the Court is asked to remit a mixed question of law and fact, which is, in my opinion, incompetent. The question of the nature and extent of the defenders' obligation for upkeep is a question of law for the consideration of the Court.

Presumably the same objection would apply whatever the source of the repairing obligation, whether it involved interpretation of the common law, or the construction of a statutory or lease provision.

(2) Under Rule 29(2) a remit is not conclusive unless it is made jointly by both parties or with the consent of both. The wording would appear to exclude a remit by the sheriff *ex proprio motu*.[33] If made by only one party, therefore, the other could object (presumably a likely occurrence) and the expert's findings would not be conclusive. The matter would have to go

---

30   (1888) 15 R 776.
31   1919 35 Sh Ct Rep 78; see also *Maclagan v Marchbank* (1911) 2 *SLT* 184; (1911) 27 Sh Ct Rep 282.
32   *McFarlane v Crawford* 1919 35 Sh Ct Rep 78 at 79 per Sheriff Welsh.
33   Welsh, *Macphail* (n 28) para 13.29.

It is submitted that a landlord receiving such an order, coupled with the committee's detailed account of their decision, will be left in no doubt about what is required of him or her in order to avoid incurring a penalty. At any rate, any landlord or tenant aggrieved by the decision of a private rented housing committee may appeal to the Sheriff by summary application within 21 days of being notified of the decision.[54] If any such appeals have raised substantive legal issues, none of them have made it into the casebooks.

It is difficult to escape the conclusion that RSEOs, in sharp contrast with their common law counterparts, have been remarkably successful in the enforcement of repairing obligations.

K. Conclusions

Specific implement, as a remedy to enforce repairing obligations in leases, has long fallen into disuse because of its long history of failure, mainly due to problems of specification and the fear of the unfair imposition of penal consequences. For a number of reasons that have been set out above, it is submitted that the remedy is worth reconsidering and has the potential to be a much more useful tool for both landlords and tenants when enforcing repairing obligations. In particular:

(i)   The greater flexibility enabled by the keep-open decisions has addressed many of the fears regarding specification and possible penal consequences. It is worth pointing out that part of the perceived problem with keep-open decrees was not only that they related to a large number of actions, but also that these actions extended over a lengthy period of time. Repairing obligations present only the first and not the second of these difficulties. As Lord Hoffmann pointed out in *Co-operative Insurance Society Ltd v Argyll Stores (Holdings) Ltd*[55] (in relation to the supposedly more restricted English remedy of specific performance) a distinction can be made between court orders requiring a defendant to carry on an activity, and those designed to achieve a result. And one of the examples which he gave of the latter was the enforcement of repairing obligations by specific performance.[56]

(ii)   The possibility of delegating technical details to a person of skill could go some way to addressing any remaining problems of specification,

---

54   Housing (Scotland) Act 2006 ss 64(4).
55   1998] AC 1; [1997] 2WLR 898.
56   1998 AC 1 at 13 per Lord Hoffmann.

provided that care is taken to confine any such remit to questions of fact. Even if the objection of one of the parties prevents the expert's decision being final, the court could nevertheless be given considerable assistance in wording a suitable decree.

(iii)   Repairing standard enforcement orders have proved to be a formidable tool by means of which private sector residential tenants can compel their landlords to carry out necessary repairs. They have operated in a similar way to specific implement, without apparently throwing up any substantial legal difficulties. The decisions of the private rented housing committees (which include legal expertise) have been thoroughly documented and their experience could provide valuable guidance for the courts in framing decrees *ad factum praestandum.* There seems no reason in theory why social tenants and commercial landlords should remain the poor relations.

The greatest potential for the revival of specific implement is probably in the case of residential tenants in the social sector, who do not of course have recourse to the Private Rented Housing Panel. Problems of disrepair in residential property have a long history in social as well has private housing, one of the most notorious examples being the severe dampness frequently experienced in sub-standard council housing.[57] For the tenant of such a property, who possibly has limited opportunities to move elsewhere, damages alone may not be an adequate remedy, and the ability to compel the landlord to carry out repairs could be invaluable.

We noted above the remarks of Lord McCluskey in *Retail Parks* that the defenders were a large commercial organisation that freely undertook their obligation with legal advice, and that they had already occupied the subjects for the purpose stated in the lease for nearly 20 years without any apparent difficulty or misunderstanding. A similar comment could be made about social landlords, particularly local authorities and housing associations. As well as being large organisations who freely undertook their obligations with legal advice, one would expect them normally to have extensive experience and expertise in executing repairs. And the meaning of "wind and water tight and in all other respects reasonably fit for human habitation" (and its common law equivalent) has been thoroughly explored in legal precedent, mainly because the statutory formulation is identical to its English counterpart, and has been so for more than 100 years.[58]

---

57   Problems thoroughly examined in P D Brown and A McIntosh *Dampness and the Law* (1987).

58   See for example the leading English case of *Summers v Salford Corporation* [1943] AC 283, [1943] 1 All ER 68.

It is also worth pointing out that the model tenancy agreement for Scottish secure tenancies recommended by the Scottish Executive[59] elaborates substantially upon the basic habitability obligation prescribed by statute, including many of the obligations spelled out in the repairing standard introduced for the private sector by the Housing (Scotland) Act 2006, and also setting out in detail the landlord's repairing obligations in relation to dampness, condensation and mould. In cases where a social landlord has adopted this model, therefore, the enforcement rights of tenants have been even more strengthened.

Specific implement has perhaps less potential in the case of commercial leases. As noted above, the standard commercial lease is the tenant's FRI (full repairing and insuring) lease, by which the landlord's common law repairing obligation has been passed on to the tenant. It is also standard for commercial leases to provide that, in the event of the tenant failing to carry out repairs, the landlord may step in and carry them out at the tenant's expense. This right also provides the legal justification for the landlord presenting an outgoing tenant with a bill for dilapidations. In these circumstances, specific implement may not be the most effective and convenient remedy. However, there may still be cases where the possibility of specific implement may be useful, for example in cases where commercial landlords may be short of the funds to carry out the repairs themselves.

In any case, any further development of the common law can only enhance the enforcement potential of repairing obligations in all types of lease. We have seen above how the development of specific implement deriving from the keep-open issues in commercial leases can be applied to assist with the enforcement of repairing obligations in residential leases. There is no reason why this type of cross-fertilisation could not work in the opposite direction, with the result that new precedents in the residential sector could establish principles applicable in other areas of lease law. Landlords and tenants of commercial and agricultural leases could therefore also benefit in the longer term.

As we saw above, specific implement is a primary remedy for breach of contract in Scotland, there is a presumption in favour of it being available, and the onus is upon the defender in any case to show why it should be denied. It is hoped that the above discussion may help to make that onus more difficult to overcome.

---

59 Scottish Executive "Model Scottish Secure Tenancy Agreement" (revised version July 2002), available at www.scotland.gov.uk/publications.

13. Two Questions in the Law of Leases

Lord Gill

A. Introduction

In his years as a practitioner and as holder of the Chair of Conveyancing at Glasgow University, Professor Robert Rennie has served his profession and his *alma mater* with distinction. His contribution to the development of our property law is fittingly recognised by the publication of this *Festschrift*. It is a privilege to contribute this essay in honour of my good and esteemed friend.

In this essay I consider the meaning and effect of the decision of the House of Lords in *Clydesdale Bank plc v Davidson*.[1] That decision raised two fundamental questions; namely, the nature of the rights of *pro indiviso* proprietors of heritable property and the nature of the tenant's right in a contract of lease. I put forward the following propositions, namely (1) that in modern Scots law, on entry or, in the case of a long lease, on registration, the tenant in every contract of lease has a right *in rem* in respect of the subjects of let; (2) that on the question of the validity of the lease in that case, the *Clydesdale Bank* case was correctly decided; (3) that the decision of the Scottish Land Court in *Serup v McCormack*,[2] being a logical extension of that decision, was correctly decided; and (4) that the *obiter dicta* of the judges in the *Clydesdale Bank* case to the effect that the invalid lease was a valid contract for occupation and management of the land were unsound.

---

1   1998 SC (HL) 51 ("the *Clydesdale Bank* case").
2   2012 SLCR 189.

    http://dx.doi.org/10.11647/OBP.0056.13

B. The Nature of the Rights of a *Pro Indiviso* Proprietor

In *Magistrates of Banff v Ruthin Castle Ltd*[3] Lord Justice Clerk Cooper, as he then was, eruditely expounded the distinction in Scots law between joint ownership, being the class of right typified by the ownership of co-trustees, and ownership in common, being the right typified by the ownership of two or more persons in whom the right to a single subject has come to be vested, each being entitled by his separate act to dispose of his separate share. I am concerned in this article with owners in common in the sense in which Lord Justice Clerk Cooper used that expression.[4] There are three defining characteristics of the relationship that governs such owners.

(1) Unanimity

Since *pro indiviso* proprietors hold the property in common, there is deemed to be unititular possession among them, each having an equal share or such proportionate share as they may agree upon.[5] The universal rule of common ownership is that there must be unanimity in decision-making affecting the subjects. This principle is based on the Roman law.[6] Bell recognised that that was the law,[7] but he advocated a principle of majority-based decision making.[8] That idea failed to find favour in the courts. In the *Clydesdale Bank* case Lord Clyde described it as "somewhat delphic" and as being "unilluminated by authority."[9] But in the context of this essay that is a side issue, since Bell insisted that there had to be unanimity in the granting of leases.[10] That has been the consistent view of the courts. It is now beyond question that a single *pro indiviso* proprietor cannot grant a lease that would be binding on singular successors.[11] Each individual proprietor has an effective veto, unless by contract he renounces it, on any proposed act of management with which he disagrees.

---

3 1944 SC 36.
4 *Magistrates of Banff* (n 3) at p 68.
5 Cf K G C Reid, "Property," in *The Laws of Scotland: Stair Memorial Encyclopaedia* vol 18 (1993) paras 22-34.
6 J Inst 3.27.3; C 10.35.2.
7 Bell, *Principles* §1072.
8 Ibid §1077.
9 *Clydesdale Bank* (n 1) at 61.
10 Bell, *Principles* §1075.
11 *Campbell and Stewart v Campbell* Fac Coll 24 January 1809; *Morrison, Petr* (1857) 20 D 276; cf *Bell's Exrs v Inland Revenue* 1986 SC 252.

(2) Use

Each proprietor is entitled to make use of every inch of the property. Therefore, no single *pro indiviso* proprietor may take exclusive possession of any part of the property unless the others consent.[12] If the land is let, each proprietor is entitled to a share of the rents.[13] No individual proprietor may obtain an excessive benefit at the expense of the other proprietors without prior agreement.[14] If he does so, he must account to them for the ordinary profits accruing to him from the period of his possession.

Nevertheless, the proprietors may validly agree *inter se* that the subjects will be possessed by one or more of their number. It is then a matter for agreement on what terms the occupying proprietor will occupy the subjects.[15] In such a contract, it is open to the proprietors to agree that in return for having sole and exclusive possession, the occupying proprietor will make a compensatory payment to the others.[16]

(3) Division and sale

In a relationship of the kind considered in the *Clydesdale Bank* case each of the *pro indiviso* proprietors can rely on the rule *nemo in communione invitus detineri potest*, a rule said by Lord Jauncey to be justified by considerations of public policy. The dissatisfied proprietor has no right to evict a co-proprietor from the subjects. His only remedy is the drastic remedy of the action of division and sale, which is derived from the Roman *actio de communi dividundo*. The right of each proprietor to enforce this remedy is absolute.[17] In an action of division and sale the court may order that the subjects should be divided up rateably or, if that is impracticable, that they should be sold and the proceeds divided.[18]

---

12   *Bailey v Scott* (1860) 22 D 1105, Lord Benholme at 1109.
13   Erskine, *Principles* 3.3.56; Bell, *Principles* §1072.
14   *George Watson's Hospital Governors v Cormack* (1883) 11 R 320.
15   *Price v Watson* 1951 SC 359.
16   *Price* (n 15), Lord Keith at 366.
17   *Brock v Hamilton* (1857) 19 D 701 at 703; *Banff Magistrates v Ruthin Castle Ltd* 1944 SC 36, Lord Justice-Clerk Cooper at 68.
18   *Brock* (n 17) Lord Rutherford at 702-03.

C. The Decision in *Clydesdale Bank Plc v Davidson*

In the *Clydesdale Bank* case the central question for the House of Lords was whether *pro indiviso* proprietors could grant a valid lease to one of their number.

The appellant was one of three *pro indiviso* proprietors of a tract of agricultural land. All three entered into a contract that purported to be a lease by which the other two let the land to the appellant. A month later, all three granted a standard security in favour of the Bank over part of the property. Some years later, they granted a further standard security over the rest of the property. The standard securities were granted in consideration of loans to the appellant only. When the appellant defaulted, the Bank enforced the securities and raised an action of removing against him. The appellant defended the action on the plea that he had a protected agricultural tenancy.

A straightforward resolution of the case was set out by Lord Jauncey to the following effect. At the date of the purported lease the appellant enjoyed a real right in the subjects entitling him to possess them jointly with the other *pro indiviso* proprietors. The contract concluded on that date neither superseded nor altered that real right. It conferred on the appellant a personal right to enforce the obligation by his co-proprietors to refrain from exercising their rights to joint possession in return for the compensatory payments. When the contract ceased to have effect, the appellant's right to possession *qua* proprietor would continue unchanged but his co-proprietors would no longer be disabled from jointly exercising their possessory rights. The contract was not a lease.[19]

Lord Clyde and Lord Hope concurred in holding that on general principles of contract a body of *pro indiviso* proprietors cannot grant a valid lease to one of their number. In doing so they adopted the reasoning of Lord Justice Clerk Ross in the court below, which was based on the view that a party cannot be both creditor and debtor in the same obligation, and that the purported lease could not validly confer on the appellant the subordinate right *in rem* of tenancy in respect of land over which he enjoyed the pre-eminent right of ownership.

---

19   *Clydesdale Bank* (n 1) at 54.

tenant the right *in rem* of tenancy, since he already had a right *in rem* as a proprietor, the contract was nonetheless a valid contract the effect of which was to confer on the appellant a personal lease, and in consequence the protection of the agricultural holdings legislation. The success of the alternative theory depends on there being favourable answers to both questions.

F. The Nature of the Tenant's Right in the Contract of Lease

(1) The common law

The common law adopted the general principle of the Roman law that the right of the lessee in the contract *locatio conductio* was prestable against the lessor, but not against a subsequent owner. The *locus classicus* in Stair is as follows:[29]

> A tack of itself is no more than a personal contract of location, whereby land, or any other thing having profit or fruit, is set to the tacksman for enjoying the fruit or profit thereof, for a hire, which is called the tack-duty; which therefore did only oblige the setter and his heirs, to make it effectual to the tacksman, but did not introduce any real right, affecting the thing set, and carried therewith to singular successors; but so soon as the thing set ceased to be the setter's, the tack could only defend the tenant till the next term of removing.

At common law, therefore, the lessee had only a right of action against the lessor and his representatives to be maintained in possession for the duration of the lease. Since feudal law did not allow a right in land to be effectual against singular successors of the proprietor without sasine, the tenant had no protection against them and could be removed from the tenancy with ease.

In that state of the law, conveyancers attempted to secure the tenant's vulnerable position in relation to a singular successor of the landlord by drawing on the analogy of sasine and conferring on the tenant a simulated form of infeftment for the purpose of creating a real right. This procedure is described with derision by Paton and Cameron as a "specious form of

---

29   Stair, *Inst* 2.9.1-2; 1.15.4. The first edition is to similar effect cf Stair, *Inst* (1st ed) 1.29.1-2.

charter and sasine."[30] It was not, and could not be, a true infeftment since the tenant's right was that of temporary occupation only.[31]

(2) The emergence of the right in rem

The Leases Act 1449

The Leases Act 1449 was passed with the specific purpose of correcting the weakness in the law that left the agricultural tenant defenceless to removal by a singular successor of the landlord.

The Act, in the Glendook version quoted by Rankine,[32] provided as follows:[33]

> It is ordained for the safetie and favour of the puir people that labouris the ground, that they, and all utheris that hes taken or sall take landes in time to cum fra lordes, and hes termes and zeires thereof, that suppose the lordes sell or annaly that land or landes, the takers sall remaine with their tackes, unto the ischew of their termes, quhais handes that ever thay landes cum to for siklike maill as they tooke them for.

Although the Act was introduced at the instance of James II to remedy the injustice of the eviction of labourer tenants at the will of the landlord, its scope was not limited to the "puir people that labouris the ground." It extended to "all utheris."

---

30   G C H Paton and J G S Cameron, *The Law of Landlord and Tenant in Scotland* (1967) 3.

31   "Of old, it was usual to sanction the right of the tenant by infeftment, and by that means he held under the real right of infeftment what is now held by mere acquisition of the subject" (*Hamilton v Hamilton* (1845) 8 D 308, Lord Jeffrey at 312).

32   *A Treatise on the Law of Leases in Scotland*, 3rd edn (1916) 132.

33   Leases Act 1449. In *Mountain's Trs v Mountain* 2013 SC 202, the First Division preferred the text given in the Records of the Parliaments of Scotland to 1707, namely
"Item it is ordanit and statute that for the saueritie and favour of the pure pupil that laubouris the grunde that thai and al uthiris that has takyn or sal tak landis in tym to cum fra lordis and has termes and yeris tharof, that suppose the lordis sel or analy thai landis, that the takaris sall remain with thare takis one to the ische of thare termez quhais handis at evir thai landis cum to for sic lik male as thai tuk thaim of befor."
A modern version of the text is as follows:
"For the security and benefit of those who work upon the land, it is decreed that they and anyone else who have rented or who shall rent lands from landlords for a fixed term shall remain entitled under their leases until the ish [termination date] thereof, nowithstanding that their landlord has sold or alienated the land, and irrespective of the identity of the transferee of the land, for the same amount of rent as was initially agreed." (Hugo and Simpson, "Lease" in Zimmermann, Visser and Reid (eds), *Mixed Legal Systems in Comparative Perspective: Property and Obligations in Scotland and South Africa* (2005) 307.

In the *Ius Feudale,* Craig interprets the 1449 Act as having conferred on the tenant a real right:[34]

> Again, a covenant sometimes appears in a tack whereby the lessor undertakes that he will not remove the tenant from his holding. Such a covenant is however personal to the lessor who enters into it; and although the original grantor of the tack (being owner of the subject at the time he granted it) is bound by his obligation not to remove the tenant, the covenant loses its force on a change of ownership and cannot be enforced against a singular successor. As has been seen, the opposite rule applies to a tack covenanted to endure for a fixed term of years, for such a tack confers a real right on the tenant and affects the subject itself, especially when (as I have explained) possession has followed upon it.

Stair,[35] Erskine[36] and Bell[37] are to the same effect. Bankton is to similar effect;[38] but Kames adheres to the view that a tack is a mere personal right that was not made real by the 1449 Act.[39]

Mackenzie describes the effect of the Act in the following way:[40]

> Tacks which before this Act were only personal rights are by this Act made real rights ... Possession is the same thing to tacks that sasines are to alienations: and of old some tacks had sasines or instruments of possession: but neither was necessary nor is now usual. And the reason why they used sasines then, being to make the tack real, and to defend against singular successors; this was no more used after the Act of Parliament by which possession makes a tack a real right.

In consequence of the 1449 Act the practice of taking sasine on a lease fell into disuse in the 15th century. Mackenzie's confident interpretation of the Act goes to the heart of the matter.

The nineteenth century controversy

The words of Sir George Mackenzie are a useful preface to the controversy that preoccupied the Court of Session as to the effect of the 1449 Act on the nature of the tenant's right. In the early nineteenth century the nature of

---

34 *Ius Feudale,* 2.10.9 (trans Lord Clyde (1934)).
35 Stair, *Inst* (1st edn), 2.9.4 and 7.
36 Erskine, *Inst* 2.6.25.
37 Bell, *Principles* §1177.
38 Bankton, *Institute,* 2.9 (1752).
39 H H Kames, *Elucidations respecting the Common and Statute Law of Scotland* (1777) 8-9.
40 G Mackenzie, *The Works of that Eminent and Learned Lawyer, Sir George Mackenzie of Rosehaugh* (1716) vol 1, 188-89.

the tenant's right became the subject of judicial controversy in the context of commercial leases.[41] The controversy was precipitated by the attempt by conveyancers to secure a debt over the debtor's tenancy by having the debtor assign the tenancy to the creditor and by the creditor's granting a sub-tenancy to the debtor. If the debtor's tenancy conferred only a right *in personam* under such an arrangement, the assignation would effectively transfer the lease to the creditor upon intimation of it to the landlord; whereas if the tenancy conferred a right *in rem*, the creditor's right to the tenancy would be perfected only upon his taking possession.

At that stage, the preponderant view of the writers was that the 1449 Act conferred a real right of tenancy.[42] In a lecture prepared for delivery in 1821-1822 Baron Hume described the far-reaching effects of the statute. Having expounded the principle that the lease, in its native and proper character, is a matter of personal contract, he describes the lease as a sort of estate or real interest in the tenant. This, he says, is a new and foreign character bestowed by the 1449 Act and is the oldest ordinance to that purpose in the law of any country of Europe.[43]

Inglis v Paul

Inglis v Paul[44] brought the controversy into the open. In that case a sub-tenant assigned his sub-tenancy to a bank in security of a cash-credit. Two days later, the assignation was intimated to the principal tenant, but not to the sub-sub-tenant who occupied part of the subjects. The bank did not enter into possession. About two years later, the sub-tenant was sequestrated. The bank thereupon intimated the assignation to the tenants of the property and required that they should pay the rents to the bank. Thereafter the trustee was elected and was granted decree of adjudication. The resulting competition between the assignee of the sub-lease, who had failed to take possession of the subjects, and the sub-tenant's trustee in sequestration was considered by the whole court.

---

41 The principal cases on the point and the origins of the Registration of Leases (Scotland) Act 1857 were usefully reviewed by W Guy, "Registration of Leases" (1908-1909) 20 *Juridical Review* 234, 239.

42 J Balfour, *Practicks* (1754) 200; Craig, *Jus feudale* 2.10.2-10; Stair, *Inst* 2.9.2; Mackenzie, *Institutions* 2.6.5 and *Observations* 37; Erskine, *Inst* 2.6.23; Bankton, *Institute* 2.9.1; W Ross, *Lectures on the practice of law in Scotland* (1792) vol 2, 476; Bell, *Commentaries* 1.65.

43 G Campbell H Paton (ed), *Baron David Hume's Lectures 1786-1822: Volume IV* (1952) 73.

44 (1829) 7 S 469.

The view of Lord Justice Clerk Boyle and seven other judges on the point was as follows:[45]

> The rule of law is, that rights are completed by delivery. In feudal subjects, this is accomplished by sasine or symbolical delivery; and in subjects which do not admit of sasine, by giving natural or civil possession. Tacks, in one respect, are personal; and in another, real rights. In a question between the landlord and the tenant or his assignees, they are personal rights; therefore, in a competition between two *bona fide* and onerous assignees, the landlord is bound to prefer him who first intimates his assignation (which is the way of completing a personal right) and to put him in possession accordingly. But, in a question with the singular successors of the landlord and the tenant or his assignee, a tack is a real right by force of the statute of 1449; and therefore it is incomplete, unless possession, natural or civil, has been attained.

Lord Balgray agreed that the bank's case failed for want of possession. He accepted that until possession followed on the assignation of the lease, the title of the assignee was not secure; but he rejected the idea that the assignation was not perfected by intimation to the landlord, but only by possession. Assignation of the lease, although quite complete as to title, might be defeated and disappointed by allowing the cedent to remain in possession. The assignee thereby exposed his right to danger and risk. But in the view of Lord Balgray, the question was not what was necessary to complete the assignee's right to the tenancy. The decision depended on different principles. This was his view:[46]

> It was constantly to be kept in mind, that a lease by the law of Scotland was nothing but a personal right. It was a *bona fide* contract for the use of land or other subject, as laid down by the civil law. It was very true that the Scotch act 1449 bestowed, from public utility, a peculiar privilege on those who held leases of heritable subjects, that they should be protected in the possession of their subjects against all persons till the contract expired, if they were in the actual possession. This was an exception from the general rule, and a privilege bestowed; but it altered not the nature of the right. To say that a lease is a real right, is a most egregious mistake in point of law. No doubt it is effectual against singular successors, and it descends to heirs; but this arises from other extrinsic and adventitious circumstances, totally distinct from the true legal nature of the right. Being a personal right, a lease naturally becomes the subject of assignation; and that assignation is perfected by intimation to the landlord or author from whom it flows,

---

45 *Inglis* (n 44) at 473.
46 Ibid at 474.

or acknowledgment by them, provided always he has originally bestowed the right of conveyance. Abstractly, therefore, the assignation of a lease is perfected, and must be perfected, by intimation to the landlord. It requires intimation to no other human being. So much is this the case, that suppose a number of intimations were made to a landlord, and it is required of him to give possession, he is bound to deliver it to the first intimated assignation. No authority can be pointed out in the law of Scotland to the contrary.

In this view Lord Balgray was supported by his First Division colleagues Lord Craigie and Lord Gillies, who expressly dissented from the majority view that the assignee acquired right to the tenancy of the subjects only by taking possession.[47]

Brock v Cabbell

A year later the point came up again in *Brock v Cabbell*[48] and was considered by a court of 15 judges including all 12 of the judges who had taken part in *Inglis v Paul*. The point arose in similar circumstances. The tenant granted an assignation of the tenancy in security to a bank. The assignation was intimated to the landlord. The bank thereupon sub-let the subjects to the former tenant who remained in possession and paid the rents. The bank at no time thereafter entered into possession. The competition was between the bank and the trustee in bankruptcy of the former tenant. In that context, the lease controversy inevitably returned.

The Lord President and five judges, four of whom had been in the majority in *Inglis v Paul*, gave the majority opinion. It begins in uncompromising terms:[49]

It is a general rule in the law of Scotland, that possession, natural or civil, is necessary to complete the transference of a real right. A tack is a real right, by force of the statute 1449, in a question been assignees and adjudgers from the tenant; and to that case, therefore, the general rule applies. This is vouched by the concurrent authority of every institutional writer, and by an uninterrupted series of decisions for more than two centuries.

Lord Fullerton concluded that the lease became:[50]

... in virtue of the statute 1449 a real right, a character uniformly assigned to it by our institutional writers and confirmed by a series of decisions which it is impossible now to disturb.

---

47   *Inglis* (n 44) at 474.
48   (1830) 8 S 647.
49   *Brock* (n 48) at 652.
50   Ibid at 661.

The conclusion of the majority was that since the bank had never taken possession of the land after the assignation, the assignation/sub-tenancy arrangement was "a collusive device to create a latent security over a real right, without change of possession."[51]

Lord Gillies again allied himself with Lord Balgray, concurring in the result advocated by the majority but challenging the general propositions that I have quoted. Their position was succinctly expressed as follows:[52]

> We consider a lease to be a right of an anomalous nature. Its creation and its transmission are to be regulated as if it were, what it truly is, a personal right. We, therefore, cannot affirm that it is the law of Scotland that an assignation of a lease duly intimated is *per se* an imperfect right, unless followed by natural or civil possession.

The usually taciturn Lord Craigie delivered an erudite opinion, lengthy by the standards of the day, that has not attracted academic attention. In it the true point of division clearly emerges. The opinion gives us an insight into the mind of a conveyancer who, even four centuries after the 1449 Act, was still influenced by the spirit of the Roman law.

Lord Craigie's opening statement makes his position clear. He quotes the 1449 Act and immediately concludes from the wording of it as follows:[53]

> Thus it appears, 1. That, by the common law, the landlord or proprietor of lands could not effectually grant a lease to endure beyond the period of his right. 2. That the extension of the right of the tenant by positive statute, and in express deviation from the common law, is confined to the case of buyers or singular successors in the property of the lands.

He then makes the claim that that is how in practice the 1449 Act has been understood. He cites three cases in which the tenant's right does not prevail against third parties who acquire the landlord's interest; namely where the land falls into the hands of the superior by virtue of a feudal casualty; or in the case of a lease granted by a wadsetter when the right of reversion has been exercised; and in the case where the right of the lessor has been set aside. In all of these cases, he says, the current leases flowing from the landlord are of no effect for ensuring possession to the lessee.

At this point, Lord Craigie has to face the fact that nearly all of the writers take a different view. This is his untroubled response:[54]

---

51   *Brock* (n 48) at 653.
52   Ibid.
53   Ibid at 654.
54   Ibid.

> It is the more necessary to attend to this, because in many of the books of authority there are expressions from which it has been inferred, that, by the statute, leases had become real rights, and that they could not in any case be effectual to third parties, unless followed with natural and actual possession. The very opposite proposition, as it humbly appears to me, is the true one.

Lord Craigie then emphasises that, properly speaking, a lessee of lands has no right to the lands. He has only a right of possession. Therefore his possession must be governed by the properly attested agreements between those who have an interest in it.[55]

As matters stood after 1830, the clear division of opinion on the controversy had been resolved in favour of the strong majority view that the right of the lessee was a real right. In that respect, the court was at one with the writers. After *Brock v Cabbell* the real right theory was not to be challenged for nearly forty years.

By 1838, the Third Report of the Law Commissioners in Scotland, of whom George Joseph Bell was one, expressed the view that the law respecting the effect of the 1449 Act on the rights of singular successors in the land was well settled by the statute and by a long series of decisions making the possession of the tenant serve the purpose of sasine on the lease, to the effect of conferring a real right independently of any record.[56] The Law Commissioners recommended[57] that it should be possible for a tenant to create a security over his lease by an assignation that would be recorded in a public register, the register being a form of publication that would make the creditor's security effectual.[58] In due course the Registration of Leases (Scotland) Act 1857 provided that the registration of a long lease, would make the tenant's right valid against singular successors of the landlord,[59] the act of registration having the same effect as entry into possession had been held to have in the case law;[60] and that on being recorded the

---

55   We can leave the opinion at this point because his Lordship then turns to questions of assignation.
56   Third Report of the Commissioners, *Conveyancing* 13 January 1838 (HMSO: London) xl. The report also states in more general terms not limited to agricultural leases, that "in order to the constitution of a real right in land, or other heritable subject, whether absolute, conditional, irredeemable, or in security, the law requires symbolic delivery of possession, or sasine, as it was termed, of which the only evidence is an instrument prepared and authenticated by a notary-public."(ibid, xxiii)
57   Commissioners, *Conveyancing* (n 56), 52.
58   Ibid.
59   1857 Act, s 2.
60   Ibid, s 16.

assignation of the lease in security constituted a "real security" over the lease.[61]

In 1845 the real right issue arose obliquely in *Hamilton v Hamilton*[62] in relation to an agricultural lease that did not contain a conventional irritancy. The question was whether the landlord could nevertheless irritate the lease for the tenant's failure to implement certain obligations *ad factum praestandum*. In finding against the landlord on that point, two of the majority judges, Lord Mackenzie and Lord Jeffrey, expressly relied on the consideration that the tenant had acquired a real right by entering into possession of the land. They held that such a right could be terminated by irritancy only where the irritancy was expressly warranted by a statutory or a conventional provision.

In 1867 in *Campbell v McKinnon*[63] Lord Kinloch in the Outer House took the view that a lease conferred only a personal right. The Inner House overturned his judgment. In the leading opinion Lord Curriehill described the principle that possession under a lease conferred real rights on the tenant as "trite law."[64] The judgment of the Inner House was affirmed by the House of Lords,[65] where Lord Westbury said that the effect of the 1449 Act was that upon entry to the land the lessee's right became real.[66]

Only a year later, the question arose again in *Edmond v Reid*.[67] In that case an agricultural tenant was bound by a residence clause. She indicated her intention not to reside on the farm. There was no irritancy clause in the lease. The landlord concluded for declarator of the existence of the tenant's obligation to reside and, if the tenant should fail to reside, for decree that she had forfeited all right to possession of the farm.

The action was defended on the ground *inter alia* that the landlord was not entitled to a declarator of forfeiture since there was no irritancy clause to support it. In pursuing that defence, counsel relied on *Hamilton v Hamilton*[68] for the submission that "a lease was a real right. Non-residence did not create an irritancy, and there was no conventional irritancy."[69] On being pressed by the court to make her intentions clear, the tenant lodged a

---

61 1857 Act, s 4.
62 (1845) 8 D 308.
63 1867 5 M 636 at 644.
64 *Campbell* (n 63) at 649.
65 *sub nom Campbell v McLean* (1870) 8 M (HL) 40.
66 *Campbell* (n 63) at 46.
67 (1871) 9 M 782.
68 *Hamilton* (n 30).
69 *Edmond* (n 66) at 783

minute that was construed as a judicial declaration that she would not fulfil the residence condition.

In the leading opinion, Lord Justice Clerk Moncreiff took the line that the landlord was not seeking declarator of irritancy at all, because the conclusions were "entirely for the future" and related solely to the effect of a subsequent refusal by the tenant to fulfil the conditions of the lease. He then turned to the real right issue. He said that he did not question the "doctrine" in *Hamilton v Hamilton*[70] that a lease conferred a real right on the tenant; but in his view the lease was nevertheless a mutual contract and was subject to the principle that no-one could take the benefit of the lease and at the same time repudiate its conditions. He followed the decision in *Drummond*[71] where the court had held that although a residence clause was not fenced with a power of irritancy, the contract would necessarily come to an end if the tenant should put it out of his power to fulfil the conditions of the lease. On that point, the Lord Justice Clerk relied on *Hamilton v Hamilton* in holding that the tenant's declared inability or unwillingness to fulfil the lease constituted a renunciation.

The other three judges concurred in the result; but the submission for the tenant, and the Lord Justice Clerk's support for the decision in *Hamilton v Hamilton*, provoked Lord Cowan and Lord Neaves. While both were content to decide the case on the basis of the tenant's declared intention not to observe the residence clause, neither was prepared to accede to the real right theory. Lord Cowan put the matter as follows:[72]

> The argument of the defender was founded on a fallacy. He said a lease was a real right, and to be assimilated to a feu-right. That is not its nature. A contract of lease is a mutual contract, and although, under the statute 1449, with some of the privileges of a real right, it does not substantially differ from a mutual contract.

Lord Neaves' view was as follows:[73]

> The defenders' counsel was in error when he argued that a lease was the same in character as a feu-contract. It is no doubt an heritable contract, on account of its being for a tract of future time. That is a totally different matter from its being a real right.

---

70   *Hamilton* (n 31).
71   1806, Mor app Tack, No 6.
72   *Edmond* (n 67) at 785.
73   Ibid.

The Act of 1449 was for the benefit of the poor people who laboured the ground. It prevented the vendees of the lessor from turning out the lessee. It declares the right followed by possession to have that effect, but that is not making it, properly speaking, a real right.

These *dicta* are the starting point for the alternative theory.

A decade later, in his *Lectures on Conveyancing*,[74] Montgomerie Bell concluded that leases at an early period were raised to the position of real rights, conferring a title of possession preferable to that of purchasers and creditors whose rights were subsequent to the date when possession was taken under the lease.[75]

(3) Twentieth century developments

The state of the law on the nature of the tenant's right in the early twentieth century is summarised in Rankine's conclusion that leases, originally and in their nature merely personal contracts, were in certain cases converted into real rights by the 1449 Act "as liberally construed by the Court."[76] That can fairly be said to be the starting point for the modern expositions of the law on the nature of the tenant's right.

The question arose again in 1949 in *Millar v McRobbie*.[77] In December 1947 the then proprietors of an arable farm granted the defender a 14-year lease with entry at Whitsunday 1948. The lease conditions provided for the customary sequence of handover arrangements by which the incoming tenant would have access to parts of the land from 1 March 1948 for the purpose of sowing and by which, in due course, the tenant would have access after his waygoing to reap his final crop. Thereafter the landlords sold the farm to the pursuer with entry at 29 February 1948. The defender duly took access to the land under green crop between late March and early May and during that period prepared and sowed the ground. The pursuer then had the defender interdicted from entering on the land on the plea that the lease was not binding on him as a singular successor of the landlords, the defender not having taken entry to the land in terms of the lease.

---

74 M Bell, *Lectures on Conveyancing*, 3rd edn, vol 2 (1882).
75 Bell, *Lectures* (n 74) 1197.
76 Rankine, *Leases*, 3rd edn (n 32) 132. This is the authoritative edition published in February 1916.
77 1949 SC 1.

In the appeal of the defender to the Inner House, counsel for the defender did not argue that his right *in personam* against the former proprietor was good against the singular successor. Instead, he argued that he had been in possession of part of the land from March onwards and that that limited possession was sufficient to confer on him the protection of the 1449 Act. The First Division refused the appeal by distinguishing between the possession that would have followed from entry at the specified date and the anticipatory or deferred occupation of certain parts of the land by which the agricultural cycle was maintained.[78]

The significance of this case is that it established that the theory that the tenant has a right *in rem*, and that the right is made effective by the taking of possession, was firmly part of the law of Scotland. That is clear in Lord President Cooper's opening statement:[79]

> It has been well settled for centuries that possession under a lease is the equivalent of sasine in relation to feudal property. Without possession the tenant is merely the personal creditor of the lessor. By entering into possession the lessee publishes to the world in general, and to singular successors in particular, the fact of his lease, and since the practice of taking sasine on a tack fell into disuse in the 15th century, no substitute has been recognised by our law for possession except registration of long leases under the Act of 1857.

In view of the classic statement of Lord Kinloch in *Wight v Earl of Hopetoun*[80] which was affirmed by the House of Lords,[81] that a lease of that kind ran from Whitsunday to Whitsunday, notwithstanding handover arrangements, the decision in *Millar v McRobbie* was inevitable. It is significant however that neither the arguments of counsel nor the opinions of the judges make any reference at all to the nineteenth century controversy.

The decision in the *Clydesdale Bank* case further affirmed that the tenant's entry into possession conferred the real right.[82]

---

78 Lord President Cooper at 6-8.
79 *Millar* (n 77) at 6.
80 (1863) 1 M 1074 at 1099.
81 *Wight v Earl of Hopetoun* (1864) 2 M (HL) 35.
82 In the most recent consideration of the 1449 Act and of s 85(1) of the 1991 Act, the First Division took that proposition for granted (*Mountain's Trs* v *Mountain* 2013 SC 202, Lord President Gill at para [10]).

G. Conclusions

(1) The personal right theory

Two influences underlay the minority view in this extended controversy. First, the Roman law in which a lease of land, as part of the wider contract of hire, conferred on the lessee only a right *in personam* against the lessor; and second, the strict feudal theory on which sasine endowed the proprietor with rights of ownership that were valid against all comers.

The essence of the argument for those judges who held to the personal right theory was simple. The tenant under the Roman contract *locatio conductio* had a right *in personam*, against the lessor only, to be maintained in possession. The purpose of the 1449 Act was to protect the tenant against removal by the landlord's singular successor. On that view, there was an interpretation of the 1449 Act that dealt with the perceived mischief in a perfectly intelligible way without the need to confect a right *in rem*; namely that the Act protected the tenant's right *in personam* by making it prestable against the singular successor. In this way the 1449 Act secured the tenant's position against the singular successor,[83] with minimal change to the existing law, while remaining true to its civilian roots.

To those who held the minority view, the analogy between the taking of sasine under a disposition and the taking of possession under a lease was at best an imperfect one. To them, the taking of possession was only the palest shadow of sasine. The idea that the mere taking of possession could confer a right *in rem* was heresy.

This line of argument came naturally to judges who were steeped in the principles of the Roman law and of feudal conveyancing. To them the taking of sasine was a significant juristic act by which the fullest rights of ownership were conferred and publicly acknowledged. The private act of taking possession under a private contract that endowed the lessee with, at most, subordinate and temporary rights in the subjects could not meaningfully be equiparated with sasine.

But this view failed to win the day. The liberal construction to which Rankine referred was favoured by most of the writers from earliest times and has had a secure place in the case law for the last two hundred

---

83   As Lord Neaves explicitly held (cf *Wilson v Mann* (1876) 3 R 527 at 532).

years. The *obiter dicta* of two judges in *Edmond v Reid* are the last judicial statements to have been made in support of the personal right theory. It is perhaps a criticism of the alternative theory that in wresting these *dicta* from that single case, Bury and Bain have failed to place their theory in its full historical context.

Over time, the 1449 Act has come to be accepted as (1) conferring a right *in rem* on the tenant in a contract that meets the requirements of a valid lease; and (2) applying to leases of subjects of all kinds.[84] Although the 1449 Act specifically refers to "lands," the courts have interpreted it as applying also to residential dwellings, minerals, quarries, ferries, harbours and salmon fishings.[85]

In their critique of the *Clydesdale Bank* case, Bury and Bain suggest that because the contract between the *pro indiviso* proprietors was held not to be a true lease, nevertheless because it regulated the terms upon which the defender would occupy and farm the subjects, it qualified as a personal lease and fell within the definition of "lease" in section 85(1) of the Agricultural Holdings (Scotland) Act 1991.

Even on the assumption that the contract in the *Clydesdale Bank* case was a valid contract between the *pro indiviso* proprietors for occupation and maintenance of the farm, there is, I think, a flaw in this line of argument. If I am right in my interpretation of the twentieth century authorities, it is beyond any reasonable challenge, in my view, that in the modern law of Scotland a contract of lease that meets the essential requirements that were agreed and re-stated in *Gray v Edinburgh University*[86] confers a right *in rem* on the tenant. On the other hand, if the contract fails to meet those requirements, it is not a lease at all.

The argument for the survival of the common law form of personal lease suggests that such a lease may attract the protection of various statutory regimes and, in particular, when it is a lease of agricultural land will be a "lease" within the definition of that term in section 85(1) of the Agricultural Holdings (Scotland) Act 1991.

For the reasons that I have given, I conclude that the common law personal lease is no longer part of the law of Scotland. But even if it were a

---

84   *Waddell v Brown* 1794 M 10309; *Campbell v Mc Kinnon* (1867) 5 M 636, Lord Deas at 651.

85   *Waddell* (n 84); *McArthur v Simpson* 1804 M 15181; *Pollock, Gilmour & Co v Harvey* (1828) 6 S 913; *Clerk v Farquharson* 1799 M 15225; *Lumsden v Stewart* (1843) 5 D 501; *Gentle v Henry* 1747 M 13804.

86   1962 SC 157.

valid form of lease, the question whether it fell with any particular statutory regime would depend on the relevant legislation. For example, it may be that under the Housing (Scotland) Acts a party may be deemed to be a tenant even if he holds under a form of tenure that is not a lease at all.[87] That however does not advance the argument.

On the assumption that a contract of the kind considered in the *Clydesdale Bank* case were to constitute a personal lease, such a lease would not necessarily come within the special definition of "lease" in section 85(1) of the Agricultural Holdings (Scotland) Act 1991.[88] *Ex hypothesi* a personal lease is good only against the lessor. It cannot therefore fit into the scheme of the 1991 Act where every lease to which the Act applies is subject to a statutory form of annual relocation[89] after the expiry of the contractual term and is good against any subsequent landlord of the holding. Moreover, the wideness of the definition of "landlord" in section 85(1) of the 1991 Act is such that the landlord may be a person who is not vested in the ownership of the land. The definitions of landlord and tenant in section 85(1) apply, of course, only for the purposes of the 1991 Act.

In any event, the results of the alternative theory would be incongruous. If a *pro indiviso* proprietor were to acquire a purported personal lease of agricultural land granted by his co-proprietors, his co-proprietors would not qualify as the "landlord" in terms of section 85(1) of the 1991 Act because under that definition all persons having a share in the title to the land constitute the landlord. Even if it were possible for the lease to be granted by the co-proprietors including himself, the lease would be unworkable. By reason of the rights of every individual *pro indiviso* proprietor that are inherent in his ownership, and by reason of the principle of unanimity to which I have referred, the appellant – on that hypothesis – could prevent *inter alia* the service upon him of any notice to quit under section 21 of the 1991 Act, any notice for a review of rent under section 13, any demand to remedy fixed equipment under section 22 and any application for a certificate of bad husbandry under section 28. That would be an unreasonable result.

---

87 As Bury and Bain (n 27) submit at their footnote 29 under reference to *Kinghorn v Glasgow DC* 1984 *SLT* (Lands Tr) 9; and *Andrew v North Lanarkshire Council* 2011 Lands Tribunal, available at http://www.lands-tribunal-scotland.org.uk/decisions/LTS.TR.2010.10.html

88 Or for that matter qualify as one of the limited duration tenancies introduced by the Agricultural Holdings (Scotland) Act 2003.

89 1991 Act, s 3.

One other aspect of the case for the alternative view is the suggestion that in the *Clydesdale Bank* case the House of Lords failed adequately to consider what constitutes one of the cardinal elements of a lease, namely a rent. The suggestion is that their Lordships took too narrow a view of rent as being a payment of money, there being wide definitions of rent given by the writers which comprehend a non-pecuniary consideration. This again seems not to advance the argument. No-one would dispute that the cardinal element of rent covers payment in money's worth; but the judges of the House of Lords were dealing with a contract which, whatever its substance or validity, purported to provide for payment of a money rent.

(2) The *pro indiviso* proprietor issue

The discussion as to the nature of the tenant's interest in a lease may in the event be futile if the contract in the *Clydesdale Bank* case was invalid on other grounds. To succeed in the alternative theory its proponents must still establish that a personal lease created by several *pro indiviso* proprietors in favour of one of their number is a valid contract. In my view, if the personal lease known to the Scottish common law had survived to the present day, the arrangement between the *pro indiviso* proprietors in the *Clydesdale Bank* case could not have been such a contract, for the good and sufficient reason that it is not possible for a party to be both creditor and debtor in a contract. The logic of this principle is recognised as a general principle of the law of contract.[90] In the specific case of leases the principle is established by a powerful tract of authority in cases such as *Price v Watson*[91] and *Kildrummy (Jersey) Limited v IRC*.[92] These authorities were reviewed and affirmed by the House of Lords in the *Clydesdale Bank* case.

Although the principle can be securely rested on logic, it is also justified by a consideration of the consequence identified in *Price v Watson*,[93] namely that the so-called tenant, as a *pro indiviso* proprietor, has rights of ownership over every inch of the subjects of let and would therefore be secure against eviction.[94]

In this discussion I am considering only the case where *pro indiviso* proprietors grant a purported lease to one of their number. In the *Clydesdale*

90   W M Gloag, *The Law of Contract*, 2nd edn (1929) 4; *Church of Scotland Endowment Committee v Provident Association of London Ltd* 1914 SC 165.
91   1951 SC 359. Cf also *Denholm's Trs v Denholm* 1984 *SLT* 319; *Bell's Exrs v Inland Revenue* 1986 SC 252; *Barclay v Penman* 1984 *SLT* 376.
92   1991 SC 1.
93   1951 SC 359.
94   Bell, *Principles* §1072; Erskine, *Principles* 2.6.53.

Bank case, in both the Inner House and the House of Lords, the court was referred to the Outer House decision in *Pinkerton v Pinkerton*.[95] That was an example of the converse case where an individual granted a lease to four joint tenants of whom he was one. Neither court found it necessary to consider the validity of such a contract. In my view, it is irrelevant to the present discussion; but it may be that the judgment of Lord Mackay of Clashfern in that case is not the last word on that subject.

Bury and Bain seek support for their argument in a statement of Lord Johnston in *Higgins v Assessor for Lanarkshire*,[96] a case where the *pro indiviso* proprietors let the subjects to one of their number, namely:[97]

> That [the tenant] could be ejected by his co-proprietors I have no doubt. *Qua* tenant, he could not avail himself of his rights as co-proprietor *pro indiviso* to resist removal at the instance of his co-proprietors ... that fact does not enable him to maintain himself in possession *qua* tenant till he is removed with his own consent.

Higgins v Assessor for Lanarkshire was a case about valuation for rating. The question was whether the rent passing under the lease was a true indicator of the annual value of the subjects on the statutory valuation hypothesis. For the answer to that question, it did not matter whether the lease was valid or not. The issue of the validity of the lease was not raised by either party to the appeal and none of the judges considered it. Lord Johnston's statement, which was plainly an *obiter dictum*, simply assumed the validity of the lease. That *dictum* was referred to in the *Clydesdale Bank* case both in the Inner House and in the House of Lords. Neither court considered it to have any persuasive value.

All of these points are raised to support the general contention that the House of Lords while ruling out the validity of the contract as a lease by *pro indiviso* proprietors to one of their number, nevertheless upheld the validity of it as an occupation and management contract and, by extension, a personal lease. This is the key element in the alternative theory; but it may be a step too far.

The House of Lords authoritatively confirmed the now uncontroversial point that the *pro indiviso* proprietors of land are entitled to agree among themselves that one of their number will have sole occupancy of the land and to agree on the terms and conditions on which he will occupy it. Such terms and conditions could include, for example, the payment by the

---

95 1986 *SLT* 672.

96 1911 SC 931.

97 *Higgins* (n 96) at 934.

occupying proprietor to the others of a sum reflecting their share of the rents that would have been received if the land had been let to a third party; or the payment of a sum representing a proportion of the net profits of the occupier's farming enterprise; and the payment by them to the occupier, at the termination of the contract, of their share of the value of the occupier's improvements.

In this way, the contract could achieve a similar result to that which would have applied if the land had been let to a third party. However, in such a contract, the parties would be, on one side, the occupier and, on the other side, the other *pro indiviso* proprietors. The contract in this case was between different parties, namely, on one side, all of the *pro indiviso* proprietors and, on the other, one of the three *qua* individual. The judges of the House of Lords regarded the purported lease document as being in itself a valid contract by which the *pro indiviso* proprietors regulated the occupation and management of the land. Those statements were plainly *obiter*. In my view, they are unsound. Since the contract was between all three proprietors and one of their number, it failed as a contract for occupation and management on the same logic on which it failed as a lease.

This objection could be dismissed as raising a mere matter of form. But the objection goes beyond that. The contract bore to be, and was intended to be, a lease. I cannot understand how, as the judges of the House of Lords seem to have implied, it fell to be read as being what it did not bear to be, and was not intended to be; namely, a contract between all three *pro indiviso* proprietors contracting as such *inter se*. It would seem to be an extraordinary interpretation of the purported lease that the parties to it, having reached *consensus* on the creation of a lease over the subjects, however mistakenly, should be held to have had the common intention of creating a contract of an entirely different kind.

Furthermore, if the purported lease could have been so regarded, I cannot see how intelligible terms could have been read into it. The contract was intended to make the appellant tenant of the land, and as such vested in the rights conferred by the contract and subject to the duties that it imposed; but subject also to the provisions of the 1991 Act and related statutes such as the Succession (Scotland) Act 1964. I fail to see how the contract could be read as having entirely different consequences for the appellant *qua* owner in occupation. On that view, therefore, I conclude that the appellant in the *Clydesdale Bank* case acquired neither a right *in rem* to occupy the land *qua* tenant, nor a right *in personam* to the exclusive occupation of it *qua* proprietor.

14. Conveyancing: A Bright Digital Future?

Professor Stewart Brymer

A. Introduction

We are all accustomed to how heritable property transactions work – and sometimes do not work. If we were creating a property transfer system from scratch today, what would it look like? Indeed, how might a conveyancing system operate in, say, 2050? Is it too fanciful to suggest that transactions will be carried out electronically from start to finish with electronic paperwork, electronic examination of title and a clean and accessible Land Register holding all information relative to land and property in Scotland with experienced property lawyers advising clients on the important aspects of the transaction assisted by trained legal executives? This essay aims to look at the conveyancing process as we know it with a view to assessing how close we are today to that vision becoming a reality.

B. Conveyancing Past and Present

Prior to the enactment of the Conveyancing and Feudal Reform (Scotland) Act 1970, the Land Tenure Reform (Scotland) Act 1974 and prior to the Land Registration (Scotland) Act 1979, there had been very little change in conveyancing law and practice. Indeed, the pace of change could be said to have been somewhat glacial. The combined effect of the aforementioned statutes was radical given the introduction of *inter alia* the Standard

    http://dx.doi.org/10.11647/OBP.0056.14

Security; redemption of feu duty on sale; and registration of title. The first two statutes were the result of earlier analysis of Scots property law by the Reid, Henry and Halliday Reports.[1]

There was little further in the way of legislative intervention in the area of property law until 2000. That was not to say that the Scottish Law Commission was not busy however.[2] The result was the enactment of the Abolition of Feudal Tenure Etc. (Scotland) Act 2000; the Title Conditions (Scotland) Act 2003; and the Tenements (Scotland) Act 2004 which all came into force on the Appointed Day.[3] If there was ever a significant date in Scots property law, that was it. We are now some ten years on from the Appointed Day and the Scottish Law Commission has completed another highly regarded review of registration law and practice.[4] The 1979 Act has been criticised over the years, most notably when it was described as having, "all the intellectual sharpness of a mashed potato,"[5] but the fact of the matter is that the Act has worked and solicitors and the public generally have benefited from registration of title. The time was right for a complete overhaul of the system however. This resulted in the enactment of the Land Registration etc. (Scotland) Act 2012 ("the 2012 Act"), Part 10 of which[6] came into force on 11 May 2014 by virtue of The Electronic Documents (Scotland) Regulations 2014.[7] These Regulations were introduced under the 2012 Act, the balance of which came into force on 8 December 2014. The Regulations prescribe the requirements for electronic signatures that will allow documents covered by the Requirements of Writing (Scotland) Act 1995 ("the 1995 Act"), with the exception of Wills and other testamentary writings meantime, to be signed by applying a suitable electronic signature and thus be both legally valid and self-proving. This means that contracts

---

1   Registration of Title to Land (Cmnd 2032: 1963) ("Reid Committee Report"); Registration of Title to Land (Cmnd 4137: 1969) ("Henry Committee Report"); and Conveyancing Legislation and Practice (Cmnd 3118: 1968) ("Halliday Committee Report"). See also *Land Tenure in Scotland: A Plan for Reform* (Cmnd 4099: 1969) (the White paper) and *Land Tenure in Scotland: A Plan for Reform* (1972) (the Green paper).

2   Report on Abolition of the Feudal System (Scot Law Com Report n 168, 1999); Report on the Law of the Tenement (Scot Law Com Report n 162, 1998) and Report on the law of Real Burdens (Scot Law Com Report n 181, 2000).

3   28 November 2004.

4   Report on *Land Registration* (Volumes 1 and 2) (Scot Law Com Report n 222, 2010)

5   Discussion Paper on *Land Registration: Void and Voidable Titles* (Scot Law Com DP n 125, 2004) para 2.24.

6   s 96 to s 100.

7   See Registers of Scotland Electronic Documents (Scotland) Regulations Consultation Report.

for the sale, purchase and leasing of land and property can be completed electronically instead of in writing with a "wet" signature being applied thereto. For more on this, see below.

There has been considerable change in the practice of conveyancing during the past 45 years. There will be some who argue that these changes have not had any major effect on the practice of conveyancing and, in any event, that the profession has adapted to change and will continue to do so. That may well be the case. Nevertheless, in a lecture given in 1998, Professor Robert Rennie said: "Some conveyancing solicitors look back to the past with nostalgia and forward to the future with a degree of trepidation." It is suggested that the full implications of the 2000, 2003 and 2004 Acts have not yet been felt and, when combined with the enabling provisions of the 2012 Act, the changes to Property law and Conveyancing law and practice in particular will be significant. There are those who believe that any change is unwelcome. The combined effect of the pace of change in today's society and developments in IT over the past 30 years dictate against that view being an acceptable position however. The World Wide Web was only created in 1990[8] and look at the effect that that has had on our lives. Who would have predicted that? These developments are exponential and all-invasive in every aspect of our business and personal lives. Is there any reason why conveyancing should be immune from such changes? I suggest not.

In a thesis written in 1989, Ian Burdon, then with Registers of Scotland, concluded that:[9]

> The present millennium began with feudalism and reliance on the literacy of the clerical elite. The vision of the beginning of the next millennium is of an automated land registration system alongside a fully integrated digital information system, unencumbered by those administrative and bureaucratic structures which serve only to impede the public.

In the preface to our book entitled "Conveyancing in the Electronic Age,"[10] Robert Rennie and I stated that we hoped that there was considerable future potential for Scotland to develop land registration coverage with additional content that meets the needs of a much more informed and information-hungry society. That is precisely what is now happening with the 2012 Act and the Scottish Government's desire to see the whole

---

8   J Ryan, *A History of the Internet and the Digital Future* (2010) 107.

9   I Burdon, *Automated Registration of Title to Land: A report for the Government Study Fellowship* (1998).

10   R Rennie and S Brymer, *Conveyancing in the Electronic Age* (2008).

of Scotland on the Land Register during the course of the next 10 years.[11] That may be seen as an ambitious target by some,[12] but is there any reason why such an objective cannot be achieved? The political will exists and Registers of Scotland have shown how responsive they can be in embracing all the statutory obligations on them under the 2000 and 2003 Acts and also under the 2012 Act. The Keeper's challenges are considerable but there is an enthusiastic and well-informed team in Registers that is engaging with its stakeholders and can see the potential that exists. The benefits of the Land Register being completed are social and economic as well as political and it is appropriate that we consider the benefits that this may bring. Change is all around us and it is suggested that it is better being involved in the change process rather than being outside the tent looking in. Life without change would mean that there would never be any progress.

So, what are the changes introduced by Part 10 of the 2012 Act and how will those changes impact on conveyancing law and practice?

(1) 2012 Act ss 96-100 ("Part 10")

Credit for what has been a formidable piece of work in the shape of the 2012 Act must go to the Scottish Law Commission and to Professors George Gretton and Kenneth Reid in particular. The profession is indebted to these two individuals. They have played a pivotal role in reforming the Scots law of property over the past 35 years while, at the same time, retaining the underlying principles established over the last 400 years. Credit must also go to the Registers of Scotland and to the Scottish Government for having the vision to progress the statutory timetable through a period of economic uncertainty.

Part 10 makes changes to the 1995 Act so as to make digital execution equivalent to a traditional "wet" signature. In essence, it e-enables all the documents referred to in s 1(2)(a) of the 1995 Act. Digital signatures are, of themselves, not new of course as the profession has had experience of using the whe undertaking transactions involving Automated Registration of Title to Land ("ARTL").

---

11   Registers of Scotland, Completion of the Land Register, Public Consultation (2014) paras 8-15, available at http://www.scotland.gov.uk/Resource/0045/00451087.pdf and Report of the Land Reform Review Group: The Land of Scotland and the Common Good (2014) para 24 ff, available at http://www.scotland.gov.uk/Resource/0045/00451087.pdf

12   "Target Set to Register all of Scotland's Land" *Scottish Legal News*, 27 May 2014.

ARTL was introduced in 2006[13] when an Order made changes to the 1995 Act for the purposes of ARTL. The introduction of this change by secondary legislation under s 8 of the Electronic Communications Act 2000 came about following a Joint Opinion of the so-called Professorial Panel (Professors Brymer, Gretton, Paisley and Rennie – Professor Reid being excused given his then role with the Scottish Law Commission) which was delivered to the then Keeper of the Registers of Scotland ("RoS") in April 2003 and later published in the *Juridical Review*.[14] Digital execution under ARTL was a necessary first step. Originally, it was proposed that a digital signature would still require to be witnessed in order to be probative. The view of the Professorial Panel was that the conferring of probative status on an unwitnessed deed was beyond the scope of a Section 8 Order. However, there is no requirement on the Keeper to only accept probative deeds in respect of land registration applications. Accordingly, the unanimous view in the Joint Opinion was that the Keeper was perfectly entitled to accept a digitally executed deed without the need for that deed to be probative. Authentication by way of a digital signature which is validated by a third party gives the degree of security that is required for those placing reliance on such deeds.

The 1995 Act was suitably amended and in his annotations to the amended 1995 Act,[15] Professor Kenneth Reid indicated that in the case of electronic documents, the distinction between probative and non-probative deeds was abandoned. ARTL was subsequently introduced and is still in use today[16] – although not as widespread as originally envisaged. There are a number of reasons why this is the case, the principal and somewhat non-technical explanation being that its operation is somewhat "clunky" and in need of an overhaul. In truth, ARTL was not embraced fully by conveyancers and was not widely used in transactions other than remortgages, Improvement Grants and certain Charging Orders. Such an overhaul will be undertaken and an upgraded version of ARTL will be launched by RoS (Registers of Scotland) in due course. This is also permitted under Part 10. In the words of Gilbert, it is easy to "carp and criticise" about anything in life and developments in the law and practice are no exception.[17] In the case of ARTL, however, one would do well to reflect on just how ground-breaking

---

13 The Automated Registration of Title to Land (Electronic Communications) (Scotland) Order 2006 (SSI 2006/491) ("the 2006 Order").

14 2005 JR 201.

15 K Reid, *Requirements of Writing (Scotland) Act 1995* (1995).

16 Over 91,000 transactions to date (as of 31 October 2014).

17 *The Pirates of Penzance; or, The Slave of Duty.*

the system was and what other benefits it will bring when upgraded as part of the move towards Scotland having a fully digitised Land Register. Could ARTL have been introduced in a different manner? With the benefit of hindsight, this is undoubtedly the case. It is hoped that ARTL Mark 2 will be introduced and that practice will develop as a result of demand from the profession. That will occur once all the other building blocks for digital transactions are in place and we see that purchasers, sellers and lenders want to transact in this way. That will complete the change process which will begin after the Designated Day for the 2012 Act when a large number of services will be provided by RoS in an electronic manner.

(2) What is a Digital Signature?

The term "digital signature" is in many ways a convenient tag for the authentication of a document by electronic means. There are many variations including machines that allow a signature to be traced which then appears on a screen. Indeed, such systems could have been adapted for use in such a way that an electronic signed deed could have accompanied an ARTL application. That is not what would be regarded as a digital signature in a technological sense however. The crucial element is not the digital signature itself but the digital certificate which provides the security for the adhibition of the signature and which thus underpins same. In strict technological terms, the certificate is used to create the digital signature which is a product of the actual document and the digital certificate together. This detail is suitably encrypted and lies behind the signature.

In the ARTL system, the digital certificates comply with the X509 standard.[18] As a general rule, the longer the length of cryptographic keys, the stronger the encryption. For example, a 20BIT key is twice as strong as a 19BIT key and so on. A digital signature with a robust encryption such as the ARTL digital certificate is therefore very secure and one might remember that in the not so recent past, a digital certificate with a key length of over 56BITs was classed as a military weapon for export purposes and special licences were required. What is important is the strength of the digital certificate. In other words, not every digital signature can be used in the knowledge that it is secure. Put simply, a cheap digital signature obtained on the internet on a credit card payment is never likely to be acceptable for the processes envisaged by Part 10 because the digital

---

18   See J R Vacca, *Computer and Information Security Handbook* (2008) 436 ff.

certificate which is used to adhibit the digital signature is simply not secure enough. Any digital signature has to be one which is backed by a digital certificate trusted by people in a business and commercial context. It is not just the technological content that is important. Of particular importance for property lawyers given the uses to which a digital signature is to be put in conveyancing transactions is the identity check which is made by the provider of the digital certificate before that certificate is issued.

As mentioned above, in a very basic sense, an electronic signature could be simply a name at the end of an email or an image of a person's written signature added to an electronic document. Neither of these would meet the terms of the requirements set out in the Regulations. An advanced electronic signature is uniquely linked to the signatory and is capable of identifying the signatory. It is created using systems that the signatory can maintain under his/her sole control. This, by necessity, means that the digital signature will only be processed by a certification authority after robust security and ID checks are carried out. An advanced electronic signature will, however, require a certification authority[19] to have verified the identity of the individual using same however.

For an electronic signature to become an advanced electronic signature it must be:

(i) uniquely linked to the signatory;

(ii) capable of identifying the signatory;

(iii) created using means that the signatory can maintain under their sole control; and

(iv) linked to the data to which it relates so that any subsequent change of the data is detectable.

An advanced electronic signature has more significant value than an electronic signature: it guarantees the integrity of the text, as well as the authentication. The juridical value it has is for integrity: one is sure the text received is the same that was sent, and that no hacker has changed it.

The only practical way to meet these requirements is to use the technology called Public Key Infrastructure ("PKI"). PKI is the technology that provides a solution for secure electronic signatures. The key components are the digital certificates that form part of the signature. These allow for the validity of an electronic signature and the identity of the signatory to be

---

19 See below.

authenticated. The electronic signature and the digital certificate are both provided by the certification service provider. The electronic signature that incorporates the digital certificate is usually held on a chip embedded within a pin protected smart card that the signatory can maintain under their sole control or held remotely and securely by a third party.[20]

The authentication of a deed or a missive by a person using a digital signature operates within PKI. There are two mirror aspects of digital signatures. From the point of view of the party who holds the signature no-one else must be able to use it. However, from the point of view of the party who is to receive and rely on the document authenticated by a digital signature, there must be a method of verifying that the document has, indeed, been digitally signed. The technology is complicated as one might expect but it essentially operates on the basis of a private key and a public key. The private key is held by the holder of the digital signature and is not made known to the other party who is to receive the digitally signed document. The public key on the other hand is available to the recipient of the document and that party uses the public key to verify simply that the document in question has been authenticated by the digital signature. A PKI infrastructure employs advanced encryption techniques. It is obvious that there must be a closed, robust and secure environment in which solicitors can interact with each other and indeed, interact with the Land Register and other bodies with a view to processing electronic dealings free from any interference by any unauthorised outsiders. Referring once again to the ARTL system, the PKI created for the Land Register is a closed tactical public key infrastructure. This means that the digital certificates were/are issued to licensed ARTL users only and cannot be used for any purpose other than for the purposes of the ARTL system.

A significant step forward was made on 11 May 2014 when the Electronic Documents (Scotland) Regulations 2014 ("the 2014 Regulations") came into force. The Regulations are a small but very important step that will help facilitate conveyancing in Scotland to be carried out electronically. The 2014 Regulations were made under powers that were inserted into the 1995 Act by the 2012 Act. The 2014 Regulations allow legal documents that the 1995 Act specifies must be in writing (other than wills and other testamentary writings at present) to take an electronic form and be legally valid.

---

20   See below.

The 2014 Regulations provide that electronic versions of legal documents governed by the 1995 Act can be legally valid if they are signed by using what is termed an "advanced electronic signature." For a document to obtain the presumption that it is has been signed by the granter, and to become self-proving, it must be signed using an advanced electronic signature, and that signature must be certified using a "qualified certificate."

The terms "advanced electronic signature" and "qualified certificate" used in the 2014 Regulations are defined in the Electronic Signatures Regulations 2002 ("the 2002 Regulations"), a piece of Westminster legislation that adopted into UK law Directive 1999/93EC of the European Parliament and Council on a Community framework for electronic signatures.

Advanced electronic signatures are issued by what is termed a "certification authority." For an electronic document to become self-proving, the documents must be signed using an advanced electronic signature that is certified using a qualified certificate. The 2002 Regulations prescribe that a qualified certificate must contain:

(i) an indication that the certificate is issued as a qualified certificate;

(ii) the identification of the certification-service-provider and the State in which it is established;

(iii) the name of the signatory or a pseudonym, which shall be identified as such;

(iv) provision for a specific attribute of the signatory to be included if relevant, depending on the purpose for which the certificate is intended;

(v) signature-verification data which corresponds to signature-creation data under the control of the signatory;

(vi) an indication of the beginning and end of the period of validity of the certificate;

(vii) the identity code of the certificate;

(viii) the advanced electronic signature of the certification-service-provider issuing it;

(ix) limitations on the scope of use of the certificate, if applicable; and

(x) limits on the value of transactions for which the certificate can be used, if applicable.

The Law Society of Scotland is currently in the process of introducing an electronic practising certificate or Smartcard which will contain within it a secure digital signature that meets the requirements for an advanced electronic signature that is certified using a qualified certificate.[21] These Smartcards will give Scottish solicitors the ability to benefit from the 2014 Regulations and sign legal documents electronically. This is being achieved by way of a phased roll-out which commenced in Summer 2014.

Trust is a key element of every PKI infrastructure. Under the ARTL system, the procedure for obtaining a Digital Signature began with a personal visit by Land Register staff in order to validate the identities of those people who were to act as local registration authorities in face to face meetings. A similar certification process is being undertaken by the Law Society and that is exactly as it should be in order to ensure that public confidence in the system is maintained.

As far as general practice is concerned, it might well be prudent for solicitors to incorporate authority from clients in Terms of Business to the effect that the client authorises their solicitor to sign missives and any other permitted document, electronically on his/her behalf. No such authority is given under current practice when adjusting missives, of course, but it is good practice at the moment to seek authority from one's client before issuing an offer or formal missive. It therefore makes sense to add a simple provision to this effect in Terms of Business.

The full effects of the change to digital signatures will not be harnessed until a secure electronic document exchange facility is available. That has been talked about for some time. The reality, however, is that such document exchange facilities already exist. The stockbroking community, among others, is well versed at dealing in this way. This is a natural progression for conveyancing and the sale/purchase of heritable property generally. It is envisaged that this will be a secure online portal or platform on which solicitors can communicate in a secure manner with other solicitors, lenders, RoS, Revenue Scotland and, indeed, their clients. Once there is a single national missive and standard styles of common conveyancing documents[22] there will be a greater opportunity for solicitors to focus on being a trusted adviser in the process which, in time, will hopefully see the Scottish system of conveyancing retain its uniqueness. There is, at present, a trend towards us having a conveyancing system that is, to all intents and purposes, the same as that which operates in England and Wales, with

---

21   The Law Society of Scotland, "Introducing the Smartcard," available at www.lawscot. org.uk/smartcard

22   See below.

exchange of contracts and chains of transactions becoming the norm. There is an opportunity now to reverse this trend.

(3) The need for client confidence

As mentioned above, The Law Society of Scotland Smartcard initiative will not have full coverage until October 2015. Commercial solutions are believed to be available however. One such solution is the Yooseful Technology Property Manager™ product.[23] This product is registered under a certification authority through Entrust.[24] To become a certification authority, an organisation must seek accreditation under the T Scheme.[25] T Scheme was initially established to provide a voluntary approval scheme for providers of the cryptographic elements necessary to underpin the use of digital signatures. This is because Government wishes people and organisations to have trust in e-commerce. The digital certificate can be embedded in a mobile phone or in a card and card reader as the case may be and can be used on a "pay as you go" basis. There are benefits of other "wrappers" offered by the providers of the digital signature e.g. indemnity insurance etc.

In essence, it is envisaged that the net effect will be a streamlining of the conveyancing process and thus satisfying the desire for the legal profession to remain as effective gatekeepers of sale and purchase transactions. People want to communicate electronically – and many do it already without fully appreciating the inherent risks that exist when transacting in an insecure manner. They are used to it and expect instant responses. Secure email exchange would be much better so that transactions are safe. It is therefore imperative that there are robust safeguards in place in order that the sale and purchase process can operate smoothly and hopefully help minimise delay and loss. This will be achieved by removing uncertainty with regard to undelivered or intercepted emails; missing deeds; delay in conclusion of missives etc. In what way is that not a good thing?

For the Law Society Secure Digital Signature to be used effectively in a conveyancing transaction, it will require to be integrated with a firm's case management software and other systems. That may not be as simple a

---

23 For more information see Yooseful Technology Limited's website available here: www. yoosefultechnology.com

24 For more information see Entrust®, Inc.'s website available here: www.entrust.com

25 For more information see the Scheme Limited's website available here: www.tscheme. org

process as it sounds and discussions are underway with case management software providers with a view to smoothing integration. Perhaps there is an opportunity for the Law Society to offer a branded secure dealing room or portal to its members as a way to effectively host the platform on which secure transactions can be carried out?

Digital signatures based on digital certification provided by a certification authority allow parties to rely on the validity of the signature. In simple terms, if you trust the certification authority, then you can trust the digital signature. The digital signature will be legally valid and admissible as evidence of the authenticity and integrity of the electronic communication. It will hopefully also speed up the process of concluding missives, and remove problems encountered with regard to delivery of letters concluding the bargain etc.[26]

As with any change in the way things are done, it will take time for digital signatures to become the norm. Put simply, we tend to trust that which we know. I am confident that practice will evolve quickly, however – especially among the younger members of the profession. Why should we and our clients not benefit from a secure way in which to sign and exchange contracts and documents? "Early adopters" will have an opportunity to develop their practices further by embracing this exciting, and entirely logical development.

Any system, whether in ARTL or in the exchange of missives or the signing of documents in a manner designed to replicate as nearly as possible the existing paper-based systems, must be based on client confidence. For so long as members of the public do not have digital signatures of a type that meet the prescribed requirements, the essential underlying element will be the authority given by a client to his/her solicitor or other agent to sign for them using a digital signature. From a policy and security point of view, the holding of a digital signature should be with an individual rather than by a firm or limited liability partnership as a whole as the latter would render the system less secure. There are, however, already developments which might result in the use of digital signatures being extended to any transaction concluded over the internet. This involves the use of a biometric.[27] A biometric solution uses physiology to reinforce the link between the person applying the digital signature and the signature itself and is, perhaps, where we will end up as further technological advances are made.

---

26   See *Park, Petitioner* 2009 *SLT* 871.
27   See L Reid and M Bromby, "Beyond the Chip and PIN" 53(7) *JLSS* (2008) 50.

Change will happen and it is suggested that it makes logical sense for the whole sale and purchase transaction to be able to be competed electronically from start to finish. Conveyancing Case Management systems are now widely used and it is envisaged that changes to these systems will increasingly make use of the technological developments that exist, especially when, as is the case with Part 10, these are underpinned by legislation. It is essential however that all new systems are introduced with care and attention especially with regard to the importance of client confidence therein. It is this that gives the solicitor an opportunity to remain central to the sale and purchase process as a "trusted adviser."

C. Conveyancing Future

(1) National Land and Property Information database

An essential requirement for an efficient system of transferring ownership of heritable property is the accuracy and availability of information relative to the property being sold and, indeed, neighbouring properties. It is essential that searches of local authority and other records are undertaken prior to the purchase of a property. Unfortunately, however, the quality of records and practices differ from local authority to local authority. This results in uncertainty and increases the potential for error and loss.[28] There are some examples of very good practice in local authorities. One such is the City of Edinburgh's planning and building standards portal.[29] Even that system still has its gaps however e.g. plans are not available in all instances and all current systems suffer from the lack of a uniform addressing database. It is nevertheless an example of what can be achieved. The introduction of the National Gazetteer as a result of a collaboration among 32 local authorities in Scotland was a significant step forward with each property being allocated a Unique Property Reference Number ("UPRN"). There is considerable potential in grouping all relevant data from both public and private sources around the UPRN.

Up to date and readily accessible information on land and property is at the very core of the conveyancing service. It has been argued for many years that it is nonsensical for solicitors to have to have recourse to multiple

---

28   See *Runciman v Borders Regional Council* 1998 *SLT* 135.
29   This is available at https://citydev-portal.edinburgh.gov.uk

data sets, some of which may not be comprehensive in their coverage or, indeed, be current. This is not in the best interests of either buyer or seller. Why should they be put at risk? It must surely be the case that in today's information-based society that all relevant data on land and property is held in a comprehensive and easily searchable database. This initiative may well be the catalyst for reform that has been required. Without it, the existing systems would grind on with little or no appetite for change. It is suggested that the availability of relevant information which is accurate and comprehensive, can be properly interpreted and can be relied upon and is readily accessible is not only consistent with the aims of Government as far as efficiency is concerned, but is also necessary as part of the Scottish Government's commitment to improve the supply of information for people when making a decision about buying and selling a home. The benefits of a national portal containing all information relative to land and property (other than title information) are significant and are achievable given the political will to do something about the present unsatisfactory nature surrounding the supply of information relative to land and property. Why should this be tolerated in this day and age when it can be avoided?

There have been a number of recent developments which have the potential to significantly improve the way in which information about Scotland's land and property is managed and made available. A number of inter-related initiatives are being, or are about to be, launched, which together with new governance arrangements, suggest that the original aims of the Scottish Land Information Service ("ScotLIS") may finally be realised.

In 2001, those involved with the ScotLIS project[30] produced the following statements of intent:

> The ultimate aim of the ScotLIS project is that of providing an integrated data set where the user obtains information from a range of providers by means of a single search enquiry. This will be facilitated by means of a gazetteer … The extent to which data from different suppliers will be integrated will be determined in the course of the ScotLIS pilot and through the ongoing development of the service.

ScotLIS never progressed beyond the pilot stage for a number of reasons, mainly to do with the available technology at the time, but also due to the way in which the organisations involved viewed their own information.

---

30 See http://brymerlegal.blogspot.se/2012/03/joined-up-land-and-property-information. html

Since then, a number of significant events have occurred including legislative change and most markedly the economic downturn which has led to serious review of the way in which the public sector will require to deliver services in future.[31]

In December 2009, Scottish Ministers signed the European INSPIRE Directive which places an obligation on them to publish information on a number of spatial data themes which contain environmental data. Those themes directly related to land and property are Addresses, Geographic Names, Cadastral Parcels and Buildings and the Directive explicitly specifies what information is required to be published and how this must be done using web services. This was a very important step on the road to the goal of joined-up property information.

In 2010, a joint venture was established between the Local Government Association and the Ordnance Survey to deliver a National Address Gazetteer for England and Wales by working collaboratively to combine the best features of the National Land and Property Gazetteer and Ordnance Survey address products. This provided for the inclusion of One Scotland Gazetteer data into the National Address Gazetteer.

The Scottish Government also established a Spatial Information Board with the remit to implement the Scottish Spatial Data Infrastructure/INSPIRE Directive requirements. The Board's membership is drawn from senior officers from Scottish Government, NDPBs, SOLACE, NHS, AGI Scotland, Edina and the Registers of Scotland. The Board reports to a National Board overseeing public sector reform in Scotland. Five theme groups were established under the Board, with one of these having the remit for Land, Property and Addresses, which include Geographic Names and Buildings and there is a clear reporting structure for land and property related information to Ministerial level. This was one of the key components missing from ScotLIS in 2001, as well as the links to other geospatial initiatives.

Scotland is well placed to develop a land and property infrastructure which will be capable of supporting greatly improved services, including e-Conveyancing and improved asset management.

Unifi Scotland[32] is a think tank that was established a number of years ago to look at ways of improving access to and use of data on Land and Property with a view to having a government-backed definitive source

---

31 For a more detailed review of the background to ScotLIS see S Brymer, "National Gazetteer for Scotland" (2008) 97 *Greens Property Law Bulletin* 1-3.

32 See http://www.unifiscotland.com/

of information. Its membership includes representatives from The Law Society of Scotland, the Royal Institution of Chartered Surveyors, RoS, the Council of Mortgage Lenders, Ordinance Survey private search companies and representatives of local and national government. The focus of Unifi is to enhance the accessibility, quality and reliability of property information and, in turn facilitate the quicker completion of property transactions. In essence, Unifi seeks to improve the current system. The progressive availability of location-based information and the ability to usefully link various sources of this through definitive addressing and intelligent mapping provides the means to improve decision making, smarten traditional ways of working and draw significant value in a way that has not been possible before. Hopefully all stakeholders will be convinced of the considerable savings that will be achieved and we can move quickly towards converting this vision into a reality.

(2) Comparative example

It is usually the case that someone, somewhere will have done, or is thinking of doing, that which you are considering. Legal systems are no different. One of the attributes of Scots law over the years is the way that it has adapted and learned from other jurisdictions. That has been hugely beneficial and the study of comparative law can bring significant benefits.

One such benefit may be capable of being found in Norway where an innovative land information project has already been introduced by the Norwegian Land Information company.[33] In Norway, the majority of municipalities have pooled their information on land and property with the Norwegian Land Information company, Ambita AS. This information is held digitally and is accessed on a "pay as you go" basis. Considerable benefits have accrued both for local government and for those who rely on the information. It is hoped that it might be possible for a pilot study of such a project to be undertaken in Scotland. This would require collaboration among local authorities, utility companies and the holders of other information on land and property.

The property information portal in Norway is called INFOLAND and it serves as an inter-operable cooperation between public and private sector, collecting layers of information necessary to the various stakeholders in the property segment, be they a private citizen, mortgage lenders and

---

33   For more information see Ambita AS's website at www.ambita.com.

credit institutions, property solicitors, surveyors, contractors and others. The INFOLAND portal connects information from the planning and property departments of the municipalities in addition to information developed on the back of this from private sector search companies and other government bodies such as environmental offices, Ordnance Survey and others. The principle behind the portal is simple. A one-step search for a property in question and all information relevant to the request is made available. The supplier (the local authority or another information provider in the portal) provides the necessary information either immediately as a pdf to be downloaded or to an email address or – in the case of non-digital documents – to a specified postal address. The simplicity of the portal's front-end function for the searcher covers a multitude of layers that also entail an administration statistic allowing the supplier to follow requested transactions. In the case of payments, a simple arrangement that allows for subscription or for credit card payments is also made available.

In short, the INFOLAND portal has functioned as a single one-stop-shop for all layers of property information in Norway since its launch in 1998 in Stavanger. It provides efficient and timesaving access to information, thereby saving money and speeding up Norwegian property transactions. It is hoped that the same result can be achieved in Scotland.

(3) Lender Exchange

Changes are also currently being made by a number of mortgage lenders with the introduction of Lender Exchange[34] by Decision First Limited, a joint venture company between Decision Insight Information Group and First Title plc. Individual lenders have been communicating their positions to solicitor firms on their lending panels.

Lender Exchange is a web portal which aims to address the issue of multiple lenders seeking similar information from solicitors in order to better manage their panel systems. The aim is to reduce costs and the administrative burden on solicitor firms while also helping the mortgage lenders minimise fraud and negligence through due diligence.

Information is gathered by Decision First and a fee is paid based on the size of the firm. Once in the system, the information need not be further updated unless there is a change to individual details such as an

---

34 For more information see Decision First Limited's website at www.lenderexchange. co.uk

amalgamation, a finding of professional misconduct etc. The obligation will be on the firm to advise of changes. Leading the way with Lender Exchange are Santander, Lloyds Banking Group and RBS, but the system is open to all mortgage lenders who wish to participate.

Lender Exchange is being promoted by mortgage lenders – not the Council of Mortgage Lenders.[35] Lender Exchange is designed to allow lenders to communicate better with solicitors on their panels by electronic means rather than the present outdated requirement that fax be used. An added benefit might be that solicitors could also be able to communicate in a secure manner with other solicitors on the portal, thus creating a secure dealing room of the type mentioned above on which conveyancing transactions can be carried out. This would be a good example of solicitors and lenders working together, irrespective of any decision with regard to separate representation. This would be a positive step forward but it is dependent upon Lender Exchange being operated in a manner which is seen to be fair to all concerned.

(4) Law Society Working Party on the Future of Conveyancing

Following the Law Society AGM in 2013, a Working Party was established to consider various issues affecting the residential property sector. The Working Party is made up of practitioners and others with interest in the residential property sector and it has managed a full meeting each month since July 2013. Various strands worthy of investigation were identified which, taken together, should enhance the way property transactions are undertaken. These include:

(i)   Standard Missives

(ii)   Standardised Documentation

(iii) Secure dealing room or portal

(iv)   Quality Badge for Conveyancers

The Working Party believes there is a clear role for a vital, progressive legal profession assisting consumers in the sale and purchase of residential property and that solicitors should seek to remain at the core of that process. That goal is best achieved however by the Law Society leading the change process from the front for the benefit of its members and citizens alike. In

---

35   For more information see the Council of Mortgage Lender's website available here www.cml.org.uk.

so doing, the Law Society is following the lead of countries like Denmark where solicitors made fundamental reforms to the way their role in the house buying/selling process operated following the removal by the Danish Government of the solicitors' monopoly in conveyancing. They now have a thriving property profession and we can usefully learn lessons from their experience.

(5) The Digital Home

With registration happening automatically following completion of an electronic process, there will, in future, be no physical delivery of title deeds. Settlement will therefore become truly symbolic with the keys being the focal point – for as long, of course, as keys are still required. We will have therefore come full circle and are effectively taking sasine! A fully integrated electronic security system covering the property and operated by a personal PIN is already a reality. Who is to say how this will develop? It is conceivable that all information relative to a property could be stored in a memory chip embedded in the property itself perhaps in the form of an In Home Display. This could be a register of all repairs and improvements carried out – including all local authority and other permissions in respect of the works. This would be an up to date record and would replace the Property Questionnaire as part of the Home Report. Until that time however, the keys and supporting documentation such as consents, guarantees, permissions and others will be delivered at settlement. These are important documents and have to be kept safe and it is suggested that these should also be recorded electronically in much the same way as a car log book is maintained.

D. So How Does the Vision Become a Reality?

We are already quite far along the road towards conveyancing transactions being completed electronically. As mentioned above, there are already companies that have developed software which can be utilised to enable agents and solicitors to collaborate, share property information and digitally sign and exchange property contracts.

The 2012 Act will also further enable electronic registration of title in the registers under the management and control of the Keeper of the Registers of Scotland. Additional regulations under the 2012 Act will follow which will e-enable ARTL Mark 2 and other such developments. It is envisaged that this will be by way of a process of evolution rather than revolution however. Practitioners will be given the opportunity to get used to accessing the registers electronically and the move towards a comprehensive ARTL process will thus evolve over time. That time period is finite however. The road map to digital conversion is being prepared.

Over a period of time, the Land Register will be cleansed of real burdens that are no longer valid and subsisting. This will be achieved by solicitors informing the Keeper of their judgment in this regard. Once done, the Land Register will be transparent and fully accessible. This, of course, also fits with the stated aim of Government to have all Scotland mapped and registered in the Land Register by 2024.

It is suggested that the electronic genie is out of the bottle and we have been afforded a glimpse of the future. We have a chance to shape that future however. Is it to be one where the solicitor remains central to the process? I do not see why not. Changes in working practices and, more importantly, in attitudes, will be required however. Conveyancing is a service and we all like to receive good service. Most solicitors provide a very good service and it is suggested that it is now time to focus on how to implement these changes and re-design our businesses accordingly. The heady days of the property boom have passed. During that period, it was almost too easy to make money from buying and selling property for clients. Looking forward, we must surely focus on quality of service and the trusted adviser concept as a means to providing a better service to our clients. I suggest that the effective introduction of changed working practices will assist that goal rather than hinder it.

Once available, e-Conveyancing (in its fullest extent) will make property transactions cheaper and quicker to complete. Such a facility may not speed up the negotiation of missives which, on many occasions, for many often oblique reasons can become very lengthy. It might just act as a catalyst however and we might get back to a situation last seen in the 1970s when missives were often concluded in a short period of time and often on a *de plano* basis. To become a reality however, there has to be a will on the part of everyone involved in the process to embrace the necessary changes and make it happen. The fact of the matter is that clients will expect change and for transactions to be processed in the most efficient way possible. Those who do embrace change once the necessary safeguards are in place should gain a competitive advantage over their rivals.

The digital clock is ticking...

15. Islamic Mortgages

Professor George Gretton

A. Theory, Practice and Fun

In most countries property law is, or at least is seen as being, dry and dull. And in most countries links between property law theorists and property law practitioners are weak. Not so here. Far from being dry and dull, property law in Scotland is, and is seen as being, exciting, fun and often – in a good sense – funny (thanks, Robert) funny. Strong links exist between theory and practice (thanks again, Robert). This paper has no laughs, but has something in it of practice and theory.

B. Introduction

I hesitate to write on Islamic mortgages for a good reason: I am unqualified to do so. To be qualified one would need to unite three qualities: knowledge of property law, knowledge of Shari'a[1] law, and knowledge of what is happening in practice. I have some of the first, but little of the second or third. So why this paper?

The main answer is that – as far as I can see – there is hardly anything published on the subject. There is a large literature on Islamic finance, all of which mentions the Islamic mortgage, but none of which seems to get

---

1   Variously transcribed into the Latin alphabet. Other forms are "Sharia," "Shari'ah," "Sharia'a" and "Shariah," where English is the destination language, and yet other forms for other destination languages, such as French *Charia* or *Chari'a*, or German *Scharia* or *Schari'a*.

     http://dx.doi.org/10.11647/OBP.0056.15

down to brass tacks – at least as far as the legal systems of the UK are concerned. The two standard English texts on mortgage law pass over the subject in complete silence.[2] The Scottish monographs are silent. If there is a periodical literature I have not found it, though there is one exception, and, to boot, a Scottish exception: Graham Burnside has written on the subject.[3] I find this paucity of discussion odd. Someone needs to do something. Islamic mortgages are not common in Scotland (less common, I think, than in England) but they are not unknown.

A subsidiary reason is that the internet is full of nonsense on the subject. Of course, the internet is full of nonsense on *every* subject, but with most subjects one can, with a bit of effort, navigate to reliable sources. Not so, as far as I can see, with Islamic mortgages in the UK context. Even seemingly respectable sites have dubious material. Here for instance is *The Guardian* on 29 June 2008:[4]

> Imagine a mortgage lender who allows you to take all the increase in the price of your home when you sell, but is prepared to share any loss if the property has fallen in value. Such a deal may seem too good to be true in the current property market, but it is exactly what a handful of banks specialising in Islamic home loans are offering.

Is that really true? I don't want to target *The Guardian*, and quote it here precisely because it is usually a respectable source, but here it goes again, on 29 October 2013, under the intriguing heading "Facts are sacred":[5]

> Islamic finance is all about sharing risk between financial institutions and the individuals that use them. To do that, the two parties are tied into a longer-term relationship with each other that is supposed to shift incentives and avoid cut and run financial deals. So, for example, sharia-compliant mortgages mean that the bank and the borrower share the risks of repayment rather than charging any form of interest.

Hmmm.

---

2   W Clark (ed), *Fisher and Lightwood's Law of Mortgage*, 13th edn (2011) (at the time of writing, a 14th edition is in the offing, but is not yet available to me); I Clarke (ed), *Cousins on the Law of Mortgages*, 3rd edn (2010).

3   "Unveiling the Islamic Mortgage" 2005 *JLSS* Dec/58; "Islamic Finance: A Scottish Lead?" 2009 *JLSS* Aug/56.

4   H Qureshi, "Sharia-compliant mortgages are here – and they're not just for Muslims," available at http://www.theguardian.com/money/2008/jun/29/mortgages.islam

5   M Chalabi, "Islamic finance for beginners," available at http://www.theguardian.com/news/datablog/2013/oct/29/islamic-finance-for-beginners. "Facts are sacred" is a heading used in the Guardian's "datablog," in reference to C P Snow's aphorism "comment is free, but facts are sacred."

So: despite my lack of qualifications for the subject, and conscious of the inadequacies of what follows, I offer some thoughts on the Islamic mortgage, mainly with reference to Scots law. Lastly by way of throat-clearing, the subject is larger than could be covered in a short paper such as the present. Indeed, it would be a good subject for a PhD. But half a loaf is better than no bread.

C. Prohibition of Interest

Judaism forbade interest, and that prohibition was received into its two daughter religions, Christianity and Islam.[6] In Christian countries the prohibition was generally accepted not only as a religious rule but also as a matter of positive law. Eventually, however, the legal ban was abandoned everywhere, though at different times in different countries.[7] In Scotland the ban ended with the Reformation (1560).[8] Turning to Islamic countries, in some (for example, Turkey) the law now permits interest: in those countries that accept Shari'a law as part of positive law, interest is legally impermissible. Pious Muslims, and Muslim organisations, seek to avoid interest, whether as debtors or as creditors.[9] Some non-Islamic financial institutions also offer what they claim to be Shari'a-compliant financial products. Such products will usually have been given the approval of a Shari'a-compliance board composed of experts in Islamic theology.

The question is not whether interest should be limited to reasonable levels.[10] In Shari'a, all interest, reasonable or unreasonable, is forbidden. What is forbidden is not the lending of money, but interest: loans are

---

6   There are also roots in Greek philosophy, especially Aristotle.

7   For an illuminating history of the European position from Roman to modern times see R Zimmermann, *The Law of Obligations* (1996) 166-77.

8   I know of no legislation lifting the ban. What happened at the Reformation was that a number of canon law rules, which had been accepted as part of the common law, were simply abandoned, other examples being the celibacy of the clergy and the prohibition of divorce. The first statute on the law of interest that I know of was the Act 1587 c 52 (APS iii 451 c 35) providing that the maximum lawful rate of interest was to be 10%. The Act expressly said that its provisions were not applicable to transactions entered into before its date. Thus between 1560 and 1587 interest was permitted and there was no maximum lawful rate. As far as I know the history of the subject (in Scotland) has never been fully studied.

9   Though in practice many Muslims do in fact borrow and lend at interest.

10   Legal limits on interest rates have been and remain common. For instance in the Roman Empire the maximum permitted rate was 12%. For a study of the current situation, see U Reifner, S Clerc-Renaud, and R A M Knobloch, Study on Interest Rate Restrictions in the EU: Final Report (2010), available at http://ec.europa.eu/internal_market/finservices-retail/docs/credit/irr_report_en.pdf

permissible so long as they are at zero interest. Nor is there any objection, in the Islamic tradition, to security for a loan. For example, there would be no objection to X lending Y money, secured by standard security – so long as the loan is interest-free. And there's the rub: whilst loans between friends and relatives are commonly interest-free, in the world of commerce no one will lend without a return. Indeed, to lend without a return is to transfer net value from lender to borrower: it is like a donation. Achieving a return without using interest is the challenge for Islamic finance, and various workarounds have been developed. (As they were in medieval Europe.[11]) How Muslims and Muslim organisations deal with the fact that interest often runs on debts *by force of law*,[12] I do not know, but that is another story.

(1) Other rules

Islamic theology imposes other restrictions, too, such as the prohibition of contracts involving uncertainty or speculation. Thus conventional insurance is forbidden, though as with interest there exist workarounds, which achieve by the back door what cannot be achieved through the front door. Another theological principle is that one transaction cannot be made conditional on another.[13] I do not understand, and so cannot explain this principle, but its influence is evident.

D. Circumventing the Prohibition

A workaround involves structuring the transaction as something other than a contract of loan. Some other type of contract has to be identified, to bring about the actual results of a loan contract. The three main workarounds[14] are to structure the transaction as (i) a contract of lease, this being called *ijara*, or (ii) a contract of sale, this being called *murabaha*, or (iii) a contract

---

11 The parallels are striking. In medieval Europe the ban on interest was circumvented easily, just as it is in the Islamic tradition.

12 There is a body of law (some of it common law and some of it statutory) whereby interest can run where a debt is not paid when due, including (but not limited to) such matters as judicial interest, interest on overdue tax, and the Late Payment of Commercial Debts (Interest) Act 1998.

13 Whether this is a separate principle, or an aspect of the previous principle, I do not know.

14 One comes across references to other Arabic terms, but it may be (I do not know) that all such other terms boil down to one of the three mentioned in the text.

partnership, this being called *musharaka*.[15] Before looking at these, a few words on terminology.

(1) Terminology: "mortgage," "debtor," "lender"

Although the terms "Islamic mortgage" and, less commonly, "Halal mortgage" are in standard use, lenders offering these products tend to prefer the term "home purchase plan," no doubt because the term "mortgage" suggests the existence of a contract of loan. (Still, the term "home purchase plan" does not work well, because it suggests that the finance is available only for house purchase. In fact it is also available where a person already owns property and wishes to raise money on the back of it.) For the same reason, the terms "debtor/borrower" and "creditor/lender" tend to be avoided. This is easily achieved, by using such terms as "the customer," "the bank" etc. In this paper, however, this terminology is not adopted.[16]

(2) Workaround (i): *ijara*

In the first type of workaround, *ijara*, the lender acquires the property and leases it to the borrower for the mortgage term, such as 25 years. The contract confers on the borrower a right to acquire ownership at the end of the term. In short, the arrangement is one that, for moveables, would be called hire-purchase, though this analogy seems never to be remarked upon.[17] Whether this method has been used to any extent in Scotland I do not know, but it is common in England. The entry in HM Land Registry shows the lender as owner, and shows the borrower as holding a registered lease.[18] The lease is usually charged to the lender by the borrower, but one may wonder how much this really adds to the lender's security, given that the lender has in any event the fee simple, coupled with all the rights of a landlord if a tenant is failing to pay the rent.

The "rent" covers both the interest and the capital payments. The rent does not relate to the value of the property, as would be the case in a genuine

---

15 These three terms are variously transliterated.

16 And for convenience in this context I use the term "mortgage" even though it is not the right term for Scots law. I beg forgiveness.

17 Hire purchase is itself a workaround, arising from a different cause, namely the inadequacy of chattel mortgage law in England, and its complete absence in Scotland.

18 Except in the unusual case of a very short-term mortgage, where the lease term will be too short to be registrable.

lease. For instance, a buyer who puts down a 50% deposit on the property would be paying less rent than a buyer of an identical property who puts down only a 30% deposit. The rent is reviewed periodically, but not in line with the changing value of the property, as would happen with a genuine rent, but in line with changing market interest rates. Typically the "rent" is linked either to LIBOR[19] or to Bank of England lending rate. The aim is to achieve, as closely as possible, the effects of a conventional mortgage.

(3) Workaround (ii): *murabaha*

In the second type of workaround, *murabaha*,[20] the lender buys the property and then immediately resells it to the borrower at a higher price, the price to be paid in instalments over a period of years. (15 years seems to be a common period for this kind of mortgage.) For instance, the property is bought by the lender for £200,000, and immediately resold to the borrower for £300,000.[21] (The difference depends partly on the length of the mortgage term and partly on market interest rates at the time of the transaction.) This latter price is paid in instalments. At the end of the mortgage term, the lender conveys title to the borrower. The "price" is in reality, though not in name, a mix of two elements: capital repayments and interest. One drawback to this scheme is that the interest rate is non-variable, for the re-sale price is fixed at the outset.

I have said that there is first a transfer by the original seller to the lender, and a later transfer by the lender to the borrower. But one could imagine a modified structure, whereby there are at the outset two transfers, one by the original seller to the lender, followed (perhaps the next day) by the transfer by the lender to the borrower, coupled with a mortgage back to the lender by the borrower. But whether this happens at all in practice I do not know. Finally, while this type of mortgage is used in England, I am not aware that there has been any use of it in Scotland.

---

19 London Interbank Offered Rate.

20 Also transliterated as *murabahah*.

21 This paper is about private law, not public law, but it may be noted that double tax is not payable: Land and Buildings Transaction Tax (Scotland) Act 2013 sch 7. These provisions reproduce ss 71A-73AB of the Finance Act 2003, the latter remaining in force south of the border. The exemptions apply not only to *murabaha* mortgages but to any Islamic mortgage involving double transfer.

(4) Workaround (iii): *musharaka*

The third type of workaround is the *musharaka*,[22] and this is of particular importance because my impression is that it is the main form in use in Scotland.[23] The word means "partnership," and the broad idea is that borrower and lender own the property as partners. It is, however, not a partnership in any sense of that term known to Scots (or English) law. Thus it is not a partnership at common law, or under the Partnership Act 1890, the Limited Partnerships Act 1907, or the Limited Liability Partnerships Act 2000. In what sense it could be described as a partnership in any sense of that word is not easy to see. Nevertheless this arrangement is marketed as being a partnership.

The only form that seems to be used in the UK is the "diminishing *musharaka*," in which borrower and lender in some sense (see below) co-own the property, and the borrower buys the lender's shares over a period of time, eventually ending up with 100%. In the meantime the borrower pays the lender interest on the diminishing balance, this interest taking the nominal form of rent. As in a conventional "repayment mortgage," the borrower's periodical payments to the lender include both capital and interest, the latter being named rent. As with the *ijara* mortgage, the rent is kept under regular review, and is linked to LIBOR or to Bank of England rate. The diminishing *musharaka* mortgage seems to be the main form of Islamic mortgage in use in Scotland.

Transferring a slice of ownership from lender to borrower every month or quarter or year would be awkward and expensive, and whilst numerous websites say that that is what happens, I am sceptical. The diminishing *musharaka* is the only type of Islamic mortgage where I have been able to study the documentation in detail. I am very much obliged to the Islamic Bank of Britain plc, which seems to have the main share of this area of finance in Scotland, for providing me with that documentation. What happens (at least under the IBB's Scottish documentation) is that the property is held by the debtor as trustee, and the borrower and lender have beneficial interests under the trust. As the borrower gradually repays

---

22   Also transliterated as *musharakah*.

23   I am most grateful to the Islamic Bank of Britain plc for providing me with its full style documentation for Islamic mortgages in Scotland.

the lender, the beneficial shares change, until eventually the borrower has a 100% share of the beneficial interest. As in the other types of Islamic mortgage, the regular payments are in substance payments of capital plus interest. The interest is called an "occupancy payment." There is a standard security over the property in favour of the bank. Though this is granted by the debtor as trustee (for title is held as trustee) it secures the obligations owed by the debtor as an individual. Thus in property law terms, this has the same structure as a conventional standard security: ownership held by the borrower, and a subordinate real right of security is held by the lender. Once the borrower has acquired 100% of the beneficial interest, the bank discharges the standard security. Of the three types, the diminishing *musharaka* comes the nearest to being the same as a conventional mortgage in everything but name.

In England, by contrast, it seems that title is usually vested in the lender, with the lender then granting a lease to the borrower in respect of the lender's beneficial share of the property. The difference between this and *ijara* is perhaps not clear to those not expert in Islamic theology.

E. Shared Risk?

It is commonly said that in Islamic finance there must be risk-sharing. This statement as such is not very informative, since in all finance there is risk-sharing: in a conventional loan, the borrower runs the risk of not being able to pay, with unfortunate consequences, and the lender runs the risk of not being paid, also with unfortunate consequences. "Sharia-compliant mortgages mean that the bank and the borrower share the risks of repayment rather than charging any form of interest."[24] As far as I can see that is not true. If the borrower defaults, the bank sells the property and takes what is due. If there is a shortfall, the borrower remains liable. I cannot be sure that this is universally the position: that would require more research than I have been able to undertake. But it may be noted that the more a financial deal protects the borrower, the more expensive it is going to be.

It seems that in an Islamic mortgage the lender and borrower are supposed to share the burden of maintenance, presumably on the basis of risk-sharing. But again this can be circumvented. For instance in the

24 See above.

IBB documentation, the borrower is bound to maintain the property, and the bank the binds itself to pay the borrower the "service change amount" (defined as "the expenses incurred by you in providing the services" – that is, maintaining the property). But at the same time any such amount is automatically met by a "supplemental occupancy payment" due by the borrower to the bank, which is of precisely the same amount.[25] There is also an obligation on the borrower to insure the property. (How that fits in with the prohibition of insurance in Shari'a law I do not know.)

F. The 20-Year Issue

The Land Reform (Scotland) Act 1974 provided that residential leases could not be for longer than 20 years.[26] That is a problem if an Islamic mortgage involves a lease, as in the *ijara*, and the term of the loan is over 20 years. How significant the problem is depends to some extent on how one interprets the rather complex provisions of the 1974 Act. It seems that the rule has in fact been a reason why there has (as it seems) been little attempt to use *ijara* mortgages in Scotland, though it should be noted that the rule in the 1974 Act does not affect non-residential property. In the IBB documentation for "diminishing *musharaka*" the interest is labelled not "rent" but an "occupancy payment" and one imagines that the 1974 Act is the reason for that terminology. Whether such words make any difference is perhaps open to debate: for instance in an English case in 1985 the House of Lords held that language designed to prevent an agreement being characterised as a lease will fail in its purpose if the agreement is in reality a lease.[27] There is an irony here: in the 1985 case an arrangement that was in reality a lease was being dressed up in the documentation as not being a lease: in (some types of) Islamic mortgages what is in reality not a lease is being dressed up in the documentation as being a lease. Although one might speculate as to what would happen if a court were to say that "occupancy payment" means rent, with the result that the 1974 Act is engaged, that is surely unlikely since (unlike the 1985 case) the underlying intention of the parties is not a tenancy anyway.

---

25 This is, at least, how I understand the documentation. The documentation is sometimes unclear to me, but the same is true of the documentation for conventional secured loans.

26 Sections 8-10. Some exceptions were introduced by the Housing (Scotland) Act 2010 s 138 but the basic rule remains. It may be added that the 1974 Act did not apply to pre-existing leases.

27 *Street v Mountford* [1985] AC 809.

The period of 20 years crops up quite often in property law, and one such instance is the rule that a standard security is redeemable after 20 years regardless of the terms of the agreement.[28] It is occasionally suggested that this rule might have negative consequences for Islamic mortgages, but in fact the rule has no greater significance for Islamic mortgages than it does for conventional mortgages,[29] and accordingly nothing more will be said here.

G. The "Lease between Co-owners" Issue

If property is co-owned, it cannot be leased to one of the co-owners.[30] Whilst this is a background issue worth noting, its importance for Islamic mortgages is probably limited. In the first place, in Islamic mortgages it does not seem that the property is in fact co-owned between borrower and lender (despite what one reads on the internet): as far as I can see title is always held (in Scotland at least) either by the borrower (solely) or by the lender (solely). In the second place, the rule does not prevent an arrangement whereby one co-owner has exclusive occupation, paying the others a periodical sum in return. That is perfectly possible: the rule merely says that such an arrangement is not a lease. Finally, it is perhaps open to debate how the rule would work out if something called a "lease" were to be entered into between those holding the *beneficial interest* under a trust. But as has been said, that seems to be rare or unknown in Scottish Islamic mortgages.

H. The "Only by Standard Security" Issue

In the years before 1970, the usual way of securing a loan over heritable property was the "*ex facie* absolute disposition." Here title was vested in the lender, and the debtor's right was a contractual: to occupy the property, and, after paying off the loan, with interest, to have the property conveyed to him/her. In the language of Roman law, this was *fiducia cum creditore*.

---

28 Land Tenure Reform (Scotland) Act 1974 s 11. The Housing (Scotland) Act 2014 s 93 confers power on the Scottish Ministers to alter this period.

29 That is also the view of the Scottish Government. See Scottish Government, Consultation on Proposals to Exempt Certain Heritable Securities from the "20 Year Security Rule" (2014), available at http://www.scotland.gov.uk/Resource/0046/00461603.pdf

30 *Clydesdale Bank v Davidson* 1998 SC (HL) 51.

The arrangement could happen in either of two ways. In the first place, Donald Debtor might own the property and then convey it to a lender. In the second place, and this was commoner in practice, it was used as acquisition finance: Donald Debtor wanted to buy a house, and would conclude missives, but would direct the seller to convey, not to him, but to his lender.

There was thus a gap between substantive reality (debtor = in reality owner, bank = in reality merely secured lender) and legal reality (bank = owner, debtor = contractual occupier). This came to be seen as undesirable. The Conveyancing and Feudal Reform (Scotland) Act 1970 did two things.[31] First, it created a new form of heritable security, the standard security. Secondly, it banned the *ex facie* absolute disposition. The reform took root. Standard securities remain with us to this day, and *ex facie* absolute dispositions are now just a memory for the old and not even a memory for the young. As a result, few today remember the prohibition. The prohibition is phrased briefly:[32]

> A grant of any right over land or a real right in land for the purpose of securing any debt by way of a heritable security shall only be capable of being effected at law[33] if it is embodied in a standard security. Where for the purpose last-mentioned any deed which is not in the form of a standard security contains a disposition or assignation of land or of a real right in land, it shall to that extent be void and unenforceable...

This prohibition seems to strike at some types of Islamic mortgage, where heritable property is granted in security of a debt, otherwise than by standard security. An argument could be set up that the statutory prohibition affects only grants by debtor to creditor, and that grants by a third party to the creditor are unaffected, which would be the state of affairs, for the *ijara* and the *murabaha*, in acquisition finance, i.e. where Donald Debtor is seeking to buy property and asks the seller to convey to the bank. This is not the place

---

31 To speak of just "two things" is of course to oversimplify.

32 Conveyancing and Feudal Reform (Scotland) Act 1970 s 9(3) and part of (4). It is quoted here in its amended form. The contrast between the brevity of this prohibition and the prolixity of the 1974 prohibition of long leases over residential property is striking.

33 Though not pertinent to this paper, I cannot resist mentioning that these two words ("at law") have always puzzled me. Presumably they were included for *some* purpose. At law – as opposed to what? Equity? This is not entirely a joke. Note that the passage says "at law" not "in law." English equity lawyers use the contrasting terms "*at* law" and "*in* equity."

to discuss that argument;[34] I will only mention that in 1970 it was taken for granted that the statutory prohibition applied to both types of case, with the result that the *ex facie* absolute disposition wholly disappeared.

The issue is most serious for the *ijara*: this seems to be exactly the sort of thing that the section 9 prohibition was aimed at. As for the *murabaha*, the argument is a good deal weaker, because although the property is conveyed to the creditor, it is then immediately conveyed to the debtor. What about the diminishing *musharaka*? If the typical English form were adopted, whereby title is vested in the bank, the section 9 prohibition would seem to apply, but, as mentioned, this form does not seem common in Scotland. Might the section 9 prohibition apply to the form described above, used in Scotland? The property itself is not granted to the bank in security of a debt, so probably the section 9 prohibition is not engaged. However, the wording of the section 9 prohibition is broad, and could be read as covering even the grant, by way of security, of even a beneficial share of property.

It might be said that the section 9 prohibition is irrelevant to Islamic finance, because the section 9 prohibition is about security for loan finance, and Islamic mortgages do not use the contract of loan. That argument does not work. Section 9 is not tied to loans but to "debt,"[35] and all Islamic mortgages use debt.

Finally on this subject, the section 9 prohibition is not some quirky fossil rule. There is a strong argument of public policy in its favour: that for the owner of heritable property to be the party that is in reality merely a lender, is an unacceptable subterfuge: the transaction should show its face.

I. The Consumer Protection Issue

Consumer protection is one of the themes of modern law. Consumers are protected[36] in credit transactions, in tenancy agreements, in standard securities and in many other areas. In a conventional mortgage, consumers are protected in a number of ways, including the provisions of the Conveyancing and Feudal Reform (Scotland) 1970, as amended over

---

34 Discussion of section 9 would take a paper to itself. It is curious that, as far as I know, it has never been subject to any published examination in detail. Furthermore, the report that led to section 9 said rather little about it. (Report on Conveyancing Legislation and Practice (Cmnd 3118: 1966), chaired by Robert's great predecessor, Jack Halliday.)

35 Defined in the broadest way: s 9(8)(c).

36 The quality of the protection is of course open to debate, but that cannot be discussed here.

the years. Are Islamic mortgages subject to the same level of consumer protection as conventional mortgages? In the case where title is vested in the debtor, and the creditor's enforcement rights are based on a standard security, the answer would seem to be affirmative. But in those structures where title is held by the lender,[37] consumer protection is weakened. The modern law on protecting mortgage debtors is based on the assumption that what is involved is a standard security.[38] If there is no standard security, and title is held by the bank, the consumer protection provisions are not engaged. If the structure is that of an *ijara* mortgage, the creditor has title and the debtor has a lease; that may engage the consumer protection provisions of lease law, but the protections are not the same. In *murabaha* it is not apparent to me that there would be any protection at all, apart from generic consumer credit protection.

J. Second Mortgages

Property can be encumbered by more than one standard security. Indeed, there is in theory no limit to the number that can be granted, though I do not recall ever having seen more than four. Subject to one or two qualifications, they rank by order of creation of the real right, which is to say by date of registration. There is no conceptual difficulty about multiple standard securities, for the groundwork lies in the theory of property law that we have inherited from the civilian tradition: the grant of a subordinate real right leaves ownership where it was. One of the drawbacks of the old *ex facie* absolute disposition was that second mortgages were problematic. A workaround was created whereby the debtor's personal right to a future conveyance (after paying off the loan) was assigned by way of security.

The same problems, and indeed perhaps even more intractable, would arise for Islamic mortgages where title is held by the lender. Whether some workaround would be possible, I do not know. If it is not possible, that is a negative. If it is possible, it would inevitably be artificial and cumbersome, as was the case with the old *ex facie* absolute disposition.[39] Even where

---

37 Structures that may fall foul of the section 9 prohibition (see above).
38 Much the same is true I think in English law.
39 Given the problems with the old *ex facie* absolute disposition, it may be wondered why it was in such common use until 1970. The short answer is that although there were alternatives, whereby the creditor had a subordinate real right and the substantive owner was also the legal owner (as in a standard security), these alternatives had significant technical disadvantages.

title is not held by the lender, there would be problems. Thus in the IBB diminishing *musharaka* the registered owner is the debtor but *qua* trustee, the beneficial interest being divided between debtor and lender. How one could pin a second mortgage on to that I am is unclear to me.

K. Insolvency Risk

In a conventional mortgage, the possible future insolvency of the creditor is not a risk for the debtor. If Donald Debtor borrows £100,000 from the Bank of Unst, Fetlar and Yell,[40] secured by standard security, and in the next financial crisis the bank becomes insolvent, and, like Lehman Brothers, is allowed to collapse, Donald Debtor is not sucked into that collapse, because he owns his property. That is one of the benefits of the system of subordinate real rights. But if property is owned by Bank of Unst, Fetlar and Yell, Donald has a problem.[41] The subject is complex, involving, among other things, the question of whether Donald can successfully argue that the bank owns the property as implied, or as constructive, trustee. That issue would require a whole paper to itself. I merely note it here as another example of the problems that may arise from adopting an artificial structure.

L. Impediments?

Holyrood:

> S2W-16368 – Brian Adam (Aberdeen North) (SNP) (Date Lodged Tuesday, May 10, 2005):

> To ask the Scottish Executive whether any impediments exist in Scots law to the provision of Islamic mortgages and, if so, what action it will take to remove these.

> Answered by Hugh Henry (Thursday, May 19, 2005):

> The Scottish Executive is not aware of any impediment in Scots law which prevents the provision of Islamic mortgages.

---

40 Actually too good a name to waste of a mere bank, I'm sure you'll agree, Robert. In future this will be a law firm. Everyone who knew them agrees that Messrs Unst, Fetlar and Yell (all LLB (Glas)) not only had a sound knowledge of the law of Scotland, but were shrewd men of business, whose success in legal practice was affected neither by Mr Unst's occasional grumpiness, nor by Mr Yell's excitable disposition.

41 Which, however, is not the case for the IBB Scottish mortgage.

An answer that has the merit of brevity. Given what has already been said in this paper, there is no need here to discuss the answer substantively, but something should be said about the question. "Impediment"? The word suggests something undesirable. Someone (such as myself) with the view that Islamic mortgages, when compared with conventional mortgages, might be undesirable, would not use such language.

M. Conclusion

Islamic mortgages aim at the same practical reality as conventional mortgages. Different words are used, to conceal the reality. That, at least, is how it seems to me. If interest-bearing mortgages are a bad thing, then Islamic mortgages are a bad thing, for Islamic mortgages are, apart from the wrapping, interest-bearing mortgages. But if, on the other hand, interest-bearing mortgages are not a bad thing, then it is better that they should be done in an open manner, and not by artificial means, producing both complexity and pitfalls. And finally, whilst I am no expert in Islamic theology, I note that those who do have such expertise frequently criticise Islamic mortgages as being mere shams.[42] What they say (albeit that I do not subscribe to Islam) makes more sense to me than the promotional brochures and videos of the institutions that offer what they call Shari'a-compliant finance, brochures and videos that the mainstream media and politicians should have a slightly more critical attitude towards.

---

42   Here is a sample: (i) http://www.islamicawakening.com/viewarticle.php?articleID=1291;
(ii)   http://sunnahonline.com/library/contemporary-issues/115-islamic-ijara-mortgages-by-hsbc-and-other-banks;   (iii)   http://www.islamicmortgages.co.uk/index.php?id=258;
(iv) http://www.islamicparty.com/commonsense/hlmort.htm

16. Completion of the Land Register: The Scottish Approach

John King

A. Introduction

Scotland can lay claim to the world's oldest, still running, public property register. Dating from 1617,[1] the Register of Sasines has witnessed the industrial revolution, the extension of the franchise and the spread of property ownership. It is a real success story; the authors of the Act got it right first time, and deed registration became a concept which was subsequently adopted, in various guises, across the world.

Scotland also has one of the most recent land registration systems by international standards. The Land Register was a late introduction to Scotland: the Land Registration (Scotland) Act 1979 ("the 1979 Act") commenced in 1981, albeit only for the operational county of Renfrew.[2] It took a further 22 years before the Land Register was extended to all registration counties in Scotland.[3] The 1979 Act has enabled the registration

---

1 Registration Act 1617.
2 Land Registration (Scotland) Act 1979 (Commencement n 1) Order 1980, SI 1980/1412.
3 The Land Registration (Scotland) Act 1979 (Commencement n 16) Order 2002, SI 2002/432, brought on to the Land Register the registration counties of Banff, Moray, Nairn, Ross and Cromarty, Caithness, Sutherland and Orkney and Zetland.

    http://dx.doi.org/10.11647/OBP.0056.16

of over 1.5 million properties in Scotland but it has not been without challenge or criticism.

One commentator scathingly described the Act as "having all the intellectual sharpness of mashed potato."[4] Consequently, within 12 years of the 1979 Act operating throughout Scotland (though doubts persisted as to whether or not it also extended to Scotland's seabed as well as its land), it has been reformed and replaced, subject to transitional provisions, by the Land Registration etc. (Scotland) Act 2012 ("the 2012 Act").

One of the key policy aims that lay behind the 2012 Act was enabling the completion of the Land Register. No timescale for completion was provided in the Act, though the Economy, Energy and Tourism Committee recommended the "setting of a target and interim targets, even if aspirational, on the face of the Bill."[5] This was not an approach that found favour with the Minister responsible for the Bill.[6] However, other factors have subsequently influenced Scottish Ministers to set a timescale for completion.

In May 2014 the final report of the Land Reform Review Group was presented to Scottish Ministers.[7] Established by the Scottish Government in May 2012, the ground had a remit to consider a broad spectrum of land reform issues. One of the areas it considered was coverage of the Land Register and it recommended that:[8]

> ...the Scottish Government should be doing more to increase the rate of registrations to completion of the Register, a planned programme to register public lands and additional triggers to induce the first registration of other lands.

Following consideration of that report, Paul Wheelhouse MSP, the Minister for Environment and Climate Change, made the following announcement:[9]

> Along with my colleague Enterprise Minister Fergus Ewing, I have asked Registers of Scotland to prepare to complete land registration within 10 years, with all public land registered within five years.

---

4   Professor George Gretton commenting on *Kaur v Singh*: see 1997 SCLR 1075 at 1085.
5   Scottish Parliament Official Report, Economy, Energy and Tourism Committee, 6 Mar 2012, col 58.
6   Land Registration etc. (Scotland) Bill: Economy, Energy and Tourism Committee Stage 1 Report – Scottish Government Response (2012).
7   Land Reform Review Group, *The Land of Scotland and the Common Good* (2014).
8   Para 32.
9   Scottish Government, "Target Set to Register all Scotland's Land" (news release), 25 May 2014.

So, some 33 years since land registration was introduced to Scotland, we now have a target for completing the Land Register by the end of 2024. This essay seeks to offer a definition of completion, considers the contrasting approaches to completion under both the 1979 Act and the 2012 Act, compares these with the English and Welsh experience and asks whether or not the legal tools exist to enable completion within the ten year target.

B. The Case for Completion

Setting aside discussion over the timescale for completion, the suggestion that a completed Land Register is desirable is likely to be met with general approval. That was certainly the emphasis of the evidence provided to the Economy, Energy and Tourism committee. They reported that there "was overwhelming support from witnesses for a Land Register that is reliable, secure and accessible and for the eventual closure of the Register of Sasines."[10]

The arguments in favour of a completed Land Register have been well rehearsed in recent years. The Scottish Law Commission (SLC) succinctly stated that "the short answer is that the Land Register is better than the Register of Sasines"[11] and then detailed why this was so. Similarly the Consultation Document on completion of the Land Register[12] ("the completion consultation document") lists the benefits. Indeed, glancing south of the Border, the website of Her Majesty's Land Registry (HMLR)[13] also lists near identical reasons why registration in the Land Register and the aim of a completed register is so desirable. So, what are the reasons?

The completion consultation document sets out four compelling reasons: transparency, cost, efficiency and national asset. Transparency is self-evident. A map-based register of title to land makes for simple interrogation and so provides ease of access to information on who owns Scotland. That, in turn, reduces the costs associated with examination of titles: it takes less

---

10   Scottish Parliament, Official Report, Economy, Energy and Tourism Committee, 6 Mar 2012, col 19.

11   Scottish Law Commission, Report on *Land Registration* (Scot Law Com n 222, 2012) vol 1 para 33.17.

12   Registers of Scotland, Completion of the Land Register Public Consultation (2014).

13   Land Registry, Practice Guide 1: First Registrations (2003) para 1.2, available at http://www.gov.uk/government/publications/first-registrations/practice-guide-1-first-registrations. One additional advantage they list is making large holdings of land and portfolios of charges more readily marketable.

time and effort to examine an entry on the Land Register than it does if a property is held under title deeds on the Sasine Register. Added to this, the SLC has highlighted[14] the growing issue that some younger conveyancers may not have the requisite knowledge of the workings of Sasine titles.

For a country of Scotland's size, it is inefficient to have two property registers. The Land Register makes it easier to transact with property, which in turn, facilitates the property market and makes Scotland attractive to foreign investment. At a macro level, transparency, ease of access and the guarantee of title adds value to the economy. That fits with the final reason provided by the completion consultation document for a completed Land Register being a national asset. Knowing who owns Scotland and having access to that information supports those public and private bodies and companies whose administrative and business activities require use of accurate title information. The Land Reform Review Group also commented[15] on the difficulties of having an informed discussion on land reform and land use in the absence of comprehensive information on land ownership in Scotland.

Though there is general consensus that a completed Land Register would be an unqualified positive for Scotland, the fact the journey to that end is set against the backdrop of a near 400-year old deeds register is to our advantage. It is more helpful to have two property registers than to simply have one incomplete Land Register. If a property is not on the Land Register, there is a very high chance it will rest on deeds in the Sasine Register. In short, except for an indeterminate but expected low volume of properties not on either register, it is generally possible, albeit at times with difficulty, to identify the title deed or potential title deed that relates to an area of land.

Contrast that with England and Wales. There is one national property register, Her Majesty's Land Register ("HMLR"), but it is not yet complete. Approximately 15% of the land mass of England and Wales is not on HMLR.[16] Tracking information on non-registered land is anything but straightforward; there may be some information in local registers or there may simply be no information available. So, as much as there are solid reasons for completing Scotland's Land Register, we should recognise that

---

14   Scottish Law Commission, Report on *Land Registration* (n 11) vol 1 para 33.18.
15   Land Reform Review Group, *The Land of Scotland and the Common Good* (n 7) Ch 23.
16   HM Land Registry, *Annual Report and Accounts 2013/14* (2014) 43.

other jurisdictions with incomplete Land Registers may look at us with envy over the continuing safety net that an old deeds register can provide.

C. What Constitutes Completion?

In being asked to complete the register within ten years, it is clearly essential that the Keeper sets out what this entails. This allows progress to be monitored and expectations to be managed. There are various interpretations that can be suggested.

First, completing the Land Register could be viewed as achieved when the Sasine Register is closed to new deeds of any type. RoS estimates that there are some 1.1 million property titles[17] remaining in the Sasine Register. The rate at which titles transfer from the Sasine Register to the Land Register has averaged at an annual rate of 40,270 first registrations over the last ten years.[18] On the designated commencement day for the 2012 Act, 8 December 2014 ("the designated day"), the Sasine Register closed to all dispositions. Over the last ten years, an average of 22,850 dispositions have been recorded each year in the Sasine Register.[19]

The 2012 Act contains powers under section 48(2) and (3) which, if used in full, could have the effect of closing the Sasine Register to all deeds. The mechanics and practicalities of this are discussed later. Of course that would not make the Sasine Register redundant; it would simply up the pace with which properties transfer on to the Land Register. In 2013-14 some 35,000 deeds were recorded in the Sasine Register, affecting an estimated 25,000 different properties and interests in land.[20] Notwithstanding the increased pace with which properties would move on to the Land Register, the fact remains that the two property registers would continue to co-exist for potentially many decades. So, closure of the Sasine Register to new deeds would not equate with a completed Land Register.

Secondly, taking the first interpretation a step further, completion could be viewed as achieved when all properties and interests held on title deeds recorded in the Sasine Register are brought on to the Land Register. Unquestionably that would be a significant achievement, as it would enable the Sasine Register to take a well-earned retirement amongst Scotland's

---

17   Registers of Scotland (RoS) estimates, current as of November 2014.
18   Based on Land Register intake figures from April 2004-March 2014.
19   Sasine Register Minute Book entries April 2004-March 2013.
20   Sasine Register Minute Book April 2013-March 2014.

national archives. However in terms of Scotland's new Cadastral Map there would still be gaps. In land registration parlance, there would still be tracts of land without a red edge delineating ownership boundaries. There would still be unregistered land and so the Land Register would not be complete.

Thirdly, the most comprehensive interpretation of completion combines interpretations (i) and (ii) and seeks to add to that the remaining unregistered land. That would provide a complete cadastral map for Scotland reflecting ownership of land, identifying long leases over land and also detailing ownership of separate tenements in that land. It is currently impossible to ascertain the full extent of land that does not fall within either the Land Register or the Sasine Register. Within RoS we have anecdotal knowledge of some such land, for example the original land holdings of St Andrews University and some City of Edinburgh Council land holdings in Edinburgh's Old Town. The full extent of unregistered land will only become apparent when all properties and interests held on title deeds recorded in the Sasine Register are in turn registered in the Land Register. Much of this land will have seen ownership transferred via charters and deeds that were executed prior to the establishment of the Sasine Register. It is also possible that some of this land will have been gifted as common good land, may be undivided commonty or may, if never alienated, remain with the Crown.

It is also inevitable that some of this notionally unregistered land will ultimately trace back to titles on the Sasine Register that were considered to have previously transferred to the Land Register. This is not surprising; aside from the difficulties in interpreting often vague Sasine deed descriptions, the prescribed application form[21] for a first registration under the 1979 Act invites the applicant to advise if they will accept the Land Register boundaries reflecting the occupied extent where that is less than the legal extent as set out in the deeds. Whilst this provision can often resolve what would otherwise be a boundary issue with a neighbouring property that also includes the same area within its title deeds, there are instances where slithers of land excluded from Land Register titles will not fall into any other titles.

An applicant may choose not to include land outwith their physical boundaries (fence, hedge etc.) within the Land Register title. This may

---

21   Land Register (Scotland) Rules 2006, SSI 2006/485, r 9(i)(a) (Part B question 2(a)).

satisfy the expectations of a purchaser in a first registration transaction but it does mean that the seller may remain, unwittingly in most cases, the owner of the excluded interest. It is not uncommon for such slithers to be considered abandoned and unused by anyone or to be possessed as part of a neighbouring property extent without being contained within the legal title for that property. Identifying and resolving these unintended consequences of the operation of land registration under the 1979 Act will be challenging, though it may be that the new 2012 Act provisions for prescriptive claimants[22] will provide a vehicle for bringing some of these strips of land on to the Land Register.

The completion consultation document sets the bar high. It favours the comprehensive interpretation. It is noted that even if this point is achieved, the cadastral map will not remain unchanged; it is a living map and registered extents will change to reflect sub-divisions and amalgamations of property.

D. Completion: Achievable or Unattainable?

All three of the above possible interpretations talk in terms of absolutes when considering what could constitute completion. The question that arises is whether or not it is practical to talk in terms of absolutes or is that an aspiration that is simply too high. The answer depends in large part on whether or not legal powers exist to enable completion or not. If the legal powers do exist, and there is a political commitment to maximising the use and effect of those powers, then absolute completion is not a forlorn aspiration. Equally, starting from a position whereby legal powers on their own would not be sufficient to achieve completion would suggest that any target ought to be more modest.

(1) England and Wales: the comprehensive register

There has long been an unsubstantiated anecdotal view amongst RoS registration staff that HMLR must be near completion. That view was informed by two factors (three if you include the absence of any research): first, the awareness that the Land Register stems from 1862,[23] and secondly the application of a little relative mathematics. The argument runs that if

---

22 Land Registration etc (Scotland) Act 2012, ss 43-45.
23 Land Registry Act 1862.

the Land Register has been in existence for over 150 years, it must be near complete if our own Land Register has 58%[24] of properties on it after a mere 33 years. Set in the context of a pub quiz for land registrars, it is doubtful if many would correctly answer 54.5% if asked to estimate the end March 2006[25] figure for land mass coverage of England and Wales. Clearly, our view has been wrong.

It has taken a considerable period of time for their Land Register to gain traction. Although the Land Registry Act 1862 established a land register for England and Wales, it did not back its introduction with any element of direct or indirect compulsion. Consequently, by 1868, only 507 titles were registered. The need for compulsion was recognised, albeit in a less than robust fashion by the Land Transfer Act of 1897; local counties could still veto the introduction of compulsory registration.[26] As a result, adoption was slow.[27]

Compulsion was to the fore in the Land Registration Act 1925, as provision was made for the Sovereign, by Order in Council, to make registration following a sale compulsory in any area.[28] It is reported that forecasts at the time suggested that compulsory registration would be extended to all areas by 1955. This was not to be and the remaining 14 areas were not brought within the ambit of the Land Registry until 1 December 1990.[29] At this point there were some 12.7 million registered titles whereas now there are some 23.8 million.[30] Before the introduction of computer mapping the Land Registry was not able to work out the percentage of land registered. So, the fully-operational English and Welsh Land Register is only some 13 years ahead of our own wholly-operational Land Register.

HMLR do now have a considerably more comprehensive range of legal triggers for registration, referred to under section 4 of the Land Registration

---

24   Registers of Scotland, *Completion of the Land Register Public Consultation* (n 12).

25   Land Register, *Annual Report and Accounts 2005/06* (2006) 14.

26   Under s 20(5)-(6), the Registry had to give 6 months' notice to the council concerned and if within 3 months the Council held a meeting with at least two thirds of councillors present that rejected compulsory registration, then the order could not be made.

27   In 1899 London County Council became the first area to adopt compulsory registration following a sale. An attempt to pass a motion to prevent this under s 20(6) was defeated by 73 votes to 35 (*The Times*, 16 Feb 1898).

28   Land Registration Act 1925 s 120.

29   Registration of Title Order 1989, SI 1987/1347, available at http://www.legislation.gov.uk/uksi/1989/1347/contents/made. These were the districts of Babergh, Castle Point, Forest Heath, Leominster, Maldon, Malvern Hills, Mid Suffolk, Rochford, St Edmundsbury, South Herefordshire, Suffolk Coastal, Tendring, Wychavon and Wyre Forest.

30   HM Land Registry, *Annual Report and Accounts 2013/14* (n 16) 11.

There is of course a sting in the tail should registration not be sought, for in the absence of registration no real right will be obtained. As the commentary to the Registration of Title Practice Book narrates, "the compulsitor is that there shall be no real right without registration."[47] There are other factors driving the time frame in which registration ought to occur: limited company standard securities over registered land require registration in the Land Register before they can be registered in the Register of Charges.[48] The protection afforded by letters of obligation and the new advance notices[49] in effect set a time-frame within which registration will, in the main, occur.

Requests for voluntary registration were permissible under the 1979 Act[50] and the Keeper was given the discretion on whether or not to accept such a request. The criterion by which the Keeper should consider such a request is that of expediency. In practice, for the period from 1981 through to the mid-2000s that criterion was tightly applied and voluntary registrations were rare. The emphasis was very much on the impact such a request would have on the Keeper and not on the needs of the applicant. As the Practice Book[51] explains: "the Keeper does not normally accept voluntary registrations unless there are obvious benefits to him." The main source of voluntary registrations related to transfers of a half *pro indiviso* share in a Sasine title. In those circumstances the Keeper would encourage voluntary registration of the remaining half share. The only other circumstance in which the Keeper would regularly accept a request was in connection with a builder or developer's title for which individual plots were about to be sold.

The reason for the reluctance to accept requests was simple: RoS was not coping with the volume of trigger-based registrations and did not want to add to the time it would take to complete those registrations. The Keeper's position began to change in the mid-2000s. There was growing acceptance that the balance of convenience was tipped too heavily in favour of the Keeper. A more relaxed and encouraging approach developed and culminated in a joint article[52] by the current Keeper and Fergus Ewing MSP, the Minister for

---

47   *Registration of Title Practice Book*, 1st edn (1981) para C02.
48   Companies Act 1985 s 410.
49   Section 58(1) of the 2012 Act provides an advance notice has effect for the period of 35 days.
50   1979 Act s 2(1)(b).
51   *Registration of Title Practice Book*, 2nd edn (2000) para 2.9.
52   F Ewing and S Adams, "All aboard the Land Register," 17 Oct 2011, available at http://www.journalonline.co.uk/Magazine/56-10/1010324.aspx

Energy Economy and Tourism, heralding an effective open door policy. The exceptions to that are limited and relate in the main to ongoing litigation affecting the property to which the request relates. In the last four years, RoS estimate that the volume of voluntary registrations has been in the region of 2000 applications per annum: about 4% of the overall volume of first registrations. That of course compares poorly with the volume of voluntary applications received by HMLR. The open door policy has been supported by some targeted marketing of voluntary registration, mostly around commercial and residential developers and large private estates.

The 1979 Act was not wholly oblivious to the future. The Act states that Ministers may provide:[53]

> ...that interests in land of a kind or kinds specified in the order... shall be registered; and the provisions of this Act shall apply for the purposes of such registration with such modifications, which may include provision as to the expenses of such registration, as may be specified in the order.

The provision has not been used. Commentary in the Practice Book describes this provision somewhat dramatically as "machinery for the elimination of the Register of Sasines."[54] In a nod to the current discussion on funding completion, the then Government did indicate the costs of closing the Sasine Register would, other than in trigger situations, be borne by the public purse.[55]

The problem with the 1979 Act approach is that it allowed for no middle ground. Triggers for registration were set in the legislation and no provision was made for the addition of further triggers. Instead, section 2(5) allowed Scottish Ministers to provide that at a certain point in time those remaining unregistered properties would be registered by the Keeper. Finding an explanation as to how this provision would work in practice is challenging. I am unaware of any detailed discussions within RoS as to its use and there were no plans to suggest to Ministers that it be used. Mindful of the costs associated with section 2(5), the Scottish Executive did suggest in 1999 that consideration of its use would be appropriate when most properties in a registration county had been registered through sale.[56] It indicated that would be the case after 10 to 15 years of land registration. That was an overly optimistic assessment of the pace of completion. In the event, the gap from a limited set of triggers to committing to full registration was considered a leap too far.

---

53   1979 Act s 2(5).

54   *Registration of Title Practice Book*, 1st edn (n 47) para C16.

55   HC Debs, First Scottish Standing Committee, 27 Mar 1979, col 13.

56   Scottish Executive, Land Reform: Proposals for Legislation (E/1999/1), Para 6.3.

Without question, the 1979 Act has advanced completion. In just under 34 years, some 1.5 million property titles have been registered, estimated at roughly 58% of all properties within Scotland.[57] This is a not inconsiderable figure given that it was April 2003 before all of Scotland was operational under the Act. For the registration counties that were first on to the Land Register, the title coverage is way in excess of the Scottish average; Renfrew stands at 76% and Dumbarton at 74%.[58] More recent converts to the Land Register, particularly those predominantly rural counties, have much less coverage. Both Ross & Cromarty and Caithness have fewest titles registered: an estimated 36%.[59] This is not surprising. Properties in the more economically active and densely populated urban areas change hands more frequently than properties in rural areas.

Under the 1979 Act triggers for registration, completion would simply not be achieved. Some properties never change hands and some transfer for no consideration. RoS forecast that registration counties would peak at around 90% title coverage based on the 1979 Act triggers.[60] Achieving 90% coverage would vary from registration county to registration county:

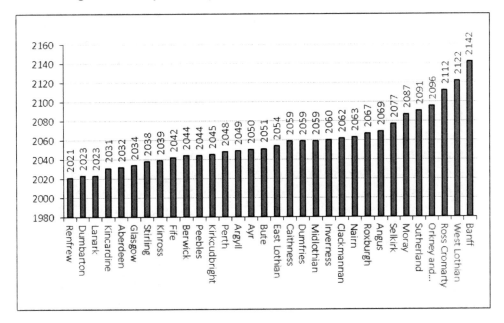

Projected completion rate with no changes

---

57   Registers of Scotland, *Completion of the Land Register Public Consultation* (n 12) para 16.

58   RoS, figures accurate to end Mar 2014.

59   Idem.

60   Registers of Scotland, *Completion of the Land Register Public Consultation* (n 12) para 26.

Between now and 2030. RoS forecast that only five registration counties would potentially exceed 90% title coverage. The majority of counties would take to 2060 to see 90% title coverage and for some of the more rural counties, such as Ross and Cromarty and Banff we could be waiting for up to 100 years and more. In short, completion would simply not happen and therein lies the driver for the changes introduced by the 2012 Act.

(3) The 2012 Act

The 2012 Act takes a markedly different approach to the bringing of properties on to the Land Register as compared with the 1979 Act. Not only does the Act provide the technical tools to further the goal of completion but underlying those technical provisions is a strategy to direct their use. The 2012 Act approach to registration moves away from the approach under the 1979 Act of listing transaction types the occurrence of which will require registration. Instead it lists those deeds to which the Register of Sasines is closed; the effect being that they must be registered in the Land Register.[61]

In an Act concerned with completion one might suspect that the list would be extensive. On the contrary it is brief. On the designated day the specified deeds to which the Sasine Register is closed number three; disposition, lease and assignation of lease. The door to the Sasine Register is left slightly ajar for those dispositions where recording in the Sasine Register is necessary for purposes of dual registration under the Title Conditions (Scotland) Act 2003.[62] Registration remains voluntary but as under the 1979 Act a real right cannot be acquired otherwise.[63]

The 2012 Act approach to registration makes no distinction between a disposition for value and a disposition for no consideration or value. Notwithstanding the additional 8500-10000 new registrations that RoS forecast will be generated by this approach, the impact on completion is marginal. The following table suggests that registration counties will achieve 90% completion earlier than would otherwise be the case but not significantly earlier.[64] Achieving 90% completion rates across Scotland would still take until the 22nd century. As under the 1979 Act, and indeed as is the case in England and Wales, some properties and interests will

---

61   2012 Act s 48(1).
62   Ibid s 48(6).
63   Ibid s 48(1).
64   RoS, Business Planning Forecast May 2014.

simply not change hands and so this new registration requirement will not deliver completion.

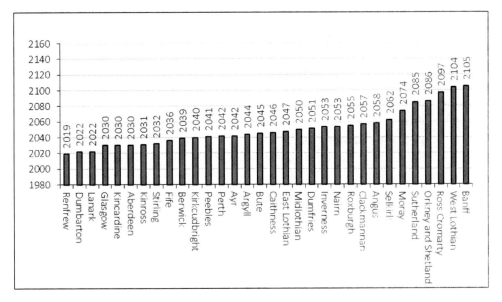

Projected impact of the 2012 Act

There is one further legislative change that the 2012 Act introduced that will aid completion, both in a direct and an indirect way. That change concerns leases. Leases are by their nature temporary. Under the 1979 Act, they enter the Land Register and then, at the end of their life, the associated entry on the Land Register is removed. The 2012 Act sets different legal requirements around leases and those requirements aid completion. It will no longer be possible to register a lease, a sub-lease or an assignation of an unregistered lease unless the plot of land to which the deed relates is also registered. Where the plot of land is unregistered, an application to register such a deed will induce registration of the owner's plot; termed "automatic plot registration."[65] On its own this will not have a major impact on completion – over the last ten years RoS has registered an annual average of 945 leases.[66] Where it will have more impact is on making landlords consider whether or not it would be more practical to voluntarily register

---

65   Automatic plot registration is required by the operation of sections 24, 25 and 30 of the 2012 Act.

66   RoS, Business Planning figures for the period January 2004-December 2013. From 1 January to 11 November 2014 some 1664 leased have been registered. The increase is in the main due to leases of airport car parking spaces.

all their land rather than simply the area affected by the lease. As a driver of voluntary registration, the impact of automatic plot registration could be significant, for it is only through voluntary registration that a landlord can retain control of the registration process for his or her land.

The 2012 Act brings about no immediate changes as far as applications for voluntary registration are concerned. The Keeper's discretion to accept or refuse such an application remains as does the test of expediency. So too does the Keeper's open door policy to voluntary applications. However, the Keeper recognises that more will be required than simply having an open door to voluntary applications if the ten year completion target is to be met. The volume of voluntary applications will have to increase substantially and the challenge for realising that will rest with the Keeper. Voluntary registration will have to be actively marketed and the Keeper will need to employ a range of different arguments to different sectors in aid of this. For some, the existence of the automatic plot registration provisions may offer an inducement to register; for others having certainty and assurance as to legal boundaries may be important: and for the wider public sector the catalyst to register will be the target set by Scottish Ministers to register such land within five years. It is the Keeper's understanding that the vehicle for this is voluntary registration.

Set against the benefits of voluntary registration will be cost. Costs will be a factor for many who are open to considering voluntary registration; the Keeper acknowledges this and the completion consultation document sought views on an appropriate level of financial incentivisation. Registration fees are only part of the overall costs; there will, in most cases, be legal costs. However, as the successful HMLR experience has demonstrated, costs are not an absolute barrier. The outcome of the consultation is not yet known.

The need to promote voluntary registration means that the legal discretion the Keeper has to refuse a request for voluntary registration is likely to prove theoretical rather than real. The 2012 Act gives Scottish Ministers the power[67] to prescribe an end to that discretion and it is thus perhaps no surprise that the Keeper favours its removal.[68] There are other strong legal reasons for ending that discretion and those reasons derive from the strategy for completion that the Act gives effect to. The completion toolkit set out in section 48 includes the power for Scottish Ministers, after due consultation with the Keeper and other appropriate

---

67   2012 Act s 27(6).
68   Registers of Scotland, *Completion of the Land Register Public Consultation* (n 12) para 30.

persons, to close the Sasine Register to standard securities on a county-by-county or all-Scotland basis. Closure of the Sasine Register in this way will create additional "triggers" that will increase the number of properties having their first registration onto the Land Register. Before this power can be enabled, section 48(7) requires that the Keeper's discretion to refuse an application for voluntary registration be removed.

The reason for this is perhaps best explained by an example. If the Sasine Register is closed to a standard security, the creditor's rights under the security can only be made real through registration of the security in the Land Register. To enable registration of the security, there must be a Land Register entry for the property. Thus, the property to which the security relates must be registered in the Land Register either before or at the same time as the security. As there is no statutory trigger for this the proprietor must apply for voluntary first registration in the Land Register. This power is helpful. Based on 2013-14 Land Register intake figures, some 6000 standard securities fell to be recorded in the Sasine Register. The table below shows the projected effect the addition of this provision to the completion armoury would have.[69]

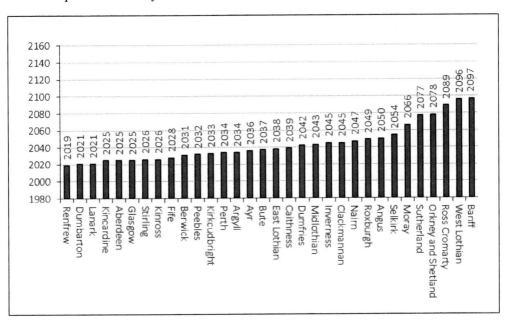

Projection completion rate inclusive of 2016 standard security changes

---

69 RoS Business Planning, May 2014.

The practicality of closing the Sasine Register to standard securities and other deed types has to be considered, and was one of the areas of focus in the completion consultation document. Certain standard securities are already a trigger for registration in England and Wales. That suggests that the market can accommodate the additional work associated with the registration of the property. In the commercial arena, the Keeper has noted that there is an increasing number of requests for voluntary registration arising from the unwillingness of certain lenders to make high end loans in the absence of a Land Register title. In any event, the fact that standard securities are dealt with specifically on the face of the 2012 Act reflects the Scottish Parliament's view that at some point consideration should be given to closing the Sasine Register to them; the issue is one of timing as opposed to principle.

Closing the Sasine Register to other deed types is more problematic and this is reflected in the completion consultation document. Many of the deeds recorded in the Sasine Register are drawn up and granted by a body other than the proprietor; the most common being discharges, improvement grants, and charging orders and the incentive to apply for voluntary registration does not exist in the same way as with a standard security. Although it is possible for automatic plot registration to be used in such cases to do so would raise a number of practical difficulties for the parties and the Keeper which do not exist for leases and assignations of leases.

To rely on voluntary registration in the same way as is envisaged should the Sasine Register be closed to standard securities is more complicated and less practical. It could also lead to less transparency; if the debtor had to voluntarily register his or her property before being able to register a discharge it may be that such deeds would simply not be registered. Registration would only be necessary at the next transfer of the property or if a fresh standard security was required. Care would also need to be exercised to ensure such a provision would not cut across other policy initiatives or the ability of, for instance, local authorities who may wish to register a charge over a property. Consequently closing the Sasine Register to other deed types would require to be supported by the immediate Keeper induced-registration (KIR) of the property that is to be subject to the deed. The Keeper's view[70] is that closing the Sasine Register to other deed types is

---

70   Registers of Scotland, *Completion of the Land Register Public Consultation* (n 12) para 27.

best left until the volume of remaining properties is of a manageable scale to allow for a prior KIR; indeed it if KIR is to be aggressively used it may be that this provision will never be used as it may have the effect of running counter to a planned programme of KIR.

The crucial point is that the 2012 Act provides for the practical closure of the Sasine Register to an increasing range of deed types at some future point; a necessary pre-requisite for completion of the Land Register though not in itself actually delivering completion. For that to happen, there requires to be a subsequent transaction affecting a property held on title deeds in the Sasine Register in order to trigger registration in the Land Register. For most properties, there will eventually be a transaction but the point at which that transaction occurs could be well in to the future. Additionally, there will remain a percentage of properties that remain off the Land Register radar. If completion is to happen in a timescale other than that determined by the natural pace of the property market, the remaining unregistered properties need to be identified and brought on to the Land Register. Identification of land not on the Land Register is straightforward. If it has not been mapped and accorded a title number under the 1979 Act (cadastral unit number under the 2012 Act) then quite simply it has not been registered.

In order that this land can then be registered, the 2012 Act gives the Keeper the power to undertake KIR.[71] This power, active from the designated day, allows the Keeper "to register an unregistered plot of land or part of that lot." No application for registration is required and nor is the involvement or consent of the owner required though the Keeper must notify the owner upon completion of registration. So is KIR the answer to the question of whether or not completion is feasible?

It is unquestionably a large part of the answer. It cannot assist with those properties whose titles are not on the Sasine Register but, in principle, it can aid identification of those properties as they will be the gap areas left in a registration county once KIR has been completed. But just how practical is KIR? The SLC are relatively positive about it:[72]

> The draft Bill accordingly makes provision for the final completion of the Register. The Keeper would simply be empowered to register any unregistered property. In practice, the Keeper would usually have enough

---

71   2012 Act s 29.
72   Scottish Law Commission, Report on *Land Registration* (n 11) vol 1 para 33.49.

information to make up the title sheet – information about boundaries, information about the identity of the owner, and information about any subordinate rights to be entered in the C and D sections as encumbrances or in the A section as pertinents. After all, when a title is registered in the Land Register, it is not (with very rare exceptions) moving out of the private realm. Title is already in another of the Keeper's registers – the Register of Sasines.

There are two key phrases in this statement: "final completion" and "usually have enough information." With a ten-year completion target, KIR will have to be used extensively. The completion consultation document envisages that through market growth, use of increased triggers, and the commitment to register public land, some 88% of Scotland's property will be registered by end 2024.[73] By the Keeper's reckoning, that leaves some 275,000 potential property titles (though some titles will inevitably include multiple properties) that require to be brought on to the register by voluntary registration or KIR. Even if the appetite for voluntary registration grows to levels experienced in England and Wales at the height of their marketing campaign, some 150,000 or more potential titles will require to be tackled under KIR. Consequently the use of KIR will not be limited to completing the final parts of the cadastral map jigsaw; it will require to play a much more extensive role.

The critical question is whether or not the KIR powers lend themselves to be used in such an extensive manner. The answer will largely be determined by the information available to the Keeper. The extent to which the Keeper will have enough information, and what can be done when she does not, was the focus of the KIR section in the completion consultation document. For urban residential properties stemming from common routes of title, the Keeper is more likely to have sufficient information as she has already carried out pre-registration title examination and, for a large number of these properties, has pre-mapped them. Fortunately, in terms of absolute numbers, these properties will form the majority of the titles that KIR will seek to register. The completion consultation document notes that there are 700,000 such property titles.[74] This does not mean that KIR will be straightforward but the challenges ought to be limited to issues other than mapping. Rural and commercial properties will be less straightforward, as indeed will be titles to minerals and other separate tenements of land, and

73   Registers of Scotland, *Completion of the Land Register Public Consultation* (n 12) para 19.
74   Ibid para 18.

findings and options for progressing KIR shared in a public consultation will it be possible to draw any definitive conclusions as to the use of KIR and the priority it should be given in delivering completion. It is, however, already clear that in offering solutions to some of the most pressing challenges the Keeper will encounter, the 2012 Act did envisage that KIR titles will not necessarily have the look and feel or the legal equivalence of other registered titles. Just how different they may be is yet to be seen but in an acceptance of that may lie the answer to completion.

E. Conclusion

Completion of the Land Register is now high on the political agenda. The continuing focus of the current Scottish Government on land reform matters has ensured a greater awareness amongst community groups, public and private bodies, professional organisations, land charities and citizens as to the information currently available on land ownership in Scotland and the central role of the Land Register in providing that information. This focus is timely, coming as it does on the heels of the implementation of the 2012 Act: legislation that has at its heart the completion of the Land Register.

Setting a ten-year target has brought an immediate focus on the completion provisions in the 2012 Act. They offer a significant improvement on the triggers for registration contained in the 1979 Act and compare favourably with the legislative framework for progressing completion that HMLR operates with. The 2012 Act provides a strategy: progressive closure of the Sasine Register to an increasing range of deeds, continued encouragement for voluntary registration, and the rolling introduction of KIR as operational counties near completion. The SLC's suggested timeframe for implementation of that strategy was not 10 years: they envisaged a longer time-scale.[78] Notwithstanding the timescale for delivering the strategy has shortened, the strategy that underpins the 2012 Act remains largely appropriate.

Achievement of the target will depend, in large part, on continuing political will; political support will be necessary if the legal powers in the 2012 Act are to be used to full effect. If the political desire to see completion continues, and signs are positive given the cross-party support for the completion provisions in the then Land Registration etc (Scotland) Bill,

---

78 Scottish Law Commission, Report on *Land Registration* (n 11) vol 1 paras 33.65-33.67.

then year-on-year progress to meeting the target will be evidenced. The powers to close the Sasine Register to deed types and those relating to KIR will be instrumental in delivering near completion. Further analysis on and options for the widespread use of KIR will be forthcoming from the Keeper. The Keeper is confident KIR can be used to drive completion but assessment of that confidence must await publication of the planned public consultation on its use.

With continuing political support completion will be well advanced by 2024 and indeed it may, at a practical level, be considered achieved. Inevitably, there will be areas of land for which no title can be readily traced and also areas where there is doubt as to where title rests. There may also be some registrations, particularly of bodies with extensive and complex landholdings where parts of that portfolio are still a work in progress. But come 2024 the completion landscape will have changed and the focus will have moved from enabling completion to ensuring Scotland maximises the social and economic benefits of a complete or near complete Land Register.

17. Primary Clients, Secondary Clients, Surrogate Clients and Non-Clients – the Expanding Duty of Care of Scottish Solicitors

Kenneth Swinton

Until the publication by Professor Rennie of his monograph *Solicitors' Negligence*[1] in 1997 there was no coherent treatment of the liability of Scottish solicitors for their negligent acts or omissions. Thereafter Professor Rennie published a volume of opinions on professional negligence[2] and has published a stream of articles which relate to the professional practice of conveyancing. He has continued to make himself available for opinion work as well as appearing as an expert witness in many cases. Law and practice has continued to develop over the last two decades and this chapter considers how factors have developed which may have expanded the duty of care over this period without seeking to provide a comprehensive update of Professor Rennie's work.

---

1   R Rennie, *Solicitors' Negligence* (1997).
2   R Rennie, *Opinions on Professional Negligence in Conveyancing – The Opinions of Professor Robert Rennie* (2004).

      http://dx.doi.org/10.11647/OBP.0056.17

A. Introduction

The fundamental duties of a Scottish solicitor have not changed over the years. However they have been subject to formal elaboration and expansion in Codes of Conduct, Standards of Conduct and Standards of Service. A solicitor is expected to place the interests of the client above her own,[3] to avoid conflicts of interest[4] and to respect the confidentiality of a client's business.[5] It is trite law that a solicitor owes those duties to a client but does not owe duties to third parties, in general. Where a solicitor acts for more than one party then she may do so only where there is no conflict or at least there is only a potential conflict of interests[6] but not an actual conflict.[7] Where confidential information is obtained from one client and it becomes of value to another client then a conflict will occur. The dilemma is whether to breach confidence and make a disclosure or to maintain the confidence and risk a subsequent claim for negligence or negligent misrepresentation.[8] There is only one course of action which is to resign the agency for one or both parties.[9]

The primary duty of a solicitor is to the client and is based on the law of agency. While the term professional negligence is commonly used this is not based on delictual liability but a breach of contract. Where a claim is made by a third party it must be based on delict. This is problematic as pure economic loss cannot be recovered in delict although it is available in cases based on negligent misstatement.[10]

Over the last two decades, a uniform series of basic contractual obligations owed by solicitors to lenders has resulted from the introduction of the Council of Mortgage Lenders Scottish Solicitors' Handbook,[11] This

---

3   Law Society of Scotland Practice Rules 2011, r B1.4.

4   2011 Rules, r B1.7; Charter of Core Principles of the European Legal Profession and Code of Conduct for European Lawyers (2008) principle C, Code 3.2.

5   2011 Rules, r B1.6; Charter of Core Principles of the European Legal Profession and Code of Conduct for European Lawyers (2008) principle B, Code 2.3.

6   2011 Rules, r B1.7.2.

7   Ibid, r B1.7.1.

8   *Bank of East Asia Ltd v Shepherd & Wedderburn* 1995 SLT 1074; *Frank Houlgate Investment Co Ltd v Biggart Baillie LLP* [2014] CSIH 79; *Marks & Spencer Group Plc v Freshfields Bruckhaus Deringer* [2004] EWCA Civ 741, [2004] 1 WLR 2331; *Prince Jefri Bolkiah v KPMG* [1999] 2 AC 222; *Bristol & West Building Society v Aitken Nairn* 1999 SC 678;*Clark Boyce v Mouat* [1994] 1 AC 428; *Leeds & Holbeck Building Society v Alex Morrison* 2001 SCLR 41.

9   See A Paterson and B Ritchie *Law, Practice and Conduct for Solicitors* (2006), Ch 7 for a discussion.

10   Rennie, *Negligence* (n 1), para 2.01 and the authorities cited there.

11   Available at http://www.cml.org.uk/cml/handbook/scotland

covers solicitors acting in the constitution of securities for lenders in relation to residential mortgages, both for purchase and re-mortgage purposes as well as many buy to let commercial loans. The existence of clear standard obligations has led to the growth of situations where solicitors have been found wanting in failing to either (a) recognise the existence of an actual conflict of interests between a purchaser client and lender client or (b) obtain the purchasing client's authority to make disclosures to the lender. Smith and Barton[12] writing in 1995 devote a whole chapter to disciplinary proceedings relating to conflicts of interest. None of the cases digested refer to conflicts between purchaser and lender. The Scottish Solicitors Discipline Tribunal has in recent years considered what appears to be a steady stream of cases where solicitors appear to have regarded their purchasing clients as the primary clients and the disclosure to the lenders of surrounding circumstances as of secondary importance.

Furthermore the Money Laundering Regulations 1993[13] imposed new obligations on solicitors to identify their clients. Those duties had not had a significant impact on practice when *Solicitors' Negligence* was published. In the intervening years the obligations in relation to prevention of money laundering have expanded considerably,[14] imposing increasingly onerous duties on solicitors to identify the clients, the source of funds and the wealth of the clients from which these funds are obtained. The intention is to prevent the legal profession and the financial system becoming conduits which assist criminals in concealing or converting the proceeds of their unlawful activities. Furthermore solicitors fall within the regulated sector and are obliged to make authorised disclosures of suspicious activity to the relevant authority under pain of criminal prosecution[15] or regulatory sanctions.[16] This has led to attempts founded on failures in a criminal or regulatory sense as evidence of a contractual or delictual failure on solicitors acting for private clients with a view to imposing civil liability, even where separate agents are instructed by the borrower and lender.[17]

---

12 I Smith and J Barton, *Procedures and Decisions of the Scottish Solicitors Discipline Tribunal* (1995).
13 Money Laundering Regulation 1993, SI 1993/1933.
14 Currently represented by the Money Laundering Regulations 2007, SI 2007/2157 and the Proceeds of Crime Act 2002, particularly Part 7 Money Laundering.
15 Proceeds of Crime Act 2002, s330.
16 Money Laundering Regulations 1993, SI 1993/1933, reg 42.
17 *Cheshire Mortgage Corporation Ltd v Grandison* [2012] CSIH 66; 2013 SC 160; *Frank Houlgate Investment Co Ltd v Biggart Baillie LLP* [2014] CSIH 79, where there was a finding against the solicitors on other grounds.

Such a possibility in the context of inadequate professional service claims has been recognised by Professor Rennie.[18] In this way, the Law Society of Scotland investigating conduct complaints or the Scottish Legal Services Commission investigating service complaints may in fact operate as a surrogate for the client in providing a basis for a negligence claim.

The consolidated Practice Rules[19] require that a solicitor should provide in writing details of the work to be undertaken at the earliest opportunity.[20] A solicitor should accordingly be aware of who their client is. Such terms of engagement will generally not only specify what work is to be done but what is not to be done. Thus it should prevent the subsequent expansion through leakage into other areas or others who might potentially later claim client status.

B. The Move to Written Terms of Business

The relationship between solicitor and client is one of agency,[21] which makes entirely appropriate the term "law agent."[22] As noted, above lenders instructing solicitors in residential lending work will impose their terms for business through the CML Handbook. It would however be unusual for consumers to impose written terms. Writing in 1996, Professor Rennie stated:[23]

> The basic duty of care owed by a solicitor is to his or her client. Similarly any specific contractual obligations are, generally speaking, owed to the client who instructs the legal task concerned.

The corollary to this simple truth is that no duty of care is owed to others in pursuit of the interests of the client. Professor Rennie noted then that the contract between solicitor and client is rarely in writing.[24] The converse is now the case as a result of the imposition of a practice rule. The terms of business on which the client instructs the agent must be set out in writing

---

18   Rennie, *Negligence* (n 1), para 11.03.
19   Law Society of Scotland Practice Rules 2011, r B4.1-4.2.
20   This is subject to certain exceptions which are not discussed here.
21   Rennie, *Negligence* (n 1), para 3.02.
22   Law Agents (Scotland) Act 1873; J H Begg, *A Treatise on the Law of Scotland Relating to Law Agents* (1873); The Scottish Law Agents Society was incorporated by Royal Charter in 1884, all indicating this then universal usage.
23   Rennie, *Negligence* (n 1), para 4.01.
24   Ibid para 3.02.

at the earliest practical opportunity.[25] There should be no doubt as to the identity of the client, therefore, in contemporary practice. Nor should there be doubt as to the nature of the work for which the solicitor has been instructed. The terms of business should set out the extent of the services to be provided and the estimated fees and outlays.[26] Setting out the scope of the engagement offers comfort to the solicitor which can prevent subsequent claims arising out of "mission creep" to other areas which were beyond the initial instructions. For example, when instructed in relation to the sale of an investment property, a solicitor may undertake the conveyancing work and exclude liability for advice in relation to taxation.[27]

There might be a temptation to include in the written terms of engagement some restriction of liability on the part of the solicitor. Such attempted limitations of liability are unlikely to be effective. Firstly, solicitors are under the general obligation to act in the best interests of clients and not to allow personal interests to affect advice to or actings on behalf of clients.[28] Secondly, under the Unfair Contract Terms Act 1977, any exclusion of liability for loss or other damage through negligence can only be given effect where it satisfies a reasonableness test.[29] In *Killick v PricewaterhouseCoopers [No1]*[30] the defendant accountants argued unsuccessfully before Neuberger, J (as he then was) that the cap on liability of £10m imposed in their terms of business was reasonable. On this basis, it is submitted that exclusions or limitations of liability in terms of business are unlikely to meet the threshold required to establish reasonableness. Furthermore, where the client is a consumer, the Unfair Terms in Consumer Contract Regulations will apply[31] provided the contract is in standard terms – in other words, where the consumer has no opportunity to individually negotiate it. If an imbalance in parties' rights and obligations to the detriment of the consumer arises from the terms of the contract it is to be regarded as *prima facie* unfair. Where, for example, a term excludes or limits liability in the event of total or partial non-performance or inadequate performance of a

---

25 Law Society of Scotland Practice Rules 2011. r B4.2.

26 Ibid.

27 In *Stevens v Hewats* [2013] CSOH 61; 2013 *SLT* 763 the agents in question had been instructed to prepare a gift of heritable property. Had the terms of engagement specifically excluded the provision of advice in relation to inheritance tax then, arguably, there would have been no basis of action.

28 Law Society of Scotland Practice Rules 2011, r B1.4.1 and B1.4.2.

29 Unfair Contract Terms Act 1977, s 2.

30 [2001] PNLR 1.

31 Unfair Terms in Consumer Contract Regulations 1999, SI 1999/2083.

contract for services, this is like to fall within the ambit of unfairness.[32] In this context, a limitation of liability clause has been held to contravene the Regulations.[33] Where the client is a commercial entity the economic balance may favour the client. The CML Handbook[34] adopts the common law standard[35] in respect of the duty of care owed by the solicitor to the lender and then imposes a series of specific and more onerous duties.[36] These may in turn be supplemented by individual lenders' own requirements and the possibility exists of transaction-specific further instructions issued with the loan papers. There is no opportunity for the solicitor to include a term which might limit her liability to the lender.

As well as providing clearer guidance to clients through having written terms of business the use of such terms should allow solicitors to avoid claims where the alleged want of due care and skills relates to a matter which is ancillary to the business undertaken – such as advice regarding surveys[37] or finance[38] in relation to a purchase. Of course those terms of engagement might seek to restrict liability to third parties. Whether this would be effective would depend on whether such a limitation of liability was reasonable.[39]

C. Identification of the Client

As noted in the previous section, the change brought about through professional practice rules requiring written terms of business has brought clarity in identifying to whom the legal services are delivered and who will be responsible for payment. However that is not quite the same thing as identification of the person who provides the instructions. Are the instructions those of the person who presents herself as the client to the

---

32   1999 Regulations, art 5 and schedule para 1 (b).
33   *West v Ian Finlay and Associates* [2014] EWCA Civ 316, in relation to the terms of business of a firm of architects.
34   CML Handbook (n 11).
35   Ibid para 1.4.
36   For example in terms of para 5.9.1, the solicitor must ask a purchasing client if the balance of the price is being provided without resort to other lending and where there is other lending to disclose this to the instructing lender. This is the case whether or not that loan is to be secured on the property and has no impact of the validity or ranking of the security.
37   Rennie, *Opinions* (n 2), p 436.
38   Ibid p 438.
39   Unfair Contract Terms Act 1977, s2; *Hedley Byrne v Heller and Partners* [1964] AC 465; [1963] 1 All ER 575; *Caparo Industries v Dickman* [1990] 2 AC 605; [1990] 1 All ER 568.

solicitor or who she represents she is? There has been no change in the underlying common law in relation to agency. However the imposition of duties in relation to anti-money laundering processes has clouded this issue. The first Money Laundering Regulations[40] in the UK came into force on 1st April 1994. Solicitors fell within the regulated sector for the purposes of the Regulations and were obliged to identify clients. A major exemption permitted solicitors to excuse existing clients from the requirements to produce documentary evidence of identity. Given the novelty of the obligations and the noted exemption it is unsurprising that Professor Rennie did not require to address these issues in 1996.

The relationship between solicitor and client is one principally governed by the law of agency. Where the solicitor is acting for a disclosed principal then the solicitor will not, in general, become personally liable to third parties.[41] The position is less straightforward where the principal turns out to be a fraudster, impersonating another. In such a situation there is scope to argue for the solicitor to incur personal liability on the basis she had no instructions from the appropriate party. Laura Macgregor suggests that where the agent has been neither fraudulent nor negligent in misrepresenting his authority, the only possible action which the third party has against the agent is the contractual action of breach of warranty of authority.[42] She indicates that the theoretical basis of the action is difficult to discover,[43] but adopts the approach taken by Gloag,[44] who refers to the principle as arising out of the contract between the third party and the agent. In this context, however, there is no effective contract between the agent and the third party. In *Scott v J. B. Livingston & Nicol*[45] Lord Coulsfield states that the normal rule is that the agent is liable in delict on the basis of breach of warranty of authority.[46] This is borne out by the earlier case of *Anderson v John Croall & Sons Ltd*[47] which is generally taken as the standard authority for this proposition in Scotland.

---

40   Money Laundering Regulations 1993, SI 1993/1933.
41   W M Gloag and R C Henderson *The Law of Scotland*, 13th edn, by H Macqueen et al (2012) para 19.27 and the authorities referred to therein.
42   L Macgregor, "Agency," in *The Laws of Scotland: Stair Memorial Encyclopaedia*, Reissue (2002) para 168.
43   Ibid.
44   W M Gloag, *Law of Contract*, 2nd edn (1929) p 155.
45   1990 *SLT* 305.
46   *Scott* (n 45) at 307.
47   (1903) 11 *SLT* 163; see also *Salvesen & Co v Rederi AB Nordstjernan* (1903) 6 F 64 9 (which was partially reversed in the House of Lords on other grounds (1905) 7 F (HL) 101; (1905) 13 *SLT* 20.

The point was raised in sharp focus in the recent case of *Cheshire Mortgage Corporation v Grandison*.[48] Lenders who were separately represented raised actions against firms of solicitors who had acted apparently for the owners of properties who raised funds from the pursuers secured over the properties. Some time after the recording of the relevant standard securities it became apparent that the persons who had instructed the solicitors in relation to representing their interests in the constitution of the securities had impersonated the true owners of the properties. The securities, based on forged signatures and false identities were worthless. The lenders sued on the basis of breach of warranty of authority.[49]

Evidence was led as to the steps taken by the agents in question to identify the persons who presented themselves as the clients.[50] In neither the Outer House nor Inner House judgments is any reference made to the purposes for which identification was being sought. The items sought would of course be familiar to anyone dealing with the anti-money laundering requirements in contemporary practice. A professional operating within the regulated sector, such as a solicitor, is obliged to carry out customer due diligence.[51] This requires sufficient proof of identity on the basis of documents obtained from reliable and independent sources.[52] The 1993 Regulations themselves do not specify what these might be. However guidance from the Joint Money Laundering Steering Group[53] is regarded as authoritative[54] and requires two forms of check – the first to identify the person and the second to tie that person to the address provided. A failure by a regulated professional to comply with these requirements is a criminal offence.[55] Furthermore it is a regulatory requirement for solicitors to comply with this regime[56] in all cases whether or not the business falls with the statutory money laundering definitions. It is surprising that there is no mention in the case of basis on which the solicitors in question collected

---

48   [2012] CSIH 66; 2013 SC 160.
49   Further claims were made based on the letters of obligation which had been issued by the "borrowers" agent. These were disposed of on the basis that a letter of obligation was granted as an ancillary obligation to those which were established in the principal contract. Where that principal contract had been reduced then the ancillary obligations must also fall: *Mason v AR Robertson and Black* 1993 SLT 773.
50   *Cheshire Mortgage Corporation* (n 48) at para 11.
51   Money Laundering Regulations 2007, SI 2007/ 2157, reg 7.
52   2007 Regulations, reg 5.
53   Available at http://www.jmlsg.org.uk/industry-guidance/article/guidance
54   It must now be approved by HM Treasury.
55   2007 Regulations, reg 45.
56   Law Society of Scotland Practice Rules 2011, r B6.23.1.

these data or whether they met the statutory and regulatory requirements. It is submitted that compliance with those standards will satisfy the common law requirement of absence of knowledge or lack of negligence necessary to make a breach of warranty of authority entirely innocent. In order for there to be a successful prosecution then a criminal standard of proof would be required. The Scottish Solicitors Discipline Tribunal also applies a criminal standard in relation to evidence. In the context of a civil action for breach of warranty of authority presumably the agent would have to address having taken reasonable steps only. In the instant case it is apparent that the identification requirements did comply with the anti-money laundering regime in place at the time.[57] What is equally clear is that while the practices of the solicitors in question met the standards in place in 2004 when the frauds occurred, the need for ongoing monitoring on a risk-based approach required under the 2007 Regulations ought to have raised suspicions about the written requests to transmit funds electronically to third parties. Once funds had been transmitted to the agent acting for the borrowers they become the property of the borrowers.[58] Arguably the solicitor would not come any duty to the lender to disclose suspicions at this point unless the security was in an "all sums due and to be become due" format. However, she must make a suspicious activity to report to the National Crime Agency.[59] Nonetheless the compliance with the statutory and regulatory requirements and the ability of an authorised person to rely on identification carried out by another such authorised person[60]were referred to in the *Cheshire Mortgage Corporation* case.[61] It was not accepted that there had been any such reliance as the business had already been introduced to the lender prior to the involvement of the solicitor for the "borrower."[62] As the court noted:[63]

---

57 *Frank Houlgate Ltd v Biggart Baillie* [2009] CSOH 165; 2010 *SLT* 527. Lord Drummond Young's opinion at para 25 dismissed claims based on the Money Laundering Regulations 2003 which have now been replaced by the 2007 Regulations.

58 *R v Preddy* [1996] AC 815; [1996] 3 WLR 255; [1996] 3 All ER 481; *R v Waya* [2012] UKSC 51; [2013] 1 AC 294; [2012] 3 WLR 1188; [2013] 1 All ER 889.

59 Proceeds of Crime Act 2002 part VII. See n 105 in relation to the timing of the duty.

60 See currently Money Laundering Regulations 2007, SI 2007/ 2157, reg 17.

61 Outer House judgment [2011] CSOH 157; 2012 *SLT* 672 at para 16 being referred to as 'KYC rules.' See further K Swinton, "The Potential for civil liability arising from failures in client identification requirements under the Money Laundering Regulations" (2011) 79 SLG 97.

62 Nor for that matter had the solicitor confirmed in writing that he consented to his identification being relied on as required by the Regulations.

63 *Cheshire Mortgage Corporation Ltd v Grandison* [2012] CSIH 66; 2013 SC 160 at para 32 per

> All that the agent is warranting is that he has a client and that client has given him authority to act. It would be quite unreasonable and inappropriate to extend this to an implied warranty that his client has a certain attribute or attributes.

While there may be circumstances where the solicitor does warrant some attribute in relation to the client which can be relied on by third parties then that will amount to a representation and will bring matters with the principle articulated in *Hedley Bryne & Co Ltd v Heller & Partners*[64] as refined in *Caparo Industries v Dickman*.[65] There may be situations where the client's identity is correctly ascertained by the solicitor but an important attribute becomes a matter of contention. In *Frank Houlgate v Biggart Baillie*[66] solicitors acted for a party who was exactly who he claimed to be. However he represented that he owned an estate which was owned by another unrelated person with a similar name. The solicitors acted on behalf of the fraudster who borrowed money on the security of the property with other agents acting for the lenders. The action was framed in part on the basis of breach of warranty of authority. For the reasons discussed above it was held there was no warranty on the part of the agents for the fraudster that he was the registered proprietor of the subjects.[67] However the solicitors were subsequently found liable on other grounds. After the security had been registered the fraud came to light and the fraudster admitted to his solicitor that the fraud had been committed. He asked for time to put matters right and repay the loan. However the fraudster used the breathing space to top up the sums advanced. The solicitor failed to withdraw from acting, advise the agents acting for the lender or make a suspicious activity report at this point under the Proceeds of Crime Act 2002.[68] It was held that the solicitor ought to have resigned the agency and disclosed the fraud to the solicitors acting for the lender, the perception in the mind of the solicitor that he was bound by client confidentiality being entirely misplaced.[69] The policy argument on which the decision is based is clear:[70]

L Clarke, delivering the opinion of the Court.

64   [1964] AC 465; [1963] 1 All ER 575.

65   [1990] 2 AC 605; [1990] 1 All ER 568. See further Rennie, *Negligence* (n 1), para 4.03 et seq.

66   [2009] CSOH 165; 2010 *SLT* 527.

67   *Frank Houlgate* (n 66) at para 28 (opinion of Lord Drummond Young).

68   *Frank Houlgate Investment Co Ltd v Biggart Baillie* LLP [2014] CSIH 79; 2014 *SLT* 1001 paragraph 9.

69   The solicitor in question was censured for his conduct and fined the maximum £10000: *Mair* [2009] SSDT 1463.

70   *Frank Houlgate* (n 68) at para 34 (opinion of Lord Menzies).

> Society expects high standards from a Scottish solicitor. Perhaps first and foremost, a solicitor is expected to have the highest standards of honesty. She is an officer of the court, and owes obligations to the client, to the court, to fellow members of the profession, and to the general public.

The legal basis on which to hang that policy provided divided opinions. In the Inner House, Lord Menzies held that once the solicitor became aware of the fraud and failed to take steps to dissociate himself from it be became an accessory to the fraud.[71] There was, in effect, a continuing implied representation to the solicitor for the lender that he is not aware of any fundamental dishonesty or fraud which might make the security transaction worthless.[72] This line of reasoning is supported by the three Lords Ordinary who gave opinions at earlier stages of the proceedings[73] and Lord McEwan sitting in the Inner House.[74] It must be taken as settling the law. Lord Malcolm however dissented from this analysis – in his view there was no need to invoke the concept of accessory to the fraud. Rather, he held that once the fraud became known the solicitor came under a freestanding duty to take reasonable care to prevent further foreseeable losses flowing from the fraudulent transaction which he had unwittingly facilitated.[75] This may be sufficient to dispose of the case in question, but had the security granted been for a fixed amount rather than 'all sums due or to become due', then this suggests that no such duty would have arisen. On the other hand if the test is accessory to the fraud then in the fixed security example the solicitor would still come under a duty of disclosure. It would be odd if the resulting obligation on the solicitor depended solely on whether the security covered further advances or not. Accordingly the analysis of all the other senators who have given opinions is preferable to that of Lord Malcolm.

D. The Primary Client and the Secondary Client

Where the same solicitor acts for both the lender and the borrower each is owed a duty of care by the solicitor. This causes no issues where the interests of the lender and borrower coincide – most obviously in ensuring

---

71 Ibid at para 45.

72 Ibid at para 43.

73 *Frank Houlgate Investment Co Ltd v Biggart Baillie* LLP [2009] CSOH 165; 2010 *SLT* 527 at para 21 (Lord Drummond Young); 2011 CSOH 160; 2012 *SLT* 256 at para 33 (Lord Glennie); [2013] CSOH 80; 2013 *SLT* 993 at para 43 (Lord Hodge).

74 *Frank Houlgate* (n 68) at para 89.

75 Ibid at para 81.

there is a good and marketable title.[76] However the Practice Rules distinguish the situation where there is potential for conflict from that where there is actual conflict. In the former situation, the rules provide a series of limited exceptions.[77] However, the primary rule must be adhered to where an actual conflict arises. In *Midland Bank plc v Cameron, Thom, Peterkin & Duncans*[78] solicitors had made representations to the lender as to the borrowing client's means. This was inaccurate and the lenders sought to hold the agents liable. Lord Jauncey in finding for the defenders established a four part test: (a) there must be an assumption of responsibility; (b) the solicitor must represent to the other party that he has the necessary skill in relation to the representation; (c) the other party must rely on the representation and; (d) the solicitor must be aware that the third party would rely on the representation. This is a straightforward restatement of the principle in *Hedley Byrne*. Lord Jauncey expressed the view that where the solicitor is engaged to prepare the security by a lender the decision to lend has already been taken and there are no other duties incumbent on the solicitor.[79] The decision in *Midland Bank* has been followed in the Irish Supreme Court case of *Doran v Delaney*[80] and has never been expressly overruled in this jurisdiction, however Rennie doubted it would be followed today.[81] That must be correct – in the post-*Caparo* era cases such as *White v Jones*,[82] *Robertson v Watt & Co*[83] and *Holmes v Bank of Scotland*,[84] step (b) in particular was absent.

Rennie, in considering the attitudes which prevailed at the time of *Midland Bank*, expressed the view that at the time the solicitor treated the purchasing/borrowing client as primary and the lending client was accorded a secondary status.[85] If that ever was true, the CML Handbook, applying to residential transactions, makes explicit the obligations on a solicitor to make disclosures. The decision to lend is now subject to revision right up until release of funds. Notwithstanding the contractual equal status of

---

76 Law Society of Scotland Practice Rules 2011, r B1.7.1 and B2.1.2: "You shall not act for two or more parties whose interests conflict."
77 See 2011 Rules, r B1.2 generally.
78 1988 *SLT* 611.
79 *Midland Bank* (n 78) at 618.
80 [1998] IESC 66.
81 Rennie, *Negligence* (n 1) para 5.01.
82 [1995] 2 AC 207; [1995] 1 All ER 691.
83 2nd Div, 4 July 1995, unreported.
84 2002 *SLT* 544.
85 Rennie, *Negligence* (n 1) para 5.01.

lease. When the intended security holder died a claim was made by his beneficiaries which claim was ultimately unsuccessful. On that basis the comments were merely *obiter* and Lord Goff's analysis must be correct. The House of Lords by a majority of three to two in *White* held that a solicitor assumed a special duty towards potential beneficiaries and if that duty was breached then liability would follow. Such a duty could be by omission and not only negligent acts of commission.[114] The House found that it was a case akin to transferred loss,[115] where the beneficiary had a loss and no claim in contract and the deceased had a claim but no loss, and that it was fair just and reasonable in all the circumstances to hold the solicitor liable which was an incremental approach.[116]

While *White* may have set a new course in England, *Robertson* was a Scottish case, hence Professor Rennie's views that this still represented the law in Scotland but that it would be unlikely to remain good law should a Scottish case be taken to their Lordships' House. However, their Lordship's intervention did not prove necessary. As recently as 1990, *Robertson* had been seen as binding and determinative of the issue by Lord Weir in *Weir v J M Hodge & Son*.[117] However *Holmes v Bank of Scotland*[118] saw Lord Kingarth sitting in the Outer House depart from the line of authorities starting with *Robertson*. The reason for so doing was an unremarked upon and unreported Inner House decision from 1995[119] decided shortly after *White* and therefore binding upon him. For his part, Lord Kingarth saw no reason why *White* should not be followed in Scotland, notwithstanding the strong dissents therein from Lord Jauncey and Lord Mustill.[120]

That the deceased had a claim but no loss and the disappointed beneficiaries did is borne out by *Matthews v Hunter & Robertson Ltd*.[121] The executor brought a claim against the solicitors alleging that they had failed to effectively revoke a survivorship destination. The executor is said to be *eadam personam cum defuncto* and if the deceased had no loss to his estate at the moment prior to his death then the estate suffered no loss either. It was held by Lord Brodie that the additional *Caparo* limb of the test, that it

114 *Hedley Byrne & Co Ltd v Heller & Partners Ltd* [1964] AC 465; [1963] 2 All ER 575; *Henderson v. Merrett Syndicates Ltd.* [1995] 2 AC 14 5, 182, *per* Lord Goff.
115 *White* (n 111) at 265 (Lord Goff).
116 Ibid at 270 citing *Caparo Industies plc v Dickman* [1990] 2 AC 605 (Lord Brown Wilkinson).
117 1990 *SLT* 266.
118 2002 *SLT* 544.
119 *Robertson v Watt & Co*, 2nd Div, 4 July 1995, unreported.
120 *Holmes v Bank of Scotland* 2002 *SLT* 544 para 19.
121 [2008] CSOH 88; 2008 *SLT* 634.

was fair, just and reasonable in the circumstances, would not be satisfied in this situation. The principle of assumption of duty has been held to extend potentially to recipients of lifetime gifts. There is a fine distinction between the sort of negligent omission as in *White* or *Holmes* and a situation where there is advice tendered negligently to a client who then acts on that advice and the resulting will or conveyance which in its own terms is perfectly in order does not produce the desired effect. In *Fraser v McArthur Stewart*,[122] which related to the ineffective legacy of a croft based on negligent advice, it was held by Lord Brailsfield that *White* was not directly in point and that the facts were distinguishable. As a result the advice and the effects of the advice were severable and there was no assumption of duty on which the disappointed beneficiaries might found. In *Stevens v Hewats*[123] on the other hand the solicitors were instructed to convey a house and associated lands by way of gift. The disponer continued to reside in the property notwithstanding the gift. Some eight years later it was discovered that the conveyance was ineffective and a new conveyance was registered. At this time consideration was also given to the gifts with reservation rules for inheritance tax and a lease drawn up at market rent whereby the donor paid rent to the donee. Unfortunately the donor did not survive the necessary seven years. Claims were made both by the executors and the donee, in relation to the additional inheritance tax which was payable. The registering of a disposition on behalf of the donee has contractual aspects of the duty of care, as noted by Lord Tyre[124] but the assertion was made by the claimants that general tax planning advice was or ought to have been provided. Lord Tyre was of the view that a stateable case had been made out on the basis of the decision in *White* but that the issue required proof.[125] In the parallel action by the executors, Lord Tyre held on the same basis as *Matthews* that no claim lay against the solicitors.[126] To date *Stevens* is the only example of the *White* principle being applied in a conveyancing context in a reported case in Scotland. It is however clear that Lord Goff's incremental approach to the extension of liability expressed in *White* is exactly that and the application of the principle of assumption of risk is capable of adaptation to a number of different situations. The law will continue to develop.

---

122 [2008] CSOH 159; 2009 *SLT* 31.
123 [2013] CSOH 61; 2013 *SLT* 763.
124 *Stevens* (n 123) at para 13.
125 Ibid at 16.
126 *Milligan's Executors v Hewats* [2013] CSOH 60; 2013 *SLT* 758.

G. Third Party Claims for Inadequate Professional Service

Inadequate professional service is now defined as "professional services provided by a practitioner in connection with any matter in which the practitioner has been instructed by a client [which] were inadequate."[127] These provisions replace earlier provisions[128] which defined such services as not of the quality which could reasonably be expected of a competent solicitor. The relationship of inadequate professional service with negligence has been a source of uncertainty since the provisions were first enacted. Professor Rennie expressed the opinion that inadequate professional service is possible without negligence but whether the converse is true remains contentious in relation to the earlier provisions.[129] Paterson and Ritchie are of the opinion that the two often overlap.[130] In terms of section 11 of the 2007 Act the Scottish Legal Complaints Commission must, in considering what is fair and reasonable in all the circumstances, take into account the law, professional rules standards and guidance and any relevant codes of practice. When the provisions were being debated before the Scottish Parliament, the minister considered that there would be serious problems with requiring the Commission to separate negligence aspects from wider aspects of inadequate professional services.[131] So overlap is the order of the day and there is no comprehensive definition of inadequate professional services. Given the compensation levels are up to £20,000 and the Commission has a number of other tools such as ordering other steps to rectify the inadequate service this is a significant remedy for those affected by inadequate professional service.[132] Furthermore there is no need to prove loss as exists in the law of negligence.[133] Such services according to the definition must relate to a matter instructed by a client there is no requirement for the person affected to be the client.

The test for service complaints is that the Commission must be satisfied that the complainer has an interest to enforce. Paterson and Ritchie suggest that the category has the potential to be broad and is capable of including

---

127 Legal Profession and Legal Aid (Scotland) Act 2007, s2(1)(b).
128 Solicitors (Scotland) Act 1980 s65(1).
129 Rennie, *Negligence* (n 1), para 11.06.
130 Paterson and Ritchie, *Law, Practice and Conduct* (n 9), para 1.04.
131 SP Committee Official Report, 23rd Meeting (Session 2), September 26, 2006.
132 Legal Profession and Legal Aid (Scotland) Act 2007, s10.
133 Rennie, *Negligence* (n 1), para 11.05.

beneficiaries (and presumably disappointed beneficiaries) in an executry, opponents in a court case or perhaps where the agent for one side delays a conveyancing matter to the prejudice of the other.[134] The Commission's ability to accept third party complaints is now circumscribed by the decision in *Council of the Law Society of Scotland v Scottish Legal Complaints Commission*.[135] A complaint was accepted in relation to a conduct matter but the principle is equally applicable to service complaints where the person making the complaint had received a letter from a firm of solicitors regarding an alleged trespass on their property on the basis of information supplied by the client. The Court held that a solicitor had a duty to represent her client and was entitled to rely on the information supplied. Furthermore a solicitor is not bound to respond to any complaint made by third parties.[136] In *Saville-Smith v Scottish Legal Complaints Commission*[137] the pursuer sought to complain against the solicitor acting for his former employer on the basis that the solicitor had both revised the letter of dismissal and had appeared in the subsequent Tribunal proceedings. This was rejected as frivolous – again illustrating a narrow approach to third party claims. While these cases may restrict the scope of complaints they do not entirely exclude it and a third party complaint by a disappointed beneficiary may be admitted with the possibility of compensation being paid to complainer in circumstances where negligence need not be proved or where there is no incidence between liability and the loss. For example, the fine distinction drawn in *Fraser* in relation to the advice and the subsequent ineffective legacy, might not trouble the Commission when considering what is fair and reasonable in all the circumstances.

H. Conclusions

The fundamental tenets of practice – fidelity, confidentiality and the avoidance of conflicts of interest – remain the same as they did two decades ago. Some measures of regulatory reform such as written terms of business

---

134 Ibid para 16.04.
135 [2010] CSIH 79; 2011 SC 94; 2011 *SLT* 31; for a similar cases see SLCC Annual Report 2011/12 case 4 letter to third party, SLCC Annual Report 2010/11 case 4 opponent's agent in court action.
136 Scottish Legal Complaints Commission, Third Party Complaints advice sheet available at http://www.scottishlegalcomplaints.org.uk/for-practitioners/guidance-advice/advice-and-information.aspx
137 [2012] CSIH 99.

may clarify the obligations undertaken by solicitors which will tend to reduce the scope for negligence and in a few restricted situations may permit the limitation of liability. On the other hand the increasing interest of the legislature in anti-money laundering measures and the reduction of financial crime have imposed duties on solicitors that have fundamentally affected practice, undermining the duty of confidentiality, as well as requiring regulatory bodies to expand the ambit of the supervision of the profession. Inevitably these duties have been seized upon by the victims of identity theft in conveyancing matters as enhancing the obligations of solicitors to third parties.

Lenders have organised themselves to require solicitors to act on their behalf subject to standard terms which are significantly more explicit than the common law standards which are preserved. The result of such explicit standards is that a 'tick-box' approach can be adopted in regulatory inspections to demonstrate compliance or otherwise with those standards without the need to explore the perimeters of common law duties which can, on occasions, appear hazy.

Finally the creation of a new simplified regime for service complaints with significantly increased limits of compensation opens the door to fairly sizeable negligence claims being dealt with as inadequate professional service claims without the need to prove loss and without the client being required to incur the potential costs involved in litigation.

There can be little doubt that the duty of care owed by solicitors to their clients and third parties has expanded since Professor Rennie wrote his authoritative work.

18. The Court and the Conveyancing Expert

Lady Paton

A. The Changing Landscape

The traditional litigation landscape once familiar to the conveyancing expert is undergoing considerable upheaval. The development of automated and electronic technologies, a question-mark over immunity from suit, and the recommendations in Lord Gill's Scottish Civil Courts Review Report,[1] are some of the changes bringing about a new and unfamiliar environment.

B. Automated and Electronic Technologies

Not every lawyer aspires to an automated and paperless world. John Mortimer possibly spoke for many when he observed through his fictional character barrister Horace Rumpole (habitué of the Old Bailey and the Uxbridge Magistrates Court):[2]

> Things, I regret to have to say it, have not improved since those distant days, and many of the faults must be laid at the door of automation. Not only have witnesses changed [replaced, for example, by recording devices]. String quartets, which were once the pride of the tea room, have now been replaced by an abominable form of mechanical music. The toasting fork has given way

---

1   Report of the Scottish Civil Courts Review (2009), available at http://www.scotcourts. gov.uk/about-the-scottish-court-service/the-scottish-civil-courts-reform

2   J C Mortimer, *Rumpole for the Defence* (1982) 108.

     http://dx.doi.org/10.11647/OBP.0056.18

to an alarming machine that fires singed bread at you like a minute gun. The comforting waitress in black bombazine has become a device that contrives to shoot a warmish and unidentifiable fluid into a plastic cup and over your trousers at the drop of a considerable sum of money. None of these engines is an improvement on the human factor, neither are trials made any easier by the replacement of the living witness with the electronic device.

Nevertheless there is a current trend in the legal world seeking to achieve an automated electronic paperless environment. The Scottish Government has published a paper entitled The Digital Strategy for Justice in Scotland,[3] setting out how digital technology will be used to transform the way in which justice services are delivered in Scotland. The government envisages fully "digitised justice systems" including digital warrants, digital recording of evidence, video-conferencing, and the creation of a secure digital platform to store all information relevant to a case. Cynics might predict that court hearings will soon consist of judges sitting alone surrounded by plasma screens, recording devices, and qwerty-keyboards, with a piece of software instead of a clerk of court, witnesses' evidence taking the form of talking heads on-screen, productions flashing up on a split screen, and lawyers' submissions being transmitted directly from offices or chambers by means of a system such as Skype, phone-conferencing, or Twitter.[4]

That may be too gloomy a view. The judiciary in the Court of Session has expressly welcomed much of the government's digital initiative. In an address at the launch of the Digital Strategy, Lady Dorrian described current problems being experienced in the courts, and possible digital solutions, pointing out *inter alia* that:[5]

> Cases are becoming more complex, with a greater array of technical and forensic evidence that requires analysis and careful presentation in court. Video evidence needs time to be examined thoroughly. Witnesses who are cited for court may not turn up on the appointed day. There may be issues around the timely disclosure of evidence. All of these factors might be mitigated by the application of digital solutions – as evidence can be collected and shared electronically, for example, or witnesses reminded of their need to attend court by text or e-mail, as now happens. [...]
>
> In any modern society, the administration of justice must retain the trust and confidence of the people it serves. And it will only do that if it keeps

---

3   Scottish Government, The Digital Strategy for Justice in Scotland (2014).

4   Something similar to the future envisaged by the Rt Hon Lord Justice Brooke, "The Courts and Judiciary in 2024" in *Now and Then, A Celebration of Sweet & Maxwell's Bicentenary* (1999) Ch 8.

5   Victoria Quay, Edinburgh, 20 August 2014, available at http://www.scotland-judiciary. org.uk/26/1301/Speech-by-Lady-Dorrian-at-the-launch-of-The-Digital-Strategy-for-Justice-in-Scotland

pace with the times, and remains relevant to the experience of the people and organisations it serves. We are now in an era, according to research published earlier this month, when Britons spend more time using technology devices than they do sleeping. If people and businesses communicate instantly by e-mail, Skype, or Facebook, they will expect public services to do likewise. [...]

[D]igital innovation will allow greater transparency in proceedings, make it easier for people to participate in the system – whether making applications, submitting documents, giving or providing evidence, paying fines – wherever they are and at a time that suits them. [...]

Changes in technology and changes in procedures cannot happen in isolation – they must be accompanied by changes in the attitude and behaviours of those using the new technology. It is very encouraging that the Digital Strategy has been the product of wide-spread collaboration across the justice system; this suggests that there is a willingness to embrace change in all quarters, at least at the leadership level. It is vital that this willingness is spread further, and that is best done by making real – for all those involved – the benefits that innovation will bring.

Certainly it must be acknowledged that a wealth of information can be stored, transported, and accessed by the use of computers and electronic technology. Pen-drives and USB sticks are becoming more common in court: thus pleadings, submissions, notes of appeal, notes of argument, case reports, statutes, rules of court and productions can be contained in an item measuring about 4cm by 2cm, easily portable and easily inserted into a computer, giving access at any time and any place to all these materials. Text-books, rule-books, bench-books, codes of conduct and other guidance can be accessed by a DVD disc, or directly online. Search and cut-and-paste facilities available on computers are very helpful to court-users. General electronic functions such as email and texting are undeniably useful, for everyone, and are currently being used for court work including solicitors' firms enrolling ancillary motions in court cases. Thus the new technology, albeit not entirely welcomed by every generation of court-user, is currently being actively incorporated into the court system.

The "wide-spread collaboration across the justice system" referred to in Lady Dorrian's address is already taking place in the world of conveyancing. For example, in October 2002 the Keeper of the Registers of Scotland consulted four conveyancing professors[6] in a project which resulted in the digital "Automated Registration of Title to Land" (ARTL).[7]

---

6   Professors Stewart Brymer, George Gretton, Roderick Paisley and Robert Rennie (Professor Kenneth Reid was not involved because he was at that time a full-time commissioner with the Scottish Law Commission). See S Brymer, G Gretton, R Paisley and R Rennie, "Automated Registration of Title to Land" (2005) JR 201-50.

7   R Rennie and S Brymer, *Conveyancing in the Electronic Age* (2008); S Brymer and I Davis,

Dispositions may be electronic, as may missives (fax or email and possibly text). Electronic signatures are now permitted.[8] Since the coming into force of the Land Registration etc (Scotland) Act 2012, a title to land may never appear as a tangible deed: its provenance may be digital and it may remain digital throughout its life. For some lawyers, these developments may give rise to anxiety and nostalgia for the traditional working environment of documentary missives, parchment-like dispositions, storage in deed-boxes, title searches in the Register of Sasines, and face-to-face settlement meetings at solicitors' offices during which deeds and cheques physically changed hands. But the new world is here, and the combination of a paperless court system and electronic conveyancing may mean that any conveyancing expert wishing to assist the court should be IT-literate,[9] reasonably skilled in computers and electronic devices, familiar with current electronic conveyancing practices, and able to give evidence (supported by productions) by video-link. Thirty years ago, those skills and qualifications were not even contemplated, far less required of a conveyancing expert. Some experts might benefit from further training, and may find themselves experiencing a steep learning curve.

C. A Question-mark over Immunity from Suit

A further upset for conveyancing experts has arisen in the context of immunity from suit. For many years it has been a well-established principle that an expert witness taking part in court proceedings has civil immunity in relation to his evidence. As explained by the Court of Appeal in *Stanton v Callaghan*:[10]

> (i) an expert witness who gives evidence at a trial is immune from suit in respect of anything which he says in court, and that immunity will extend to the contents of the report which he adopts as, or incorporates in, his evidence; (ii) where an expert witness gives evidence at a trial, the immunity which he would enjoy in respect of that evidence is not to be circumvented by a suit based on the report itself; and (iii) the immunity does not extend to

---

"Automated Registration of Title to Land ('ARTL')" in R Rennie (ed), *The Promised Land: Property Law Reform* (2008) Ch 9; G L Gretton and K G C Reid, *Conveyancing*, 4th edn (2011) para 8.23-8.25.

8   Requirements of Writing (Scotland) Act 1995, ss9B(1) and (2), as introduced by the Land Registration etc. (Scotland) Act 2012, s97(2). For discussion, see R Rennie and S Brymer, "A Bold Step Forward" 2012 *JLSS* 32-33; R Rennie and S Brymer "E-missives: What Now?" 2014 *JLSS* 18-19.

9   J Irving, "Survival in the IT Age" 2000 *JLSS* 18-19.

10   [2000] QB 75 at 100.

protect an expert who has been retained to advise as to the merits of a party's claim in litigation from a suit by the party by whom he has been retained in respect of that advice, notwithstanding that it was in contemplation at the time when the advice was given that the expert would be a witness at the trial if that litigation were to proceed.

That was the position in Scotland: the immunity enjoyed by expert witnesses was part of a greater immunity enjoyed by those involved in court cases.[11]

However the law has changed, certainly in England. The Supreme Court in *Jones v Kaney*,[12] by means of what might be seen as judicial legislation,[13] decided by a majority of three to two that an expert witness giving evidence in court should not be immune to an action for professional negligence.[14] Lord Hope and Lady Hale dissented. Lord Hope saw no principled basis for removing immunity from expert witnesses. He relied upon the Scottish case *Watson v McEwan*,[15] pointing out that *Watson* remained binding in Scotland, and that witness immunity in Scotland was a devolved matter. Thus the accepted view is that the decision in *Jones* is not binding in Scotland, where *Watson* remains binding until appropriate legislation is enacted by the devolved Parliament.[16] While some may agree with Lord Phillips, who led the majority in the Supreme Court, that experts will not be discouraged from giving opinions or evidence if immunity is removed,[17] many would disagree.[18] Accordingly the approach adopted by the majority of the

---

11   Stair, *Inst* 4.1.5.

12   [2011] UKSC 13; [2011] 2 AC 398.

13   R Rennie, S Brymer and D Reid, "The End of Immunity for Expert Witnesses?" 2012 Scottish Law Gazette 37-40.

14   Thus overruling *Stanton v Callaghan* (n 10).

15   [1905] AC 480.

16   Rennie et al (n 13).

17   R Jackson and J Powell, *Professional Liability* (7th ed) by J Powell and R Stewart (2011) para 2-110; Rennie et al, "The End of Immunity" (n 13), although the authors went on to identify a potential problem as follows: "If ... the evidence of the expert for the client [is] clearly rejected by the court, the likelihood is that the client will be found liable in expenses. One hopes that the removal of immunity (should it ever come to Scotland) would not then result in a subsequent claim against the expert on the losing side. If that were the case, would we all then be hunting for an elusive super expert able to say that no expert of ordinary competence could ever have given that particular opinion?"

18   Including the Earl of Halsbury LC in *Watson v McEwan* (n 15); Salmon J in *Marrinan v Vibart* [1963] 1 QB 234 at 237; Lord Wilberforce in *Roy v Prior* [1971] AC 470 at 480; Simon Brown LJ in *Silcott v Commissioner of Police of the Metropolis* (1996) 8 Admin LR 633 at 637; Lord Hoffmann in *Taylor v Director of the Serious Fraud Office* [1999] 2 AC 177 at 214; and Lord Hope in *Jones* (n 12) at para 165: "It is one thing to be liable to a wasted costs order at the instance of the court itself, or to proceedings by a professional body for professional misconduct. It is quite another to be at risk of worthless but possibly embarrassing and time-consuming proceedings by a disgruntled and disaffected litigant in person."

Supreme Court in *Jones v Kaney* must bring a frisson of apprehension to those in Scotland offering their services as expert witnesses, even although the effect of the decision has not hitherto come north of the border.

D. Case Management and the Conveyancing Expert

Following upon the success of the new rules of court for personal injuries actions,[19] there has been general recognition that a similar case management approach would be beneficial in other types of cases. As is noted in Lord Gill's Report of the Scottish Civil Courts Review:[20]

> We are satisfied that, with the exception of certain specified types of action, all actions in the Court of Session and the sheriff court should be subject to judicial case management. On the lodging of defences, a case should be allocated to the docket of a particular judge or sheriff. A case management hearing should be fixed shortly thereafter. This would normally take place by means of a telephone conference call. Parties would make submissions as to further procedure and any other matters arising, such as disclosure of documents. The judge or sheriff would identify the factual and legal issues in the case and decide what form of case management is most appropriate. In complex cases this may take the form of active judicial case management akin to the commercial model ... with further case management hearings as the case progresses. In straightforward cases the court might decide that a timetable and related orders akin to the case-flow procedure under Chapter 43 would be appropriate. In that event, no further case management hearings would be required. In certain cases a mixture of these techniques would be appropriate.

One outcome of increased case management might be the ordering of experts to hold discussions, exchange reports and/or prepare a minute of admissions or a joint statement.[21] Thus the modern conveyancing expert should be prepared to participate in such a meeting, treading the fine line between fulfilling his duty to the court while protecting his client's interests (a task made more difficult by being in a private consultation without the immediate supervision of the presiding judge.)[22] As Lord Hope commented in *Jones v Kaney*:[23]

---

19   Rules of the Court of Session 1994, Ch 43.
20   Report of the Scottish Civil Courts Review (n 1), Ch 5, para 48.
21   A L Stewart, "Evidence," in *The Laws of Scotland: Stair Memorial Encyclopaedia,* Reissue (2006) para 179; and see the procedure adopted in *Jones* (n 12).
22   For example, one expert might seek to exert pressure on the other: cf *Jones* (n 12).
23   *Jones* (n 12), para 156.

[I]t is plain that the paid expert owes duties to the client by whom he is being paid. If he agrees for a reward to prepare a report and to present himself in court to give evidence, he is obliged to do those things and to take reasonable care when he is doing so. He must make the necessary investigations and preparations for the giving of that evidence. Nevertheless when it comes to the content of that evidence his overriding duty is to the court, not to the party for whom he appears. His duty is to give his own unbiased opinion on matters within his expertise. It is on that basis that he must be assumed to have agreed to act for his client. It would be contrary to the public interest for him to undertake to confine himself to making points that were in the client's interest only and to refrain from saying anything to the court to which his client might take objection.

E. The Conveyancing Expert and Alternatives to Court

Lord Gill's Report of the Scottish Civil Courts Review notes that:[24]

ADR [alternative dispute resolution] in general provides a valuable way in which the burden on the civil courts can be lifted. More importantly, it provides an opportunity for dispute resolution in cases where the confrontational process of litigation is inappropriate. It is therefore a valuable complement to the work of the courts. [...]

Mediation may, in some cases, offer advantages over litigation, particularly in cases where it is important to preserve relationships. [...]

[Quoting, with approval, Dame Hazel Genn] "ADR cannot supplant the machinery of justice precisely because, in civil cases, the background threat of litigation is necessary to bring people to the negotiating table ... a well-functioning civil justice system should offer a choice of dispute resolution methods."

Conveyancing disputes concerning boundaries, real burdens, titles, servitudes, prescriptive possession and other similar problems, are classic examples of disputes which respond well to these flexible, less formal, dispute-resolution procedures. The opinion of a respected conveyancer will frequently resolve the issues, without the need to go to court. Meetings and joint consultations can assist in achieving a mutually acceptable outcome. By contrast, formal court proceedings can be protracted, wearing, and expensive, as Rennie has pointed out:[25]

[E]ven if [clients] win, there will be expense involved on an extrajudicial basis... If matters go to court [it should be emphasised to clients] that civil litigation is for the very rich or very poor and that if they lose they will be

---

24 Report of the Scottish Civil Courts Review (n 1), ch 7, para 20-22.
25 R Rennie, "Boundary Ddisputes Rrevisited" 2013 *SLT (News)* 189-94, at 193.

liable not only for their own expenses both judicial and extrajudicial but for the other side's judicial expenses.

Thus a valuable ADR service is currently being provided by practising conveyancers, professors, and other members of academic staff.[26] The result is not only the satisfactory resolution of many disputes, but also a great saving of resources, both the courts' and the parties'. In this context, the conveyancing expert can be regarded as, in effect, assuming the mantle of "the court."

F. In a Changing Landscape, some Classic Principles Remain

It is some comfort that, amidst all the changes and upheavals, certain well-established principles continue to apply in relation to the role of the conveyancing expert in court.

(1) Assistance for the court

Once in court, the conveyancing expert is not the final arbiter. His role is to provide assistance to the judge.[27] As Lord Justice-Clerk Cooper emphasised in *Davie v Magistrates of Edinburgh*[28] (a case involving scientific evidence):[29]

> Expert witnesses, however skilled or eminent, can give no more than evidence. They cannot usurp the functions of the jury or judge sitting as

---

26   See, for example, D Cusine, *Conveyancing Opinions of JM Halliday* (1992); R Rennie, *Opinions on Professional Negligence in Conveyancing* (2004).

27   Even although instructed and paid by one party. See however the reservations expressed in F Davidson, *Evidence* (2007) para 11.27; and the views stated in I Macphail, *Evidence* (1987) at para 17.27: "It is sometimes maintained that the system whereby in adversary procedure each party adduces its own expert evidence is objectionable... In [certain] countries ... the court is permitted to select experts to inform it of their opinion based on their own particular knowledge and experience. Recently, in countries whose practice is based on an adversary rather than an inquisitorial system, the question whether the device of the court expert should be adopted has been widely discussed. It is not generally employed in Scotland, where conflicts of opinion between experts are adjudicated upon frequently and apparently without embarrassment by both judges and juries. (Footnote 90: A rare example, if not a unique case [of a court expert] is *Irvine v Powrie's Trs* 1915 SC 1006, where the professor of chemistry in Edinburgh University was appointed by the court for the limited purpose of supervising the parties' experts while they removed specimens of paper and ink from a registered deed which the pursuer sought to reduce on the ground of forgery.)"

28   1953 SC 34.

29   *Davie* (n 28) at 40.

(iv) The existence but not the name of any other client of the expert with competing interests;

(v) Whether the expert has worked with the expert instructed by the opposing party (if known).

13. Any actual or potential conflict of interest must be reported to the solicitor as soon as it is raised or becomes apparent and the assignment must be terminated.

Despite the existence of such guidelines, difficulties can arise. A recent action for damages for alleged professional negligence[44] illustrates a failure fully to comply with principles 12(c) and 13 of the Code of Practice. In that case, property consultants and architects/planners gave evidence in court concerning the loss which the pursuers alleged they had suffered. Lord Woolman felt obliged to make the following observations:[45]

> During cross-examination, Mr A [of Keppies, Glasgow, Architects and Planners] disclosed that although there is no formal association, his firm has had links with the defenders since 2004. The name "Keppie" appears on the main door of the defenders' offices. Keppie has used rooms within to hold meetings. The defenders' website states that Keppie is able to offer planning services.
>
> Individuals must think carefully before accepting instructions to act as an expert witness. The court expects them to be scrupulously impartial. In this instance, Mr A's links with the defenders should have been notified at a much earlier stage.

Another illustration of a problem (in effect a breach of the third proposition of *The Ikarian Reefer*) was referred to in *McTear v Imperial Tobacco Ltd*[46] at para 5.10. An expert witness in a criminal trial[47] had made an assumption which was neither justified nor disclosed to the court. Lord Justice General Emslie stated that, as a result, the witness had been discredited. He observed:[48]

> This was, in our judgment, conduct on the part of an expert witness which demonstrated a complete misunderstanding of the role of scientific

---

44 *Hawthorne v Anderson* [2014] CSOH 65; and see too *Liverpool Catholic Archdiocese Trs v Goldberg (No 3)* [2001] 1 WLR 2337 at page 2340, where the court refused to admit the evidence of an undoubted expert who was also a long-standing friend of the defendant

45 *Hawthorne* (n 44) at para 84 and 85.

46 *McTear* (n 40).

47 *Pierce v HM Advocate* 1981 SCLR 783.

48 *Pierce* (n 47), quoted with approval by Lord Caplan in *Elf Caledonia Ltd v London Bridge Engineering Ltd*, 2 September 1997, unreported at 225, referred to by Lord Nimmo Smith in *McTear* (n 40) at 139.

witnesses in the courts, and a lack of the essential qualities of accuracy and scientific objectivity which are normally to be taken for granted.

G. Conclusion

In conclusion, much is expected of both the court and the conveyancing expert in the twenty-first century. Neither can afford to rely solely upon traditional or well-established practices or technology. Each must acquire new competences which were not even envisaged in the latter part of the twentieth century, yet each must retain and abide by the well-tried principles and practices expected of both court and expert when an expert witness gives evidence. The result is a challenging but fascinating and ever-developing area of the law.

19. The Role of the Expert Witness in Professional Negligence Litigation

Gerald F Hanretty QC

A. Introduction

Expert or skilled witnesses are objectionable. Needless to say, that observation is not directed towards the characters, qualities, learning or experience of those not infrequently called to assist parties and the court in litigation. Rather, the leading of such evidence necessarily results in material being presented to the court which is, by its nature, opinion evidence and accordingly objectionable – and, in the absence of justification, therefore inadmissible.

Issues in relation to the admissibility and use of opinion evidence have long been the subject of debate throughout the English-speaking world. Indeed, in the 21st-century it is worthwhile reflecting upon the observations of J P Taylor in the third edition of his work *A Treatise on the Law of Evidence*:[1]

> Perhaps the testimony which least deserves credit with the jury is that of skilled witnesses. These gentlemen are usually required to speak, not to facts but to opinion; and when this is the case, it is often quite surprising

---

1   J P Taylor, *A Treatise on the Law of Evidence as Administered in England and Ireland,* 3rd edn (1858) 54.

     http://dx.doi.org/10.11647/OBP.0056.19

to see with what facility, and to what extent, their views can be made to correspond with the wishes or the interests of the parties who call them.

It is likely to be the position that such an observation would be thought by most to remain valid, at least in part. However, what has not much been discussed is the role of the expert in modern dispute resolution other than analyses of the principles to be adopted by experts in the conduct of their duties with only a little practical guidance for practitioners in relation to the choice of experts.

B. The Conventional Analysis

Although litigation by its nature puts in issue partisanship on the part of expert witnesses, in reality, those giving evidence within the realm of professional negligence litigation are highly regarded. In a relatively small jurisdiction like Scotland, it is unsurprising that professional integrity, impartiality and sound judgement are highly prized. Accordingly, challenges to skilled witnesses are most often advanced by challenging the empirical material upon which opinions are advanced or by denouncing the expert opinion as an exercise in usurping the function of the court itself. The importance of instructing expert witnesses who command respect from within their professions cannot be overemphasised.

Of course, the Court jealously guards the role society calls upon it to perform. The classic exposition of the expert's function might be found in the familiar guidance provided by Lord President Cooper in *Davie v Magistrates of Edinburgh*.[2]

More recently, it appears to have been thought necessary to elaborate upon the role of the expert witness. Although discussed within the context of a criminal appeal the observations made in *Wilson v HM Advocate*[3] provide general guidance on the matter. It is worthwhile considering at length the court's opinion in relation to expert evidence in its adoption of Lord President Cooper's *dicta* and its application in a more modern context:[4]

At this point, in view of the significance of (certain) testimony in this case, we should now consider what we believe to be the proper character of

---

2   1953 SC 34 at 40.

3   2009 JC 336.

4   *Wilson* at para 58-63.

expert evidence, and in particular attempt to describe our understanding of its nature and effect on the conclusions we should draw. In general, of course, opinion evidence is not admissible in our criminal courts; witnesses may only under normal circumstances give evidence about matters within their direct knowledge. The evidence of an expert witness is an exception to this rule. It is not possible to provide an absolute direction as to what constitutes legitimate subject-matter for expert opinion. However, two general principles will normally give some guidance. First, the subject-matter under discussion must be necessary for the proper resolution of the dispute, and be such that a judge or jury without instruction or advice in the particular area of knowledge or experience would be unable to reach a sound conclusion without the help of a witness who had such specialised knowledge or experience. Secondly, the subject-matter in question must be part of a recognised body of science or experience which is suitably acknowledged as being useful and reliable, and properly capable of reaching and justifying the opinions offered, and the witness must demonstrate a sufficiently authoritative understanding of the theory and practice of the subject. The nature and scope of expert opinion evidence cannot at any one point in time be exhaustively defined.

The effect of expert opinion evidence can perhaps be described with more precision. The role of the expert witness, and his duties and responsibilities, have been subject to much judicial comment. In *National Justice Campania Naviera SA v Prudential Assurance Co Ltd (The Ikarion Reefer)*,[5] Cresswell J listed a number of such duties and responsibilities, *inter alia*:

1. Expert evidence presented to the court should be, and should be seen to be, the independent product of the expert uninfluenced as to the form or content by the exigencies of litigation.

2. An expert witness should provide independent assistance to the court by way of objective unbiased opinion in relation to matters within his expertise.

3. An expert witness should state the facts or assumptions on which his opinion is based. He should not omit to consider material facts which could detract from his concluded opinion.

4. An expert witness should make it clear when a particular question or issue falls outside his expertise.

To this might be added a requirement that an expert witness should in particular explain why any material relevant to his conclusions is

---

5   [1993] 2 Lloyd's Rep 68; [1993] FSR 563; [1993] 37 EG 158.

ignored or regarded as unimportant. Although the categories of duty and responsibility described by Cresswell J in the Ikarion Reefer case were concerned with civil matters, these rules are equally applicable to criminal cases.

In addition, particularly in criminal cases, other duties and responsibilities have been recognised by the courts. For example, the court will expect in a criminal matter that an expert's report must state the facts upon which opinions are based, and if assumptions are made, these must be clearly identified. Reasons must be given for conclusions. Whether instructed for the prosecution or defence, the principal duty of an expert witness is to the court, and this overrides any duty he owes to the party which instructed him. Again, explanations should be given for the basis on which all relevant material is either accepted or rejected.

It therefore follows that a judge or jury is not bound by the opinion evidence tendered by an expert witness. There are clear principles under which such evidence is admitted. In *Davie v Magistrates of Edinburgh* Lord President Cooper said (p 40):

> Expert witnesses, however skilled or eminent can give no more than evidence. They cannot usurp the functions of the jury or the Judge sitting as a jury ... Their duty is to furnish the Judge or jury with the necessary specific scientific criteria for testing the accuracy of their conclusions so as to enable the Judge or jury to form their own independent judgment by the application of these criteria to the facts proved in evidence. The scientific opinion evidence, if intelligible, convincing and tested, becomes a factor (and often an important factor) for consideration along with the whole other evidence in the case, but the decision is for the Judge or jury. In particular the bare ipse dixit of a scientist, however, eminent, upon the issue in controversy, will normally carry little weight, for it cannot be tested by cross-examination nor independently appraised, and the parties have invoked the decision of a judicial tribunal and not an oracular pronouncement by an expert.

Although in modern practice (as in the present case), expert evidence is routinely appraised and cross-examined, the position essentially remains that an expert witness's opinion is only a factor (albeit an important one) in the decision of a judge or jury.

It is abundantly clear therefore, and has been for many years in our courts, that an expert witness is not in the position to provide the court with a statement of unqualified conclusions about the question of fact on which his opinion bears. If he does so, the effect of his testimony may well be much diminished. In this context, it is perhaps worth noting that an expert witness is in a particularly privileged position in our courts. Prior to the decision, he is the only person permitted to express an opinion. Other witnesses must confine themselves to facts. Further, an expert witness will routinely rely on assumptions, hearsay evidence, his impression of testimony that he has not heard, and reports, statements and other secondary sources of information, all of which might be incompetent in a court of law if presented as factual evidence. It is therefore of the utmost importance that any expert witness carefully describes the source and assesses the worth of all material on which his opinion is based. We refer to the case of *Gilmour v HM Advocate*[6] (paras 79, 80).

If the approach taken by the court is a paradigm warning to experts in relation to empirical fact lying within the province of the decision-maker, more recent guidance has been given reiterating the court's duty to make findings as opposed to simply adopting an expert's views. In *Kennedy v Cordia (Services) LLP*[7] Lord Brodie considered the admissibility of expert evidence in a personal injuries action arising out of the pursuer's fall in icy conditions:[8]

> In the present case the dispute that had to be resolved was whether, on the basis of the essentially uncontroversial primary facts, as a matter of law, the reclaimers [the defender employers] were under a duty to take a particular precaution (providing attachments to footwear and ensuring their use) and, had they taken that precaution, whether the respondent would have suffered injury. That was something that the Lord Ordinary was fully equipped to do without any instruction or advice; it was squarely within his province as judicial decision-maker. No additional expertise was required. It may be that a judge has personally never carried out a risk assessment of any kind. That does not mean that, having heard evidence of the nature of the activity being assessed and having been provided with a document recording the risk assessment, he cannot determine whether or not the assessment was "suitable and sufficient" in terms of regulation 3(1) of the [Management of Health and Safety at Work Regulations 1999]. It is the job of a judge to hear evidence about matters with which he may previously have been totally unfamiliar and, on the basis of that evidence, come to conclusions of fact and then apply the relevant law to these facts. In *Midland Bank Trust Company Limited v Hett Stubbs & Kemp* [1979] 1 Ch 384 (a case of alleged negligence on the part of a solicitor engaged to carry out a conveyancing transaction) Oliver J was faced with a similar situation to that which faced the Lord

---

6 [2007] HCJAC 48; 2007 *SLT* 893; 2007 SCCR 417.

7 [2014] CSIH 76.

8 *Kennedy* at para 15.

Ordinary here. In what has become a much-quoted passage, he said this, at p. 402:

'I must say that I doubt the value, or even the admissibility, of this sort of evidence, which seems to be becoming customary in cases of this type. The extent of the legal duty in any given situation must, I think, be a question of law for the Court. Clearly if there is some practice in a particular profession, some accepted standard of conduct which is laid down by a professional institute or sanctioned by common usage, evidence of that can and ought to be received. But evidence which really amounts to no more than an expression of opinion by a particular practitioner of what he thinks that he would have done had he been placed, hypothetically and without the benefit of hindsight, in the position of the Defendants, is of little assistance to the Court whilst evidence of the witness's view of what, as a matter of law, the solicitor's duty was in the particular circumstances of the case is, I should have thought, inadmissible, for that is the very question which it is the Court's function to decide'.

C. The Realities of Modern Practice

Bearing in mind the foregoing admonitions, what then is the role of the expert in professional negligence litigation? Perhaps, notwithstanding the quantity of judicial ink addressing the issue, the reality is rather more prosaic. Each of the cases mentioned above in reality identifies the professional obligations incumbent upon experts. They do not, and are not intended to, discuss the pragmatic and practical aspects of the role. Moreover, as society has become more complex and more aspects of business and private life are thought to lie within the province of one profession or another, the need for expert opinion where things are perceived to have "gone wrong" has increased exponentially. Indeed, it is not unreasonable to suggest that in a developed, economically active society there shall be an increasing need for the advice of those who engage in the wide variety of professional activities now commonly encountered. The historical categorisation of "professions" and "trades" is probably an anachronism which fails to address the societal changes wrought by demographic, scientific and clinical advances over the last two centuries. Why might a computer programmer not be asked to explain her decision to write a particular line of code which thereby exposed the computer user to an increased threat from an obscure but identified virus? If the decision was a consequence of a judgement weighing the risks, advantages and disadvantages of such a piece of code, is such not a matter for expert analysis? Of course, such an example demonstrates the need not for one role for the expert witness but rather a multiplicity of roles arising in relation to such a scenario.

Experience suggests that there are at least four and possibly five distinct roles which the expert might be called upon to perform in the context of dispute resolution/litigation. Plainly, much will depend upon the nature of the expertise under scrutiny. In addition, especially within the context of claims against those who have professional indemnity insurance, the professional under challenge will, more often than not, have the benefit of experienced insurers and solicitors. As a corollary, those who feel aggrieved may well require to instruct solicitors who are less familiar with either the profession or professional branch concerned or the constraints of litigation in such a context.

(1) The investigator

If the issue truly arises out of the carrying out of some professional skill or art the detail of which is a mystery to those unskilled in such it must be axiomatic that some investigation will be likely. Obviously, in many cases the basic facts will have been fully explored by the legal teams involved. For example, the allegedly negligent conveyancer's file will have been recovered and pored over. The client's precognition will have addressed the solicitor's mandate. The lender's terms of engagement will have been considered.

In reality, the expert will frequently identify issues which require to be investigated before any concluded view might be taken in relation to breach of duty. Examples might be found of cases where a solicitor's knowledge of his client's intentions in relation to development of a property may or may not be relevant where a material period of time has elapsed during which the possibility of development could reasonably be discounted as a matter to be drawn to the attention of potential lenders.[9] Such knowledge may or may not be apparent to the solicitors instructed but might reasonably be anticipated to be the sort of issue which an expert might, in an appropriate case, bring to the client's and his solicitor's attention.

Likewise, it is not uncommon where losses are sought to be recovered in relation to claims arising out of events many years previously for experts to suggest avenues of attack or defence where law or practice has in the meantime changed. Examples can be found in the field of conveyancing

---

9   *Leeds and Holbeck Building Society v Alex Morrison & Co* 2001 SCLR 41.

relating to letters of obligation, the necessity for site visits and the requisites for a competent and sufficiently comprehensive report on title. Practice in relation to each of these aspects of day-to-day conveyancing has drastically altered over the last ten years. Diverging views in relation for example to standard forms of clauses in missives has resulted in the need for creation of organisations such as the Standard Missives Joint Working Party of the Edinburgh Conveyancers' Forum. An expert relying on what is perceived to be a standard clause in modern practice would in all likelihood be providing a pretty poor opinion if he or she were to suggest that the Working Party's suggestions are indicative of practice in earlier years.

It also ought to be borne in mind that experts may be engaged not only in relation to whether or not there has been negligence/breach of duty but whether any admitted breach has been causative of loss. In many cases, the quantum of damages will necessarily demand investigation by experts. The input of the forensic accountant exemplifies the role of expert/investigator. Invariably, such an expert will be provided with basic documentation in relation to the performance of individuals or companies. In the real world however such experts frequently advise on the recovery of documents the existence of which is beyond the ken of mere lawyers.

For the avoidance of doubt, it is not suggested that the investigator expert don a forensic trenchcoat and fedora. Indeed, it is no part of the expert's function to effectively dig about to find material which might support his side's position. Such would, having regard to the dicta mentioned above, be anathema. The instructing solicitor must do all within his power to carry through such investigations as the expert identifies. Plainly, steps should already have been taken to ensure that the information initially provided to the expert is as complete as possible. The investigator expert does however require to address the issues in the case and in so doing must take steps to ensure that his opinion satisfies the proper requirements of the court in relation to a presentation of the whole factual matrix necessary for the just determination of the cause.

(2) The gatekeeper

The role of the expert as gatekeeper remains to some extent unrecognised. However, the importance of this role cannot, it is submitted, be underestimated.

Claims of professional negligence have diverse consequences. In the first place, the professional reputation of individuals is invariably placed in the public domain for dissection. In the second place, the ability of individuals to earn a living may well be adversely affected. In the third place, the costs of professional practice may substantially increase in consequence of claims or a claims history. The consequences for individuals and firms can be dire.

It is the first consequence that more often than not has greatest impact on people. Professional men and women often consider the making of a claim against them as a personal attack. He or she might often think of such a claim as being a challenge to his or her *raison d'être*. The emotional consequences might outweigh even a significant pecuniary disadvantage. It follows that such claims ought not ordinarily to be advanced unless they have some proper foundation.

It has been recognised in Scotland for many years that the proper conduct of professional negligence litigation demands that no such claim be advanced before the court unless there is available to the pursuer and his advisers suitably qualified expert opinion that supports the existence of certain professional practices or duties and that same have been breached to the pursuer's detriment. The point has been made forcefully in a number of decisions relating to vexatious litigants. In *Lord Advocate v McNamara*[10] the opinion of the court was delivered by Lord Reed. He made the following remarks in relation to the advancing of claims against professionals in the absence of appropriate opinion evidence:[11]

> As we have explained, these proceedings were based on allegations of professional negligence which were unsupported by the opinion of anyone qualified to express an opinion on that issue. It is not suggested that they were instituted in the expectation that such support could be obtained; nor does there appear to have been any attempt to obtain such support. In those circumstances, we consider that we are entitled to conclude that the proceedings were instituted without any reasonable ground and were vexatious.

More recently, Lord Woolman had cause to discuss the requirements for an expert witness to support a claim in relation to a counter-claim arising out of alleged professional negligence in the related case of *Tods Murray WS v Arakin*.[12] He stated:[13]

---

10 [2009] CSIH 45; 2009 SC 598.
11 *McNamara* at para 54.
12 2010 CSOH 90.
13 *Arakin* at 90-93.

The pursuers emphasised the vital importance of a party being in possession of an appropriate expert before making allegations of professional negligence. They contended that in the absence of such a report, it is an abuse of process to institute and persist in such proceedings.

In response, Mr McNamara argued that in respect of some of the allegations, no expert was required. This was most clearly put in the defenders' Note of Argument, which stated "sometimes matters of misconduct are just so blatant they require no experts' view to demonstrate that this is the case."

I reject that approach. In my view, allegations of professional negligence require to have a proper foundation. Without such underpinning, the court is not in a position to make a finding in favour of the defenders (Walkers Evidence, third edition para. 16.3). As a solicitor must always exercise a measure of judgement in fulfilling his duties, it is not enough to say that he has failed to implement his instructions. The allegation must always be buttressed by a report from an appropriate witness, which states that the course taken was one that no solicitor exercising ordinary skill and care would have taken.

In the absence of such a rule, it would be open to a party to make whatever assertions he or she chose, however spurious or mistaken. In my view, that is just what has happened here.

Lest it be thought that the rules in Scotland in relation to the stringency inherent in requiring the production of an expert report are to any extent inconsistent with *Midland Bank Trust Company Limited*,[14] it should be noticed that in England and Wales a not dissimilar approach in relation to the need for expert support is adopted in modern practice.[15] However, for completeness' sake, it should be noticed that an exception is made in that jurisdiction in relation to some claims arising out of negligent conveyancing[16] although same is probably explicable by reference to technical differences in conveyancing practice.

The requirement for an expert report supporting a claim necessarily creates the role of gatekeeper expert. It probably goes without saying that those with a sceptical approach might consider that the necessity for such a role to be borne in mind by the expert witness is indicative of protectionism or cronyism. On the other hand, it is submitted that the views provided by both Lord Reed and by Lord Woolman amply demonstrate the necessity of such a role if the court is to exercise its jurisdiction equitably and efficiently.

---

14 *Midland Bank Trust Company Limited v Hett Stubbs & Kemp* [1979] 1 Ch 384.
15 *Pantelli Associates Ltd v Corporate City Developments Number Two Limited* [2010] EWHC 3189.
16 *Brown v Gould & Swayne* [1996] EWCA Civ J0124-3.

(3) The mediator

Within the context of disputes relating to professional liability it is, by the nature of things, by no means unusual for experts also to be engaged in mediation practice. However, the individuals concerned will be at pains to recognise the very distinctive role of the mediator in a mediation process from other aspects of their professional practices including the provision of expert opinion.

It is perhaps interesting to observe that the overlap in areas of expertise between mediators and expert witnesses is sometimes thought to be a necessary subject for analysis.[17]

For present purposes the mediator expert remains principally a witness. What has changed in the course of the last 20 years is an increasing reliance by the court upon experts to reduce the scope of dispute. In particular, since the introduction to the Court of Session of commercial actions the court has made demands upon parties to narrow the scope of any controversy and, where appropriate, to demonstrate that steps have been taken towards agreeing evidence.

Rule 47.12 of the Rules of the Court of Session 1994 makes provision for Procedural Hearings in commercial causes. Rule 47.12(2)(h) provides that the court may direct:

> that skilled persons should meet with a view to reaching agreement and identifying areas of disagreement, and may order them thereafter to produce a joint note, to be lodged in process by one of the parties, identifying areas of agreement and disagreement, and the basis of any disagreement.

Needless to say, in many professional negligence claims there will be substantial areas of agreement. However, inasmuch as such disputes not infrequently require to be resolved by reference to the exercise of a professional judgement there will always remain scope for disagreement. This rule nonetheless requires a meeting. Such meetings will, no doubt, be approached in a positive fashion. Experience suggests that such meetings effectively operate as a form of informal mediation. That may well be desirable.

An understandable desire to reduce the scope of disagreement is bolstered somewhat by the provisions of Rule 47.12(2)(i) which provides that the court:

---

17 See for example C Haselgrove-Spurin, "The role of the mediator," available at http://www.nadr.co.uk/articles/published/mediation/RoleOfTheMediator.pdf

may appoint an expert to examine, on behalf of the court, any reports of skilled persons or other evidence submitted and to report to the court.

The position in the Sheriff Court is arguably even more demanding in as much as rule 40.12(3)(m) of the Ordinary Cause Rules 1993 empowers the sheriff to make any order which the sheriff thinks "will result in a speedy resolution" of the case!

What ought to be borne in mind by expert witnesses is that they cannot indulge in advocacy. To do so would plainly run counter to the whole ethos of the expert witness.

Mention was made above of the significance of professional judgement on the part of those whose actions are being criticised. Inasmuch as professional judgement necessarily connotes the possibility of a range of different actions/advice on the part of the individual concerned it must at least be possible for expert witnesses to effectively mediate in a way which reduces the breadth of the professional judgement challenged. Such a form of "mediation" has the significant advantage of narrowing the issues in dispute to the point where, if appropriate, certain evidence might be agreed or, where possible, compromise arrived at.

A necessary *caveat* must be stated. It is no part of the expert witness role to indulge in negotiation. She cannot enjoy any such mandate. More importantly, notwithstanding the professional obligations upon the expert to assist the court as outlined above, any such expert will nonetheless still require to answer to his client. There will be occasions where the expert witness risks professional embarrassment by failing to observe the limits imposed upon her to confine opinions advanced to the four walls of the litigation concerned and the factual matrix under consideration.

(4) The quantifier

When discussing the role of expert witnesses in professional negligence cases it is inevitable that the focus will be on the merits of the claim. In reality, many litigations focus as much upon the question of causation and the quantum of damages as upon primary liability.

The quantifier expert will be required to opine on the pursuer's position but for the negligence/breach of duty complained of. In many cases, as suggested earlier, the nature of the breach of duty dictates that the quantifier expert shall be one and the same person who speaks to the merits. That will not always be the case. Frequently, within the context for example of clinical negligence claims, a number of areas of expertise arise for consideration. The birth of a baby born with cerebral palsy may well focus upon the action or inaction of an obstetrician. The prognosis for the child, damaged and undamaged, will be addressed by others such as neonatal paediatricians and paediatric neurologists.

Lest it be thought that the quantifier expert's role is in some way lesser than that of those providing opinions on the merits of a claim, the position in the real world is far more demanding. It is frequently the case that at the point in time at which the disgruntled client asserts that the professional's negligence occurred many alternative ways forward might have been in contemplation. It is certainly not uncommon for example for developers of land to consider a number of different possibilities for development when acquiring a site. An error in relation to the extent of the title obtained may require the consideration of a series of different hypotheses as to how the land would otherwise have been developed. For example, planning considerations may have impacted upon the number of plots which might have been marketed. Such might plainly have impacted upon the profit to be generated by the development. Equally, planning conditions may have rendered an otherwise profitable part of a developer's land bank of no worth whatsoever.

Indeed, in certain respects the quantifier expert's function is particularly difficult. The discussion above in relation to the development value of land is an obvious example. The developer will invariably suggest that he would have adopted whatever scheme would have maximised the profit to be generated. The obligation on the expert however will necessarily require him to test that proposition. To fail to do so would be a dereliction of his obligations to the court as well as to his client. But in fulfilling his obligations he will necessarily risk being perceived as taking views adverse to those of his client. Moreover, the quantifier expert will almost invariably also be an investigator expert. It is not always the position that the client assists in providing information which might have a consequence of reducing the value of the claim being advanced. Of course, the preceding observations arise within the context of the expert witness retained on behalf of the claimant. Similar considerations will arise nonetheless for those instructed and retained in respect of the defence of such claims.

Another complicating factor for the quantifier expert arises from the need to consider the quite distinct issue of mitigation of damages. It is trite to observe that the onus of proof in relation to a failure to mitigate damages rests upon the defender. Although issues in relation to mitigation might have been identified by defenders in appropriate cases it will frequently be the quantifier expert who is charged with forming a view on the steps which might properly have been taken by the claimant when presented with the breach of duty hypothetically conceded to have taken place.

(5) The communicator

It is implicit throughout the foregoing that expert witnesses are reasonably anticipated to be well-respected, vastly experienced and of obvious integrity. All of those attributes however are, within the confines of dispute resolution, almost valueless in the absence of an ability to relay complex factual material, explain sometimes ethereal concepts and address all manner of hypotheses which might be advanced in discussion with the decision-maker.

Of particular worth in the expert witness is a demeanour which is empathetic to the role of the decision-maker. Equally, he or she should be capable of communication in a fashion which is neither arrogant nor submissive.

D. The Choice of an Expert Witness in the Real World

It will be apparent that the demands made upon expert witnesses are many and varied. The scepticism which is sometimes applied to expert evidence is, for the most part, balanced by the need to repose confidence in those witnesses skilled in the multiplicity of professional roles found in modern society.

This discussion is intended to broaden issues surrounding the instruction of expert witnesses in professional negligence claims. It highlights the diverse skill set which ought to be found in the well instructed expert's toolbox. It may assist experts in recognising the different roles that they perform at a subconscious level.

Inevitably, professional negligence litigation is testing of all those involved in whatever role and at whatever level. What is most important is that such litigations are conducted in a way which reflects the nature of the issue at hand. Professionalism, propriety, integrity and diligence require to be deployed throughout.

20. Robert Rennie:
A Bibliography

Compiled by Bernadette O'Neill

1972

Floating Charges: A Treatise from the Standpoint of Scots Law unpublished thesis (University of Glasgow).

1988

"Non-Oil Related Minerals and Reservation Clauses" *Law Society of Scotland PQLE Paper* (1988).

1992

"Introduction to Commercial Missives" in Law Society of Scotland PQLE *Commercial Missives Seminar* (1992) vol 80 4-23 (Edinburgh: Law Society of Scotland).

Book review of P Robson and K Miller *Property Law* (1991) (1992) 37(12) *JLSS* 476-77.

1993

"Mandates, Assignations and Arrestments" (1993) 38(5) *JLSS* 185-86.

"A Matter of Interest" (1993) 38 (9) *JLSS* 363-65.

"Letters of Obligation – A Classic Dilemma" (1993) 38(11) *JLSS* 431-33.

"Missives – Penalty Interest Clauses" with D J Cusine (1993) 38(11) *JLSS* 450-51.

"Warrandice: A Guarantee With Small Print" (1993) 5(Oct) *PropLB* 6-8.

Missives with D J Cusine (Edinburgh: Butterworths/Law Society of Scotland).

 http://dx.doi.org/10.11647/OBP.0056.20

1994

"Inhibitions, Standard Securities and Further Advances" (1994) 39(2) *JLSS* 52-54.

Book review of A J McDonald *Conveyancing Manual* 5th edn (1993) (1994) 39(4) *JLSS* 121.

"Negligence, Instructions and the Lender's Need to Know" (1994) 39(4) *JLSS* 135-38.

"Conveyancing - What's Coming?" (1994) 39(12) *JLSS* 450-53.

"Dead on Delivery" (1994) 19 *SLT* 183-89.

"Possession: Nine Tenths of the Law" (1994) 26 *SLT* 261-65.

"The Theory and Ethics of Irritancy" (1994) (3) *JurRev* 283-91.

1995

"Negligence, Securities and the Expanding Duty of Care" (1995) *JLSS* 40(2) 58-61.

"The Requirements of Writing (Scotland) Act 1995" with D J Cusine (1995) 40(6) *JLSS* 221-225.

"Coal Mining Inquiries" with S Brymer (1995) 40(6) *JLSS* 238-39.

"Certificate of Title: Legal Context" (1995) 40(10) *JLSS* 377-79.

Book review of D M Walker *The Law of Contracts and Related Obligations in Scotland* 3rd edn (1995) (1995) 40(12) *JLSS* 466.

Book review of A Barr J M H Biggar A M C Dalgleish and H J Stevens *Drafting wills in Scotland* (1994) (1995) 18 *SLT* 170-71.

Book review of D M Walker *The Law of Contracts and Related Obligations in Scotland* 3rd edn (1995) (1995) 40 *SLT* 369.

"The Acquisition of Crofts" (1995) 63(2) *SLG* 63-66.

"The Feudal System – Going, Going, Gone?" (1995) 4 *JurRev* 321-31.

"The Requirements of Writing (Scotland) Act 1995" (1995) 5 *JurRev* 445-52.

"Grabbing the Proceeds of Sale of the Family Home" (1995) 17(Sep) *FamLB* 2-3.

"Rescission of Missives" (1995) 17(Oct) *PropLB* 2-4.

The Requirements of Writing with D J Cusine (Edinburgh: Butterworths/Law Society of Scotland).

"Letters of Obligation – Legal Lubrication" (1995) 1(1) *SPLQ* 76-82.

1996

"Alluvio in the Land Register: Shifting Sands and the Thin Red Line" (1996) 5 *SLT* 41-44.

"Keeping the Price and the Property: Sharp v Thomson" (1996) 1 *JurRev* 68-71.

"Law Reform at the University" (1996) 41(6) *JLSS* 221-22.

"The Professional's City?: Lawyers of the City and the University of Glasgow" (1996) 41(8) *JLSS* 304-06.

"Requirements of Writing: Problems in Practice" (1996) 1(3) *SLPQ* 187-96.

"Setting Missives up – and Apart" (1996) 19(Feb) *PropLB* 2-4.

1997

Solicitors' Negligence (Edinburgh: Butterworths/Law Society of Scotland).

"Prescriptive Possession in the Sasine and Land Registers" (1997) 2(4) *SLPQ* 309-15.

"The Sellers' Remedies" (1997) 26(Apr) *PropLB* 1-3.

"The Sasine Register and Dispositions A Non Domino" with AM Falconer (1997) 42(2) *JLSS* 72-74.

"Sharp v Thomson: The Final Act" (1997) 42(4) *JLSS* 130-34.

"Negligence and the Duty to Disclose – A Turning of the Tide" (1997) 42(10) *JLSS* 405-07.

Professor McDonald's Conveyancing Manual 6th edn with A J McDonald, S Brymer and D J Cusine (Edinburgh: T & T Clark).

1998

"Non-Feudal Landholdings in Scotland" with D O'Donnell (1998) 3(1) *SLPQ* 31-51.

"The Tragedy of the Floating Charge in Scots Law" (1998) 3(3) *SLPQ* 169-79.

"Conveyancing Case Law: Some Unexpected Results" (1998) 3(4) *SLPQ* 278-85.

"Faxed Missives – The Distinction Between Constitution and Transmission" (1998) 32(Mar) *PropLB* 2-3.

"Fraud and Forgery, and the Land Register" (1998) 36(Nov) *PropLB* 1-3.

"The Future of Conveyancing" (1998) 43(12) *JLSS* 21-23.

"The Reality of Real Burdens" (1998) 19 *SLT* 149-53.

Scottish Conveyancing Legislation (ed) with M Meston, R R M Paisley, K G C Reid and D J Cusine (Edinburgh: W Green) [loose leaf service regularly updated].

Annotations in *Scottish Landlord and Tenant Legislation* D Brand (ed) (Edinburgh: W Green).

1999

"Abolition of the Feudal System" (1999) 12 *SLT* 85-92.

Book review of A Wightman (ed) *Scotland: Land and Power – The Agenda for Law Reform* (1999) (1999) 38 *SLT* 325-26.

"Negligence: Liability of Each Individual Partner to the Firm" (1999) 4(1) *SLPQ* 13-18.

Missives with D J Cusine 2nd edn (Edinburgh: Butterworths/Law Society of Scotland).

2000

"Conclusion of Missives in the Modern Age" (2000) 5(4) *SLPQ* 346-55.

"The Modern Missive" (2000) 8 *SLT* 65-70.

"To Sharp v Thomson - An Heir" (2000) 31 *SLT* 247-51.

Book review of G L Gretton & Reid *Conveyancing 2nd edn (1999)* (2000) 45(2) *JLSS* 43.

Book review of *Registration of Title Practice Book* 2nd edn (2000) (2000) 45(12) *JLSS* 44.

2001

"Boundary Disputes" (2001) 13 *SLT* 115-19.

"Leasehold Casualties" (2001) 27 *SLT* 235-39.

"Solicitors' Negligence and the Judgement of Solomon" (2001) 6(2) *SLPQ* 95-102.

"Statutory Personal Bar - Rei Interventus Replaced" (2001) 6(3) *SLPQ* 197-203.

"Solicitor's Negligence: Third Parties Join the Queue" (2001) 6(4) *SLPQ* 304-13.

Minerals and the Law in Scotland (Welwyn Garden City: EMIS Professional Publishing).

Book review of C H Agnew *Crofting Law* (2000) (2001) 5(2) *EdinLR* 264.

Review of *Professor McDonald's Conveyancing Case Notes CD-ROM Production* (Dundee University) (2001) 46 (1) *JLSS* 40.

2002

"Mineral Rights" (2002) 7(1) *SLPQ* 1-9.

"Solicitors' Negligence: Rearguard Action" (2002) 7(2) *SLPQ* 87-96.

"The Role of the Expert Witness in Negligence Claims" (2002) 39 *SLT* 317-321.

Standard Securities with D J Cusine 2nd edn (Edinburgh: Butterworths/Law Society of Scotland).

2003

"A Matter of Opinion" (2003) 48(5) *JLSS* 32-35.

"In My Considered Opinion: A Decade of Disputed Advice" (2003) 48(8) *JLSS* 26-29.

"The End of Conveyancing As We Know It" (2003) 48(11) *JLSS* 15-18.

"House Rules" with L Freedman (2003) 17(27) *Lawyer* 23.

"Standard Securities" (2003) 71(1) *SLG* 26.

Land Tenure Reform (Edinburgh: Thomson/W Green).

2004

"Last Piece of the Jigsaw" (2004) 49(3) *JLSS* 26-27.

Book review of KGC Reid *The Abolition of Feudal Tenure in Scotland* (2003) (2004) 49(3) *JLSS* 59.

"Waste Paper" with G Gretton, R R M Paisley and S Brymer (2004) 49(5) *JLSS* 54-57.

"How Much Law, Anyway?" (2004) 49(8) *JLSS* 60-63.

"Will We Leave It to the Software?" in "What Next For Conveyancing?" with D Reid, R Mackay and S Brymer (2004) 49(11) *JLSS* 18-19.

"Solicitors' Negligence: Dealing With Tricky Twosomes" (2004) 6 *SLT* 33-36.

"Widening the Duty of Care" (2004) 40 *SLT* 245-49.

Land Tenure in Scotland (Edinburgh: W Green).

Opinions on Professional Negligence in Conveyancing: the Opinions of Professor Robert Rennie (Edinburgh: Thomson/W Green).

2005

"Control of Land in the Post-Feudal era" (2005) 16 *SLT* 89-91.

"The Race to the Registers Revisited" (2005) 50(7) *JLSS* 53-55.

"Memorial and Opinion Intus Re: Automated Registration of Title to Land" with S Brymer, G Gretton and R Paisley (2005) *JurRev* 201-50.

Land Tenure and Tenements Legislation 2nd edn (Edinburgh: Thomson/W Green).

"Conveyancing" in *The Laws of Scotland: Stair Memorial Encyclopaedia*, Reissue (Edinburgh: LexisNexis)

2006

"Standard Missives and Negligence" (2006) 12 *SLT* 65-69.

"Solicitors' Negligence: The Specialist and Best Practice" (2006) 35 *SLT* 225-30.

Book review of G L Gretton and K G C Reid *Conveyancing* 3rd edn (2004) (2006) 51(5) *JLSS* 48.

"Purchase Options in Leases" with D Bell (2006) 51(5) *JLSS* 49-50.

"Opinion for the Law Society of Scotland Relative to Special Mandates for the Adhibition of Digital Signatures" available at http://www.lawscot.org.uk/media/88205/opinion_of_prof_rennie.pdf

2007

"What sort of Lawyers Do We Want?" (2007) 1 *SLT* 1-4.

"Real Burdens – A Question of Interest" (2007) 14 *SLT* 89-93.

"Noting Title in a Non Feudal Era" (2007) 22 *SLT* 157-62.

Solicitors' Negligence (Edinburgh: Butterworths/Law Society of Scotland).

Book review of A C Ferguson *Common Good Law* (2006) (2007) 52 (2) *JLSS* 45.

2008

The Promised Land: Property Law Reform (ed) (Edinburgh: Thomson/W Green).

"Barker v Lewis on Appeal" (2008) 12 *SLT* 77-79.

"Claims and The Credit Crunch" (2008) 36 *SLT* 239-44.

"An Idea Whose Time Has Gone" with L Freedman (2008) 53(9) *JLSS* 68-69.

Conveyancing in the Electronic Age with S Brymer (Edinburgh: Thomson/W Green).

"Supplementary Opinion by Professor Robert Rennie for the Law Society of Scotland Relative to Special Mandates for the Adhibition of Digital Signatures" available at http://www.lawscot.org.uk/media/88202/artl-supplementary-opinion.pdf

2009

"Counting the Costs in Tenements" (2009) 23 *SLT* 137-40.

"Marching Towards Equity – Blindfolded" (2009) 32 *SLT* 187-92.

Land Tenure and Tenements Legislation 3rd edn (Edinburgh: W Green).

2010

"Folly, Guilt and More Folly: The McCaig Cases" in J P Grant and E Sutherland (eds) *Scots Law Tales* (2010) (Dundee: Dundee University Press).

"Land Registration and the Decline of Property Law" (2010) 14(1) *EdinLR* 62-79.

"Solicitors` Negligence - New Developments" (2010) 29 *SLT* 159-64.

"The Ice Cream Man Cometh" (2010) 30 *SLT* 165-68.

"Law v Practice: Royal Bank of Scotland Plc v Wilson" (2010) 40 *SLT* 219-24.

Book review of K S Gerber *Commercial Leases in Scotland* (2009) (2010) 14(1) *EdinLR* 170-72.

Book review of W M Gordon and S Wortley *Scottish Land Law* 3rd edn vol 1 (2009) (2010) 55 (4) *JLSS* 51.

2011

"Pre-2004 Real Burdens – The End Game" (2011) 23 *SLT* 163-68.

"Enforcement of Missives" (2011) 24 *SLT* 169-73.

"Interest Enforced" (2011) 28 *SLT* 217-21.

"Interpretation of Commercial Missives" (2011) 37 *SLT* 273-79.

"Missives in Motion" with S Brymer (2011) 56(12) *JLSS* 32-33.

"Property Law: How the World Changed at Martinmas" in E E Sutherland, K E Goodall, GF M Little, and F P Davidson (eds) *Law Making and the Scottish Parliament: The Early Years* (2011) (Edinburgh: Edinburgh University Press).

Book review of M Higgins, *The Enforcement of Heritable Securities* (2010) (2011) 15(3) *EdinLR* 510-11.

2012

"The 20 Year Rules and the McLetchie Amendment" (2012) 16(1) *EdinLR* 114-16.

"The Lodge with Three Names: Lubbock v Feakins" (2012) 16(3) *EdinLR* 438-45.

"The End of Immunity for Expert Witnesses?" with S Brymer (2012) 80(2) *SLG* 37-40.

Book review of G L Gretton and K G C Reid *Conveyancing* 4th edn (2011) (2012) 57(2) *JLSS* 7 [full version available online at bit.ly/xKU264].

"A Bold Step Forward" with S Brymer (2012) 57(3) *JLSS* 32-33.

"A More Flexible Approach to the Scottish Principle of Warrandice" (2012) *LNB News* 55.

2013

"Warrandice – The Threat of the Threat of Eviction" (2013) 4 *SLT* 27-29.

"Boundary Disputes Revisited" (2013) 27 *SLT* 189-94.

2014

"E-missives: What Now?" with S Brymer (2014) 59(1) *JLSS* 18-19.

"Lender Exchange Ahead" with S Brymer (2014) 59(2) *JLSS* 33 [fuller version available online at bit.ly/xKU264].

2015

Leases with S Brymer, T Mullen, M Blair and F McCarthy (Edinburgh: W Green/ Scottish Universities Law Institute).

Index

.

This book need not end here...

At Open Book Publishers, we are changing the nature of the traditional academic book. The title you have just read will not be left on a library shelf, but will be accessed online by hundreds of readers each month across the globe. We make all our books free to read online so that students, researchers and members of the public who can't afford a printed edition can still have access to the same ideas as you.

Our digital publishing model also allows us to produce online supplementary material, including extra chapters, reviews, links and other digital resources. Find *Essays in Conveyancing and Property Law* on our website to access its online extras. Please check this page regularly for ongoing updates, and join the conversation by leaving your own comments:

http://www.openbookpublishers.com/isbn/9781783741472

If you enjoyed this book, and feel that research like this should be available to all readers, regardless of their income, please think about donating to us. Our company is run entirely by academics, and our publishing decisions are based on intellectual merit and public value rather than on commercial viability. We do not operate for profit and all donations, as with all other revenue we generate, will be used to finance new Open Access publications.

For further information about what we do, how to donate to OBP, additional digital material related to our titles or to order our books, please visit our website: http://www.openbookpublishers.com

OpenBook Publishers
Knowledge is for sharing

CPSIA information can be obtained at www.ICGtesting.com
Printed in the USA
LVOW10s0858080516

487239LV00006B/63/P

9 781783 741472